National Welfare Benefits Handbook

22nd edition

Marcus Revell
David Simmons
and
Lynn Webster

Child Poverty Action Group

Acknowledgements

We would like to thank the following people for their help in preparing the *Handbook*. We are grateful to Don Flynn and Gary Vaux; and the DSS officers with whom we have had many helpful discussions. We would especially like to thank the staff in CPAG's Citizens' Rights Office for their careful checking of the manuscript at each stage and for their helpful suggestions and support; thanks also to Julia Lewis and Richard Kennedy for their editorial and production work, to Mary Shirley for her accurate and interpretative typing of the manuscript and for her help with checking final proofs; to Catherine Dawson and Maggie Phelps for their conscientious indexing of the book; to Dale Russell and June Taylor at Boldface Typesetters for the high quality and speed of their work, and to The Bath Press for reliably meeting a very tight printing schedule.

© CPAG Ltd 1992
British Library Cataloguing in Publication Data
National Welfare Benefits Handbook – 22nd ed. (1992-93)

    1. Social security – Great Britain –
Periodicals 2. Income maintenance programs Great Britain –
Periodicals
I. CPAG Ltd
361.6'0941   HD7165.A/

ISBN 0-946744 38 6

Contents

MEANS-TESTED BENEFIT RATES

Income support applicable amounts

Personal allowances

under 18* (usual rate)	£25.55
under 18* (in certain circumstances)	£33.60
aged 18-24	£33.60
aged 25 or over	£42.45
Single parent	
under 18* (usual rate)	£25.55
under 18* (in certain circumstances)	£33.60
aged 18 or over	£42.45
Couple	
both under 18*	£50.60
one/both over 18*	£66.60
Dependent children	
under 11	£14.55
aged 11-15	£21.40
aged 16-17*	£25.55
aged 18	£33.60

*For eligibility of under-18s and calculating amounts, see pp50-56.

Premiums

		From October 1992
		£
Family	£ 9.30	
Lone parent	£ 4.75	
Pensioner		
single	£14.70	16.70
couple	£22.35	25.35
Enhanced pensioner		
single	£16.65	18.65
couple	£25.00	28.00
Higher pensioner		
single	£20.75	22.75
couple	£29.55	32.55
Disability		
single	£17.80	
couple	£25.55	
Severe disability		
single	£32.55	
couple (if one qualifies)	£32.55	
couple (if both qualify)	£65.10	
Disabled child	£17.80	
Carers	£11.55	

Some claimants have their applicable amount calculated differently. This applies to the following groups:

Claimants who are only entitled to the urgent cases rate – see p36
Claimants who are voluntarily unemployed – see p45
Claimants on government training schemes – see p47
Claimants on strike – see p58
Claimants in residential care or nursing homes – see p72
Claimants in hospital – see p82
Claimants who are prisoners – see p85
Claimants without accommodation – see p86

Housing benefit applicable amounts
Personal allowances and premiums as for income support, *except*

single person aged 16-24	£33.60
lone parent under 18	£33.60
lone parent premium	£10.60

Community charge benefit applicable amounts
Personal allowances and premiums as for income support, *except*

lone parent premium	£10.60

Family credit

Adult credit	£41.00
Child credit	
under 11	£10.40
age 11-15	£17.25
age 16-17	£21.45
age 18	£29.90
Applicable amount, ie, threshold level	£66.60

Social fund payments

Maternity expenses	£100.00
Cold weather payment	£6.00

Capital limits

Income support	£8,000.00
Family credit	£8,000.00
Housing benefit	£16,000.00
Community charge benefit	£16,000.00
Disability working allowance	£16,000.00

Disability working allowance
Adult credit

single	£42.40
couple/lone parent	£58.80

Child credit

under 11	£10.40
age 11-15	£17.25
age 16-17	£21.45
age 18	£29.90
Applicable amount (ie, threshold level)	
single	£39.95
couple/lone parent	£66.60

NON-MEANS-TESTED BENEFIT RATES

Earnings replacement benefits

	Claimant £pw	Adult dependant £pw	Child dependant £pw
Unemployment benefit			
under pensionable age	43.10	26.60	
of or over pensionable age	54.15	32.55	10.85*
Sickness benefit			
under pensionable age	41.20	25.50	
of or over pensionable age	51.95	31.20	10.85*
Invalidity pension	54.15	32.55	10.85*
Invalidity allowance			
higher rate	11.55		
middle rate	7.20		
lower rate	3.60		
Statutory sick pay			
higher rate	52.50		
lower rate	45.30		
Severe disablement allowance	32.55	19.45	10.85*
Age-related addition –			
higher rate	11.55		
middle rate	7.20		
lower rate	3.60		
Statutory maternity pay (lower rate)	46.30		
Maternity allowance	42.25	25.50	
Invalid care allowance	32.55	19.45	10.85*
Widowed mother's allowance	54.15		10.85*
Widow's pension	54.15		
Non-contributory widow's benefit	32.55		10.85*
Retirement pension			
Category A	54.15	32.55	10.85*
Category B for a married woman	32.55		10.85*
Category B for a widow	54.15		10.85*
Category B for a widower	54.15		10.85*
Category C for a person not a married woman	32.55	19.45	10.85*
Category C for a married woman	19.45		10.85*
Category D	32.55		10.85*

Benefits for the severely disabled

	£pw
Attendance allowance	
higher rate	43.35
lower rate	28.95

Disability living allowance

Care component	
Higher	43.35
Middle	28.95
Lower	11.55
Mobility component	
Higher	30.30
Lower	11.55

Industrial injuries benefits

Disablement benefit – variable, up to 100%	88.40

Industrial death benefit

Widow	
higher permanent rate	54.15
lower permanent rate	16.25
Widower	54.15
Child	10.85*

Benefits for children

		£pw
Child benefit	(for only or eldest child)	9.65
	(for other children)	7.80
One parent benefit		5.85
Guardian's allowance		10.85*
Child's special allowance		10.85*

* These are reduced by £1.10 for any child for whom you receive the higher rate of child benefit.

Income tax allowances

	pa	*pw*
Personal allowance	£3,445	£66.25
Married couples allowance	£1,720	£33.08
Additional personal allowance for caring for children	£1,720	£33.08

National Insurance contributions

gross weekly earnings

Below £54	Nil
£54-£405	2% on the first £54 and
	9% on the rest, up to £405

This is the 'contracted-in' rate for Class 1 contributions. For other NI rates, see CPAG's *Rights guide to non-means-tested benefits*, Chapter 12.

PART I
Introduction

Chapter 1

An introduction to means tests

This *Handbook* covers only those benefits which are 'means-tested'. This chapter explains:

1 Which benefits are means-tested (below)
2 How means tests work (p5)

1 WHICH BENEFITS ARE MEANS-TESTED

(i) Non-means-tested and means-tested benefits

Non-means-tested benefits are those paid with only limited consideration of how much money you have (your 'means' of support), provided you satisfy certain basic conditions such as being available for work, disabled or widowed.

The main earnings-replacement benefits are unemployment benefit, sickness benefit and invalidity benefit, severe disablement allowance, maternity allowance, invalid care allowance, widows' benefits and retirement pensions. Other non-means-tested benefits are intended to contribute towards the extra costs of bringing up children or of disability. They include child benefit, attendance allowance, industrial injuries benefits and disability living allowance.

Entitlement to some of the earnings-replacement benefits depends on you having paid sufficient social security contributions; for other non-means-tested benefits there is a requirement that you should have lived in Great Britain for a certain length of time.

None of these non-means-tested benefits is covered in detail in this *Handbook* (although the main benefit rates are included at the front of the book). For further information, you should look at CPAG's *Rights guide to non-means-tested benefits* (15th edn, 1992/93, £5.95 post-free from CPAG Ltd, £2.25 for claimants).

By contrast, entitlement to **means-tested benefits** does not depend on your having satisfied any contribution conditions or conditions of past residence. Instead it depends on your satisfying certain basic conditions but also on your income and capital being sufficiently low. The intention is to limit entitlement to those who are most in need. This involves quite detailed investigation of your means. The ways means tests work are outlined on p5 and there are different tests for the different benefits.

The means-tested benefits covered in this *Handbook* are:
- [ ] income support (IS) (p7);
- [ ] family credit (FC) (p129);
- [ ] disability working allowance (DWA);
- [ ] housing benefit (HB) (p151);
- [ ] community charge benefit (CCB) (p213);
- [ ] social fund (SF) payments (p285);
- [ ] remission of National Health Service charges (p333);
- [ ] free milk and vitamins (p343);
- [ ] free school meals and other education benefits (p345);
- [ ] housing renovation grants and other local authority grants and services (p347);
- [ ] discretionary payments for the disabled (p351).

Entitlement to some of these benefits may depend on whether or not you are in full-time work, but not all of them (see below).

It is also important to note that some benefits are administered by the Benefits Agency on behalf of the Department of Social Security (DSS) but that others are administered by local authorities or other bodies (see below).

(ii)   Means-tested benefits for people at work

Income support is restricted to those who are not working full-time (which usually means for 16 hours or more a week), and some of the other benefits are restricted to those already receiving IS. Family credit and disability working allowance are restricted to those who are working full-time. Other benefits – including housing benefit – may be claimed whether you are working or not.

Benefits only for people *not* **in full-time work:**	**Benefits only for people in full-time work:**
income support	family credit
social fund cold weather payments, community care grants and budgeting loans	disability working allowance
free school meals	

Benefits for people irrespective of whether they work:
housing benefit
community charge benefit
social fund maternity payments, funeral payments and crisis loans
education benefits (other than free school meals)
housing renovation grants
all other benefits not in the above lists

(iii) The administration of means-tested benefits

The administration of the various benefits described in this *Handbook* varies enormously depending on who is responsible for it.

☐ The Benefits Agency administers IS, FC, DWA and the SF on behalf of the DSS. Initial claims should be made and dealt with locally but London claims are dealt with centrally by large centres in Glasgow, Belfast and Wigan. All FC and DWA claims are sent to an office in Blackpool.

☐ Local authorities (usually district councils outside London) administer HB, CCB and housing renovation grants. HB and CCB are often administered by the same office.

☐ Local education authorities (county councils and metropolitan boroughs outside London) administer education benefits.

☐ The National Health Service administers health benefits but the Benefits Agency deals with any investigation of your means.

☐ Various other bodies deal with the other benefits covered in Chapter 26 of this *Handbook*.

Contacting benefit offices

Detailed advice about claiming and how decisions are made in the case of each benefit will be found elsewhere in this *Handbook*. However, there is some basic guidance about dealing with offices which applies to all benefits.

Writing to your office is nearly always the best way to have your case dealt with. It is easier for the person dealing with your case and it ensures there is a permanent record of what you said. A letter enables you to cover all the relevant points clearly and systematically.

You should always put your name, address, the date and any official reference number at the top of your letter. If possible, make a copy of it. You should also keep all letters and forms sent to you, even if the information is disappointing. They may help you or your adviser later to work out whether any decision can be challenged.

If there is a delay in getting a reply, you can telephone to find out why, but it may be better to write a short reminder and only telephone if you still receive no response.

Nevertheless, on occasion, **telephoning your benefit office** may be necessary. If you are a London claimant, try your branch office first. If you have to ring the centre in Belfast, Glasgow or Wigan, you are only charged the local rate. Be ready to give your surname and any reference number. Try to get the name, title and telephone extension number of the person you speak to as this may be useful in the future. Make a brief note of what is said together with the date. If the information is important, follow up the telephone call with a letter confirming the points that have been made so that any misunderstanding can be cleared up. You could ask the office to write to you but they are usually reluctant to do so merely to confirm a telephone conversation.

Visiting your office enables you to have a detailed conversation with someone. However, check the opening times first. Many offices are very busy and you can expect a long wait if you do not have an appointment. An appointment can usually be arranged by telephone. Take along any documents which might possibly be relevant as it is frustrating to be asked to return because you are unable to provide one small item of information. Again, follow up any important meeting with a letter confirming the points you have made or ask the office to confirm in writing any advice to you. It is a good idea to take a friend or relative with you, not only for moral support, but also as a witness to what is said.

If you are a London claimant, you can go to your local branch office to discuss your claim. They will contact the social security centre in Belfast, Glasgow or Wigan if necessary.

Complaints

Ways of formally challenging decisions are explained elsewhere in this *Handbook*. However, you may want to complain about the way your case is dealt with simply to get a quicker decision or to have something properly taken into account.

If you are dissatisfied with the way someone is handling your case, you should contact a more senior official within the relevant department. Relatively junior staff usually deal with most cases so it may be enough to contact a supervisor. Above the supervisors, there will be an office manager. Benefit Agency offices also have a customer services manager, and you could try speaking to her/him.

Ultimately, there are government ministers including the Secretary of State for Social Security.

Local authority offices are the responsibility of a senior officer (the Chief Executive, the Treasurer, the Director of Education or whoever – the relevant officer's name or title usually appears on letter-headings). In turn, those officers are responsible to councillors and you can write to one of your local councillors or the chair of the relevant council committee. Government departments also monitor local authorities so, if all else fails, you can write to the relevant minister – ie, the Secretary of State for Social Security for HB, the Secretary of State for Education for education benefits, and the Secretary of State for the Environment in other cases.

A similar approach can be taken in the case of NHS benefits which are ultimately the responsibility of the Secretary of State for Health.

Emergencies

If you have lost all your money or there has been a similar disaster, it is possible to get help at any time.

Any local police station should have a contact number for Benefit Agency staff on call outside normal office hours. In London there is a special Benefit Agency office open in the evenings and at weekends for emergencies. It is Keyworth House, Keyworth Street, London SE1 (tel: 071-407-2315 or, during the day, 071-620-1456).

There will also be a duty social worker who can be contacted via your local council or the police.

2 HOW MEANS TESTS WORK

For some benefits there are complicated rules for assessing your needs and resources. Some other benefits are payable once you have qualified for a different means-tested benefit (known as a 'passported' benefit). Yet other benefits are 'discretionary' – in other words, there are no set rules for deciding whether your means are sufficient but your means are one consideration when it is being decided whether to award the benefit.

(i) The main non-discretionary benefits

The following benefits have complicated rules for calculating your needs and resources:
- [ ] income support;
- [ ] family credit;
- [ ] disability working allowance;
- [ ] housing benefit;
- [ ] community charge benefit;
- [ ] health benefits (other than free milk and vitamins);
- [ ] housing renovation grants.

However, it is not always necessary to consider all the benefits separately because, except in the case of FC and DWA, you automatically satisfy the means test for the other benefits if you qualify for IS.

With the exception of FC and DWA, all the benefits have similar ways of taking account of your needs. These involve adding up personal allowances for each member of the family and then adding on extra amounts to take account of extra expenses you may have because of your circumstances. For IS, HB and CCB, these amounts are known as 'applicable amounts' and, where they are set figures, they are covered in Chapter 17. However, there are special rules for special groups of claimants, particularly for those claiming IS. Health benefits and housing renovation grants have similar rules.

All the benefits (including FC and DWA) also have similar ways of calculating resources to take into account both your income and your savings and other capital assets. Parts of your income and capital may be disregarded. If you have too much capital, you are not entitled to any benefit at all. If you have a lesser amount of capital, it may reduce the amount of benefit to which you are entitled because it is treated as producing an income. The main rules for calculating resources are set out in Chapters 18 and 19 although, again, there are variations for health benefits and housing renovation grants.

Once your needs and your income have been calculated, your benefit can be worked out. In the cases of IS and health benefits, that is simply done by deducting your income from your needs. In the cases of HB, CCB and housing renovation grants, there are more complicated formulae which take into account the amount of your rent, community charge or estimated cost of repairs, as well as your other needs and your income and which allow you to qualify even though your income is above IS level. These formulae are set out in the relevant chapters elsewhere in this *Handbook*. Each one produces the result that the higher your income, the less benefit you receive while, at the same time, those with incomes substantially above IS level receive some help.

FC and DWA are also calculated on the basis of a complicated formula which is based on your maximum FC/DWA which takes into account your family's size but which is not intended directly to represent your needs. Again, the object of the formula is that you should be entitled to some benefit even though your income is substantially above IS level.

(ii)   Passported benefits

Some benefits do not have their own means tests. Instead, to be entitled to such benefits, it is simply necessary that you are entitled to another 'passported' benefit. These are:

Benefit	Passport
SF maternity expenses payments	IS, FC, DWA
SF funeral expenses payments	IS, FC, DWA, HB, CCB
Health benefits	IS, FC
SF cold weather payments	IS
SF community care grants and budgeting loans	IS
Free school meals	IS
Housing renovation grants	IS

In the case of all SF payments, it is a further condition of entitlement that your capital is not above a certain level. In the case of community care grants and budgeting loans, you must still persuade the social fund officer to exercise her/his discretion in your favour as these are also discretionary benefits.

For free school meals there are no other tests. If you are entitled to IS, your children are entitled to free school meals; if you are not, they are not.

IS also acts as a passport to the Independent Living Fund although others with income less than the IS applicable amount also qualify.

(iii)   Discretionary benefits

Where a benefit is discretionary, the means of the claimant are obviously crucial in deciding whether or not to award the benefit. SF crisis loans, budgeting loans and community care grants are paid on a discretionary basis, although certain rules also have to be followed. To get a budgeting loan or community care grant, a claimant must be entitled to IS.

Where local authorities have the power to make payments for things like school uniforms, they could do it on a purely discretionary basis but often have local means tests similar to the IS means test.

Many of the benefits covered in Part X of this *Handbook* are discretionary.

PART II
Income support

Chapter 2

The basic rules of entitlement

This chapter covers:

1 Introduction to IS and basic rules (see below)
2 Age (p9)
3 Full-time work (p9)
4 Full-time and part-time education (p12)
5 Availability for work (p14)
6 Presence in and temporary absence from Great Britain (p18)

1 INTRODUCTION

Income support (IS) is the main benefit for people with a low income. However, it is not paid to people in full-time work who can claim family credit (see p129) or DWA (see p139) instead.

If you pay rent or a community charge you may be entitled to housing benefit (see p151) and community charge benefit (see p213), as well as IS.

If you are entitled to IS you also qualify for:
- ☐ health service benefits such as free prescriptions (see Chapter 25 – p333); *and*
- ☐ education benefits such as free school meals for your children (see Chapter 26 – p345).

You may also qualify for social fund payments (see Chapters 20 – 24 – pp285-331).

(i) The principal conditions

You can claim IS if you satisfy the following rules:

☐ Your income is less than your applicable amount (which is the amount, fixed by law, intended to cover your day-to-day living expenses – see p236). When calculating your benefit, some of your income may be ignored but you may also be treated as having income you do not really receive (see p246).

☐ Your savings and other capital must be worth £8,000 or less. Some capital (in particular, your home) may be ignored, but you may also be treated as having capital you do not really possess (see p272).

☐ Neither you nor your partner (see below) can be in full-time paid work (see p9). Note that you can claim if you are temporarily away from full-time work because, for example, you are sick.

☐ You are not in full-time education (although there are exceptions to this rule – see p12). However, if you are studying part-time, you may qualify (see p14).

☐ You are at least 16 (although 16- and 17-year-olds have to satisfy extra rules – see p52).

☐ You are signing on as available for work (see p38) and actively seeking employment (see p40), unless you are not required to do so because you are, for example, sick, aged 60 or more, a single parent, etc (see p16). If you cannot satisfy these rules you may be able to get a reduced rate of IS on hardship grounds – see p18.

☐ You are present in Great Britain (although there are exceptions to this rule – see p18).

There are some groups of claimants to whom special rules apply. Those rules are covered in Chapter 5.

You do not have to pay National Insurance contributions to qualify for IS.

(ii)   Who you claim for

You claim for your 'family' which consists of:
☐ you; *and*
☐ your partner (if any) who is
  either   your husband or wife, if you are living together,
  or   a person of the opposite sex to whom you are not married but with whom you are living as husband or wife (see p229); *and*
☐ any children for whom you are responsible (which may include children who have left school – see p233).

The amount of money you receive therefore takes account of the number of people in your 'family' (see p227). When calculating the amount of IS to which you are entitled, income and capital belonging to your partner are normally treated as yours. There are special rules for dealing with income and capital belonging to your children (see pp247 and 256).

(iii)   How to claim

You must claim IS in writing, either on Form A1 which you can obtain free from your local Benefits Agency office or, if you are signing on as unemployed, on Form B1 which you can obtain free from your local unemployment benefit office. If you get the form by telephoning or writing to the Benefits Agency office, your claim will generally be treated as having been made when you asked for the form. For more detailed advice about claims and how they are dealt with, see p100.

You are usually paid from the week of your claim, but your claim can be backdated for up to a year if you have good reason for claiming late. You are paid weekly or fortnightly by giro or by order book and usually in arrears. For information about payments, see p106.

You may be able to get a crisis loan from the social fund to tide you over until your benefit is paid (see p314).

You will have to make a separate claim to your local authority for housing benefit (see p185) and for help with your community charge (see p219).

2 AGE

You have to be 16 or over to make a claim for IS. [1]

> If you are 16 or 17 you have to satisfy extra rules (Chapter 5). You must also satisfy the basic rules described in the rest of this chapter.

If you are at school or college, see pp11-13. Once you are 18 or over you get IS in the normal way, provided you satisfy the basic rules of entitlement (see below).

3 FULL-TIME WORK

The rules below apply to claims made after 7 April 1992. Prior to this date full-time work was work for 24 hours or more a week. If you worked between 16-24 hours a week shortly before, and soon after 7 April you may still be able to get IS. See the rules on transitional provisions below.

(i) The definition of full-time work

You cannot usually get IS if you or your partner are in full-time paid work. This means working 16 hours or more each week. Paid work includes work for which you expect payment. [2] Paid lunch hours count towards the 16-hour total. [3]

Where your hours fluctuate, your weekly hours are worked out as follows:

☐ If you have a regular pattern of work, the average hours worked throughout each work 'cycle' or pattern is used. For example, if you regularly work 3 weeks on and 1 week off, your hours are the average over the 4-week period.

☐ Where there is no pattern, the average over the 5 weeks before your claim is used, or a different period if this would be more accurate.

☐ If you have just started work and no pattern is yet established, the number of hours or average of hours you are expected to work each week is used. [4]

Appeal if you think the average was calculated unfairly (see p118).

Exceptions to the 16-hour rule

You will be treated as in full-time work and thus *not* entitled to IS even if you work less than 16 hours a week, if: [5]
- [ ] you are off work because of a holiday. If you do not get any holiday pay – eg, because you have not worked for the company long enough – you could try for a social fund payment (see p314);
- [ ] you are away from work without a good reason;
- [ ] you are unemployed but have received pay in lieu of wages or in lieu of notice or holiday pay from your last job or an 'ex gratia' payment in recognition of loss of employment (see p253); [6]
- [ ] you or your partner are involved in a trade dispute for seven days or less. [7]

You are not treated as in full-time work if you work 16 hours or more and: [8]
- [ ] you are mentally or physically disabled and because of this
  - your earnings are 75 per cent or less of what a person without your disability would reasonably expect to earn, working the same hours in that job, or in a comparable one;
  - your hours of work are 75 per cent or less than a person without your disability would reasonably be expected to do in that or a comparable job;
- [ ] you work at home as a childminder (see p258);
- [ ] you are on a government training scheme (Youth Training (YT) or Employment Training (ET), see p47);
- [ ] you are working for a charity or voluntary organisation or you are a volunteer and are giving your services free (except for your expenses). Where you receive any nominal payment (even one of £5 or less which would be ignored under the rule for disregarding part of your earnings), you could be counted as in full-time work. The only way round this is for the organisation to pay you for a specific number of hours a week and for you to be a volunteer for the remainder of the time (but see p270 on notional income);
- [ ] you or your partner are involved in a trade dispute and it is more than 7 days since the dispute started (see p58). This will also apply for the first 15 days following your return to work after having been involved in a trade dispute;
- [ ] you are caring for a person (whether or not you receive invalid care allowance), who is either receiving or who has claimed attendance allowance or disability living allowance. In the latter case, you will only be treated as not in full-time work for 26 weeks after the claim for attendance allowance or until the claim is decided, whichever is the earlier;
- [ ] you are working, whilst living in a residential care or nursing home, or a local authority home. This applies during temporary absences from the home too. It only covers people who are being paid at the special rates for people in homes (see pp72-79 and pp80-82);
- [ ] you work as a part-time firefighter, auxiliary coastguard, member of the territorial or reserve forces, or running or launching a lifeboat;
- [ ] you are performing duties as a local authority councillor.

You are not treated as in full-time work while you are on sick, maternity or paternity leave. Under these circumstances, you may therefore be entitled to IS, but any pay you receive from your employer will affect how much IS you get (see p250).

If you are working part-time or on short-time you may qualify for IS – for details, see pp40 and 44.

(ii) Transitional provisions for IS claimants

For the purpose of qualifying for IS the definition of full-time work after 7 April 1992 will remain 24 hours or more a week if you satisfy the following conditions:[9]

☐ In the week before 7 April 1992:
- you were working 16-24 hours; *and*
- you, or your partner, were entitled to IS.

☐ In at least one of the eight weeks before 7 April 1992:
- you were working 16-24 hours; *and*
- you, or your partner, were entitled to IS,
provided that not more than eight weeks after that week
- you were again working 16-24 hours; *and*
- you, or your partner are entitled to IS.

☐ Before 7 April 1992, you, or your partner, stopped getting IS because one of you started working for 24 hours or more for a period that lasts not more than 12 (or 8 in certain circumstances) weeks (called the 'permitted period' – see below) and which ends after 7 April 1992, *and*
- you were working 16-24 hours in the week before that period started; *and*
- you again work 16-24 hours, and you, or your partner, are entitled to IS in the week after the period ends.

☐ You, or your partner, before 7 April 1992 started government training or a course at an employment rehabilitation centre, which training or course ends after 7 April 1992, *and*
- you were working 16-24 hours, and you, or your partner, were entitled to IS in the week before the training or course started; *and*
- you again worked 16-24 hours, and you, or your partner, are entitled to IS not more than eight weeks after the training or course ends.

('Working 16-24 hours' – this includes people whose hours of work vary but who work on average at least 16-24 hours a week.)

Ending of transitional protection

This transitional protection will be lost and you will be subject to the usual 16-hour rule if for more than eight weeks:
☐ you stop working for 16-24 hours; *or*
☐ you, or your partner, stop getting IS.

However, in calculating this eight weeks, the following will be ignored:
☐ Up to 12 (or 8 – see below under 'permitted period') weeks if the reason you, or your partner, stopped getting IS was because you, or your partner, started working for 24 hours or more.
☐ Any period during which you, or your partner, were attending a government training course or an employment rehabilitation centre plus the next eight weeks after the end of the course.

'Permitted period'

This will usually be 12 weeks, but it will only be 8 weeks if you, or your partner, have now stopped working for 24 hours or more, *and*
☐ as a result, your IS is subject to a voluntary unemployment deduction; *or*
☐ you worked for 24 hours or more for less than six weeks;* *or*
☐ at any time during the 26 weeks before you started working for 24 hours or more, you were a student in relevant education or working for 24 hours or more.*
* If this applies and you are nor disqualified from unemployment benefit due to the trial period provisions (see *Rights Guide*), the permitted period is 12 weeks.

Working children

The definition of full-time work remains as 24 hours or more per week for children who are included in your claim both before and after 6 April 1992 and who work between 16-24 hours and have earnings which are disregarded in part. This only applies for as long as the child is part of your family (see p233).

4   FULL-TIME AND PART-TIME EDUCATION

People in full-time education cannot usually qualify for IS, but there are some exceptions. You may be able to claim if your course is part-time. The rules of entitlement depend partly on your age. If you have a partner who is not studying, s/he could claim IS instead.

(i)   Under 19 in full-time education

Relevant education

If you are under 19 and at school or college you are usually counted as being in relevant education. This means the course is 'non-advanced' (up to and including A-levels or higher level Scottish certificate of education) and lasts more than 12 hours a week not counting homework or other unsupervised study and meal breaks. [10] While you are in relevant education, your parents can get child benefit for you and claim for you if they get IS (see p233). You cannot get IS yourself [11] unless: [12]
☐ you have a child for whom you can claim (see p233);
☐ you are so handicapped that you are unlikely to get a job in the next 12 months;
☐ you are an orphan, and have no one acting as your parent;
☐ you have to live away from your parents and any person acting in place of your parents because you are estranged from them, or you are in physical or moral danger or there is a serious risk to your physical or mental health.
   A 'person acting in place of your parents' includes a local authority or voluntary organisation if you are in care, or foster parents.
   'Estrangement' implies emotional disharmony, [13] where you have no desire to have any prolonged contact with your parents or they feel similarly towards you. It is possible to be estranged even though your parents are providing some financial support;

☐ you live apart from your parents and anyone acting as your parent(s), and they are unable to support you and they are in prison, unable to come to Britain because of immigration laws, or chronically sick or mentally or physically disabled. This covers people who:
- could get a disability premium or higher pensioner premium; *or*
- have an Armed Forces grant for car costs because of disability; *or*
- are 'substantially and permanently disabled';

☐ you are a refugee and have started a course to learn English in order to obtain employment during your first year in Britain. This will apply for up to nine months.

If any of the above apply you can get IS without having to sign on. 16- and 17-year-olds qualify in the same way as 18-year-olds. Check p56 for how much you get.

Treated as in relevant education

You continue to count as being in relevant education until the end of the holiday after the term in which you leave. If you leave school before the legal school-leaving date, you will be treated as having stayed on until that date. The day on which you cease to be treated as in relevant education is called the **terminal date** but your parents continue to get benefit for you until the end of that week. You are able to get benefit in your own right from the Monday following your terminal date (and if you are 16 or 17, you must satisfy the extra rules described from p52). This Monday is also the first day of the **child benefit extension period** during which, if you cannot get IS, your parents can go on claiming child benefit and IS for you (see p234).

Time of leaving school	*Terminal date*
Christmas	First Monday in January
Easter	First Monday after Easter Monday
May/June	First Monday in September

You can claim earlier if you are 19 before the appropriate terminal date. [14]

If you return to school or college solely to take exams, you will be counted as in full-time relevant education. So if you leave school at Easter and return to take exams in the following term, you will not be able to claim IS until the first Monday in September. [15] If you are 16 or 17 you will also have to fulfil extra conditions (see p52).

You can get benefit earlier if you were able to get IS while at school or college or if you come within one of the qualifying groups during the final vacation.

Advanced education

If your course is advanced you will be treated as a student [16] and will not usually be entitled to IS (but see (ii) below).

(ii)   19 or over and in full-time education

If your course is full-time you will be treated as a student regardless of the level of the course. [17]

Whether a course counts as full-time depends on the college. Courses that appear part-time may be classed as full-time by the college authorities, but any course which is over 15 hours a week can be classified as full-time. There is no universally accepted definition of what constitutes a 'full-time' or 'part-time' course. Definitions are often based on local custom and practice within education authorities, or determined by the demands of course validating bodies, or by the fact that full-time courses can attract more resources. The college or university's definition is not absolutely final, but if you want to challenge it you will have to produce a good argument showing why it should not be accepted. [18]

You cannot claim unless you are: [19]

☐   a single parent or foster parent; *or*

☐   getting a training allowance; *or*

☐   a student from abroad and entitled to an urgent cases payment because you are temporarily without funds (see p65); *or*

☐   a disabled student and you satisfy one of the following conditions:

  –   you qualify for the disability premium or severe disability premium (see pp240 and 243);

  –   you are unlikely to get a job within a reasonable period of time compared to other students because of your disability and you were getting IS immediately before 1 September 1990;

  –   you made a claim for IS after 1 September 1990 and at some time in the 18 months before claiming you were getting IS as a disabled person under 19 in non-advanced education, or as a disabled student;

  –   you qualify for a disabled student's allowance because you are deaf.

☐   a couple who are both full-time students and who have a child, but only during the summer vacation, and provided they satisfy the normal rules for getting IS.

Pensioners do not count as students and therefore can continue to claim.

If you stay on to finish a course of non-advanced education at school or college until after your nineteenth birthday, you will only qualify for IS if you come into one of the groups listed above, even though – as long as you were under 19 – you would have received IS as a dependant or in your own right.

(iii)   Studying part-time

You may be able to get IS while studying part-time if you qualify under the 21-hour rule or by satisfying the availability for work test. Whether a course is counted as part-time depends on its actual length if you are under 19, or how it is described by the college if you are 19 or over (see (ii) above).

The 21-hour rule

You will still be treated as available for work and thus entitled to benefit if: [20]

☐   you continue to actively seek work (see p43); *and*

☐ the course lasts 21 hours or less a week, not counting meal breaks and unsupervised study; *and*

☐ you are prepared to give up the course immediately a suitable job comes up; *and*

☐ *either* for the three months immediately before the course you were unemployed or sick and getting IS, unemployment benefit or sickness benefit, or you were on a Youth Training (YT) course;

  or in the last six months before the course, you were unemployed or sick and getting the above benefits for a total of three months altogether, or you were on a YT course for a total of three months and, sandwiched *between* these spells, you were working full-time or earning too much to qualify for benefit.

The three months on a YT course will only count if they are *after* the terminal date (see p13 for what this means).

The course must[21] be held at a recognised educational institution; *or* be similar to a course of training run by the Employment Service for which a training allowance would be paid.

It can be advanced (post A-level) or non-advanced.[22]

You cannot qualify under this rule if:

☐ you are 19 or over and your course is called full-time; *or*

☐ you are under 19 and your course is advanced.

Studying and available for work

If you cannot pass the test for the 21-hour rule you might still be able to claim IS provided you can convince the unemployment benefit office that you are willing and able to take a job, and they consider you are 'available for and actively seeking work' (see p39). You must be prepared to give up the course if a job comes up.

You cannot qualify under this rule if you are under 19 and the course is non-advanced and over 12 hours a week.

5 AVAILABILITY FOR WORK

(i) People who have to sign on

If you are under 60 you will usually have to sign on at the unemployment benefit office as available for full-time work and show that you are actively seeking work in order to get benefit.[23] By signing on you are saying you are available to take up a full-time job of 16 hours or more a week. If you are physically or mentally disabled you will be expected to do as much as you can normally do given your health.[24] If you are working part-time you must be willing to make up your hours. Some people do not have to sign on in order to get benefit (see below). You can also get IS on hardship grounds (see p18).

For more details about your IS entitlement if you have to sign on, see p38.

(ii)   People who do not have to sign on[25]

You do not have to sign on if you come within one of the following groups:

Age

☐   You are aged 60 or more.

☐   You are aged 50 to 59 and have no prospect of getting full-time employment. You must not have had a full-time job in the last 10 years, and not have been required to sign on during that time. This rule is aimed mainly at women who are widowed or divorced and whose children have grown-up.

Sick and disabled people

☐   You are incapable of work because of illness or disability. You will be treated as incapable if:
  -   you are receiving statutory sick pay; *or*
  -   you are applying or have applied for sickness benefit, invalidity pension or severe disablement allowance and your evidence of incapacity is accepted. You must make a claim for one of these benefits even if you know you would not qualify – eg, because you do not have enough contributions. If your doctor's evidence is accepted you will be treated as incapable of work, and get IS without signing on.

☐   You are appealing a decision by the Benefits Agency not to treat you as incapable of work and your own GP continues to give you sick certificates. Until your appeal has been decided you continue to get full IS without signing on.[26]

☐   You are mentally or physically disabled and because of this your earnings capacity or the number of hours you can work is reduced to 75 per cent or less of what a person without your disability would earn in the same job (see p10).

☐   You are registered blind. If you regain your sight you will continue to be treated as blind for 28 weeks after you have been taken off the register.

☐   You are working while living in a residential care or nursing home (see p10).

Carers and people with childcare responsibilities

☐   You are a single parent claiming for a child under 16. Once the child is 16 you will have to sign on unless you are exempt from doing so on other grounds.

☐   You are a single person fostering a child under 16 through a local authority or voluntary organisation.

☐   You are looking after a child under 16 because their parent or the person who usually looks after them is temporarily away or ill.

☐   You are claiming for a child under 16 and your partner is temporarily out of the UK.

☐   You are taking a child abroad specifically for medical treatment.

☐   You are pregnant and unable to work; or there are 11 weeks or less before your baby is due, or your baby was born not more than 7 weeks ago.

☐ You are looking after your partner, or a child under 19 for whom you are claiming, who is temporarily ill.

☐ You receive invalid care allowance, or the person for whom you care either receives or has claimed attendance allowance or the highest or middle rate care component of disability living allowance (DLA). In the latter case, you will be entitled to IS without signing on for up to 26 weeks from the date of the claim for attendance allowance/DLA or until the claim is decided, whichever comes first. If you cease meeting these conditions you can claim IS without signing on for a further eight weeks. If you are now claiming IS, having ceased caring for a disabled person you are also exempt from the need to sign on during the eight weeks after you stopped being a carer.

See p233 to check when you can claim for a child.

Pupils, students and people on training courses

☐ You qualify for IS while in full-time non-advanced education (see p12).

☐ You are a disabled student and you satisfy one of the following conditions:

– you qualify for the disability premium or severe disability premium (see p240 and p243); *or*

– because of your disability you would be unlikely to get a job within a reasonable period compared to other students, and you were getting IS immediately before 1 September 1990; *or*

– you claimed IS on or after 1 September 1990 and at some time during the 18 months before claiming you were getting IS as a disabled person under 19 in full-time non-advanced education, or as a disabled student; *or*

– you qualify for a disabled student's allowance because you are deaf; *or*

– it is accepted and you have requested a supplementary requirement, allowance or bursary payable under education mandatory awards (in Scotland, allowances and bursaries) regulations. [27]

☐ You are a single parent student.

☐ You are on a government training scheme and receive a training allowance (see p47).

☐ You are attending a compulsory Open University residential course.

Others

☐ You have to go to court as a JP, juror, witness or party to the proceedings.

☐ You have been remanded in custody, or committed in custody for trial or to be sentenced.

☐ You have just come out of prison, or youth custody. You will not be required to sign on for seven days from the date of your discharge.

☐ You are a refugee who is learning English in order to obtain employment. You must be on a course for more than 15 hours a week and, at the time the course started, you must have been in Britain for a year or less. You will not be required to sign on for up to nine months.

☐   You are a 'person from abroad' and are entitled to the urgent cases rate of IS (see p65).
☐   You are involved in a trade dispute or have been back to work for 15 days or less following a trade dispute (see p58).

If you are not in one of the groups listed above, you will have to sign on as available for work to get benefit, or apply on grounds of hardship (see below).

If you are claiming as a couple, and one of you does not have to sign on, this partner should probably be the claimant (see swapping the claimant – p101).

If your partner is the claimant, you do not have to sign on, but you may wish to do so voluntarily if you are unemployed and looking for work. Signing on gives you a National Insurance credit which helps safeguard future entitlement to benefits. It also enables you to take advantage of any special concessions in your area for the unemployed. If you have been signing on for six months, you may be able to qualify for employment training (see p47).

(iii)   Payments to avoid hardship[28]

You may get IS at a reduced rate if you would normally have to sign on as available for work to get benefit, but for some reason you do not satisfy the availability test (see p39) and you or a member of your family will suffer hardship if IS is not paid. You might come within this category if you are caring for someone who is not a member of your family and not entitled to attendance allowance, but you cannot continue to look after them unless you get IS; or if you are not allowed to sign on for religious or cultural reasons – eg, it is considered inappropriate for women to work outside the home.

You cannot use the hardship provision to get benefit if you are a student.

Under this rule you will not have to be available for[29] and actively seek work but your benefit will be reduced by the **voluntary unemployment deduction** (for how this is calculated, see p47).[30]

6   PRESENCE IN AND TEMPORARY ABSENCE FROM GREAT BRITAIN

Normally you can only get IS while you are living in GB. If you have recently come to this country from abroad you may get less benefit (see p64). If you go abroad temporarily, benefit can continue to be paid for up to four weeks, but if you are taking a child abroad for medical treatment it can be paid for up to eight weeks. To qualify for IS while abroad you must have been entitled to IS before you left the country, continue to satisfy the conditions for getting IS while away and not expect to be away for more than a year.[31]

Under the four-week rule you must also fall within one of the following groups:[32]
☐   you are going to Northern Ireland. (If you have to be available for work as a condition of getting IS, you will probably end up getting benefit for the first two weeks only. If you are going there long term, you should sign on at your local office in Northern Ireland and claim IS there);

☐ you and your partner are both abroad and your partner is paid a pensioner premium, higher pensioner premium, disability premium or severe disability premium;

☐ you are incapable of work and are not signing on on the day you go away and you have been continuously incapable for the previous 28 weeks;

☐ you are incapable of work because of illness or disability and you are going abroad specifically for treatment of your illness from an 'appropriately qualified person'. Before you go you should check that the Benefits Agency accepts that this rule applies to you;

☐ you are not required to sign on. However, this does *not* apply to you if you do not have to sign on because you are:
  – at school;
  – involved in a trade dispute, or for the first 15 days after you have returned to work following the dispute;
  – receiving an urgent cases payment of IS as a 'person from abroad' (see p65);
  – a discharged prisoner.

Under the eight-week rule you must be taking a child abroad specifically for medical, physiotherapy or similar treatment from an 'appropriately qualified person'. The child must be counted as part of your family. If you were required to sign on as a condition of getting benefit before leaving Britain, this requirement automatically ceases while you are abroad [33] (see p16).

If you are a member of a couple and you qualify for IS for up to four or eight weeks, your benefit will be paid to you on your return, but you can ask for it to be paid to your partner during your absence instead. If you are not entitled to IS while abroad or you have already used up your four or eight-week entitlement, your partner will have to make a claim in her/his own right (see p232). If it is your partner who goes abroad, your benefit is reduced after four weeks (eight weeks if your partner is taking a child abroad for medical treatment). You will then be paid as if you were a single claimant or single parent but your joint income and capital counts.

While you are temporarily out of the country, you may be entitled to housing benefit to cover your rent, and community charge benefit towards your community charge (see p154 (HB) and p217 (CCB). If your IS stops, you must claim these benefits separately.

Chapter 3

How your benefit is calculated

This chapter covers:

1 The basic calculation (see below)
2 Housing costs (p22)
3 Transitional payments (p31)
4 Urgent cases payments of income support (p35)

1 THE BASIC CALCULATION

The amount of IS you get depends on your needs – called your 'applicable amount' – and on how much income and capital you have. If you have capital of more than £8,000 you will not qualify for IS at all, but remember, not all capital counts. Any capital you have over £3,000 is assumed to produce an income and will reduce the amount of benefit you get. For the rules on capital, see p272.

There are **three stages** involved in working out your IS – see below.

(i) Calculate your 'applicable amount'

This is the amount you and your family are considered to need each week to live on. It is very low, so check whether you might be able to get a social fund payment to help with special expenses (see p291). Your applicable amount consists of:

☐ **personal allowances** for each member of your family; *plus*
☐ **premiums** for any special needs; *and*
☐ **housing costs**, principally for mortgage interest payments. (Most housing costs are not included in your IS applicable amount and are met separately by housing benefit, see p151.

The detailed rules about how to calculate personal allowances and premiums are on p236. Housing costs met by IS are described on p22.

(ii) Calculate your income

This is the amount you have coming in each week from other benefits, part-time earnings, maintenance etc. Most income counts in full, but some is ignored (see p272).

(iii) Deduct the income you have from the amount you need

The answer you get will normally be the amount paid as your IS.

Your applicable amount consisting of:	minus	Your income	=	Your IS
Personal allowance(s) Premium(s) Housing costs				

Example

Ms Hughes is a single parent aged 27 and she has a daughter aged 8. She has no housing costs to be covered by IS. Her applicable amount is:

£42.45	personal allowance
£14.55	personal allowance for child under 11
£ 9.30	family premium
£ 4.75	lone parent premium
£71.05	Total

Her income is £9.65 (child benefit including £1 addition for first or eldest child)

Her IS is £71.05 (applicable amount) minus £9.65 (income) = £61.40

Different rules apply to you if you are:
- ☐ in local authority residential accommodation (p80);
- ☐ in a residential care home or nursing home (p72);
- ☐ in hospital (p82);
- ☐ a prisoner (p85);
- ☐ a person without accommodation (p86);
- ☐ 16- or 17-years-old, (p52);
- ☐ a person from abroad, (p62);
- ☐ affected by a trade dispute, (p58);
- ☐ voluntarily unemployed, (p45);
- ☐ on a government training course, (p47).

People who are members of, and fully maintained by, a religious order do not get any IS at all.

You may get more than your normal IS entitlement because you are receiving **transitional protection** (see p31).

2 HOUSING COSTS

If you pay rent or live in board and lodging or a hostel you will normally receive housing benefit to cover your housing costs (see p151). Other housing costs are met as part of your IS 'applicable amount'. These are:[1]

☐ mortgage interest payments (see p24);

☐ interest under a hire purchase agreement to buy your home (see p24);

☐ interest you pay on a loan for repairs and improvements to your home (see p26);

☐ rent or ground rent (in Scotland, feu duty) if you have a long lease of more than 21 years;

☐ rent if you are a Crown tenant (minus water charges);

☐ payments you make if you are part of a co-ownership scheme;

☐ service charges. This covers charges paid to your landlord for a service which s/he provides, for example, cleaning of common areas. Owner-occupiers can also be liable for such charges under the terms of their lease. A 'service' is something which is agreed and arranged on your behalf and for which you are required to pay. Thus if you own a flat, and your lessor arranges the exterior painting of the building every three years and you are required to meet your share of the cost, your IS includes this as a service charge. Such charges only count if they relate to the provision of adequate accommodation.[2] Charges for major repairs and improvements carried out by a lessor and for which you are responsible do not count as service charges.[3] Charges made for services provided by an outside authority do not. Therefore charges for water and sewerage services paid to a water board are *not* covered.[4] However, you could argue that a bill for services provided by an outside authority counts if you are due to pay these as a condition of continuing to occupy your home, and they are necessary to ensure adequate accommodation;

☐ payments for a tent you live in and the site it is on;

☐ any other similar housing costs not listed above which are not met by HB (see p158) – eg, interest on unpaid road charges.[5]

Your IS will not include the following:

☐ housing costs which are covered by HB;[6]

☐ water rates. You are expected to pay for these from the rest of your IS. If you are a Crown tenant and your housing costs incorporate water charges, these will be deducted from your housing costs. If you do not know how much your water charges are, they are estimated as though you were not a Crown tenant and that amount is deducted;[7]

☐ the cost of heating, hot water, lighting and cooking where these are included in your housing costs.[8] The following amounts will be deducted from your housing costs:

heating	£8.60	cooking	£1.05
hot water	£1.05	lighting	£0.70

You will be expected to meet these from the rest of your IS. However, if you can produce evidence of an actual or approximate charge for fuel, that amount will be deducted instead;

☐ the cost of service charges that are listed on p161.[9] (But note that you *can* get help with certain service charges – see above);

☐   the costs of any repairs and improvements (of a similar kind to those listed on p27). However, if you take out a loan to pay for these items your housing costs include the interest on the loan (see p26). [10]

(i)   When can housing costs be paid?

You must satisfy the following two conditions:

☐   The housing costs you pay are for the home in which you and your family normally live. [11] If you have to make payments on two properties, the Benefits Agency will pay your housing costs for both in very limited circumstances (see below). Your home is defined as the building or part of the building in which you live and includes any garage, garden, outbuildings, other premises and land which it is not reasonable or practicable to sell separately. [12]

☐   You are responsible for paying these housing costs. This does not mean you have to be legally liable. [13] You are treated as liable if:

–   you have to pay them to someone who is not in your household (see p228 for meaning of 'household');

–   you share the responsibility to pay with other people in your household in practice (but not your partner or a 'close relative' – see p74 for meaning) and it is reasonable to treat you as sharing. [14] If you share, your proportion of the costs is covered;

–   the person who is liable is not paying and you have to pay the housing costs instead in order to keep your home. This only applies if that person is your former partner or it is reasonable for you to pay. [15]

If payments for housing costs have been waived because you have paid for repairs or redecoration, which are not normally your responsibility, you can still get IS for them for up to eight weeks. [16]

There are special rules if you and your partner are involved in a trade dispute, see p60.

Where you have to pay costs for two homes you will get IS for both if:

☐   you left your old home through fear of domestic violence and it is reasonable that you should get payments for two homes. [17] 'Violence' includes violence in your old home *or* from a former member of your family. Fear of a racial attack should be covered by this rule as long as the attack would take place *in* the old home; *or*

☐   your partner unavoidably has to live away from home as a student or while on a government training course (Employment Training (ET) or Youth Training (YT), see p47) and it is reasonable to pay both costs. [18] A single person or single parent who is a student or on YT or ET and who qualifies for IS, only gets her/his housing costs for their normal or term-time home, but not both; [19]

☐   you are moving and you have to make payments on both homes. Your housing costs are met for up to four weeks. [20] If you have had to move to temporary accommodation while repairs are done to your normal home, you only get help with the home for which you have to make payments. [21] If you have to pay for both you get the housing costs of your normal home.

If you became liable for housing costs before you moved in, your IS can include these costs for up to four weeks, if you could not move in because: [22]

☐   you were waiting for adaptations for a disability; *or*

☐   you were waiting for the result of a social fund application for help with removal costs and expenses involved in setting up home (eg, furniture and bedding), and you have a child under six or your benefit includes a pensioner, higher pensioner, disability, severe disability or disabled child premium; *or*

☐ you became responsible for the housing costs while in hospital or in 'local authority residential accommodation' including sponsored places (see p80).

You must have claimed IS before you moved in, or if you claimed and your IS did not include housing costs, you should reclaim within four weeks of moving in. [23]

If you are not covered by the above rules, you can only get your housing costs met when you 'normally occupy' the premises as your home. A person who has never actually lived in their home does not 'normally occupy' it. [24] It is arguable that moving in furniture and spending a night in the home could count as living there.

If you are away from home temporarily but are still entitled to IS and you do not let your home, your housing costs will continue to be paid if you intend to return, and are unlikely to be away for longer than 52 weeks (the time-limit is slightly relaxed if you cannot control when you will return – eg, you go into hospital). Payments will cease once you have been away for 52 weeks. [25]

Those students who qualify for IS, but who are away from their term-time home during the summer vacation, will not have the housing costs on that home met unless the reason they are away is because they are in hospital, or their term-time home is also their normal home. [26]

(ii)   Mortgage payments

An amount for mortgage payments is included in your IS applicable amount under the rules described below. From May 1992 there will be changes to the way in which this is paid (see p106).

Your applicable amount does not cover capital repayments, only the interest on a mortgage, hire purchase agreement or any other loan taken out in order to buy your home. [27] (We use the term **mortgage** to refer to all such loans or agreements.) Special rules apply for the first 16 weeks that you claim IS (see p25). The cost of associated insurance premiums is not covered. Thus, claimants with an endowment mortgage will not get the insurance element paid and should consider changing the terms of their mortgage. [28] Most people pay mortgage interest after deduction of income tax but, if this does not apply, you are allowed the full amount of your payments. Otherwise, you get the net amount you actually pay. [29] Where interest is charged at more than one rate you receive the aggregated amount. [30] The amount actually charged by the lender is met as long as there is proof of the sum involved, even if that sum differs from the figure calculated by the Benefits Agency. [31]

You will only be paid the interest where you have: [32]

☐ taken out the mortgage in order to buy a home; *and/or*

☐ taken out a second mortgage or loan in order to repay the original mortgage, which was itself taken out in order to buy a home (sometimes called 're-mortgaging'); *and/or*

☐ taken out a loan for the cost of repairs or improvements (see p26).

Where a loan is taken out wholly or partly for other purposes (eg, to finance a business), the proportion of the interest payable on that part of the loan is not met except where the claim is made by a separated partner.

Separated couples

Where a couple separate and one partner buys out the other's share in the home, the additional repayment burden is met.[33] The claimant is, in effect, acquiring an additional interest in the home. (This would also apply to other claimants who bought an additional share of their home.)

If your ex-partner is not paying the mortgage, you can have the mortgage interest met as part of your benefit.[34] You can also be paid interest on a loan which is not for house purchase (eg, it could be for a car), provided your partner cannot or will not pay it, and it is secured on your home.[35] It does not matter whether the loan was taken out jointly with your partner or by one of you alone.

If you discover that your ex-partner has not been paying the mortgage as you assumed, you should ask for your benefit to be reviewed to include the mortgage interest that has not been paid.

A second loan
Interest on a second loan will only be paid to the extent that the interest on the earlier loan would have been met by IS. For example, if the amount outstanding on your first mortgage was £20,000 and you took out a second one of £25,000 to repay the first, you will only get the interest on £20,000 of the second loan met by IS.

Interest on arrears of a mortgage cannot be met[36] except where these arise:[37]
☐ during the 16 weeks after you first claim IS, when mortgage interest repayments are only covered partially (see below); *or*
☐ from interest payments some or all of which are deferred for at least two years under the terms of your loan, and which you are liable to meet.

The 16-week rule
You will get only 50 per cent of the mortgage interest for the first 16 weeks of your IS claim. However, if you or your partner are 60 or over there will be no reduction.[38] If either of you reach 60 during the first 16 weeks the restriction will be removed. If you come off IS during this 16-week period, see below. After 16 weeks, you will get the full amount of your mortgage interest.[39]

Periods when you are not on IS
So that you can qualify for full mortgage interest more quickly, you can be treated as being in receipt of IS for certain periods when you are not on IS, or you are not the person claiming (if you are, or were, a couple). These periods both count towards the first 16 weeks and enable you to qualify for the full mortgage interest straightaway in certain circumstances. You will be treated as being in receipt of IS as follows:[40]
☐ during a gap up to and including eight weeks between two IS claims;
☐ during the time when your partner was claiming on her/his own, provided you claim IS within eight weeks of becoming a couple;
☐ during the time when your ex-partner was claiming, and you claim IS within eight weeks of separating;
☐ during the time when your partner was claiming, if you take over the claiming role;
☐ during the time when someone else was claiming for you as a dependent child. But you must claim within eight weeks of this, and you must also be claiming for another child for whom s/he used to get benefit;
☐ for any period when you were not getting IS, but as a result of a review or appeal it was decided that you should have been receiving it.

Once you have qualified for the full mortgage interest as above:

☐ you or your partner can take a full-time job for twelve weeks or less, and you will be able to reclaim IS and get the mortgage interest paid in full.[41] But the normal eight-week break will apply (see above) if you or your partner leave the job voluntarily or are sacked and the voluntary unemployment deduction is applied (see p45), or if the person who took the job was, in the six months before that, in full-time work, in relevant education or a student.[42]

☐ you or your partner can attend a government training course (YT or ET), or attend an employment rehabilitation centre, and even though you may come off benefit as a result, you continue to be treated as though you are on IS while there. If you have to reclaim IS when the course is finished you get the mortgage interest paid in full immediately.[43]

If you do not qualify for IS because the 50 per cent rule means your income is higher than your applicable amount, but you would get IS if your mortgage interest was counted in full, make a second claim for IS between 16 and 20 weeks after the date of your original claim. Similarly, if your benefit was ended on review or appeal, re-claim between 16 and 20 weeks after the date of your claim that led to the original award. You will then be entitled to receive benefit (calculated on the basis that all your mortgage interest is included in your IS assessment) starting 16 weeks after the date of that original claim.[44]

If you use payments from a mortgage protection policy (taken out to insure against the risk of being unable to meet your mortgage payments) to cover the mortgage interest not met by IS, this money will be ignored as your income[45] (see p269).

After 16 weeks you will get 100 per cent of your mortgage interest payments[46] (but see p30 for tenants who buy their own homes, and p29 for 'excessive' housing costs). You also receive the additional interest payable on the arrears of interest that have accumulated during this period.[47]

Capital repayments

Your IS does not include your mortgage capital repayments. Many lenders are prepared to accept interest-only payments for a while. Local authorities are encouraged to do so in the case of single parents and have been advised to extend this practice to all cases of mortgage arrears.[48] If your local authority refuses to waive capital repayments ask the Department of the Environment (2 Marsham St, London SW1) to intervene. If your loan is from a building society, contact the head office of the society, and if that does not resolve the problem, ask the Building Societies Association (3 Savile Row, London W1X 1AF) to conciliate.

If you have to pay the capital, you may be able to increase your income by a small amount by taking in lodgers (see p265 for how this will affect your IS). Payment made direct to the lender from relatives, friends or a charity towards the capital repayments[49] will be ignored (see p271 and p282). There is a similar rule if the payment is made by a liable relative[50] (see p92).

If you use payments from a mortgage protection policy to meet your mortgage capital repayments these will be ignored as your income.[51]

(iii) Loans for repairs and improvements

All claimants (not just owner-occupiers) are entitled to receive IS to cover the interest on loans taken out to pay for repairs and improvements to their home. The loan should be used for the repairs within six months of its receipt, or longer if such a delay is reasonable. The same 50 per cent restriction for the first 16 weeks on IS applies as in the case of loans to buy a home[52] (see pp25-26).

Repairs and improvements are defined as:[53]
- [ ] major repairs necessary to maintain the fabric of the dwelling occupied as the home; *and also*
- [ ] putting in bathroom fixtures like a washbasin, bath, shower or toilet;
- [ ] damp-proofing;
- [ ] providing or improving ventilation or natural light;
- [ ] providing or improving drainage facilities;
- [ ] putting in electric lighting and sockets;
- [ ] putting in heating, including central heating;
- [ ] putting in storage facilities for fuel and refuse;
- [ ] improving the structural condition of the home;
- [ ] improving facilities for storing, preparing and cooking food;
- [ ] insulation;
- [ ] other improvements which are reasonable in the circumstances (eg, adaptations to the home for a disabled person[54]).

If the loan included the cost of necessary redecoration following any of these works, the interest on that part of the loan should also be met by IS. External redecoration on its own could be an improvement or major repair.[55]

If you have to pay a service charge for repairs and improvements it is not covered by IS, but under this rule you can take out a loan and be paid interest.

For information about housing renovation grants, see p347.

(iv) When your housing costs will not be met in full

Your housing costs may not be met in full if:
- [ ] part of the loan was taken out for business purposes (see p24);
- [ ] your home is used for both business and domestic purposes and neither part can be sold off separately. It is therefore classed as a 'mixed' or 'composite hered-itament', and not just a private dwelling. Broadly you only get help with the interest payable on that part of the property used for domestic purposes.[56] You may need further advice from your local authority or from the Institute of Revenues, Rating and Valuation (41 Doughty St, London WC1N 2LF).
- [ ] you have non-dependants living in your household (see below);
- [ ] your housing costs are 'excessive' (see p29);
- [ ] you are a **tenant** and buy your own home (see p30).

Deductions for non-dependants

A **non-dependant** is a person who normally lives with you and who is not part of your family for IS purposes (see p227) – eg, a grown-up son or daughter. A person is *not* a non-dependant if s/he:[57]
- [ ] is liable to pay you or your partner in order to live in your home – eg, a sub-tenant, licensee, or boarder. This also applies to other members of their

household. The payment must be on a commercial basis. A low charge does not necessarily mean that the arrangement is not commercial; nor do you not have to make a profit. An arrangement between friends can be commercial[58]. Close relatives (see p74) count as non-dependants even if they pay for their accommodation;

☐   is someone, other than a close relative (see p74), to whom you, or your partner, are liable to make payments on a commercial basis (ie, as a sub-tenant, licensee, boarder) in order to live in their property. Other members of their household do not count as non-dependants either;

☐   jointly occupies your home and is a co-owner or joint tenant with you or your partner. Your joint occupier's partner is not a non-dependent. Close relatives (see p74) are treated as non-dependants unless they had joint liability prior to 11 April 1988. Joint liability between close relatives which begins later only counts if it existed on or before you first lived in the property (or your partner did if s/he is the joint tenant/owner);

☐   is employed by a charitable or voluntary body as a resident carer for you or your partner and you pay for that service (even if the charge is only nominal). If the carer's partner also lives in your home, s/he will not count as a non-dependant.

A person can be treated as living with you only if they share any rooms except a bathroom or toilet or common access areas – eg, hall or landing, or, in the case of sheltered accommodation, other common rooms.[59] Thus, this includes people who share the use of a kitchen. But a person who is separately liable to pay rent to a landlord is not counted as living with you.

If you have a non-dependant living with you, a set deduction is usually made from your housing costs whether or not s/he makes a contribution towards the cost of the accommodation. The amount varies according to the age and circumstances of the non-dependant.

No deduction is made from your benefit for a non-dependant who is:[60]

☐   16 or 17 years old;

☐   18 to 24 years old and on IS;

☐   getting a YT allowance;

☐   a full-time student. This also applies during the summer vacation unless s/he has a job during that time;

☐   currently staying in your household but whose normal home is elsewhere.

☐   a joint tenant or co-owner with you or your partner, even if that person is a close relative;

☐   not living with you because s/he is in prison or has been a hospital inpatient for over six weeks.

No deduction is made from your benefit if:[61]

☐   a deduction is already being made from your housing benefit;

☐   you or your partner are registered blind or treated as blind (see p240) or getting attendance allowance (or equivalent benefit paid because of injury at work or a war injury) or the care component of disability living allowance.

A deduction is made from your benefit for each non-dependant in your household unless exempted as above.[62]

Circumstances of non-dependant	*Deduction*
18 or over, in full-time work with gross weekly income of:	
– less than £65	£4.00
– between £65 and £99.99	£8.00
– between £100 and £129.99	£12.00
– £130 or more	£18.00
18 or over and not in full-time work	£4.00

For the meaning of 'full-time work', see p9. Remember that if you are off sick or on maternity leave you do not count as being in full-time work (even if you are on full pay).[63] Gross income includes wages before tax and National Insurance are deducted plus any other income you have including benefits (but not attendance allowance or disability living allowance).

Couples and joint occupiers

☐ Only one deduction is made for a married or unmarried couple who are non-dependants.[64] Where each member of the couple would attract different deductions because of different circumstances the higher one is made. The total gross income of the couple is taken into account when deciding whether the lower deduction applies.

☐ Deductions for non-dependants are divided between joint occupiers, taking account of the number of joint occupiers and the proportion of living costs paid by each. Joint occupiers who are a couple count as one person.[65]

'Excessive' housing costs

You cannot have your full housing costs paid if it is decided that your housing costs are 'excessive'.[66] Account must be taken of the amount deducted from your housing costs for non-dependants living with you (see above).

The amount allowed for your housing costs can be restricted if:[67]

☐ your home, excluding any part that is let, is larger than is required by your family, any foster children and any non-dependants when compared to suitable alternative accommodation. The needs of everyone living in your accommodation must be considered. For example, if anyone needs additional space (ie, because of a disability), this should be taken into account. If you have a child in care, or an elderly or disabled relative who normally lives in a residential home but who regularly comes to stay with you, it is reasonable that you should have a spare room for this purpose; *or*

☐ the immediate area around your home is more expensive than other areas in which there is suitable accommodation; *or*

☐ your housing costs are higher than those of suitable alternative accommodation in the area. ('Area' here refers to the immediate neighbourhood[68] – see below.)

No restriction should be made and your housing costs should be met in full if it is unreasonable for you to move. When deciding this, the Benefits Agency will consider:[69]

☐ the availability of suitable accommodation. ('Availability' means it must actually exist, and it must be suitable for you);

☐ the level of housing costs in the area. An area is 'something more confined, restricted and compact than a locality or district . . . It might consist of . . . a number of roads, refer to a neighbourhood and even to a large block of flats. It is not capable of precise definition';[70]

☐ your circumstances and those of your family – in particular, your age, health, employment prospects and the possible upheaval in the education of any children living with you if you had to move.

Other circumstances may be worth pointing out (eg, particular difficulties you have in finding accommodation because of your family's size, your need to be near a relative to care for them or near members of your family or friends for support, the number of times you have had to move recently). It is also reasonable to argue that you should be able to remain in a home where you have lived for many years, but which is now larger than you need because, for example, there has been a death in the family, or you are now separated or divorced.

The fact that you have been told by the Benefits Agency that full mortgage interest would be paid is a factor that the adjudication officer should consider when deciding whether to limit housing costs.[71] Your inability to obtain another mortgage to buy another house is also relevant. Rented accommodation is not necessarily a satisfactory alternative if as a result you lose entitlement to IS. It would therefore not be reasonable to expect you to move unless you could be sure you could obtain a mortgage to buy an alternative property.[72]

There should be no restriction during the first six months you claim IS, provided you could afford the payments when you took them on. This should also cover a person who was a member of the family when the mortgage was taken on. So if the payments were affordable when taken on by a couple who later separated leaving one partner in the home, this rule should apply. The six-month period will be extended for up to a year if you are making every effort to find somewhere cheaper to live.[73] If your benefit is reviewed, the six-month periods should run from the date of the review.

If restriction is appropriate your housing costs are limited to the cost of a home of suitable size or expense. You would get no housing costs if the equity in your home is sufficient to buy the alternative property outright.[74]

Tenants who buy their own homes

If you buy the home which you currently rent, and your housing costs go up, you may not get your new housing costs met in full.

If you sought advice from the Benefits Agency *before* buying and were told *wrongly* that your mortgage interest would be met in full, you will still be caught by this rule. You will have to take legal action for misadvice to recover any loss. It will help if the advice from the Benefits Agency was given to you in writing.

If you did not have security of tenure (ie, the landlord had the right to make you leave without giving any reason), your new housing costs will be assessed in the normal way for owner-occupiers – ie, the increase will be paid unless you fail the other tests relating to 'excessive' housing costs – see p29.

If you did have security of tenure as a private tenant or a council tenant (ie, you were protected by the law against eviction by the landlord), the amount for your housing costs will be restricted to the amount of the rent used to calculate your HB before you bought your home.[75] If, subsequently, the cost of your mortgage or loan rises again, you will be allowed the increase in the assessment of your housing costs. If you buy the home jointly with one or more non-dependants, you will be treated as jointly responsible for the housing costs. Your allowance for housing costs will be a proportionate share of the new housing costs. [76] If you had security of tenure and your share of the new housing costs is more than the rent used to calculate your HB, you only receive that lower amount.

If a member of the household who is a non-dependant buys the home, you will not be treated as responsible for the housing costs.

The restriction is removed if there is a major change in your family's circumstances which makes it inappropriate for there to be a limit on the amount allowed for your housing costs – eg, if as a single parent you lose a part-time job and with it the £15 earnings disregard (see p255). The limit is also lifted once you have stopped getting IS for at least eight weeks and then claimed again. [77]

You will not be caught by this provision if you were not claiming benefit during the week in which you became 'liable to complete' the purchase – ie, when contracts were actually exchanged between buyer and seller. [78]

3 TRANSITIONAL PROTECTION

(i) Introduction

Some claimants are paid more than their basic IS entitlement because they receive an amount of transitional protection. Transitional protection was created when IS replaced supplementary benefit in April 1988. Its purpose was to prevent those on supplementary benefit suffering a sudden drop in income because of the different way in which IS was calculated. Later changes to the IS rules have also caused some claimants to be worse off, and they too received transitional protection. It is a payment to cover the difference between the reduced benefit rate and the amount received prior to the change.

Payments were introduced at five different stages and are as follows:

☐ **Transitional additions from 11 April 1988** for people claiming benefit immediately before and after this date. [79] If you have been receiving IS since its introduction you may still be entitled to a transitional addition (see p32). You could be getting a transitional addition on its own.

☐ **Transitional payments [80] from 30 May 1988** for those who were:
  – not entitled to IS between 11 April 1988 and 30 May 1988 because the capital rules were less generous than for supplementary benefit; *or*
  – temporarily absent from home at the changeover to IS. (See p34 for details.)

☐ **Protected sums for people who were boarders** on 10 April 1989 [81] (which is when boarders began to have their housing costs met by HB and not IS). You will only be getting this now if you are in supported lodgings. For all other boarders the protection was only temporary, lasting 13 weeks or 12 months. The protected sum was part of your applicable amount.

☐ **Protected sums for people living in hostels [82]** on 9 October 1989 (which was when hostel residents began to have their housing costs met by HB and not IS). The protected sum was part of the applicable amount. It has been phased out gradually.

☐ **Protected personal allowances [83]** from 12 September 1988 for couples where one member was under 18 prior to this date. At that time a change in the rules meant that if one partner of a couple was under 18 a reduced personal allowance was paid. This protection is no longer likely to apply as affected couples will now be over 18.

This section gives the rules for those types of transitional protection which are still current. If you are assessing entitlement for a past period and need to refer to the rules for boarders, and couples where one was under 18, see the 19th edition of the *National Welfare Benefits Handbook*. The rules relating to protected sums for hostel dwellers were described in *Welfare Rights Bulletin 91*. If you do not have these items we can supply a photocopy of the relevant parts. Write to CPAG, 1-5 Bath Street, London EC1V 9PY.

(ii) How transitional protection affects your current benefit

Although transitional protection is no longer relevant to most claimants, you may need to know about it to:
- [ ] check the amount you are currently receiving to see if it is correct; *or*
- [ ] calculate your IS for a past period.

If you are trying to make a backdated claim for benefit (see p102) or to have your benefit reviewed because you think that you were paid the wrong amount (see p105), you will need to check any transitional protection. It is possible to increase the amount of your current transitional protection by reviewing the amount of supplementary benefit paid[84] to you, or making a late claim for that benefit in order to qualify for transitional protection.[85] Supplementary benefit was paid at a higher rate than IS for many claimants because it included additional payments to cover special needs – eg, extra heating, charges for domestic assistance, extra baths, clothing needs.

For more information on other payments available and on supplementary benefit in general, see the 17th edition of the *National Welfare Benefits Handbook*.

(iii) Transitional additions from 11 April 1988

These transitional additions were the most widely available. They applied to all claimants who were entitled to supplementary benefit immediately prior to 11 April 1988 and who continued to claim its successor, income support. Only prisoners and people who had no fixed address could not qualify.[86]

Transitional additions were calculated by comparing your total benefit income in your benefit week which started between 4 and 10 April (Week 1) with that in your subsequent benefit week (Week 2).[87]

Your total benefit income[88] for the first week included all the social security benefits which you received (excluding HB) and any extra-statutory payments which were paid for that week. Mobility and attendance allowance were excluded if they were disregarded for supplementary benefit. If you were subject to a voluntary unemployment deduction (see p45) the full and not the reduced amount of benefit was used. If you were getting HB for rates prior to the changeover, £1.30 was added to this total (£1 if you were single and under 25).

You then calculated your total benefit income in the second week at the rates applicable after 11 April 1988 (again excluding housing benefit, and mobility allowance/attendance allowance if they were disregarded for IS). If this figure was lower than that of the previous week, you received a transitional addition equal to the difference. [89] It was possible to receive a transitional addition on its own if the only reason that you were not entitled to IS was because your income exceeded your applicable amount. Transitional additions count as IS. [90]

Special rules applied if you:

☐ received a domestic assistance addition of more than £10 per week (see below);

☐ lived in hostel or board and lodging accommodation but were absent for up to 13 weeks at the point of changeover to IS, or left this accommodation temporarily after this point;

☐ lived in a residential care or nursing home but were temporarily absent at the introduction of IS, or at a later stage;

☐ had a partner who had been in hospital for over 52 weeks.

If you need information about these refer to the 19th edition of the *National Welfare Benefits Handbook*.

Transitional additions were intended to reduce over time as your IS entitlement increased. If you received a large transitional addition you may still be getting it, albeit at a reduced rate. The addition stops altogether if it is reduced to nil (see below), or if you cease to be entitled to IS unless the only reason for this is that your income exceeds your applicable amount [91] (see p227). In this case, you may be left with a transitional addition on its own.

Transitional additions reduce: [92]

☐ each time your applicable amount increases if you receive both IS and a transitional addition;

☐ by the excess of your income over your applicable amount where this causes you to stop being entitled to IS;

☐ by increases in your income if you are getting a transitional addition only;

☐ where you are getting a transitional addition only but become entitled to IS because your applicable amount goes up. The reduction is the difference between the increase in your applicable amount and the previous amount by which your income exceeded your applicable amount.

However, increases in your **applicable amount** due to the following are ignored: [93]

☐ the increases in the applicable amounts for children and the family premium introduced in October 1991;

☐ a child or young person in local authority care coming to stay in your household, unless they have remained for over eight weeks;

☐ admission into a residential care or nursing home, or residential accommodation, for eight weeks or less;

☐ receipt of the enhanced pensioner premium if it was included in your applicable amount during the week commencing 9 October 1989;

☐ the end of the voluntary unemployment deduction;

☐ you or your partner joining or leaving an ET or rehabilitation course.

However, if your applicable amount goes down because, for example you go into hospital – and it is later restored to its original amount on your return home – this should not count as an increase of your applicable amount. Any increase must take your applicable amount higher than it was in your second benefit week (see above). Thus temporary reductions and increases are ignored. [94]

Any increase in your **income** due to receipt of a training allowance or the increases in child benefit in October 1991 is also ignored.

You will be able to requalify for a transitional addition[95] if you cease to be entitled to IS, plus a transitional addition for less than eight weeks as long as you are receiving more than £10 per week.

If you lose your transitional addition because you or your partner have started full-time work, this period is extended to twelve weeks and your transitional addition can be for any amount. However, the requalifying period is again reduced to eight weeks if, when you go back on to IS you are:

☐ subject to the voluntary unemployment deduction; *or*

☐ you worked for less than six weeks; *or*

☐ you were a student or doing another job in the six months prior to this one.

(iv) People getting domestic assistance additions prior to 11 April 1988

The calculation of transitional additions was different if you received a domestic assistance addition of £10 or more as part of your supplementary benefit.[96] The transitional addition was:

☐ your total benefit income in Week 1 (see p32); *minus*

☐ the domestic assistance addition; *minus*

☐ your total benefit income in Week 2 (see p32), excluding any severe disability premium (SDP), if any; *minus*

☐ the difference between the domestic assistance addition and the SDP *but only if the former was lower.*

In addition to a transitional addition, people getting the domestic assistance addition of £10 or more could get a **special transitional addition**.[97] If their addition was more than their SDP the difference was payable as a special transitional addition. Special transitional additions stop when:

☐ you are not entitled to IS for reasons other than that your income exceeds your applicable amount;

☐ you go into hospital, residential care/accommodation or a nursing home;

☐ it has reduced to nil.

If you requalify within eight weeks it can be reinstated. If you are not entitled to IS because you or your partner have started work, a 12-week period may be allowed (see (iii) above). If you only receive a special transitional addition it will reduce as your income rises, unless the rise is due to receipt of a training allowance, or to the increase in the amount of child benefit payable from October 1991.

(v) May 1988 transitional payments

Under the supplementary benefit scheme the value of the following capital could be ignored for at least six months:

☐ the home where you and your partner were living prior to splitting up;

☐ property which you were trying to gain possession of through legal proceedings;

☐ property which you were trying to sell;

☐ property which you could not live in until essential work was done.

Since 30 May 1988, these have also been ignored for IS. If you qualified for supplementary benefit prior to 11 April 1988 and would have been entitled to IS but for this changed capital rule, you should have received:

☐ an extra-statutory payment to compensate you for the period 11 April 1988 to 29 May 1988;

☐ an enhanced applicable amount which includes an element equal to the transitional addition you would have received had you qualified for IS during the week commencing 11 April 1988. [98]

You may still be receiving this transitional protection as part of your IS.

You also receive an enhanced amount of IS if you were entitled to a greater or lesser amount of benefit prior to, or after, 11 April 1988 (or both), because you or a family member were:

☐ temporarily in hospital, residential care/accommodation or a nursing home;

☐ in local authority care;

☐ abroad receiving medical treatment;

☐ staying with someone else who was contributing to your maintenance. [99]

You could only benefit from this if your benefit was altered for less than eight weeks. You receive extra applicable amount equal to the difference between your 'normal' supplementary benefit in the week prior to 11 April 1988 and your IS in the first week after you (or your family member) return home.

This latter protection is lost if you lose entitlement to IS for at least 8 weeks (12 weeks if you lost entitlement because you returned to full-time work – see p34(iii)). However, if you go from IS onto an Employment Training scheme you will count as still being entitled to IS for that period. [100]

4   URGENT CASES PAYMENTS

(i)   Who can claim?

If you do not satisfy the normal rules for getting IS, you may nevertheless be able to get an urgent cases payment if you come within one of the following groups: [101]

☐ you are a 'person from abroad' and you meet certain conditions (see p65);

☐ you are treated as possessing income which was due to be paid to you but which has not been paid (see p270). If you were due to receive a social security benefit but it has not yet been paid you will not be treated as possessing it. The income you are treated as possessing must not be readily available to you and there must be a likelihood that if you do not get a payment, you or your family will suffer hardship. [102]

Even if your partner is entitled to ordinary IS you can claim urgent cases payments instead if the amount you received would be higher.

It is important to note that an urgent cases payment is a payment of IS and thus you are automatically eligible for other benefits – see p6.

If you do not come within these rules but have no money, you may be able to get a crisis loan from the social fund (see p314).

If you are not entitled to IS because you cannot sign on, but you are likely to suffer hardship without help, [103] see p18.

(ii)   How much you can get

Applicable amounts

Urgent cases payments of IS are paid at a reduced rate. Your applicable amount is:
- [ ] a personal allowance for you (and your partner). It is paid at 90 per cent of the personal allowance that would have been paid had you qualified for IS in the normal way; *plus*
- [ ] full personal allowances for any children; *plus*
- [ ] premiums and housing costs, if any, and any 'protected sum' paid because you were a boarder prior to 10 April 1989[104] (see p31).

If you are living in a residential or nursing home (private or local authority), you receive 90 per cent of the personal allowance for you (and your partner) *plus* full personal allowances for any children *plus* the amount normally allowed for your accommodation. [105]

If your benefit is reduced because you are treated as voluntarily unemployed, the voluntary unemployment deduction (see p45) is applied before the 10 per cent urgent cases reduction.

Income and capital

Almost all of your capital and income is taken into account before an urgent cases payment is made.

Income

All your income counts, including income that is usually ignored, except the following: [106]
- [ ] assumed income from capital between £3,000 and £8,000 – ie, your 'tariff income' (see p266);
- [ ] income you are treated as having if you are applying for an urgent cases payment for that reason;
- [ ] any housing benefit and/or community charge benefit;
- [ ] any payment made to compensate you for the loss of entitlement to housing benefit supplement or housing benefit;
- [ ] any payment from each of the Macfarlane Trusts or Independent Living Fund;
- [ ] payments made by haemophilia sufferers to their partner, or children out of money originally provided by one of the Macfarlane Trusts. If the sufferer has no partner or children, payments made to a parent, step-parent or guardian are also disregarded, but only for two years. These payments are also disregarded if the sufferer dies and the money is paid out of the estate;
- [ ] payments arising from the Macfarlane Trusts which are paid by a person to a haemophiliac partner, or to their child(ren).

Certain income is treated as capital if you get IS under the normal rules (see p274). [107] However, if you apply for an urgent cases payment the following is treated as income:

☐ any lump sum paid to you not more than once a year for your work as a part-time firefighter, part-time member of a lifeboat crew, auxiliary coastguard or member of the Territorial Army;

☐ any refund of income tax;

☐ holiday pay which is not payable until more than four weeks after your job ended;

☐ any irregular charitable or voluntary payment.

Capital [108]

Your capital is calculated in the usual way but the following is also taken into account:

☐ money from the sale of your home which you intend to use to buy another;

☐ the liquid assets of a business (eg, cash in hand);

☐ arrears of the following: mobility allowance, mobility supplement, disability living or disability working allowance, attendance allowance, IS, family credit, supplementary benefit or family income supplement, or any concessionary payments made to compensate for non-payment of any of these benefits;

☐ money which had been deposited with a housing association and which is now to be used to buy a home;

☐ up to £200 of a training bonus received after being on employment training (see p50);

☐ a refund of tax on a mortgage or loan taken out to buy, or to do repairs and/or improvements to your home.

Chapter 4

The unemployed and people on government training schemes

This chapter covers:

This chapter deals with people under 60 who are unemployed and required to sign on as a condition of receiving benefit and also those on government training schemes.

See p16 for circumstances in which people under 60 do not have to sign on to get benefit.

1   SIGNING ON

You will have to see a new client adviser at the unemployment benefit office, and complete form B1 and then sign on generally once a fortnight, in order to get benefit. By signing on, you satisfy the normal requirement to claim IS by attending in person at an unemployment benefit office. [1] When you sign on, you say that you are available for work and that is usually accepted as sufficient evidence of your availability at first (see p39). However, if for any reason you have failed to sign on, but have now made a late claim (see p102), your failure to sign on does not mean that you were not available for work. You will then need to tell the unemployment benefit office that you were looking for work and provide copies of any letters of rejection etc.

Even if you think you do not need IS, it is worth claiming in case you are not entitled to unemployment benefit, or if the latter takes time to come through. If your claim is successful, your IS will be paid fortnightly in arrears two days after your signing-on day so you may have to wait up to 16 days. If you have no money you should try for a crisis loan from the social fund (see p314). Do *not* be put off applying even if you are told by a receptionist or counter clerk that you will not get any help.

People under 18 who are eligible for IS and who have to sign on also have to register at the JobCentre or Careers Office. [2] For who decides whether you are available for work, see p42.

2 AVAILABILITY FOR WORK

(i) What 'available for work' means

You are treated as available for work if:[3]

☐ there is a reasonable prospect (in the foreseeable future[4]) of your obtaining the kind of work you say you are available to do – but there are exceptions to this general condition (see below); *and*

☐ you are willing and able to accept (generally at once) any offer of work.

It must be work you can reasonably be expected to do, for which you expect to be paid and which is 24 hours or more a week, or as much as you can normally do given any mental or physical disability.[5]

If you can only be available within 24 hours because you are doing voluntary work, or within 14 days if you are attending a work camp organised by a local authority or charity for helping the community, or not immediately because you work part-time in emergency and rescue services, you are still treated as available.[6]

(ii) How to fill in Form UB671

When you sign on, you will be asked to complete a questionnaire on Form UB671. This is designed to test whether you are:

☐ genuinely available for work – ie, whether you are restricting the type of job and level of pay you will accept, the hours you will work and how far you are prepared to travel etc; *and*

☐ able to take up work straightaway – eg, if you have children to look after during work hours, what care arrangements have you planned?;

☐ trying to find work.

When filling in Form UB671:

☐ indicate both the type of job you would like and also what you would be prepared to accept;

☐ where you are asked for the minimum wage or salary you will accept, you should put the going rate for that job. If in doubt put 'the going rate';

☐ state that you will be flexible about hours and travel (but be sure you are willing to be this flexible);

☐ even if you have a child or adult dependant at home, you still have to show that you could take a job at a moment's notice in order to be available. If you do not already have a childminder or carer lined up you should give the name of someone (eg, a friend or relative) who can provide care at least temporarily (but *not* someone who has to be available for work).

The Benefits Agency only counts you as not available for work if the conditions you have laid down about the type of work you will accept mean that you have no reasonable chance of getting a job.[7] Your chances will depend partly on how long you have been out of work which affects the decision on whether to treat you as available for work.[8]

Your benefit should not be stopped if you have laid down conditions and:[9]

☐ the only reason you have no real chance of getting a job is because of temporary adverse industrial conditions in the area; *or*

☐ they are reasonable in view of your physical or mental condition; *or*
☐ they relate to the type of work you usually do. This rule applies only for a 'permitted period' of up to 13 weeks – it may be less depending on your skills, training and qualifications, how long you have been in this work and whether this type of work is available. The 13 weeks run from the first day you claimed unemployment benefit after last being in full-time work. If you have not been entitled to unemployment benefit at all since becoming unemployed, the 13 weeks run from the first day you claimed IS after leaving full-time work or vocational training in your usual line of work, or after ceasing to be incapable of work. If you have never worked, or do not have a 'usual occupation', you do not get a permitted period. [10]

Your benefit can be withheld when you first claim, or later when your case is reviewed. If you are willing and able to work and think you have a chance of getting a job within the conditions you have specified, you should appeal (see p118). You might also be able to get your benefit reinstated by widening the conditions under which you are prepared to take work.

(iii)   Part-time work

If you are in part-time work or on a part-time course (see p14) you may still be treated as available for work and entitled to IS. Your earnings (and the part-time earnings of your partner) are taken into account when calculating the amount of IS you receive (see p250). If you are required to sign on for work to get benefit you must be able and willing to make up your hours to 16. [11] If you are mentally or physically disabled, the required number of hours is the number you are capable of working (up to 16). [12]

Even if you are not counted as unemployed for purposes of claiming unemployment benefit because your earnings are too high (ie, £54 or more), you can still claim IS if you satisfy the above rules.

(iv)   People treated as not available for work [13]

You will be treated as not available for work and therefore will not qualify for IS if any one of the following apply to you:

(a) without good cause you have refused to apply for, or take a suitable job, *and the vacancy still exists*;

(b) you have failed to take up a reasonable opportunity of employment *which is still open to you*. This is wider than the condition above and would cover, for example, deliberately failing to attend an interview;

(c) you are aged 18-44 and single, or a member of a childless couple and your partner is also under 45 and you have failed to take up a reasonable offer of local short-term work. This does not apply to single parents, or if you or your partner is pregnant or mentally or physically disabled;

(d) you fail to attend a second interview about your work prospects under the Restart Scheme (see p42);

(e) you have been refused unemployment benefit because you have not completed the part of the form dealing with availability for work properly;

(f) you are a student, unless you are disabled (see p14 for meaning), a single parent, or a single person looking after foster children, or you are receiving a training allowance, or you are a student from abroad who is entitled to an urgent cases payment because you are temporarily without funds (see p65);

(g) you have a current work permit. [14] (If it has expired you will need advice about your position in the UK – see p64.) You might also have difficulties claiming if you are an EC citizen and have been here for more than six months and are without a job, and you have no current residence permit (but see p67).

You will continue to be treated as unavailable for work: [15]

☐ under (a), (b) and (c) above, for 26 weeks or until the vacancy is filled, which-ever is shorter. When the vacancy is filled you are paid a reduced rate of IS – ie, with the voluntary unemployment deduction applied (see p45). In the case of (c) you will not be treated as unavailable for work until 14 days after you were given written notice of the short-term work;

☐ under (d) above, until you attend an interview or are no longer required to do so (see p42);

☐ under (f) and (g) above, for as long as these paragraphs apply to you.

If you have been refused IS and you have a partner who could qualify for IS because s/he is signing on or is entitled to IS without signing on, you should swap the claiming role, and you will not lose benefit. If your IS includes a transitional addition (see p32), you will need to calculate whether you are worse off by losing the transitional addition.

(v) Good cause for refusing a job

You are allowed to refuse a job if you have 'good cause'. [16] This is not defined for IS purposes but unemployment benefit legislation can be used where it is helpful. [17] For example, a person who has finished a training course within the last month can argue that s/he has good cause for turning down a job unrelated to the training.

Examples of good cause that are generally accepted are:

☐ the work might cause serious harm to your health, or cause excessive physical or mental stress;

☐ you have a religious or conscientious objection;

☐ you are responsible for looking after someone in your household, which would make it unreasonable to expect you to take a particular job;

☐ the time it would take to get to work and back is excessive – ie, over an hour each way, or less if your health would suffer or you are responsible for looking after another member of your household;

☐ the costs that would necessarily arise if you took the job, excluding childcare costs, are too high. [18]

Low pay does not, of itself, make a job unsuitable, [19] but you should argue that you have good cause for refusing a job if the pay (after travel expenses) would be less than IS.

(vi) Checking your availability

Claimant advisers

At any time during your claim, a claimant adviser may check your availability.

Claimant advisers are based at the unemployment benefit offices and JobCentres and their function is to ensure that claimants signing on are both genuinely available for work and making suitable efforts to find work. They are particularly likely to check on:
- [ ] young people;
- [ ] people who fail to attend Employment Training;
- [ ] people who have been unemployed for some time (particularly where there is evidence that they have not been actively looking for work);
- [ ] people with young children;
- [ ] carers (eg, those looking after a disabled relative).

A claimant adviser normally follows the same procedure for interviewing as under the Restart Scheme (see below). If you fail without good reason to attend the second interview, your benefit will be suspended.

Interviews with claimant advisers can be difficult. You should take along any evidence that shows you have made a real effort to find work (eg, a list of the jobs for which you have applied and the replies you have had). If you are unfit or have any particular problems (eg, a prison record) which make it hard for you to get a job, explain this too.

The government has said that another role of claimant advisers is to make sure that the claimant is getting the most appropriate benefit to which s/he is entitled. If you are very disabled and it is particularly difficult for you to get a job, the claimant adviser might suggest that you should not sign on, but should get benefit as a person who is unfit for work. However, you should not be pushed to do this if you really want to go on looking for work. Nor should you take work which is unsuitable, given your health.

Restart

Under the Restart Scheme, if you have been unemployed for six months or more you are called for an interview by staff at the local JobCentre in order to examine your attempts to find work, and any difficulties you have with a view to discussing retraining or job opportunities. You are allowed to take another person with you to the interview – eg, to interpret or to provide you with moral support. Your benefit will be stopped if:
- [ ] you are invited in writing to attend a Restart interview and fail to do so; *and*
- [ ] within 14 days of failing to attend a Restart interview you are invited in writing to a second interview; *and*
- [ ] without good reason, you do not attend the second interview. [20]

Your benefit is stopped from the date of the second interview, and can be stopped for as long as you fail to turn up for that interview, unless the notice to attend is withdrawn. If you think you had a good reason for not attending, you should write explaining why, and appeal against the stopping of your benefit. If you do this you should also make a fresh claim.

(vii) Who decides whether you are available for work

Decisions about whether you are available for work are normally made by the unemployment benefit office, and the officer at the Benefits Agency which pays IS usually follows that decision. Where the question about your availability for work cannot be decided immediately by the unemployment benefit office, you are treated as 'not available' in the meantime.[21] When this happens, the adjudication officer (AO) should automatically check whether:[22]

☐ you could be entitled to IS without signing on (see p16); *or*

☐ you should be paid IS to avoid hardship (see p18). You may have to remind the officer to do this.

If the AO at the unemployment benefit office decides at a later date that you *are and were* available, you should receive full IS backdated to the date of your claim.

Where you actually refuse a job offer or the opportunity of work (see p41) the officer at the Benefits Agency may decide, independently of the unemployment benefit office, whether or not you should be treated as available for work.

3   ACTIVELY SEEKING EMPLOYMENT

(i)   What 'actively seeking employment' means

You must be taking active steps to find work each week in which you are unemployed.[23] These steps include:

☐ applying for jobs by letter or telephone in response to advertisements;

☐ getting information about possible jobs from employers, registered employment agencies, and advertisements in newspapers etc;

☐ registering with an employment agency.

To be treated as actively seeking work the Employment Service would normally expect you to take at least two 'active steps' each week. For example, you could buy a newspaper to look through the job advertisements, *and* write to an employer asking for information about a job.

You are expected to take whichever steps are most likely to lead to an offer of a job. When deciding whether you have taken reasonable steps to find work the unemployment benefit office must take account of:[24]

☐ your skills, qualifications, any health and physical or mental limitations;

☐ the length of time since you were last in work;

☐ the attempts you have made to find work in previous weeks;

☐ any jobs which are available and where;

☐ whether you are on a training course or studying;

☐ whether you are doing voluntary work;

☐ the time spent helping in an emergency;

☐ whether you are homeless, and attempts you have made to find accommodation;

☐ any other circumstances that affect your ability to seek work.

You are **automatically treated as actively seeking work** in certain weeks including:[25]

☐ the first week you claim unemployment benefit, or claim IS because you do not qualify for unemployment benefit;

☐ the last week in which you are unemployed;

☐ two weeks while you are on holiday in the UK as long as you notify the unemployment benefit office in advance and can be contacted by them. You must fill in a form giving details of where you are staying;

☐   the first five weeks of an employment programme or training course that lasts at least three days a week and for which you are not paid a training allowance;
☐   if you are blind, up to four weeks of a guide-dog training course that lasts at least three days a week;
☐   up to eight weeks during which you are setting yourself up in self-employment under the Enterprise Allowance Scheme;
☐   up to three weeks of an Outward Bound Course that lasts at least three days a week;
☐   any week in which for three days you are treated as available for work because you are a lifeboatman, part-time fireman, or have helped in an emergency.

You do not have to be actively seeking employed earner's employment. You are also treated as actively seeking work if you are trying to take up self-employment for which you will get help through the Enterprise Allowance Scheme. [26]

(ii)   Checking you are actively seeking work

You may be required to attend an **Actively Seeking Work Review** at which your attempts to find work will be discussed. Keep a record of visits you make to JobCentres and agencies, and any other non-written enquiries you make about jobs, so that you can show what you have been doing to find work. Also keep advertisements you have followed up, copies of letters you write and any replies from employers and organisations about jobs.

If you cannot read or write you should tell the adviser at the JobCentre. The adviser may suggest you ask a friend or relative to help you keep a record of what is said, although a written record is not essential. The JobCentre may also suggest organisations able to help a person who speaks little or no English.

If the claimant adviser is dissatisfied with your efforts to find work, your unemployment benefit (if any) is suspended and your IS reduced (see p45). An AO then decides whether you did satisfy the test for actively seeking work. If you disagree with the decision you should appeal.

You may be able to get IS paid on hardship grounds instead (see p16). If you have been getting unemployment benefit only, you should make a new claim for IS on Form A1.

4   WORKERS ON SHORT-TIME

You may be entitled to IS when laid-off, if your hours of work (or, if your hours fluctuate, your average hours), have fallen below 16 hours a week. [27] When deciding the number of hours you work, the AO will have to decide whether to take into account the hours you work when you are not on short-time, or the hours you work now that you are on short-time. The question is whether your short-time working has become normal. You must sign on at the unemployment benefit office for the days you do not work and be accepted as available for, and actively seeking, work. If you receive a guarantee payment under the Employment Protection (Consolidation) Act 1978 or under a collective agreement or wages order, this will count as earnings and will be taken into account accordingly. [28]

5 THE VOLUNTARY UNEMPLOYMENT DEDUCTION

In certain circumstances you can be counted as 'voluntarily unemployed'. You will be disqualified from receiving unemployment benefit and will only be paid a reduced rate of IS. The disqualification can last for up to 26 weeks and the reduced rate of IS will last for the same period. [29] If you do not get unemployment benefit (eg, because you do not have sufficient contributions), you will still get reduced IS. [30] The decision to disqualify is taken by the AO at the UBO. The Benefits Agency assumes you are voluntarily unemployed in the meanwhile.

(i) When the deduction applies

You are treated as voluntarily unemployed if you have: [31]
(a)   lost your job because of misconduct; *or*
(b)   left your job voluntarily without good cause; *or*
(c)   without good cause refused to apply for, or take, a suitable job; *or*
(d)   without good cause failed to take up a reasonable opportunity of employment; *or*
(e)   without good cause failed to follow reasonable recommendations made to help you find suitable employment; *or*
(f)   lost a place on Youth Training (YT) because of misconduct, or given up a place without good cause; *or*
(g)   without good cause, refused or failed to take up training approved by the Department of Employment. In practice this affects 18-year-olds who refuse to take up a YT place. The Employment Training Scheme is not compulsory (but see p48). Also, see p46 if you refuse to take a Restart course.

You should not be penalised if you had a good reason for leaving a job. Some examples of when your benefit should not be reduced are: [32]

☐   you have left one job to start another which fell through, through no fault of your own;
☐   you left your job because of bad working conditions, or because of difficulties over pay, such as a refusal of your employer to pay the accepted rate for the job;
☐   you left or refused a job because you could not manage it – eg, it involved working at heights;
☐   you had to put up with racist abuse or sexist remarks and harassment;
☐   you left a new job between 6-12 weeks after starting it. This 'trial period' rule applies only where you have been out of work and not in full-time education or training for at least 6 months before trying the new job.

See CPAG's *Rights guide to non-means-tested benefits* for more information about what misconduct means, and when a person has good cause for leaving a job.

Good cause includes the points noted on p41 but you should not be penalised if you have turned down a job because: [33]

☐   it is work of a kind you do not usually do and you are still within your 'permitted period' (see p40);
☐   it is a job that is available only because of a trade dispute;
☐   it is not related to the type of work for which you have just finished training for

at least two months. You can only use this argument for four weeks after the course ends;

☐ the job is one you found out about yourself, unless you were also formally told about the job at the UBO, or you worked for the same employer less than a year ago and your pay and conditions will only be as good as before.

If you refuse without good cause to apply for, or take, a job, or fail to take up a reasonable opportunity of employment and the vacancy is *still* open, you are treated as not available for work (see p34), and will not be entitled to IS at all, except on hardship grounds. As soon as the job is taken, you can no longer be treated as 'not available' for work but you can still be counted as voluntarily unemployed. You are paid IS[34] but it is reduced by the voluntary unemployment deduction.

The reduction can be made for up to 26 weeks.[35] Very often the maximum period is imposed automatically but each case should be examined on its merits. If you have been disqualified from unemployment benefit, your IS will be reduced for as long as the unemployment benefit disqualification lasts.[36] You should appeal if you disagree with either the period of the reduction or the reduction itself, or both – eg, you think you had good cause for giving up or refusing a YT place; or you left your job because of bad working conditions; or you dispute that it was misconduct which lost you your job. In many cases appeals result in the 26-week period being reduced.

If you have lost unemployment benefit because of disqualification you should appeal that decision. If you win, the period of reduction of your IS will be reviewed accordingly – see p118 on how to appeal.

If you are disqualified and your partner could claim IS, they should consider claiming instead to preserve your entitlement in full (see p101).

(ii)   Restart courses and the voluntary unemployment deduction[37]

This section only applies if you fail to take up the opportunity of a job or a place on a training scheme.

If you are unemployed you may be required to attend a short course intended to improve your chances of getting work by increasing motivation and self-confidence. If you fail to attend all or part of one of these courses, your benefit may be reduced by the voluntary unemployment deduction (see p45).

The rule does *not* apply to a course which:

☐ is provided by the Secretary of State; *and*

☐ *either*   provides training for employment or is concerned with acquiring work experience;

    or   is longer than five weeks.

Your benefit will be reduced if you do not attend an appropriate course, and:

☐ you have been unemployed and entitled to unemployment benefit and/or IS for two years without a break, or during that time have been in work for periods of less than 57 days. (Periods when your benefit is reduced by the voluntary unemployment deduction do not count); *and*

☐ you have been notified of the course.

There are exceptions. Your benefit will not be reduced if you fail to attend the course for one of the following reasons:

☐ you are ill or physically or mentally disabled and therefore not able to attend the course, or your attendance would put at risk other people on the course;

☐ the time it would take to travel to the course would normally be more than one hour each way;

☐ you are caring for someone else in your household who is unable to look after themselves and there is no one else to do this and it is not practical to make arrangements for another person to provide the care;

☐ you have to go to court including attending as a witness or a juror;

☐ you are arranging your partner's or relative's funeral;

☐ you are involved in a domestic emergency;

☐ you are providing help with others to people in an emergency, including a fire, flood, explosion, railway or other accident or natural catastrophe;

☐ you are involved in an emergency as a lifeboatman or part-time fireman.

(iii)   Calculating the reduction in benefit

Your IS is reduced by 40 per cent of the personal allowance for a single claimant; this is the voluntary unemployment deduction.[38]

A smaller reduction of 20 per cent is made where:[39]

☐ you, your partner or child is pregnant or seriously ill; *and*

☐ you have savings of no more than £200.

The following table shows the amount by which your benefit is reduced:

Claimant	40 per cent reduction	20 per cent reduction
Single claimant or couple under 18 where normal benefit rate is £25.55	£10.20	£5.10
Single claimant or couple under 18 where normal rate is £33.60	£13.45	£6.70
Single claimant 18-25 or couple where one is 18-25 and the other under 18, and benefit rate is £33.60	£13.45	£6.70
Single claimant 25 or over		
Couple if both are 18 or over	£17.00	£8.50
Couple if one is under 18 but eligible for IS		

6   PEOPLE ON GOVERNMENT TRAINING SCHEMES

The Employment Service administers two government training schemes for which training allowances are paid. They are Youth Training (YT) and Employment Training (ET).

You are entitled to claim IS while on a government training scheme if your training allowance is less than your IS applicable amount (see Chapter 17). You do not have to sign on in order to qualify for benefit.[40] The amount of training allowance you receive varies according to the scheme you are on and, in the case of ET, it also varies with personal circumstances.

(i)   Youth Training (YT)

Most 16- and 17-year-olds are required to register for work or YT at the JobCentre or Careers Office and sign on at the Careers Office or unemployment benefit office.[41] This includes those aged 16 or 17 who are not eligible for IS in their own right and who must register in order to enable their parents or a responsible adult to get IS for them as dependants for a limited period[42] (see p234). They do not have to sign on. Young people aged 18 and over must sign on at the unemployment benefit office if they have to be available for work in order to get benefit. They may be offered a place on YT.

You will be expected to accept an offer of a place unless there is good reason for your refusal. If you turn down a place without good reason your IS will be subject to the voluntary unemployment deduction[43] (see p42) or you may be refused a bridging allowance if under 18 (see p57).

Young people aged 16/17 who have not been able to find a place on YT by the end of the child benefit extension period (see p53) and who would not be regarded as suitable for YT (eg, because of a disability or learning difficulties) may be given a placement of up to six months on initial training. The trainee will be eligible for a training allowance and IS top-up if appropriate.

Youth Training allowance and IS top-up

The YT training allowance is £29.50 for 16-year-olds and £35 for those aged 17 and over. If you are single and living at home without housing costs to meet, your allowance usually exceeds your IS applicable amount and so you do not qualify for an IS top-up. Trainees who are likely to qualify for IS are young people with a dependent child and young people whose IS includes a disability premium. They include claimants whose severe disablement allowance ceased when they went on YT but who continue to receive the disability premium.[44] When calculating your IS entitlement, the training allowance will count in full except for:

☐   any reimbursement of travelling expenses;[45]

☐   any 'living away from home' allowance, but only to the extent that you are not getting housing benefit to cover the cost of your temporary accommodation.[46]

If you are a couple and one of you is away from home while doing the course, see p232 for how your benefit is calculated.

Some participants in YT schemes have the legal status of employees (and are normally given contracts of employment). They do not qualify for IS because they are in full-time work.

(ii)   Employment Training (ET)

ET is not compulsory. Although you may be offered an ET place at a Restart interview (see p42), you are not obliged to take it. The government has stated that you will not be disqualified from getting benefit if you do not want to take part, or decide to leave ET early. But ministers have also said that 'if an unemployed person persistently refuses all offers of help, it may well raise doubts about their availability for work'. The benefit office will therefore consider a refusal of a place within the general context of your history of trying to find work.

Training allowances and income support

You are paid a training allowance and training premium of £10 while on ET. You get the premium on its own if you are the partner of a person who is eligible for ET (eg, a married woman returning to work) or you have not been getting benefit in your own right. The premium is ignored when calculating your IS, HB, FC, DWA and CCB. [47]

Training allowances are paid at different rates according to your circumstances. In effect, you continue to receive the same amount as before you went on ET, plus the training premium.

If you were only getting unemployment benefit before you started ET, you receive a training allowance equal to that (£43.10) plus the training premium.

If you were getting IS you get the same amount as your previous IS, but only part of it is treated as the training allowance. The remainder is your IS and allows you to retain rights to passported benefits (eg, maximum housing benefit, free school meals, social fund payments etc – see p7). The basic training allowance will usually be set at the level of whichever National Insurance benefit you received, or would have received had you been entitled to a contributory benefit, before you joined ET. However, it can be lower so that your IS is enough to allow you to continue to have certain deductions made from it – eg, for fuel direct, social fund repayments. You also get the training premium.

If you were receiving reduced IS before joining ET because of voluntary unemployment (see p45) you will receive an allowance equal to your *full* benefit plus the premium, once on the training course. When you finish ET you will go back on to reduced benefit again only if the course lasted for a shorter time than the number of weeks your voluntary unemployment deduction was due to run. (For example, if your deduction was due to run for a further 20 weeks when you started ET and the ET place was for 15 weeks, your benefit would then be reduced for five weeks after you finished ET.)

If you are still receiving a transitional payment as part of your weekly benefit, you will continue to receive this while on ET. However, you may lose all or part of your transitional protection if your circumstances change (see p33). The training premium will not affect your transitional payment.

If you have a mortgage you must persuade your lender to accept interest-only payments. Some lenders require regular statements confirming your unemployed status. Unemployment benefit office staff are told not to sign any statement which implies you are unemployed while you are on ET, but they can give you a letter stating that you are on ET and how much you get. The Building Societies Association has said that this should not be a problem and that interest-only payments will continue to be acceptable.

If you are one of a couple your partner's earnings will affect the amount of benefit you receive while on ET if you get the full training allowance. Remember that your partner can earn £5 (or £15 if entitled to the higher disregard – see p255) without it affecting benefit. If your partner gets a full-time job you will lose your allowance and go on to the premium only. Your partner may be able to claim family credit (see p129).

If you do extra work *on top* of the hours covered by your training plan, £5 (or £15) paid for that additional work will also be ignored[48] under the earnings disregard rules (see p255).

If you receive only a small amount of IS, the impact of earnings and other payments which are not ignored could have the effect of pushing you off IS altogether. You would then not be entitled to full housing benefit or 'passported' benefits (unless you qualified under the low-income rules (see p333)) or free school meals.

If your circumstances change while on ET, you should tell the unemployment benefit office and your allowance will be adjusted so that you receive an amount equal to the IS to which you are now entitled, plus the training premium. Form ET103 gives you a breakdown of how your allowance is made up. If you are not on IS and your circumstances change so that you qualify for IS while on ET (eg, you joined the scheme at 24, and are now 25) you must tell the unemployment benefit office and you will be given a claim form for IS. Your allowance will then be adjusted accordingly.

Other payments made to ET trainees

Certain expenses will be met by the training manager and will not affect your IS (or FC) entitlement. These are:[49]

☐ any reimbursement of **travelling expenses**. However, you are expected to pay the first £4 from your benefit, although the training manager can cover this as well. You can also get travelling expenses to take a child to nursery or the child-minder etc, but again you are expected to pay the first £4. If the training manager opts to meet these costs in full, your IS will not be affected. The maximum amount paid for travelling will normally be £50 a week, but where there are exceptional circumstances the amount can be increased – eg, necessary taxis and escorts for trainees with disabilities. You will also be allowed the cost of a return journey every two weeks if you have to live away for a full week;

☐ any **'living away from home' allowance**, but only to the extent that you are not getting housing benefit to cover the cost of your temporary accommodation. Your lodging costs will be met in full up to a maximum of £50 a week. A higher amount can be paid in exceptional circumstances – eg, when local accommodation costs are very high.

While on ET you should not have to pay for **protective clothing, books or equipment etc**, that you need. These expenses should be met by the training manager. However, if it is normal practice at your workplace for the trainee to buy these items, the Department of Employment can make a payment of up to £100. It will be paid to the training manager.

A training bonus (not normally more than £200) can be paid if you complete your training action plan or get a recognised vocational qualification. How much you get is up to the organisation with which you are placed. The bonus is not taxed and will not count as weekly income for IS purposes.[50] Any bonus in excess of £200 *will* count as capital and could therefore make a difference to your benefit if you are near the capital limit (see p272). (This rule also applies to FC, DWA, HB and CCB, but see p279.[51])

Training managers have discretion to make **additional payments**. They can pay an extra £10 without IS being affected because the payments are treated as charitable or voluntary payments (see p263). They can also recompense you for other expenses, but these will be taken into account for IS.

Your IS may not be affected if you receive payments in kind and/or the payments are made to a third party for you (see pp271 and 282).

Chapter 5

Special rules for special groups

This chapter covers:

1 16/17-year-olds (see below)
2 People affected by a trade dispute (p58)
3 People from abroad (p62)
4 People in private or voluntary residential care and nursing homes (p72)
5 People in local authority residential homes (p80)
6 People in hospital (p82)
7 Prisoners (p85)
8 People without accommodation (p86)

1 16/17-YEAR-OLDS

Income support is usually only paid if you are 18 or over. The Benefits Agency assumes that 16/17-year-olds who do not have jobs or youth training (YT) places are supported by parents or other adults (who can claim IS for young people who are still at school or college – see p233). If this does not apply to you, you can only get IS if you fulfil the special rules in this section.

16/17-year-olds who are still at school or following a non-advanced course at college are usually disqualified from claiming IS themselves because they are regarded as being in full-time education, but there are exceptions (see p11).

16/17-year-olds who have left school or college are also usually disqualified from IS. However, some can qualify until they are 18 (see below). Others can claim during the child benefit extension period (see p53), and those who are sick or who have recently been released from serving a custodial sentence may also claim for other short periods (see p54). For those who do not qualify under any of those rules, discretionary payments may be paid to avoid hardship (see p54). There are special rates of benefit for 16/17-year-olds (see p56).

Those between jobs or YT may qualify for bridging allowances (see p57).

(i) Claiming until you are 18 [1]

You can get IS at any time while you are under 18, if you satisfy the usual conditions *and* at least one of the following: [2]

☐ You are a single parent or single foster parent with a child under 16.
☐ You are one of a couple with a child for whom you can claim. [3]
☐ You are looking after a child under 16 while her/his parent or equivalent is temporarily away or ill.

☐ Your partner is temporarily out of the UK and you claim for a child under 16.
☐ You are taking a child abroad for treatment (see p19).
☐ You are caring for your partner or child who is temporarily ill.
☐ You receive invalid care allowance, or are caring for someone who has claimed or gets attendance allowance or disability living allowance (see p17).
☐ You are pregnant, and unable to work, or for a period starting 11 weeks before the baby is due and up to 7 weeks after the birth.
☐ You are blind (see p14).
☐ You are incapable of work or training and a doctor says this is likely to last more than 12 months.⁴ If less, see below. Remember you have to make a claim for any sickness benefit even though you may not qualify, in order to get benefit without signing on (see p16).
☐ You are a disabled student who does not have to sign on (see p17).
☐ You are on a government training course and getting a training allowance.
☐ You are a refugee learning English for at least 15 hours per week – you can get IS for up to 9 months. You must have been in Britain for a year or less when you started the course.
☐ You are a person from abroad entitled to urgent cases payments (see p65).
☐ You have been temporarily laid off but are available to return to your job.⁵

If you qualify as a member of a couple with a child, you will have to sign on unless you are exempted (see p16). You will also have to sign on if you qualify as temporarily laid off. In all other cases, people in the above groups do not have to sign on.

(ii) Claiming during the 'child benefit extension period'

If you are not entitled to claim under the above rules but it takes you some time to find a job or a YT place after leaving school, you may be able to claim IS for a period called the 'child benefit extension period'. It begins on the Monday after your 'terminal date' after you leave school or college (see p13) and ends three or four months later.

The child benefit extension periods for 1992/93 are:

First day	*Last day*⁶
Monday 13 January 1992	5 April 1992
Monday 4 May 1992	26 July 1992
Monday 14 September 1992	3 January 1993
Monday 4 January 1993	4 April 1993

You can get IS during this period if you register for work or YT at the Careers Office or JobCentre,⁷ and are:
☐ a member of a married couple whose partner is 18 or over, or is registered for work or YT, or is eligible for IS until 18 (see above); *or*
☐ an orphan with no one acting as your parent (which includes a local authority or voluntary organisation if you are in care, or foster parents if you have been boarded out); *or*
☐ living away from parents and any person acting as your parent, and immediately before you were 16 you were in custody, or in care (and not living with parents

or a close relative while in care – see p74 for meaning of 'close relative'); *or*
☐ living away from parents and any person acting as your parent, and instead are living elsewhere:
  - under the supervision of the probation service or a local authority; *or*
  - to avoid physical or sexual abuse; *or*
  - because you need special accommodation because of mental or physical illness or handicap; *or*
☐ living away from parents and any person acting as your parent, where the parents or other person is unable to support you because they are:
  - in custody; *or*
  - unable to enter Great Britain because of the immigration laws; *or*
  - 'chronically sick or mentally or physically disabled' (for meaning, see p13);
☐ having to live away from parents and any person acting as your parent, because:
  - you are estranged from them; *or*
  - you are in physical or moral danger; *or*
  - there is a serious risk to your physical or mental health.

(iii) Claiming for short periods after the child benefit extension period

Even though you are not otherwise entitled to IS, you can claim after the end of the child benefit extension period if:[8]
☐ You are **incapable of work and training under YT** because of physical or mental illness or disability and your incapacity is likely to last *less* than a year. You will get IS until you recover (see p16 for how you prove you are incapable of work).
☐ You are in one of the groups which qualify during the child benefit extension period (see above) and have been **discharged from custody**. You must register for work or YT and will then be entitled to IS for up to eight weeks.
☐ You have to live away from your parents (or anyone acting as your parent) and you are living independently following a stay in local authority care.
  IS can be paid for up to 8 weeks. This applies where you have left school even if you contrive to be treated as in relevant education (see p13).

(iv) Discretionary payments to avoid hardship

If you do not come within the above groups and you have little or no money you should make a claim for a discretionary payment of IS. The Secretary of State has the power to award a payment in order to avoid severe hardship.[9] Payments should be to prevent '*unavoidable* severe hardship'. So a person who refuses a YT place is unlikely to get a discretionary payment unless there was good reason for the refusal. Decisions to award discretionary payments are made by the staff at the Severe Hardship Claims Unit (see Appendix 1) on behalf of the Secretary of State. The following factors should be taken into account when deciding whether to award IS and for how long. They are:
☐ your health and vulnerability (eg, whether you would be at risk of turning to crime in order to obtain money to live – this will be the case where there is a threat of, or actual, homelessness);

☐ whether you have income and/or savings which would normally be ignored for the purposes of calculating your IS entitlement;

☐ your prospects of getting a YT place;

☐ the opportunities for finding casual work in the area where you live. Casual work may not be a realistic option if you are homeless;

☐ whether you have friends or relatives who would accommodate or support you. (If you know that in practice they would not agree to do so you should make this clear in your claim. You should not be refused a discretionary payment just because you live at home);

☐ your financial commitments and what would happen if you did not meet them. It is accepted that in certain circumstances young people getting the bridging allowance (see p57) will qualify for a discretionary payment. If you are a young couple only getting IS at the single person's rate (see p57), you may also be eligible in certain cases. Each case of low income should be considered on its merits.

The Secretary of State has been willing to make discretionary payments until a YT place is found for those who have been unable to find a place by the end of their child benefit extension period, or by the end of the eight-week period covered by the bridging allowance.

The Secretary of State has also taken note of the particular difficulties of people with behavioural problems, and Benefits Agency offices are instructed to refer cases to the Senior Medical Officer if the claimant has no GP, or if the information from the GP is inadequate or a certificate is refused.[10] The Senior Medical Officer will then decide whether the person should be treated as incapable of work and training and therefore paid under the special rules (for meaning of 'incapacity for work', see p16). Meanwhile a discretionary payment should be considered.

Getting a discretionary payment

Sign on at the Careers Office or unemployment benefit office in the normal way. The latter should not turn you away just because you are under 18. Complete Form B1 (see p100 for information about claiming). On the form, under Part 12 'Other Information', state that you are claiming on grounds of severe hardship. Take the form, together with any other information about your circumstances, to the local Benefits Agency office.

The Benefits Agency *must* interview you (unless it is absolutely clear you could not get IS – eg, because your capital is over £8,000). They must decide whether you can get IS under the special rules for 16/17-year-olds. **If you do not qualify, they must:**[11]

☐ contact the Careers Office to confirm you are registered for YT and when a YT placement might be found. They check on your attitude to YT and whether you have refused placements in the past. If so, they will ask why; *and*

☐ refer your case (usually by telephone and straightaway) to the special unit in Glasgow that decides claims for discretionary IS. (See Appendix 1.) Before doing so they will gather information about you to help the Glasgow unit decide your application. As well as basic details about where you live, your financial situation and whether you are sick, disabled or pregnant, they will check why you think hardship will result if no payment is made, whether friends or relatives could help you out, what you have been doing since you left school, and your attitude to YT.

There must be no delay in referring claims to Glasgow, who should give a decision within 24 hours of receiving all necessary information from the local office.

If the local office refuses to refer a case to Glasgow or there are unnecessary delays you should complain to your MP.

If you are awarded IS on the grounds of severe hardship, it is paid in arrears in the normal way. If you need money urgently you should apply for a social fund crisis loan (see p314). If you have already applied for a loan and been turned down but have since been told you will get IS, you should re-apply for a crisis loan to tide you over.

If there is insufficient information to decide your claim, the Benefits Agency may either:

☐ make a provisional decision allowing benefit to be paid for one or two weeks; *or*
☐ make a decision later when they have the necessary information. In this case you may be paid from the date you first claimed on grounds of hardship.

You should be awarded benefit for as long as the hardship continues. However, awards are often only for 2-4 weeks and you may need to reapply. Your chances of getting a YT place are crucial in deciding the length of the award, but, in practice, awards are rarely made for longer than eight weeks. Many young people are wrongly forced to rely on repeated hardship awards. If you are advised that you are unlikely to get a YT place within the period of the hardship award, you should take up the matter with the Glasgow Office and, if necessary, complain to your local MP. In addition, contact the guarantee liaison officer at the Training and Enterprise Council (in Scotland, the Local Enterprise Company) about arranging a YT placement. The Benefits Agency should also liaise with this officer, particularly if a young person has to claim a hardship payment more than once.

Your local office works out the amount of your benefit entitlement.

If you need to claim discretionary IS, try to get as much evidence as you can to back up your case. About 70 per cent of the claims made each week on hardship grounds are successful. There is no right of appeal against a refusal because the decision is made on behalf of the Secretary of State, but you should complain to your MP if you are refused and think you will suffer hardship and you could consider judicial review (see p127).

The Secretary of State has the power to withdraw your discretionary IS at any time. [12] If you lose your discretionary IS and you believe severe hardship will result, you should complain to your MP. The Benefits Agency can also recover discretionary IS if it is decided that you have misrepresented or failed to disclose a material fact and benefit has been paid as a result. [13] If you think they are wrong, you can appeal – see p118.

(v) Rates of benefit paid to 16/17-year-olds

Single people and single parents

There are two levels of payment: [14]
- lower rate   £25.55
- higher rate   £33.60

You qualify for the higher rate if: [15]
(a) you qualify for the disability premium; *or*
(b) you come within one of the groups on pp53-54 who get IS during the child benefit extension period, or for a limited period after the child benefit extension period; *or*
(c) you come within one of the groups on pp52-53 who can get IS until they are 18, and your situation is similar to a person who qualifies under (b) above apart from the requirement to register for YT or work. For example, a single parent living at home will get £25.55 (plus the allowance for her child etc); a single parent who has to live away from home because s/he is estranged from her/his parents and any other person acting as her/his parent will get £33.60 (plus the allowance for her/his child etc); *or*
(d) you come within one of the groups on p12 entitled to IS although in relevant education, and your situation is similar to a person who qualifies under (b) apart from the requirement to register for YT or work. For example, you live on your own because you have no parents and no one acting as your parent and you are still at school; *or*
(e) you get a discretionary payment of IS to prevent hardship (see p54) and your situation is similar to a person who qualifies under (b) whether or not you are required to register for YT or work. For example, you are living away from home to avoid physical abuse, the child benefit extension period is ended and you do not have a YT place and therefore get IS on hardship grounds.

Couples [16]

The amount paid to couples depends on the age of the partners and whether one or both of them would be eligible for IS as a single person. 'Eligible' includes eligibility for IS on hardship grounds.
Benefit will be paid at either the normal rate for couples or at a reduced couple rate or at the single person rate appropriate to the age of the other partner.
The rates for couples are set out below:

☐ One aged 18 or over and the other under 18 and eligible for IS £66.60
☐ Both under 18 and either both are eligible for IS, *or* one is
responsible for a child, *or* they are married and each is either
registered for YT or eligible for IS £50.60
☐ One aged 25 or over and the other under 18 and not eligible for IS £42.45
☐ One is 18-24 and the other under 18 and not eligible for IS £33.60
☐ Both under 18 and one is eligible for IS at the higher rate for under-18s £33.60
☐ Both under 18 and one is eligible for IS at the lower rate for under-18s £25.55

(vi) Bridging allowances between jobs or YT

Bridging allowances are paid at the discretion of the Secretary of State for Employment while you are between jobs or YT places. They are not social security payments. [17]
If you are registered disabled with the Department of Employment (ie, you have a green card) you can also get a bridging allowance immediately after the end of the

child benefit extension period (see p53). To get a payment, you must[18] be under 18, not entitled to IS or unemployment benefit and have left a job or YT. You must also have registered for work or YT at a JobCentre or Careers Office.

The bridging allowance is £15 per week or £3 per day. It can be paid for up to eight weeks (40 days) in a 52-week period, unless you are registered disabled with the Department of Employment when no time-limit applies. If you do not use up eight weeks' worth of bridging allowance, you can claim again within the 52-week period and get an allowance for the rest of the eight weeks. If you are liable to pay rent you will get maximum housing benefit while receiving the bridging allowance. But it counts as income for IS.

If you refuse a suitable YT place, the Department of Employment can refuse to pay you a bridging allowance on the grounds that you are voluntarily unemployed. The unemployment benefit office will be asked to decide whether this applies in your case.

You claim the bridging allowance on Form BA1 which you can pick up at the Careers Office (or JobCentre) where you register for YT. You must fill in parts A to C (the staff complete part D), giving the date you registered. You must take the form to the unemployment benefit office within the next two days. The allowance is paid fortnightly by giro. You will have to sign on fortnightly and register for YT.

2   PEOPLE AFFECTED BY A TRADE DISPUTE

If you are involved in a trade dispute your right to income support is affected. You will either receive a reduced amount or nothing.

(i)   Involved in a trade dispute

You will be treated as involved in a trade dispute if you have lost employment as a result of a stoppage of work due to a trade dispute at your place of work.[19] You will not be treated as involved in a trade dispute if:

☐   your employer dismisses you during the course of a trade dispute.[20] If this happens you will not have lost your job due to a stoppage of work, but because you have been sacked;

☐   you can show that the stoppage of work is not at your own **place of work**, but in a separate section or department[21] – eg, in the case of a colliery canteen worker who lost her employment during the 1984 miners' strike, it was held that the trade dispute was not at *her* place of employment;[22]

☐   you can show that you are not 'directly interested' in the dispute.[23] You will have to show that you have nothing to gain either financially or in connection with your conditions of work;

☐   you are dismissed due to redundancy during the stoppage. You will no longer be treated as involved in a trade dispute and will be able to claim unemployment benefit and/or IS in the normal way.[24]

If at any time during the trade dispute you:

☐   become incapable of work; *or*

☐   you are pregnant and your baby is due within six weeks; *or*

□   you have had a baby less than seven weeks ago;
– you will not be counted as involved in the dispute. [25] You will get full IS until your incapacity ends or until seven weeks after the birth of your child. [26]

The decision as to whether you are involved in a trade dispute for the purposes of IS is made by an adjudication officer at the Employment Service [27] and until then, your IS is suspended (see p103). [28]

(ii)   The amount of benefit

You will not be entitled to any IS if you are involved in a trade dispute and you are single, or a couple without children and both of you are involved in a trade dispute. [29] A single parent, or a couple with children who are both involved in a trade dispute, will be eligible for some IS. In the case of a couple where only one partner is involved in a trade dispute, the other partner and any children will be eligible for IS (see below).

A person who is involved in a trade dispute does not have to sign on in order to get benefit. [30] You should therefore claim IS direct from your local Benefits Agency office, telling them that you are out of work because of a trade dispute.

You will not be entitled to any IS immediately but will be treated as in full-time work for a period of seven days following the stoppage of work, or, if there is no stoppage, from the date you or your partner withdrew your labour. [31] If you are getting IS and your part-time earnings stop because you are involved in a trade dispute, the seven-day exclusion period will not apply but your IS will be reassessed according to the rules for people on strike. [32]

Payment of IS will be made weekly in trade dispute cases. [33]

Your applicable amount will consist of the following: [34]

For a single parent who is involved in a trade dispute:	the normal personal allowances for the children, *plus* the family premium and lone parent premium, *plus* disabled child premium, *plus* housing costs, if appropriate.
For a couple without children where only one is involved in a trade dispute:	half the personal allowance for a couple, *plus* half the couple rate of any premium payable for the person not involved in the dispute, *plus* housing costs, if appropriate.
For a couple with children where only one is involved in a trade dispute:	half the personal allowance for a couple, *plus* half the couple rate of any premium payable for the person not involved in the dispute, *plus* the normal personal allowances for the children and the family premium, *plus* disabled child premium, *plus* housing costs, if appropriate.

| For a couple with children where both are involved in the dispute: | the normal personal allowances for the children, *plus* the family premium, *plus* disabled child premium, *plus* housing costs, if appropriate. |

Where the person involved in the trade dispute is normally responsible for paying the housing costs, other member(s) of the family will be treated as responsible for these instead[35] (even if the only other member is a child), unless they too are involved in a trade dispute.

Your capital and income will be calculated as follows:
A person involved in a trade dispute is assumed to receive £22.50 strike pay whether or not s/he in fact gets any.[36] If both members of a couple are involved in a trade dispute only one amount of £22.50 is deducted. Any actual payment from a trade union of up to £22.50 in total is ignored, even if both members of a couple are involved in a trade dispute.[37] Other capital and income will be treated in the way described on pp246 and 272 except that the following will be taken into account in full as income:

☐ any tax refund due because of the stoppage of work;[38]

☐ any payment made under sections 1, 27 or 29 of the Child Care Act 1980 (in Scotland, sections 12, 24 or 26 Social Work (Scotland) Act 1968);[39]

☐ all charitable or voluntary payments (whether regular or irregular, with no £10 disregard for regular payments) except any payment from the Macfarlane Trusts or the Independent Living Fund;[40]

☐ any payment of income in kind except any payment from the Macfarlane Trusts or the Independent Living Fund;[41]

☐ holiday pay which is not payable until more than four weeks after your employment ends or is interrupted[42] (this will count as earnings and will therefore attract an earnings disregard – see p250);

☐ any advance of earnings or a loan made by your employer.[43] Where these payments are earnings, they will attract an earnings disregard.

Any other payments that are obtained because the person involved in the trade dispute is currently unemployed will also be treated as income and counted in full.[44]

(iii)   Benefit loans on return to work

If you return to work with the same employer, whether or not the dispute has ended, you can receive IS for the first 15 days back at work, in the form of a loan.[45] You will not be treated as in full-time work for this period[46] nor be required to sign on[47] and you will no longer be disqualified from getting benefit for yourself. If you are a member of a couple you will not be entitled to IS if your partner is in full-time work.[48] Your income (including any earnings you receive from your employer) will be calculated in the same way as if you were still involved in the dispute (see above) except that any payment in kind or income tax refunds will be ignored, and there will no longer be any deduction from your benefit for assumed strike pay.

Any IS that you are awarded will be paid in advance.[49] You may not get IS if you are entitled to less than £5.[50]

Repayment of the loan

Any IS paid during your first 15 days back at work can be re-claimed from your employer.[51] Your employer will deduct the sum to be repaid from your earnings. If this is not practical (eg, because you are currently unemployed) it can be recovered directly from you.[52]

When awarding you IS on return to work the Benefits Agency will at the same time decide the amount of your **protected earnings** – ie, the level below which your earnings must not be reduced by repayment of your IS loan.[53] Your protected earnings level is equal to:[54]

☐ your applicable amount excluding housing costs; *plus*
☐ £27 (£8 if you live in a hostel); *less*
☐ child benefit.

No deduction will be made if your 'available earnings' (see below) are less than £1 a week above your protected earnings level. If they are £1 or more above, your employer will deduct half of the excess above your protected earnings level. If you are paid monthly, you work out your weekly protected earnings level and multiply by five to get your monthly protected earnings level. If your monthly earnings are less than £5 above this level, no deduction will be made. Otherwise, half the excess over your monthly protected earnings level will be deducted. If your earnings are paid daily, the amount of your protected earnings and the £1 figure are divided by five to determine the amount (if any) of the deduction. The calculation can be adjusted as appropriate where your wages are paid at other intervals.[55]

Your '**available earnings**' are the whole of your earnings, including sick pay, after all 'lawful' deductions have been made.[56] These include tax and National Insurance contributions, trade union subscriptions and any amount being deducted under a court order. Any bonus or commission if paid on a different day is treated as paid on your next normal pay day.[57] If you are paid more than one lot of wages on one pay day, your protected earnings level and the £1 figure will be multiplied to reflect this.[58]

A deduction notice will be sent to your employer by the Benefits Agency setting out your protected earnings level and the amount of IS to be recovered.[59] If you have not actually received the IS and you can satisfy your employer that you have not, no deduction should be made.[60] Your employer can begin making the deductions from the first pay day after receiving the notice and must start doing so one month after getting it.[61]

A deduction notice will cease to have effect if:

☐ it is cancelled; *or*
☐ you stop working for that employer; *or*
☐ your IS loan has been repaid; *or*
☐ 26 weeks have passed since the date of the notice.[62]

If you stop work, another deduction notice can be sent if you get another job and part of your IS loan is still outstanding.[63]

You should tell the Benefits Agency within 10 days if you leave a job or start another while part of your IS loan remains unpaid.[64] If you fail to do so you can be prosecuted.[65] It is a criminal offence for your employer to fail to keep records of deductions and supply the Benefits Agency with these.[66] If your employer fails to make a deduction which should have been made from your pay, the Benefits Agency can recover the amount from your employer instead.[67]

(iv)   Other benefits during a trade dispute

☐   You can get a social fund payment for help with the cost of **baby things** (see p285), **funeral expenses** (see p287) and **travel expenses** to visit a close relative or a member of the same household who is ill[68] (see p311).

☐   A crisis loan can only be awarded in cases of **disaster** or for items needed for **cooking or space heating**.[69] Budgeting loans are not available to strikers.[70]

☐   Strikers and their families may be entitled to **free prescriptions, free dental treatment and free glasses** (see Chapter 25), even if they are not on IS.

☐   If you are on strike and your partner undergoes kidney dialysis, or has to follow a vital but expensive diet for other health reasons, it may be possible to argue that this should be covered under the NHS Act 1977.

3   PEOPLE FROM ABROAD

In IS law the phrase 'person(s) from abroad' is used to describe certain people with limited leave or without leave who are not entitled to IS at the full rate. However, this Handbook uses the phrase more broadly to describe any immigrant regardless of status or entitlement to IS. Where it is used in its technical sense it is in inverted commas.

You do not have to be British to get IS. This section describes the special rules that apply to people from abroad.

(i)   Immigration issues which affect entitlement

Entitlement to IS depends on either immigration status or citizenship.

People with 'right of abode' are not subject to immigration control – ie, they can enter the United Kingdom freely at any time regardless of how long they have been away, and their passport is not stamped on entry. They are entitled to full IS in the normal way. People in this group are:

☐   British citizens; *and*

☐   some Commonwealth citizens if they have a parent born in the UK; *and*

☐   women who are Commonwealth citizens, and who were married before 1 January 1983 to men who were born in the UK, or who were registered or naturalised as British, or who are Commonwealth citizens with a parent born in the UK.

People subject to immigration control can be divided into two groups:

☐   People who are legally 'settled' in the UK – ie, here with indefinite 'leave' to remain, with no restrictions on taking employment. ('Leave' means permission to stay in the UK.) They are entitled to full benefit.

☐   People with 'limited leave'. This means your stay in the UK is subject to either a time-limit or a restriction on your right to take employment or both. Many people who have limited leave are admitted to the UK subject to an additional restriction that they shall not have recourse to public funds and, if this applies, they will not be entitled to IS.

A list of who can claim IS is given below. People not able to claim because of immigration status may in certain circumstances be able to get an urgent cases payment instead (see p65). If you are a couple and only one of you can claim, see p65.

The public funds test

Under the immigration rules some people are admitted to the UK on condition that they do not rely on public funds. The term 'public funds' covers IS, housing benefit, family credit and housing under Part III of the Housing Act 1985 (Housing the Homeless). It does not include any of the other benefits described in this book. Nor does it include the non-means-tested benefits – eg, unemployment benefit, child benefit and disability living allowance.

If your terms of entry require that you should have no recourse to public funds, you may have a right under social security and other legislation to claim IS urgent cases payments, housing benefit and family credit, but a claim for these benefits could affect your right to remain in the UK or obtain an extension of stay, so it may be unwise for you to claim. See below on getting further advice.

There are close links between the DSS and the Home Office. Claims for benefit are often reported to the Home Office (see p71). If you are unsure about your right to claim public funds or whether it would be wise to claim, you should get advice first – from the Joint Council for the Welfare of Immigrants (tel: 071 251 8706) or a law centre or independent advice centre dealing with immigration problems – before making a claim for benefit.

(ii) People entitled to full IS [71]

You will be entitled to full benefit if:
- [ ] you are not subject to immigration control; *or*
- [ ] you have no restrictions attached to your stay; *or*
- [ ] you have limited leave under the immigration rules, but the terms of your entry are not subject to there being 'no recourse to public funds'; *or*
- [ ] you have 'exceptional leave' – ie, you were admitted with the permission of the Secretary of State outside the terms of the immigration rules and your leave has not expired. In these circumstances, you have a right to claim IS whether or not the terms of your entry refer to there being no recourse to public funds (see above). (This does not apply to immigrants given temporary admission while seeking asylum.)

In practice this means you will be entitled to claim IS if: [72]
- [ ] you are a British citizen;
- [ ] you are a British Overseas citizen with right of re-admission to the UK;
- [ ] you have right of abode, or a certificate of entitlement to right of abode, in the UK. This may include a certificate of patriality;
- [ ] you are here without any time-limit on your stay or you have been granted indefinite leave to enter or remain in the UK (but if you are sponsored, see p66);
- [ ] you have exceptional leave to remain;

☐   you are a citizen of the Channel Islands or the Isle of Man;
☐   you are a British Dependent Territories citizen, British Overseas citizen, British Protected person or British subject with indefinite leave to remain;
☐   you have been granted refugee status or political asylum (but if you have applied for refugee status, see p70);
☐   you are a national of a Common Market country (but see p67);
☐   you are a national of a country that signed the European Convention on Social and Medical Assistance (1953) – ie, Iceland, Malta, Norway, Portugal, Sweden or Turkey (but, if you have applied to vary your leave or are appealing against a refusal of leave – see p63, and if you have to be available for work – see p71);
☐   you are a national of Cyprus or Austria, but if you have to be available for work, see p71;
☐   you hold a current work permit but are not required to be available for work (see p71);
☐   you have been granted foreign husband or wife status, and have been given permanent leave to stay (but if you do not yet have permanent leave, see p69). If you are a couple and only one of you has the status to claim, see (iv) below.

(iii)   People not entitled to full IS

You are not entitled to ordinary IS if you come into one of the following groups: [73]
(a)   you have limited leave and your terms of entry are subject to there being no recourse to public funds. (This includes visitors, most students, fiancé(e)s, husbands/wives during the probationary 12 months, businessmen and self-employed persons, writers, artists, ministers of religion, persons of independent means and their dependants);
(b)   you have been granted temporary admission to the UK because you are an asylum seeker;
(c)   you are waiting for the Secretary of State's decision on your immigration status;
(d)   you have remained in the UK beyond the period covered by your limited leave;*
(e)   you are subject to a deportation order;*
(f)   you are an illegal entrant.*
* There is close liaison between the DSS and the Home Office. If you have remained here after your limited leave has expired, or are subject to a deportation order, or are an alleged illegal entrant, neither you nor your partner should claim unless you have already contacted the Home Office in order to regularise your position.

If you do not qualify for IS, you will not get benefit for a child regardless of their status.

Couples or single parents who are not 'persons from abroad' and who qualify for IS but who have children who come within the above groups will nevertheless be paid benefit in the normal way including allowances for the children and appropriate premiums. [74]

If you are in one of the above groups, you may qualify for an urgent cases payment [75] (see p65). If you have a partner who is not excluded from claiming IS, s/he could claim instead. If both of you qualify you will have to decide who should claim. If your partner can claim but you are an overstayer, illegal entrant or subject to a deportation order, make sure you regularise your immigration position first before s/he claims.

(iv) Couples who can get reduced IS

If you are a couple with one partner who qualifies for IS, that partner should claim benefit (but see (iii) (d), (e) or (f) above).

You will get the applicable amount (personal allowance plus premiums as appropriate), for each member of the family who does not come within the groups listed in (iii), provided the claim is made by a person who *is* entitled. You will also have your housing costs met. [76] Although you do not get any benefit for the 'person from abroad' her/his income and capital wil nevertheless count when IS is assesssed. As no IS is paid for the 'person from abroad' they will not usually be treated as having recourse to public funds.

If the partner who comes from abroad would qualify for an urgent cases payment (see below), financially it may be better if s/he claims this for her/himself and the other members of the family. But in so doing you will be having recourse to public funds so you should get immigration advice before claiming.

(v) Urgent cases payments for people from abroad[77]

If you are not entitled to ordinary IS, you may be able to get an urgent cases payment. See p35 for how your urgent cases payment is calculated, and how your capital and income will be treated.

You are entitled to an urgent cases payment if:

☐ your terms of entry refer to there being no recourse to public funds, but your source of funding from abroad has temporarily stopped. Provided that you have been self-supporting during the period of limited leave, and there is a reasonable chance that your funds will be resumed, you can get an urgent cases payment for up to 42 days during any one period of limited leave. If your leave is extended, the extension will be treated as part of the same period of limited leave;

☐ you are waiting for a decision on your application for leave to remain in the UK to be varied, provided you would not be subject to the public funds test if your leave were to be varied – eg, you are applying for indefinite leave. You are entitled to urgent cases payments until you are sent the decision; and for a further 28 days after that, if you have the right to appeal against the decision;

☐ you are waiting for the result of an appeal you have made under the Immigration Act;

☐ you have overstayed your leave, and have applied to the Home Office to remain here, provided you would not be subject to the public funds test if your stay were to be extended. The urgent cases payment lasts until the date you are removed from the UK if your application is unsuccessful or, in the case of a successful application, until the decision is sent to you;

☐ you have been served with a deportation order (under section 5(1) of the Immigration Act 1971), but your removal from the UK has been deferred *in writing*;

☐ you are not subject to a deportation order, but have been given permission to stay, pending the removal of another person who is subject to a deportation order but whose removal has been deferred *in writing*;

☐ you are an illegal entrant, but have been notified by the Home Office *in writing* that you can stay here;

☐ a direction has been made seeking your removal from the UK, but your removal has been deferred *in writing*;

☐ you have exhausted all rights of appeal to remain here, but you have been allowed to stay while representations are made to the Home Secretary;

☐ you have been granted temporary admission or you are waiting for the Secretary of State to make a decision on your immigration status. The urgent cases payment will last until leave is granted or you are removed from the UK, or until a decision is made on your immigration status.

In practice, where the regulation assumes the decision will be in writing, the Home Office does not put it in writing. If you have difficulty getting benefit as a result, seek advice from a local advice centre and ask them to contact CPAG.

If you are disputing your removal from the UK you will be entitled to an urgent cases payment until removal from the UK or until leave to remain is granted.

Nationals from countries that signed the 1953 European Convention (see p64), even though normally entitled to full IS, are only able to get urgent cases payments when applying for variation of leave which would not be subject to the public funds condition, or are awaiting the result of an appeal against the refusal of leave.[78]

Urgent cases payments are a type of IS so will help you to qualify for other benefits, but they are also 'public funds' so a claim might affect your immigration status (see p63 on public funds and further advice).

(vi)   Sponsorship and undertakings

A person wishing to enter the UK may be sponsored by a relative or friend living in this country. The sponsor provides the British High Commissioner or Embassy with evidence of their ability to maintain and accommodate the person from abroad for the period of any leave granted. A sponsored entrant can nevertheless claim IS as long as they have indefinite leave to remain – ie, have been admitted for permanent settlement. If you claim, you may be asked questions about the sponsorship arrangements but payment of benefit should not be delayed. The Benefits Agency should not ask *you* to try to obtain the payments from your sponsor.

Sponsors who are liable to maintain

Sponsors *may* be asked to give an undertaking that will commit the sponsor to a financial responsibility for support and accommodation. This is different from a sponsorship declaration which does not necessarily bind the sponsor. An undertaking is not mandatory and should only be given if the applicant from abroad or sponsor is specifically asked for one. In practice, few sponsors are asked.

An undertaking is only binding if the agreement was made under the terms of the Immigration Act 1971 and on or after 23 May 1980.[79] A sponsor is not liable if the sponsorship was made outside the terms of the Immigration Act 1971 – eg, for a special voucher holder.

A sponsor who is liable remains financially responsible for as long as the sponsee remains in the UK, even if the person's immigration status is changed. However, if the sponsee becomes a British citizen, the sponsor ceases to be responsible. The payments made to maintain the sponsee will be treated as liable relatives' payments in the same way as for a separated spouse (see p91).

Failure to maintain

If the person you are sponsoring claims benefit and also gets a social fund loan, the Benefits Agency may recover the loan from you.

If you are liable but fail to maintain the sponsee, the Benefits Agency has the power to recover from you whatever amount of benefit has been paid to the person for whom you are responsible. Where a sponsor cannot afford to maintain the person from abroad, the Benefits Agency should not pursue the matter. This was confirmed in a parliamentary answer (15 February 1989), when Mr Peter Lloyd (the Parliamentary Under-Secretary of State for Social Security) stated that liability to maintain would be enforced 'wherever necessary' and '*where [the sponsor] has the means*'. The Benefits Agency works out how much the sponsor can pay in the same way as for liable relatives (see p96). They can take legal action to force the sponsor to pay in the same way as for liable relatives, although with one recent exception neither CPAG nor the Joint Council for the Welfare of Immigrants has heard of any prosecutions. If you are prosecuted, see Appendix 2 for details of who to contact.

(vii)   The rights of EC citizens

The Treaty of Rome allows for the free movement of people within the EC. An EC citizen may be admitted to the UK for the following reasons:
☐   to take up employment ('workers');
☐   to establish a business or be self-employed;
☐   to provide or use a service – eg, education.
An EC citizen who is seeking work is also allowed to enter. A person wishing to provide or receive a service has a right of residence, which will last for the duration of the service provided or received. Those taking up employment or setting up a business also have a right of residence here.

EC citizens are admitted subject to the public funds requirement but they nevertheless have rights to claim full IS. All EC citizens can claim IS for as long as they are exercising their right to be here under the Treaty. They must satisfy the normal rules of entitlement.

EC workers and IS

A 'worker' is a person who:
(a)   is in employment, including part-time employment; *or*
(b)   has become unemployed, not through choice, and is willing to take another job; *or*
(c)   has been employed in the UK but has become permanently disabled through illness or injury; *or*
(d)   has worked here and is now aged 60 (or 65 if a man);[80]
(e)   has been admitted to the UK in order to seek work.[81]
It does not include a person who is voluntarily unemployed, or a student (but see below). A person who has spent a very brief time in work as a proportion of their time in the UK may not count as a worker.[82]

You normally prove your right of residence with a **residence permit** which the Home Office grants once you take employment, but the permit itself does not give you right of residence.[83] You have that just by being an EC worker. If you do not have a permit the Benefits Agency should still pay you IS if you can show that you are exercising your Treaty rights as a worker.[84] If you come within groups (a), (b) and (e) above, you also have to be genuinely seeking work and not be voluntarily unemployed.[85]

The 1988 Immigration Act contains a section which brings UK law in line with the Treaty of Rome. Though this section has not been formally implemented, the rights of EC national workers are those prescribed by the Freedom of Movement provisions in the Treaty of Rome. Because of this, EC nationals who are workers do not require leave to enter or remain in the UK. This happens already as EC nationals do not have their passports stamped on entering the UK. You cannot become an overstayer because you have no leave to overstay. You are therefore entitled to full IS.[86] If IS is refused you should appeal. If you are claiming as a part-time worker, you could also argue that this discriminates against non-British EC nationals and is in breach of the Treaty of Rome and EC Regulations.[87] Benefit should be paid irrespective of any restrictions under UK law if these conflict with your rights under EC law.

Other EC citizens with 'right of residence'

People with right of residence should have equal access to benefit in member states.[88] This covers people who are self-employed or in receipt of services. There may be a time-limit on their residence.

EC citizens not covered by the treaty

EC nationals not exercising their Treaty rights are subject to UK immigration law. They are also entitled to IS so long as they are here with leave, but must satisfy the normal rules of entitlement and the Home Office may ask them to leave if they claim. Students, retired people and others who have not worked in the UK, do not have the equal access to benefit rights that accrue to workers.[89] (Note that retired people who have worked here count as workers.)

If you are subject to UK immigration law and overstay your leave you are not entitled to IS and may be asked to leave the UK. However, as long as you are signing on and available for work and have not become voluntarily unemployed, you can argue you are a worker and you cannot be deported as an overstayer.[90] However, if you seek to return to the UK and have had recourse to public funds in the past, and not been in work since then, you could be refused entry if it is felt that you are not genuinely coming for an EC purpose (see p67).

(viii)   Foreign fiancé(e)s, spouses and children

Wives entitled to claim IS on entry

Most foreign spouses are not able to claim benefit until they have been settled in the

UK for over a year. Some women who have acquired right of abode in the UK by marriage (see p60) have a right of entry to the UK without being subject to the public funds test and can claim benefit immediately on entry if they satisfy the normal rules of entitlement (see p62).

Foreign fiancé(e)s and spouses admitted subject to the public funds test

The status of foreign fiancé(e)s and spouses changes up to four times in a period of 18 months. For most of that time they are not supposed to have recourse to public funds *and* another person (usually the spouse (to be) or another member of the family) is expected to maintain her/him. The chart below sets out the position. A person entering the UK as a foreign husband/wife enters the chart at stage 3.

	Status	**Entitlement**
Stage 1	Foreign fiancé(e) admitted to UK for a period of up to six months in order to marry a British citizen, or any other person settled in the UK. Her/his entry is subject to the condition that s/he does not take employment, and the requirement that s/he shall 'not have recourse to public funds'.	No IS or urgent cases payment payable
Stage 2	Fiancé(e) marries and applies to the Home Office for variation of leave. S/he remains subject to the above conditions.	No IS or urgent cases payment payable
Stage 3	Fiancé(e) is granted up to 12 months stay normally from the date of that decision. A husband/wife entering the country will be given an initial 12 months leave from the date of entry. In each case s/he can work but not draw public funds.	No IS or urgent cases payment payable
Stage 4	S/he applies for variation of leave before the expiry of the 12 months.	Urgent cases payment can be made
Stage 5	S/he is granted indefinite leave to remain.	Entitlement to full IS.

At stage 4 above, the 'person from abroad' is legally entitled to claim an urgent cases payment when applying for variation of leave. However, a claim for an urgent cases payment in those circumstances could affect the person's right to obtain permanent leave. In practice, neither CPAG nor the Joint Council for the Welfare of Immigrants know of any cases where a claim for an urgent cases payment has led to the refusal of indefinite leave.

Home Office practice and the immigration rules differ on what should happen during this 12-month period (see Stage 3 above). The rules state that the couple should maintain themselves and their dependants without recourse to public funds. In practice, the Home Office advises the person from abroad by letter that there is no objection to the spouse based in the UK claiming public funds to which s/he is entitled in her/his own right. S/he can therefore claim IS for her/himself (and a child dependant), but nothing for the spouse from abroad. There would, of course, be no difficulty if the partner were to claim a non-means-tested benefit – eg, unemployment benefit, including the allowance for the adult dependant from abroad, as this does not count as public funds.

Some fiancé(e)s and spouses are admitted as 'visitors'. Visitors are not entitled to benefit and are subject to the public funds test. A fiancé(e) or spouse may apply for variation of leave having entered the UK as a visitor.

Children admitted for settlement

Children admitted to the UK to join parent(s) settled here are usually given indefinite leave on entry and the parent is able to claim full benefit for them. However, if they enter with a parent who is given 12 months leave, they are also granted 12 months leave. During that time, they are subject to the public funds test and the settled parent cannot claim for them. After 12 months they are granted indefinite leave (along with the parent) and benefit can be paid in the normal way.

(ix) Applying for refugee status or political asylum

If you apply for refugee status or political asylum at the port of entry you will usually be granted temporary admission. You will not be entitled to full IS but will be able to claim an urgent cases payment while the Home Office is considering your application[91] (see p66). Citizens from countries which have signed the European Convention (1953) who seek refugee status may be admitted as visitors. They can apply for variation of leave and will qualify for an urgent cases payment.[92]

Sometimes, a person applying for refugee status may be detained on entry and refused temporary admission. Her/his solicitor may then apply for bail. Once s/he is released on bail the person from abroad will then be entitled to an urgent cases payment while her/his case is being considered.

Immigrants already in the UK and who apply for refugee status are entitled to an urgent cases payment[93] (see p65).

If you are entitled to urgent cases payments you do not have to be available for work. However, six months after you have applied for refugee status you can apply to have any restrictions on your right to take employment lifted and work instead of claiming IS.

You will need a National Insurance number (which can be issued purely for benefit purposes regardless of your immigration status – see p100). A person from abroad is expected to send her/his passport with the application for the National Insurance number. As your passport is likely to be with the Home Office or you may not have one, you may have to supply the local Benefits Agency with alternative identification or to give a sworn affidavit regarding your identity.

Illegal entrants, overstayers or people subject to deportation orders do not usually have conditions attached to their stay and can therefore take up employment without getting special permission. Check your rights first with an agency with knowledge of immigration law (see p71).

Once you have been granted refugee status (or exceptional leave to remain) you are entitled to full IS subject to the normal rules.

Asylum seekers may want help from the social fund. You can apply for help with the cost of buying basic necessities such as winter clothing etc, through the social fund (see pp291-321).

You may find it helpful to contact the Refugee Council at Bondway House, 3 Bondway, London SW8 and the Joint Council for the Welfare of Immigrants for further advice about immigration issues.

(x) Availability for work

Some people from abroad safely escape the restrictions on entitlement to IS which are linked to immigration issues, but fall foul of the general rule that you have to be 'available for work' to get benefit (see p39).

If you have a work permit, you will not be considered to be available for work, because you are not immediately available for work.[94] The reason for this is that any prospective employer has to check with the Department of Employment and Home Office before being able to employ you. You will, however, get benefit when sick.

You will not be treated as available for work if the terms of your entry do not allow you to work.

People from abroad who are claiming urgent cases payments do not need to be available for work.[95]

(xi) Investigation of entry status[96]

The claim forms (A1 and B1) for IS include the following questions:

☐ Have you come to live in the UK in the last five years?

☐ Has anyone you are claiming for come to live in the UK in the last five years?

You will be required to state on the form the nationality of the person who has come from abroad, and the Benefits Agency will usually call you for interview unless you or the member of your family concerned:

☐ is British; *or*

☐ is from Eire, Channel Islands or the Isle of Man; *or*

☐ is known to be sponsored; *or*

☐ has already had their immigration position investigated.

At the interview, you will be asked about your immigration status and that of your family, and passports, identity cards, travel documents and letters from the Home Office may be examined.

The Benefits Agency may notify the Home Office that you are getting IS if you are:

☐ an EC citizen (from Belgium, Denmark, France, Greece, Ireland, Italy, Luxembourg, Holland, Portugal, Spain and West Germany);

☐ a citizen of a European Convention country (from Iceland, Malta, Norway, Sweden and Turkey);

☐ any other person from abroad who is currently not entitled to ordinary IS on grounds of immigration status, and you have made an application to change your status or length of stay or appealed against a decision regarding your status. If there is a dispute about your status – eg, the Benefits Agency says your leave to remain here has expired, while you say it has been extended – you should appeal (see p118). The adjudication officer has to produce, for the tribunal, documentary proof from the Immigration and Nationality Department of the Home Office to back up her/his statement about your status. [97] A tribunal must usually accept the immigration authority's rulings on a person's status. [98] However, it can look at the question of whether a person needs leave to be in the UK if the answer is not clear. [99] Thus, where a dispute concerns an EC citizen and entitlement to IS, the tribunal should not feel bound to accept the Home Office view. You should argue:

☐ that under EC law an EC worker does not require leave to enter the UK;
☐ that although changes to British law are included in the 1988 Immigration Act but not yet implemented, *the requirements of the Treaty of Rome override British law*. These require freedom of movement within the community, therefore leave is not necessary;
☐ that the requirements of the Treaty of Rome are recognised, in practice, as leave is not granted by the British immigration authorities to EC citizens. Instead they are admitted freely and their passports are not stamped on entry;
☐ that when considering the question of leave, the tribunal or Commissioner should be willing to refer the matter to the European Court of Justice for a preliminary ruling on whether leave is required.

If the Benefits Agency delays payment of benefit while checking details about your identity and immigration status and, as a result, you suffer hardship, ask a local advice agency to contact CPAG.

(xii)   Divided families

Where your spouse is living abroad, and unable to come to the UK (eg, because of the UK immigration laws or for practical reasons), you will be able to claim benefit in your own right. This is because your spouse is not a member of your 'household' (see p228). You will be treated either as a single claimant or as a single parent if your children are here. If the children in the UK are treated as the sole responsibility of the parent abroad, the children will be likely to have limited leave, and the parent here will not be able to claim for them.

If you are waiting for a husband or wife and/or children to join you here you are expected to be able to maintain and accommodate them without help from public funds (see (vi) above). It would therefore be unwise for you to claim IS, housing benefit or family credit as they may be refused entry clearance.

If your partner was living here but has gone abroad for a short period – eg, because of a death in the family – see p101 on swapping the claimant role. If your child has gone abroad, see p234 for the effect on your benefit.

4   PEOPLE IN PRIVATE OR VOLUNTARY RESIDENTIAL CARE AND NURSING HOMES

A residential care or nursing home is a residential home that is private or run by a voluntary body. If you live in one of these, your IS is worked out in a special way. The normal rules about 'applicable amounts' (see p20) do not apply. There are also other special rules.

(i) What counts as a residential care or nursing home

A home counts as a residential care home for IS if it: [100]

☐ is required to be registered as such under the Registered Homes Act 1984; *or*

☐ is run by the Abbeyfield Society; *or*

☐ in Scotland, is registered under the Social Work (Scotland) Act 1968 or run by a registered housing association and provides care similar to that given in a registered home; *or*

☐ provides board and personal care because of old age, disablement, alcohol or drug dependency or mental disorders (but see p74) and is managed by a body (other than a local authority) constituted by Act of Parliament, or incorporated by Royal Charter; *or*

☐ provides board and personal care for less than four persons and has at least two carers, each working for a minimum of 35 hours a week with the residents, with one person available throughout the day and one on call at night. Each carer must have no other employment and at least one year's relevant experience. These small homes may register on a voluntary basis, but will only get treated as residential care homes if they meet the above standards.

If you are living in a home for less than four people which does not comply with the standards, you may still get the same benefit as a person in a residential care home, for as long as you remain resident in the home and need care because you are disabled or elderly or because of past or present mental illness or drug/alcohol dependence. To get this benefit: [101]

☐ you must have been receiving (or been entitled to [102]) supplementary benefit as a residential care home resident in the same home on 26 July 1987; *and*

☐ your benefit on 10 April 1988 must have been calculated as though you were living in a residential care home (or would have been but for your temporary absence as long as you were away for not more than 52 weeks [103]).

Personal care usually means the kind of care and assistance a relative would give to a disabled and elderly person – eg, help with washing, dressing and ensuring medicines are taken.

The benefit entitlement for people living in some types of homes – eg, group or cluster homes – may be unclear. In some cases they are not treated as living in residential accommodation (see p80) or in a residential care home and this can be to their advantage. Claimants who had been resettled from a longstay hospital in an end-of-terrace house owned by the local health authority were able to get IS paid at the ordinary rate plus premiums (see p236), instead of the hospital pocket money allowance (see p82). The decision to treat them in this way hinged on two main factors: [104]

☐ the level of the claimant's independence (ie, they were responsible for their own money, fuel bills were sent to them in their own name, they registered separately for poll tax and obtained exemptions);

☐ health and medication services and general care were received through normal community provision.

Where mentally handicapped claimants spend the day in a large residential care home but spend the night in a small house where they live with one or more of the carers from the main unit, in a less institutional environment, a different issue arises. The small unit is then the claimant's home and it is a residential care home only if it is registered or it fulfils the conditions for homes of less than four people (see above). Time spent by the carers at the main unit arguably should count towards the 35 hours and not as 'other' employment because there is only one institution albeit spread over different premises. Care does not actually have to be provided in the place where the claimant lives. [105]

A home counts as a nursing home for IS if it: [106]
☐ is registered as such under the Registered Homes Act 1984, the Nursing Homes Registration (Scotland) Act 1938 or the Mental Health (Scotland) Act 1984; *or*
☐ provides nursing services and is managed by a body constituted by an Act of Parliament or incorporated by Royal Charter.

Where a residential or nursing home has already been registered, and a new person has taken over the management of the home, it will continue to count as registered, provided a new application to register has been made and not turned down. [107]

(ii) People not counted as living in a residential care or nursing home

You will not get IS at the residential care or nursing home rate if:
☐ the person who runs the home is a 'close relative'. [108] **Close relative** means a parent, parent-in-law, son, son-in-law, daughter, daughter-in-law, step-parent, stepson, stepdaughter, brother, sister or the partner of any of these. Sister or brother includes a half-sister or half-brother. [109] An adopted child ceases to be related to her/his natural family on adoption and becomes the relative of her/his adoptive family. [110] Where the home is run by a limited company of which the 'close relative' is a director, this rule does not apply; [111]
☐ the arrangement is not on a commercial basis. [112] Adjudication officers are advised to interpret broadly the meaning of 'on a commercial basis', and not just rely on whether or not a profit is being made. If the intention is to cover the cost of food plus a reasonable amount for accommodation, the arrangement should be considered to be a commercial one. A charity or individual might charge enough to make ends meet, but not necessarily to make a profit; [113]
☐ you are aged 16 or over but under 19, and are in care – except where you yourself are paying someone other than the local authority for your accommodation; [114]
☐ you are on holiday and have not been away from where you usually live for more than 13 weeks. [115] 'On holiday' would not include a period of respite care or convalescence; [116]
☐ you are going into a residential care or nursing home in order to take advantage of the allowances paid to residents of these homes. [117]
☐ you are in a home run by a body constituted by Act of Parliament (except a local authority) or by Royal Charter, and the personal care you receive is *not* because of old age, disablement, mental disorder, alcohol or drug depencency; [118]
☐ your home changed from being a local authority home to a residential care home while you were living there (or temporarily away). If the local authority is still

obliged to provide accommodation for you and you stay in the same home, your IS is calculated as if you are in a local authority home (see p80). This rule applies from 12 August 1991. [119]

If any of the above apply, you will get IS at the ordinary rate, including premiums.

If your local authority is sponsoring you in the home you will count as being in local authority residential accommodation and get benefit accordingly (see p80). But see also 'topping-up' payments (p78).

(iii) Applicable amounts in residential care and nursing homes

Your applicable amount consists of an amount for **personal expenses** and an **accommodation allowance** to cover all or part of the charge made by the home. You will not be entitled to any premiums.

Personal expenses [120]

These are as follows:

Single claimant	£12.20
Couple	£24.40
Dependent child aged	
18 +	£12.20
16-17	£ 8.50
11-15	£ 7.35
0-10	£ 5.00

The accommodation allowance

The amount you receive will cover the weekly charge for your accommodation including meals and services, where these are provided, but only up to a maximum or ceiling set by parliament. [121]

If you have to pay for some meals separately, your accommodation allowance will include for each person, either an amount to cover the actual cost of the meals if they can be provided by the home, [122] *or*, if not,

☐ £1.10 for breakfast
☐ £1.55 for lunch
☐ £1.55 for dinner

unless your meals taken outside the home cost less.

If you pay additional charges for heating, attendance needs, extra baths, laundry or a special diet you follow for medical reasons, these will be included in the accommodation allowance. [123] You will not get the cost of these meals and/or extra services met in full if your accommodation charge plus the cost of meals or extra services is more than the maximum (see below).

If you receive housing benefit towards part of your accommodation charge this will be deducted from that charge and reduce your IS accordingly. [124]

Maximum accommodation allowances – ceilings [125]

Your accommodation charge (including any charges for additional services and meals) will usually only be met up to a 'ceiling'. This maximum varies depending on the type of home you are in and the type of care you receive. [126] You may find that the total amount you have to pay the home is not covered by your IS.

If you are in a residential care home the ceiling varies according to the level or type of care the home is registered to provide, or if the home is not registered, according to the care you receive. [127] The type of care depends on the health conditions and/or age of the residents. If more than one ceiling applies, the amount is decided as follows: [128]

☐ where the home is registered to provide the type of care you get, you will receive the amount that is allowed for that type of care;

☐ if the care you receive is different from the type the home is registered to provide, you will receive the allowance for the lower or lowest of the categories of care which the home is registered to provide;

☐ in any other case you will receive the amount appropriate to the care you receive.

Residential care homes

Health condition/age	*Amount payable*
Old age	£175.00
Past or present mental disorder but excluding mental handicap	£185.00
Past or present drug or alcohol dependence	£185.00
Mental handicap	£215.00
Physical disablement if under pension age, or, if over pension age, claimant had already become disabled before reaching 60 (65 if a man)	£245.00
Very dependent elderly (ie, over pension age and had become physically disabled after reaching 60 (65 if a man)	£175.00
Over pension age and registered as blind, getting war or industrial constant attendance allowance or qualifies for higher rate attendance allowance or the highest care component of disability living allowance	£205.00
Any other condition	£175.00

* *These amounts are increased by £25 per week for homes in the Greater London area.*

Nursing homes

Health condition	*Amount payable*
Past or present mental disorder but excluding mental handicap	£270.00
Mental handicap	£275.00
Past or present drug or alcohol dependence	£270.00

Nursing homes (*cont.*)

Health condition/age	Amount payable
Physical disablement, if under pension age, or if over pension age, claimant had become disabled before reaching 60 (65 if a man)	£305.00
Over pension age and had become physically disabled after reaching 60 (65 if a man)	£270.00
Terminal illness	£280.00
Any other condition (including elderly)	£270.00

* *These amounts are increased by £35 per week for homes in the Greater London area.*

The following definitions apply when deciding which maximum applies to you:

'**Mental disorder**' is defined as 'mental illness, arrested or incomplete development of mind, psychopathic disorder, and any other disorder or disability of mind' (s55 Registered Homes Act 1984).

'**Mental handicap**' is defined as 'a state of arrested or incomplete development of mind which includes impairment of intelligence and social functioning', (reg 1(2) Residential Care Homes Regulations 1984). 'Senility' is not mental handicap but can amount to a mental disorder. [129]

'**Disablement**' is defined as meaning that you are 'blind, deaf or dumb or substantially and permanently handicapped by illness, injury or congenital deformity or any other disability prescribed by the Secretary of State' (s20(1) Registered Homes Act 1984).

If you are in a nursing home the ceiling varies according to the type of care you receive there. If the home provides more than one type of care you will get the ceiling appropriate to the care you receive. [130] The type of care depends on the health conditions and age of the residents.

Some homes may be registered both as a residential care and a nursing home. In these cases your maximum accommodation allowance will be decided according to whether you are receiving residential or nursing care.

Getting more than the ceiling

You can get more than the ceiling if one of the following applies:

☐ the home is in Greater London, in which case the allowance can be increased by up to £25 for each member of the family aged 11 or over, £35 extra in the case of nursing homes; [131]

☐ you have lived in the same accommodation for over 12 months and could afford it when you moved in. You will get your full accommodation charge for up to 13 weeks after you claim or after you apply for a review of your claim [132] if you are trying to move but need time to find somewhere else given the lack of availability of suitable accommodation and your and your family's personal circumstances (eg, your age, health, employment prospects and the effect on children of changing schools). If you have any disregarded income you will have to put this towards the charge first. [133] The 13-week rule does not apply if you are being accommodated by the local authority because you are homeless or under the authority's duty to promote the welfare of children;

☐ you were living in a residential care or nursing home on 28 April 1985 and you now qualify for IS. The Secretary of State can decide to give you a higher allowance to avoid hardship [134] if:

– you have continued since then to live in a residential care or nursing home (apart from any 'temporary absence', which means up to 52 weeks for a person over pensionable age, or 13 weeks in any other case [135]); *and*
– on that date you met all or part of the weekly charge from your own income and/or capital, or from other sources which are no longer available; *and*
– since then, the local authority has never paid for you to be in a home.

In this case your accommodation allowance will be:

either   the amount of your weekly accommodation charge on 28 April 1985 plus £10;

or   an amount made up of:

– the amount estimated as the reasonable weekly charge (see note below) for the accommodation on 28 April 1985, *plus*
– £26.15, *plus*
– an extra £19.10 or £28.60 if you were entitled to attendance allowance at the lower or higher rate respectively on 28 April 1985.

You will get the lower of these two amounts, and this will continue for as long as it is more than your accommodation allowance under the present rules. [136]

☐ you have been living in a home since before 29 April 1985 and were paid extra supplementary benefit from that time until 11 April 1988. This protection continued under IS. For details of who got protection under IS see p32.

Money from other sources

☐ Your local authority may have agreed to pay the difference between your IS accommodation allowance and the charge you have to pay the home. This '**topping-up payment**' can only be paid if you live in a residential care home, not a nursing home. To qualify you must be under pension age, or if you are over that age the local authority must have been paying the topping-up allowance for two years before you reached 60 (for women) or 65 (for men). [137] The payment will not affect your IS (and you will not be counted as living in residential accommodation – see p80).

☐ You may be receiving money from other sources – such as a charity or relatives – to help you pay for the part of your accommodation charge above the limit. This will also be ignored as income provided you *do* use it to pay the balance of the charge. [138] This would apply where the health authority makes a topping-up payment to a nursing home resident to meet the cost of separate charges for services (eg, heating, attendance and meals) that take the overall accommodation charge above the ceiling.

(iv) Moving in or out of residential care or nursing homes

☐ If you are getting IS and you go into a home for eight weeks or less (eg, for respite care) you get IS for being in the home from the date you go in, whatever day of the week it is. [139]

☐ If you are in the home for only a few days but have to pay a full week's charge, your IS covers all of it. [140] Similarly, if you leave the home for less than a week, your claim is not reviewed and you continue to get full IS at the care home rate. [141]

☐ If you are in the home temporarily, you are also paid housing costs for which you are liable on your normal home. [142] If you pay rent you continue to get housing benefit while you are in the home.

☐ If you are a single parent and temporarily in a home you are paid the residential care or nursing home rate of IS for a single person, plus:

either the ordinary IS allowances for children if they are not living in the home;

or the rates for children on p75 if they are living with you in the home;

plus the family premium, lone parent premium and any premiums for the children. [143]

You are also paid your normal housing costs.

☐ If someone in your family is temporarily away from the home the family still counts as being there as long as either you or your partner remain in it. [144]

☐ IS can cover a retaining fee payable while you are temporarily away from the home, but only up to 80 per cent of your normal accommodation allowance. [145] It is paid for up to four weeks if you normally live there, are away for at least a week and do not have to sign on (see p16) or for up to a year if you have temporarily gone into hospital or local authority residential accommodation. You are not covered by this rule if the residential accommodation does not provide board or it is for the rehabilitation of alcohol or drug users (see p80). [146]

☐ If you are a couple and one of you is temporarily in a residential care or nursing home and the other is living in the family home, or if the other one of you is also temporarily away from home (in hospital, or a residential care or nursing home, or residential accommodation), see p232.

☐ If you are a couple, and one of you goes into a home permanently, you will cease to be treated as a couple (see p232). [147] The partner in the home will be paid benefit as a resident and the other partner will be assessed as a single claimant or single parent as appropriate. However, you are still treated as liable to maintain one another and may be asked to contribute to your partner's upkeep if you are not on benefit.

Remember that if you are moving out of a home to live in the community you may get a community care grant (see pp300-314).

5 PEOPLE IN LOCAL AUTHORITY RESIDENTIAL HOMES

(i) What counts as residential accommodation

It must be provided by the local authority's social services department under the National Assistance Act 1948 (usually called Part III accommodation) or under the NHS Act 1977. Homes for the elderly are usually but not always established under the National Assistance Act. Accommodation for people suffering or recovering from ill health (whether physical or mental illness) is usually provided under the NHS Act 1977 and only counts as residential accommodation if *some* board is provided. [148]

'Board' usually means the provision of some cooked or prepared meals, the cost of which is included in the weekly charge for the accommodation. [149] Catering facilities which the resident has the option to use should not count as 'board' and neither should 'pay as you eat' schemes. If you live in a hostel provided under this legislation and you have access to board you will therefore count as being in residential accommodation.

If you live in a private or voluntary residential care home but are sponsored by the local authority, it will be treated as residential accommodation. This also applies if a local authority transfers ownership of a care home on or after 12 August 1991. Residents continue to be treated as in residential accommodation. In Scotland, similar accommodation is provided under s27 of the NHS (Scotland) Act 1947, s59 of the Social Work (Scotland) Act 1968 and s7 of the Mental Health (Scotland) Act 1984. Local authority residential accommodation is a means-tested service and the authority will assess you for a contribution according to your income and capital. [150] Any income you receive above the personal allowances listed below may be taken as your contribution, as well as £43.30 of the personal allowance. This rule also applies to people who are sponsored in full by local authorities in residential care homes.

You will not be treated as in residential accommodation if: [151]

☐ you are in a home for the rehabilitation of alcoholics or drug addicts that is registered under the Registered Homes Act 1984 (you will be paid on the basis that you are living in a residential care home, see p73); *or*

☐ you are in a home which does not provide board (see above). You will be paid the ordinary rate of IS personal allowance and will be able to claim housing benefit (see p151). Some people living in hostels will fall into this category.

The amount of IS you get while in local authority residential accommodation depends on whether you go there temporarily or permanently and whether you are single or part of a couple.

Your benefit may include an extra amount if you were paid as a hostel-dweller before 9 October 1989. See p31 for more information on transitional protection.

(ii) Temporary stays in residential accommodation

☐ **If you are a single person** you will have an IS allowance of £54.15 plus housing costs for your normal home, if appropriate. [152]

☐ **If you are a single parent** you will have an IS allowance of £54.15 plus the personal allowance for each child for whom you were receiving benefit before going into the home, a family premium, a lone parent premium and housing costs for your normal home, if appropriate. [153]

☐ **Couples where both are in residential accommodation** will have an IS allowance of two lots of £54.15 plus their housing costs for their normal home, if appropriate. [154]

☐ **Couples where one member is temporarily in residential accommodation**, will receive £54.15 for the partner in the home and a single claimant's allowance for the other partner. [155] Where the partner not in the home is excluded from IS (eg, because s/he is in full-time work) but the couple cannot afford to pay the residential accommodation charge, they will cease to be treated as a couple and the partner in the home will get the £54.15 IS residential accommodation allowance. [156]

☐ There were some gaps in **transitional protection** for people in residential accommodation which have been corrected – in particular, May 1988 payments and boarders' transitional protection (see p31) have been extended to single people, couples and single parents when they go into residential accommodation temporarily.

(iii) Permanent stays in residential accommodation

☐ **If you are single or a single parent** you will get a personal allowance of £10.85 plus £43.30 for your accommodation. [157]

☐ You will receive double this amount if you are a **couple and both of you are living permanently in residential accommodation**. [158] If one of you goes into **hospital**, you will continue to get your normal benefit, but if you are single you will just get £10.85. [159]

☐ If you are a **couple and one partner has become permanently resident** in residential accommodation, you will no longer be treated as a couple. [160] The partner in the home will receive the residential accommodation allowance of £54.15 (see above), while the other partner will be assessed as a single person or single parent, as appropriate.

☐ If you are a **couple and normally live in residential accommodation but one of you is temporarily away**, you should get your benefit calculated in the normal way.

(iv) Other changes to your benefit

☐ If your child is living with you in the home you will receive the normal personal allowance for her/him. [161]

☐ If you are getting disability living allowance or attendance allowance when you go into residential accommodation, it will stop after four weeks. [162]

☐ If you are getting IS and you go into residential accommodation for eight weeks or less (eg, for a period of respite care) you will lose your ordinary IS and be paid an IS residential home allowance from the date you enter the home regardless of which day of the week you go into the home. [163]

6 PEOPLE IN HOSPITAL

If you, your partner or child goes into hospital, your IS will be reduced after a few weeks. Other benefits – eg, sickness benefit – are also reduced while you are in hospital so your IS may not go down as much as you expect, and you may even qualify for IS for the first time because of reduced income. Alternatively, you may lose your IS altogether if you have other income.

If you live in residential accommodation your benefit changes only if you are single (see above). Special rules apply to people who normally live in residential care and nursing homes when they go into hospital (see p84).

If you are a member of a couple and one of you is in hospital and the other is also temporarily away from your normal home, check p231.

(i) Housing costs

You will continue to get these until you have been in hospital for one year unless you are the claimant and the Benefits Agency believes that you are likely to be in hospital substantially longer than 52 weeks.[164] If you have a partner, son or daughter who is eligible for IS, they could claim instead and get the housing costs covered. For how your housing benefit is affected, see p175.

After 52 weeks you will cease to get your housing costs met. If you are a couple, and one of you remains at home, you are treated as two separate people and the partner at home will get housing costs met (see p231).[165]

(ii) Single people in hospital

After four weeks any attendance allowance you receive stops and you therefore lose your severe disability premium.[166] Otherwise your IS remains unchanged for your first six weeks in hospital.[167] A carer would also lose their carer's premium.[168]

After six weeks your applicable amount will be reduced to £13.55 personal allowance[169] plus any housing costs (see above).

After 52 weeks you will lose any IS housing costs and only get a personal allowance of £10.85.[170] You can be paid less than this if:[171]

☐ you are unable to look after your own affairs (eg, mentally ill or senile) and another person has been appointed to act on your behalf; *and*

☐ the IS is paid to the hospital at the request of the appointee, or to the hospital as the appointee; *and*

☐ a doctor who is treating you certifies that you will not be able to make use of all or part of your benefit, and that it cannot be used on your behalf.

This rule could leave you without any income at all, though your relatives and the hospital staff should be consulted about how much you should receive. Your appointee could refuse to allow the Benefits Agency to pay the hospital direct. S/he could receive payments on your behalf instead to make sure you get the money.

(iii) Single parents in hospital

After four weeks any attendance allowance you receive stops and you therefore lose your severe disability premium. [172] Otherwise your IS remains unchanged for your first six weeks in hospital. [173] A carer also loses her/his carer's premium. [174]

After six weeks your applicable amount will be £13.55 personal allowance *plus* your children's personal allowances, *plus* the family, lone parent and disabled child premiums, [175] *plus* housing costs (see above).

If your child is also in hospital, see p84.

After 52 weeks you continue to receive the same amount unless you are no longer treated as 'responsible' for your children (see p233). In this case you will just get the £10.85 personal allowance, and your children may be able to claim in their own right even if aged 16 or 17 and still at school (see p12).

(iv) Couples

The amount paid for a couple depends on whether they have children and whether one or both of them is in hospital.

After four weeks if the person who goes into hospital receives attendance allowance, or the care component of disability living allowance, this will stop and you will lose the carer's premium if paid, [176] but all other premiums, including severe disability premium, will continue to be paid. If it is the carer who goes into hospital they cease to qualify for invalid care allowance (ICA) and therefore lose the carer's premium. If, as the carer, you qualified for ICA less than 22 weeks before going into hospital, the carer's premium could be withdrawn as soon as you go into hospital. [177]

After six weeks your usual applicable amount including all other premiums will be reduced by £10.85 if only one adult is in hospital. [178] (This also applies if both of you are in hospital but only one of you has been there for over six weeks.)

If both of you are in hospital for over six weeks your applicable amount will be £27.10 personal allowance for you both, *plus* personal allowances for your children, if any, *plus* family and disabled child (if any) premiums *plus* housing costs (see p82). You lose the severe disability premium.

After 52 weeks if one or both of a couple are in hospital, you count as separate claimants. [179]

If only one partner is in hospital s/he will be paid a personal allowance of £10.85 and the other member will be assessed as a single claimant or a single parent, as appropriate. If both members of a couple without children are in hospital they will each be paid a personal allowance of £10.85 only. [180]

If both members of a couple with children are in hospital, one will be treated as responsible for the children and receive £13.55 personal allowance for her/himself plus the children's personal allowances and disabled child premium, if any, *plus* the family premium. [181] The other will just be paid the £10.85 personal allowance.

If a child is also in hospital, see below.

(v) Children

If your child goes into hospital, your benefit stays the same for 12 weeks. After that the IS personal allowance you receive for the child will be reduced to £10.85. [182] Any premiums you receive in relation to the child remain in payment. Even if your child loses the care component of disability living allowance because s/he has been in hospital for over 12 weeks, you still get a disabled child premium for her/him, as long as s/he continues to be treated as a member of your family (see p233). [183]

The rule about adjustment to IS for a child in hospital applies equally where both parent(s) and child are in hospital.

(vi)   People in residential care or nursing homes

If you go into hospital for six weeks or less, [184] you will still get your personal allowance and your accommodation allowance as long as you still have to pay the charge for the home – or a reduced allowance if the charge is reduced. If you are single, do not have to pay the charge, and do not intend to return to the home, you will get IS in the normal way as a hospital patient. If you do intend to return but do not have to pay the charge, you will get your personal allowance as a home resident, *plus* meals allowance, if any.

After six weeks in hospital (12 for a child), the following rules apply: [185]

☐   The personal allowance for an adult in hospital is £13.55.

☐   The personal allowance for a child who has been in hospital for over 12 weeks will be £10.85.

☐   A single claimant, or a couple without children who are both in hospital, will receive £13.55 or £27.10 respectively *plus* either an amount for a retaining fee in respect of the home or an amount for housing costs, but not both. [186]

☐   For as long as another member of the family remains in the residential care or nursing home, an accommodation allowance will continue to be paid taking account of any reduction in the charge, and personal allowances at the residential care and nursing homes rate will continue for each member of the family still in the home or in hospital for six weeks or less (12 in the case of children).

☐   Where children do not live in the home while their parent(s) or only parent is in hospital, the benefit of the parent(s) is calculated in the usual way for patients (see above) except it will include either an amount for a retaining fee in respect of the home or an amount for IS housing costs, but not both. [187]

(vii)   Patients detained under the Mental Health Act

Single people detained under the Mental Health Act 1983 (in Scotland, Mental Health (Scotland) Act 1984), who were in prison immediately before their detention receive a weekly allowance of £10.85. [188]

(viii)   Going in and out of hospital

☐   The date of the change to your IS applicable amount depends on whether your IS is paid in advance or arrears. [189] If you are paid in arrears, the first reduction will take place from the first day of the benefit week in which you will have been in hospital for six weeks (not counting the day of admission). If your IS is paid in advance, the change will take effect from the first day of the benefit week which coincides with, or follows, the date when you will have been in hospital for six weeks. In the first case you could *lose* up to six days' full benefit; in the second you could *gain* up to six days' full benefit.

☐ Separate stays in hospital less than 28 days apart will be added together in calculating the length of time you have been in hospital. [190]

☐ Days at home: If you or a member of your family stop being a patient for any period of less than a week you should be paid your full IS for the days you are at home. [191]

☐ The days that you leave and return to hospital are not counted as days in hospital in the above circumstances. [192]

☐ Other benefits:

   – **Furniture and clothing:** You may be able to get a social fund payment for these when you come out of hospital, and for clothing if you are going into hospital (see Part IX). You should apply before you are due to leave hospital to give the Benefits Agency time to deal with your application.

   – **Fares to hospital:** See p342 for patients' fares and p310 for visitors' hospital fares.

   – **Transitional payments** can be affected by a stay in hospital but may be reinstated on the person's return to their home, see p33.

7 PRISONERS

You count as a prisoner if you are in custody on remand, or are serving a custodial sentence. [193]

If you are in prison, you are not entitled to IS apart from housing costs in certain limited circumstances (see below). [194] If you are married, or living as husband and wife, your partner will be able to claim benefit as a single claimant or single parent as appropriate while you are in prison. [195]

If a dependent child becomes a prisoner, you will not get any benefit for them. [196] If you have no other children you will no longer qualify for a family premium and/or a lone parent premium.

Housing costs covered by IS (see p22), will be paid while you are remanded in custody or committed in custody for trial or to be sentenced. [197] Benefit will be paid direct to the person you are liable to pay. You will also be entitled to housing benefit for rent or a lodging charge if you pay either of these (see p154).

If you are only likely to be in prison for about a year you can get housing benefit for up to 52 weeks (see p140). [198] However, you will not get help with IS housing costs such as mortgage interest, after sentence.

If you are granted leave shortly before release, you will not be entitled to IS nor will any person with whom you are staying be entitled to IS for you. However, they may be able to get a community care grant to help towards your living expenses (see p305). A community care grant may be awarded even if the amount is less than £30.

The Prison Department can make a payment for home leave where the prisoner's family is not getting IS, but does not have sufficient money to support the prisoner while on leave; they can also pay for board and lodging during a period of temporary release for a prisoner regarded as homeless.

When you are discharged you may receive a discharge grant which will be treated as capital and will not generally affect your right to be paid IS. [199] For the first seven days after your discharge (including the day of your discharge) you will not be required to sign on as a condition of getting benefit[200] (see p16). If you need help with the cost of basic essentials (eg, clothing, furniture, or rent in advance), you may be able to get a social fund payment (see p285).

Help with the cost of **visiting a close relative in prison** comes from the Home Office. For this purpose, 'close relative' means husband, wife (including an established unmarried partner), brother, sister, parent and child. Adopted and fostered children and adoptive and foster parents are included. It is normal policy to cover the travel costs (including an overnight stay and meals allowance where necessary), of up to 13 visits in a 12-month period if you are receiving IS or family credit. If your income is low but above IS level, the Home Office may pay part of the cost. Your income will be assessed in the same way as for health benefits (see p333). You apply for help with the cost of visits on Form F2022 obtainable from your local Benefits Agency office, or from the Assisted Prison Visits Unit, Calthorpe House, Hagley Road, Birmingham B16 8QR, tel: 021-455-9855. There is no right of appeal against a refusal by the Home Office of fares or a warrant for a visit but you could take up the matter with your MP.

8   PEOPLE WITHOUT ACCOMMODATION

Benefit should not be refused just because you do not have an address. You are entitled to the normal IS personal allowance (see p237) for your weekly living expenses. You will not be paid an allowance for a child dependant. You will not get any premiums for yourself, your partner or children.[201] Claimants known to stay in the area should be paid their benefit by giro or order book in the normal way, but if you are 'likely to move on or mis-spend your money' you may be required to collect your benefit on a daily or part-week basis.[202]

The *Adjudication Officers' Guide* defines 'accommodation' to include anywhere that is habitable and capable of being heated, and where you can sit, lie, cook and eat.[203] People in tents etc may therefore not be 'without accommodation' and could get premiums.

If you can get accommodation – eg, in board and lodging or a hostel – you will get your normal personal allowances and premiums (if any) and you should apply for housing benefit for the board and lodging or hostel charge. If you need help with travel costs to accommodation you have been offered, you may be able to get a social fund payment (see p310).

People with no fixed abode, and no income, may initially require a crisis loan (see p314). The Benefits Agency may decide the claimant has an unsettled way of life and refer her/ him to a voluntary project centre as an alternative. This is the practice of some Benefits Agency offices but should only be used with the client's consent and if a place is available. IS should not be refused or delayed if the claimant is unwilling to take the 'advice' being offered, or is not interested in being resettled.[204]

Chapter 6

Maintenance payments

This chapter is divided as follows:

This chapter deals with the liability of one person to maintain others and the effect any maintenance payments have on IS, but it covers only heterosexual couples who have split up and the parents of children. Some of the provisions also affect sponsors who have signed undertakings to maintain people from abroad; the implications for them are dealt with on p66. The treatment of maintenance payments will change significantly from April 1993. A summary of the changes is given in section 5 (see p98).

1 INTRODUCTION

(i) Claiming after a relationship breakdown

It often happens that a marriage or other relationship breaks down but that the parties remain living under the same roof, living separate lives. In such a case, you can both make separate claims for IS (and other means-tested benefits) and should not be treated as a married or cohabiting couple, provided that you keep separate households (see p228).

(ii) Single parents

If you are a single person responsible for a child or young person under 19 who is living in your household and for whom you can claim (see p233), you are entitled to have the **lone parent premium** included in your applicable amount (see p239) and are entitled to have £15 of your net earnings disregarded (see p255). It is not necessary for you to be a parent of the child or young person.

While you are claiming for a child under 16, you are not required to be available for work and to sign on. Nor can any voluntary unemployment deduction be made if you lose a job through misconduct, etc.

As a single parent, you are likely to be able to claim **one parent benefit** which is an increase of child benefit paid at the rate of £5.85 per week. Again, it is not necessary to be a parent of the child. If you are married, it is not usually paid until you have been separated from your husband or wife for 13 weeks (for full details, see CPAG's *Rights guide to non-means-tested benefits*). If you do claim one parent benefit, it is taken into account in full as income so you are no better off unless your total income is then sufficient to lift you off IS altogether. However, it is unwise to claim one parent benefit if that means you will be just off IS because, apart from the IS, you would lose entitlement to free school meals and also access to community care grants or budgeting loans from the social fund. This is because those payments all depend on your being entitled to IS. Your IS will not be reduced if you choose not to claim one parent benefit to which you could be entitled. On the other hand, it is a good idea to claim one parent benefit if you are soon going to take full-time work and will no longer be entitled to IS anyway. This is because you would then have the use of the one parent benefit as soon as your entitlement to IS ended. If you are already receiving one parent benefit when you claim IS or you later make a claim, make sure that the Benefits Agency office dealing with your IS claim knows so that you are not overpaid. The IS authorities do not always find out automatically, and overpayments in those circumstances are generally recoverable (see p112).

If you claim IS within three months of the birth of a child, claim a maternity payment from the social fund (see p285).

(iii)   Young mothers

If you are under 16, you cannot claim IS but can claim child benefit and one parent benefit and also health benefits (see p333). If your parents (or someone else) are entitled to include you in their family (see p233), they can also include your baby in their family for the purpose of a claim to IS or other means-tested benefits and they can claim a maternity payment from the social fund (see p285) if they are entitled to IS or FC.

If you are over 16 but have not been entitled to IS because you are under 19 and still in relevant education, you can make a claim for IS as soon as your baby is born (see p12).

(iv)   Liable relatives

The following (together with sponsors of people from abroad – see p66) are expected by the Benefits Agency to make maintenance payments if they have the means and are known as 'liable relatives':[1]

☐   a husband or wife. This includes one from whom you are separated;
☐   a divorced man or woman;
☐   a parent of a child or young person under 19;
☐   a person who has been maintaining a child or young person under 19 and can therefore reasonably be treated as a parent.

The Benefits Agency usually tries to ensure that such people are paying maintenance (see p89). Any payments they do make are taken into account in a particular way (see p91).

However, it is important to note that the Secretary of State cannot take proceedings against a person to pay maintenance for either an ex-husband or ex-wife (ie, after decree absolute of divorce). They do not usually take proceedings against people on IS as their income is too low.

(v) The interview ('naming the father')

If you are a single parent, or have children whose other parent is not your present partner or you are a separated spouse, your claim is referred to a 'liable relative officer' once it has been decided that you are entitled to IS. If you claim in person, you may be interviewed there and then, but otherwise the liable relative officer tries to arrange an interview within ten days of your claim.

The purpose of the interview is to find out who and where any liable relative is so that s/he may be approached by the Benefits Agency about paying you maintenance.

There is no penalty if you refuse to help the liable relative officer. You do not have to name any liable relative or say where they are. This may change from April 1993 – see p98.

If you have just separated and appear to have sufficient funds to be going on with, it may be suggested that no benefit should be paid to you until the liable relative has been contacted and asked whether s/he intends to pay maintenance. This is wrong. You should insist on being paid benefit on the basis that you have no maintenance until you receive some. You should make it clear that you will report any maintenance that is paid.

If you want to make the first approach to your former partner, you should ask the liable relative officer not to contact him/her until you have done so. If you do not want your former partner to be contacted at all, you should explain why. The liable relative officer should take account of any fear of violence or other similar consideration when deciding whether to do so.

Officers are instructed not to suggest that there is any penalty for failure to co-operate, but interviews are now conducted on the assumption that you will co-operate. The advantages of obtaining a maintenance order are stressed and so is the Secretary of State's power to obtain one. You are given an explanatory leaflet. It is a good idea to get independent advice from a solicitor (you can get legal aid which is free if you are on IS) about whether to obtain a maintenance order yourself or, if the Secretary of State knows enough, whether to leave it to him. Generally it will be better to do it yourself.

Remember that your benefit cannot be reduced or withheld if you decide not to give the liable relative officer any information although things may change in April 1993 (see p99). If you think you are being put under too much pressure to provide information, you should complain (see p116).

2   YOUR RIGHT TO MAINTENANCE PAYMENTS

(i) Obtaining an order

It is quite possible to have voluntary maintenance payments and never to go near a court. However, you may be unable to agree an amount of maintenance in which case a court order is necessary.

You can obtain an order against your spouse or former spouse or against any other parent of any of your children. A person other than a parent who is looking after a child can sometimes get an order against a parent, and a person over 18 (in Scotland, over 12) but still in full-time education can obtain an order against his/her own parent. Orders can be obtained from a magistrates' court, county court or the High Court (in Scotland, where maintenance is known as aliment, the sherriff's court or the Court of Session). Maintenance can be in the form of regular 'periodical payments' or a lump sum or both and, on divorce, a court has wide powers to transfer property. An order for periodical payments in the county court or High Court can be registered in a magistrates' court so that payments are made through that court.

Detailed advice about maintenance orders is beyond the scope of this *Handbook* and you should see a solicitor. Legal aid is available and advice is free if you are receiving IS. However, some advice is given here about the benefit implications of orders.

(ii)   The advantages of a maintenance order

The obvious advantage of a maintenance order which is high enough, is that it increases your income. Since periodical payments are taken fully into account as income, an order does not help while you are receiving IS unless it lifts you off IS altogether. However, there are still advantages in getting an order if you are not intending staying on IS for ever. It is always easier to get an order if you do not delay for too long and it is useful to have the maintenance available as soon as you cease to be entitled to IS rather than having to make an application then and waiting some months for it to be heard. If maintenance is not likely to be paid regularly, an interim order is best avoided because it cannot usually be diverted to the Benefits Agency (see p91).

(iii)   The disadvantages of a maintenance order

If you are staying on IS, it is unwise to have a maintenance order which takes your income to a level which just disqualifies you from IS. This is because you may lose more by way of free school meals or access to social fund community care grants or budgeting loans (which all depend on you remaining entitled to IS) than you gain from the maintenance order.

An order which is irregularly paid also means your benefit has to be adjusted frequently, although you can get round that by having the order diverted to the Benefits Agency (see p91).

There may be other disadvantages, unconnected with IS, such as the creation of difficulties over access or the risk of violence in retaliation.

(iv)   Liable relatives on low incomes

A court ought not to order maintenance to be paid if that would force the payer below subsistence level, but subsistence level might be taken as less than IS level.[2] However, there needs to be a good reason for pushing someone below IS level (such as substantial disregarded earnings or capital) and, in practice, courts usually leave people with a bit more than they would receive on IS.[3] If a liable relative has an income slightly above IS, the Benefits Agency's own formula for deciding how much can be afforded (see p96) can be used as a starting point. [4]

Any liable relative on IS should have the maintenance order varied to a nominal sum and should ask the court to remit any arrears attributable to the period when they were on IS.

Furthermore, it is wrong for a court to decide that a person on IS is not trying hard enough to get work and to impose a maintenance order as though they were in work unless a voluntary unemployment deduction (see p45) is being made from benefit. [5]

(v)   Payment of maintenance to the Benefits Agency

If maintenance is payable through a magistrates' court (including orders made in the county court or High Court but registered in the magistrates' court) and it is paid irregularly, you can authorise the clerk to pay it to the Benefits Agency when it does arrive and, in return, the Benefits Agency gives you an order book for the amount of IS you would receive if no maintenance was being paid. An interim order in the county court or High Court cannot be registered in the magistrates' court. However, diversion is also possible if payments are made to a county court or the High Court under an attachment of earnings order.

The Benefits Agency does not usually accept this sort of arrangement unless payments have actually been missed, but may if you have a good reason for wanting it done and you explain why. If payments have been missed, diverted payments are convenient both for you and the Benefits Agency as they mean that your benefit does not have to be adjusted every time a payment is either made or fails to arrive.

(vi)   Variation and enforcement of maintenance payments

Once an order has been made, either party can ask for it to be varied to take account of changes of circumstances. It is always then open to a liable relative to ask for any arrears to be remitted.

A court can order the payment of arrears by a certain date or at a certain weekly rate and a liable relative who refuses to pay can be imprisoned as a last resort.

The Secretary of State can now ask a court to enforce an order which is in your name and can intervene to object to a variation application or an application to remit arrears (see p97).

3   THE EFFECT OF MAINTENANCE ON BENEFIT

Courts can order either regular periodical payments or else a lump sum to be paid either in one go or by instalments. If you are receiving IS, it is not usually a good idea to have a lump sum instead of periodical payments because most lump sums are treated as income at a sufficiently high level to disqualify you from benefit altogether even if they are for amounts well below the usual capital limit of £8,000. However, some lump sums are treated as capital and are not affected by this rule.

(i)   Periodical payments

Periodical payments are:[6]

☐ any payment made, or due to be made, regularly whether voluntarily or under a court order or other formal agreement;

☐ any other small payment no higher than your weekly IS;

☐ any lump sum which is made instead of regular payments either as payment in advance or to cover arrears (but not including any arrears due before the beginning of your entitlement to IS).

All periodical payments are treated as income and are taken fully into account to reduce your IS except:[7]

☐ payments in kind (unless you or your partner is involved in a trade dispute);

☐ boarding school fees (but see p247);

☐ any payment to or for a child or young person who has left your household;

☐ any payments arising from disposing of property (which would normally be capital – see below);

☐ payments made to someone else for the benefit of you or a member of your family (such as mortgage capital payments) provided that it is reasonable to ignore the payment and it is not used for food, ordinary clothing or footwear, fuel, your eligible rent (see p157), eligible community charge (see p217), or those housing costs that could be met through IS. It is well worth appealing in a case where a payment is not ignored on this ground because a tribunal may take a different view as to what is reasonable.

Periodical payments which are received on time are each spread over a period equal to the interval between them. Thus, monthly payments are spread over a month. They are multiplied by 12 and divided by 52 to produce a weekly income figure.[8]

(ii)   Arrears of periodical payments

Arrears due during your claim

If payments are not received while you are claiming IS, they should not be treated as income. Then when a payment does arrive and it includes a lump sum for arrears (or in advance), the payment is spread over a period calculated by dividing it by the weekly amount of maintenance you should have received.[9]

Example

You should receive £80 per month. It is not paid for three months and then you receive £200.

£80 per month is treated as producing a weekly income of:

$$£80 \times \frac{12}{52} = £18.45$$

The £200 is taken into account for:

$$\frac{200}{18.45} \text{ weeks} = 10.85 \text{ weeks}$$

You are therefore assumed to have an income of £18.45 for the next ten weeks and six days. The maintenance payments due to you are still two weeks and one day in arrears (£40).

If a payment is specifically identified as being arrears for a particular period, it will, in practice, often be taken into account for a forward period from the week after you inform the Benefits Agency about it. However, it ought to be attributed to the past period which it was intended to cover, unless it is 'more practicable' to choose a later week. [10] In this case the Secretary of State can recover the full amount of extra benefit paid to you while maintenance was not being received. [11] (This can still be done when you receive a payment after your claim ends which is for arrears of maintenance that should have been paid while you were still claiming.) If the amount of benefit you were receiving then and are receiving now are both greater than the weekly amount of maintenance, it does not matter whether the adjudication officer spreads the payment over the period when payment should have been made or forwards from a date after the payment was received.

However, for some people it does make a difference and you should argue for the payment to be spread over whichever period is more advantageous to you. This will depend on the amount of IS you would otherwise receive, the amount of the payment and whether any other periodical payments are being made.

Example
You should have been receiving maintenance at the rate of £25 per week but eight weeks are missed and you have to claim IS at the rate of £15 per week to top-up your part-time earnings. You reduce the number of hours you are working and your entitlement to IS then increases to £30 per week. You then receive a payment of arrears of maintenance which includes £200 to make up the missing eight weeks from before your IS was increased. However, you do not receive any further maintenance payments.

If that payment were taken into account at the rate of £25 per week for eight weeks from the date it was made, you would lose all £200. However, if it were attributed to the period when the maintenance ought to have been paid in the first place, you would lose only £120 (£15 × 8) because that is all the benefit you were paid then. If you can pay £120 to the Benefits Agency, you have a very good argument that it is not 'more practicable' to spread the payment forwards rather than over the past period. You should appeal if it is not accepted.

On the other hand, if you started to receive regular maintenance payments from the date the arrears were received, you would be better off having the payment of arrears being spread forwards. This is because the new maintenance payments would reduce your IS to £5 per week so that taking the arrears into account for eight weeks would cost you only £40 (£5 × 8).

Arrears due before your claim

If the arrears are for a period before your claim they are not treated as a periodical payment. Adjudication officers tend to treat the payment as a **lump sum** derived from a liable relative so that it is treated as income rather than capital except to the extent that you have already spent it. This means that it is spread over a future period (see p95). You should argue that the regulations do not exclude arrears from the definition of periodical payments[12] just to have them brought back into the calculation as other liable relative payments. The regulations intend that they should be excluded from the liable relative provisions altogether and the payment is to be treated as capital (or as disregarded income if you are receiving current periodical payments). Any other interpretation is unfair and gives the Secretary of State an unwarranted windfall at your expense.[13]

(iii)   Lump sums treated as capital

If you receive a lump sum from a liable relative (see p88) which would, if it were capital, take your capital to no more than £8,000, it is better if it can be treated as capital rather than income. (If it is more than £8,000, you will not receive any benefit whether it is treated as capital or income, although you might be able to re-claim sooner if it were capital.)

However, only the following lump sums can be treated as capital:[14]

☐   any payment arising from a 'disposition of property' (see below) in consequence of your separation, divorce, etc;

☐   any gifts not exceeding £250 in any period of 52 weeks (and not so regular as to amount to periodical payments);

☐   any payment in kind (unless you or your partner is involved in a trade dispute – see p60);

☐   any payment made to someone else for the benefit of you or a member of your family (such as special tuition fees) which it is unreasonable to take into account – you can appeal to a tribunal who may take a different view from the adjudication officer about what is reasonable;

☐   any boarding school fees (but see p247);

☐   any payment to or for a child or young person who has left your household;

☐   any payment which you have used before the adjudication officer makes her/his decision provided that you did not use it for the purpose of gaining entitlement to IS – it should not be taken into account if you have used it to clear debts such as your solicitor's bill;

☐   any other payment if the liable relative is already making periodical payments equal to
    –   your IS if the payments include payments for you;
    –   your child's applicable amount and any family and lone parent premium if the payments are only for a child.

If the periodical payments stop or fall below that level, what is left of the lump sum is taken into account as income (see p95).[15]

'Disposition of property'

It is vital to distinguish between payments arising from a disposition of property and those that are not. 'Property' is not confined to houses and land, but includes any asset such as the contents of your former home or a building society account. There is a 'disposition' when those contents are divided up or your former partner buys out your interest. [16] Therefore, any lump sum which is paid in settlement of a claim to a share in any property is treated as capital. It is only those lump sums which are paid instead of income which are liable to be treated as income. [17] It is important to take this into account in any negotiations with your former partner and you should make sure your solicitor knows about this rule.

It is best if any court order is drawn up so as to record that any lump sum is in settlement of a claim to an interest in property. However, this is not essential and the Benefits Agency should accept a letter from your solicitor explaining why a lump sum was asked for and agreed.

Note that the proceeds of sale of your former home may be disregarded altogether for a period of time (see p276). Other capital, such as the home itself and its contents, may also be disregarded (see p275). There is therefore an advantage, while you are on benefit, in asking for a greater share of the home and accepting less in the way of capital or income which would be taken into account to reduce your benefit.

(iv) Lump sums treated as income

All other lump sums are treated as income and are spread over a period so as to disqualify you (or your child) from IS for as long as possible.

If you are not also receiving periodical payments, the lump sum is treated as producing a weekly income equal to: [18]

☐ if the lump sum is for you or for you and any children, your IS + £2;
☐ if the lump sum is just for a child or children, the personal allowance for you and each child for whom you get maintenance, any disabled child premium, family premium or lone parent premium, and any carer's premium if it is paid because you are caring for a disabled child for whom you receive maintenance.

However, if your IS entitlement plus £2 would be less than this amount (eg, because you had other income), the lower amount is used. This means that the lump sum disqualifies you from IS for a longer period.

If you are receiving periodical payments (see p92), the income is calculated as being the difference between the periodical payment and:

☐ the amount of IS plus £2 which would be paid if you did not get the periodical payment when it is paid for you alone or you and your children;
☐ the child's personal allowance plus family premium and lone parent premium if payment is just for a child.

If the lump sum is just for your child, only periodical payments for the child are taken into account. If the periodical payments are varied or stop, the calculation is done again taking the balance of the lump sum into account. [19]

The lump sum is treated as producing that income for a period beginning on the first day of the benefit week in which the payment is received and lasting for a number of weeks calculated by dividing the amount of the payment by the weekly income. The period can start in a later week if that is more practical. [20]

Example
You receive a lump sum of £2,000 just for your two children aged 13 and 8 and no periodical payments. Neither child is disabled.
The lump sum is treated as producing a weekly income of:

£21.40	(personal allowance age 13)
£14.55	(personal allowance age 8)
£ 9.30	(family premium)
£ 4.75	(lone parent premium)
£50.00	

Your IS is reduced by £50.00 per week for:

$$\frac{2,000}{50.00} \text{ weeks} = 40 \text{ weeks}$$

If, while you are disqualified, your circumstances change so that your entitlement to IS would be higher, or the benefit rates are altered, ask the Benefits Agency to recalculate the period of your disqualification using the new figures.

Arrears of periodical payments due before your claim are often treated as being a lump sum so as to disqualify you from benefit. However, you should argue that that is wrong (see p93).

4 THE SECRETARY OF STATE'S RIGHT TO MAINTENANCE PAYMENTS

(i) Liability to maintain

It is important to note that not all 'liable relatives' (see p88) whose payments affect IS in the way described above are 'liable to maintain' claimants so as to enable the Secretary of State to obtain maintenance from them.

For the purposes of court proceedings, you are liable to maintain only your spouse and your children for as long as IS is being paid for them.[21] You are not liable to maintain your ex-spouse after you have been divorced (unless you sponsored her/him when s/he came from abroad, see p66). Nor are you liable to maintain children over 16 who are claiming in their own right or any children over the age of 19.

(ii) Interviewing a liable relative

Following the interview with the claimant described on p89, the liable relative officer interviews the liable relative to judge whether maintenance can be expected. There is a standard formula used to decide how much a liable relative can afford. This formula has no statutory basis and is used only as a starting point for negotiations. The theory is that, after maintenance has been paid, a liable relative should be left with 15 per cent of her/his take-home pay above what s/he would have on IS.

Example
You take home £200 per week and live alone in a flat paying £40 per week rent and £10 per week community charge.
The calculation is:

Applicable amount	£ 42.45
Rent	£ 40.00
80% community charge	£ 8.00
15% take-home pay	£ 30.00
TOTAL	£120.45
Total take-home pay	£200.00
less	£120.45
You are considered able to afford	£ 79.55

In practice, liable relative officers also take into account any hire purchase commitments and other debts you have because the courts certainly do so.

If you are prepared to make a realistic offer of maintenance, the liable relative officer leaves you to make voluntary payments or your former partner to take any court action. Even if you could pay more, the officer will be satisfied with an offer which is sufficient to take your former partner and children off benefit, since that is all the Secretary of State could obtain in court (see below).

If you do not make a large enough offer, you are informed that the Secretary of State can bring you to court.

(iii) Enforcing a claimant's maintenance order

If there is already an order in favour of, or for the benefit of, a claimant *who is a parent*, or an order in favour of the claimant's children, the Secretary of State may do anything to enforce or vary the order which the claimant could do (see p91). (This includes applying to have the order registered in the magistrates' court.) Nevertheless, any maintenance which then has to be paid is paid to the claimant (unless diverted – see p91). [22]

Furthermore, if the Secretary of State notifies the relevant court officer that he wishes to be informed of any application by either the claimant or the liable relative to vary the order, enforce it or have any arrears remitted, he will be given that information and is entitled to take part in the proceedings. [23]

(iv) An order for the Secretary of State

The Secretary of State may obtain an order against any person who is liable to maintain a claimant or a member of the claimant's family (see p227). The application is heard in a magistrates' court. [24]

If the claim is for maintenance in respect of your spouse, the court is entitled to refuse an order if your spouse has been guilty of adultery (without your acceptance), cruelty or desertion. [25] However, the behaviour of your spouse does not affect your duty to support your children.

The fact that there was an agreement that your former partner would not ask for maintenance is not a bar either, [26] although all the circumstances must be taken into account. [27]

Since this power is there only to relieve the Secretary of State of the duty to maintain people through paying IS, the maximum amount the court can order you to pay is the amount of benefit being paid for your spouse or children.

However, even if you are not liable to support the other parent of your children, the court can still make an order which not only requires you to pay the equivalent of your child's personal allowance, any child disability premium, any family premium, any lone parent premium and any carer's premium related to care for your child, but also any personal allowance (but not any other premium) applicable to that parent. [28] The order is still made in respect of the child only, it is just that the amount is based on the assumption that maintaining the other parent is for the benefit of the child. If it is plain that the other parent would be receiving benefit anyway because, for example, s/he is incapable of work, you could argue that it was unreasonable for you to have to contribute to her/his maintenance. This power to include the amount of the parent's personal allowance in the order does not apply unless at least one child is under 16.

When the claimant ceases to be entitled to IS, the order may be transferred to her/him if any child is still under 16. [29]

(v) Prosecution

As a last resort you can be prosecuted if IS is paid as a result of your persistently refusing or neglecting to maintain your spouse or children. This is uncommon.

You can even be prosecuted for failing to maintain yourself! This is even rarer.

In either case, the maximum penalty is three months' imprisonment or a fine of £1,000 or both. [30] If you are charged with such an offence, see a solicitor. Legal aid may be available to help meet the cost.

5 CHANGES PLANNED FROM APRIL 1993

The system for enforcing and collecting maintenance payments is to change from April 1993 and you need to be aware of these changes when negotiating maintenance with your ex-partner.

The changes mean that more separated partners will be required to pay maintenance for their children, the amounts payable will be higher and claimants of IS/FC/DWA will be obliged to co-operate in obtaining maintenance. The rules only affect maintenance for children. The main changes proposed are:

☐ Collection of maintenance for children is to be administered and collected through an organisation called the Child Support Agency. The role of the courts will be greatly reduced.

☐ If you are on IS, FC or DWA, you will be obliged to authorise the Secretary of State to take action to recover maintenance. You are also required to help the Agency trace the child's parent and provide any information you can to enable them to decide how much maintenance should be paid. You can only escape this obligation if, by giving this authorisation, you or any child(ren) living with you would be likely to suffer harm or undue distress.

If you fail to co-operate your benefit could be reduced.

☐ There will be a rigid formula for calculating how much maintenance is due. It is legally binding and is based on income support rates. It aims to get enough maintenance to take you off benefit altogether. The absent parent is allowed to retain some income to cover her/his expenses, but no allowances are made for the cost of any step-children and, after maintenance payments, s/he could be left with little more than IS rates of income.

☐ The Agency expects all absent parents to pay regular maintenance payments to support their child(ren). This applies even where a capital settlement has been reached between partners instead of an ongoing maintenance agreement. In this circumstance you can be made to make regular payments *as well as* the lump sum already paid.

☐ If the Agency decides that maintenance should be paid and your partner defaults, s/he can be asked to pay interest on any arrears. Deductions can be made from her or his earnings to cover any maintenance and any arrears. If this fails (because, eg, the person is unemployed or in irregular employment) legal proceedings can be taken and bailiffs could seize their goods. Ultimately s/he could be sent to prison.

☐ Parents on IS who are single or in a childless couple, and who are not sick or disabled themselves, will be expected to contribute a small amount towards the maintenance of children of a previous relationship. This will be deducted from their IS.

Although these provisions are not yet law, you may find that Liable Relatives Officers are beginning to adopt similar tactics when negotiating maintenance. Make sure you remind them of the current legal position.

Chapter 7

Claims, reviews and getting paid

This chapter is about how income support (IS) is administered. It covers:

1 Claims (see below)
2 Decisions and reviews (p103)
3 Payments of benefit (p106)
4 Overpayments and fraud (p112)
5 Complaints about Benefits Agency administration (p116)

See Chapter 2 for who is entitled to claim. If you are in urgent financial need but your local Benefits Agency office is closed, see p4.

1 CLAIMS

(i) DSS reorganisation

In April 1991, DSS implemented major changes to the administration of the benefits system. Law and policy on social security are still made by the DSS but administration and decision-making has been delegated to the Benefits Agency. This agency has offices up and down the country, called branch offices, where you can make a claim or discuss your case. Branch offices are grouped together and managed by a district office and for each group of districts there is a territory with its own director.

As a claimant you should only need to deal with your local branch office and this is where your claim should go. You can obtain leaflets and information and there are benefit advisers to give advice and help with claims, and who have access to your computerised records.

London claimants have their claims dealt with by **social security centres** set up to deal with work which does not require face-to-face contact with the public. There are three centres, in Glasgow, Belfast and Wigan. Although the benefit centres decide your claim, you should still use your branch office to make initial claims or if you have any queries about your claim. If you have to telephone such a centre, your call will be charged at the local rate. Branch offices may have free numbers which you can use. If you have a National Insurance number, it should speed up your query if you quote it.

(ii) How to make a claim

It is helpful to have a National Insurance number if your claim is to be computerised. If you do not have one you may experience some delay, because your claim is dealt with manually. You can get one by applying to the contributions agency. You need to provide evidence of your identity.

If you are a single person, a single parent or in a lesbian or gay couple, you claim on your own behalf. If you are counted as a couple (see p229) you must choose which one of you will claim for you both. If you cannot agree, the Secretary of State decides.[1] You can change which partner claims, provided the partner previously claiming is agreeable.[2] It can be worth swapping – eg, if it would entitle you to a disability premium (see p240), or if one partner is about to go abroad (see p19) or otherwise lose entitlement (eg, become a student), or, if one partner is exempt from signing on (see p16). But if you get transitional protection because you used to get supplementary benefit (see p31), you will lose this if you swap.

The Secretary of State can authorise an 'appointee' to act on behalf of someone who cannot claim for themselves – eg, they are mentally ill or senile.[3] If this happens, the appointee takes on all the responsibilities of the claimant. Normally this would only apply from the date the appointment is agreed, but if you act on someone's behalf before becoming their official appointee your actions can be validated in retrospect by your appointment.[4] You can become an appointee by applying in writing to the Benefits Agency. You must be over 18.

The claim form

A claim for IS must be in writing and on the appropriate form[5], which is obtainable, free of charge, from your branch office.[6] If you are unemployed get Form B1 from the unemployment benefit office. All other claimants should get a form from their local Benefits Agency office, or by filling in the tear-off slip in Benefits Agency leaflet IS1 available from your local post office. The form should tell you the address to which it must be sent, once completed.

If you just write a letter, or send in the wrong form, the Benefits Agency will send you an IS form. Similarly, if you don't fill in the IS form properly they will return it to you. If you get it back to them correctly filled in within a month, you will count as having claimed on the date they got your first letter or form.[7] The Secretary of State can extend this one-month period if he thinks it reasonable[8] – eg, because you were ill.

If you want to change anything on your claim form you can usually do so at any time before they have made a decision on your claim.[9]

If you want to withdraw your claim, notify the office to which you sent it.[10]

Information to support your claim

You can be asked to supply any 'certificates, documents, information or evidence' considered relevant to your claim or to an issue arising from your claim – eg, birth certificate, rent book, or bank statement.[11]

In some cases the Benefits Agency may refuse to accept evidence that you are who you say you are. This is more likely to happen if you are black, Irish or a traveller. If this happens you should appeal, as the regulations do not specify which documents are to be accepted as evidence.

If you cannot or will not provide the information, the adjudication officer must go ahead and decide your claim within a reasonable length of time, on the basis of the details it already has;[12] if you think the Benefits Agency is delaying a decision unreasonably, see p104. If you are unable to provide information and the adjudication officer decides against you, you should appeal.

If you are one of a couple, the Benefits Agency can ask your partner to give written confirmation that s/he agrees to you making the claim and that the information you have given about her or him is true. This is usually done by your partner signing on the claim form where indicated.[13]

You may be on benefit for quite a long time, during which your circumstances may change. You must tell the benefit office, in writing, of any change which you might reasonably be expected to know might affect the right to benefit.[14] Keep a copy of the letter you send reporting such changes.

If you fail to report a change and, as a result, you receive too much benefit, the Benefits Agency may take steps to recover the overpayment (see p113) or even treat this as fraud (see p116).

(iii)   The date of your claim

Your claim is usually treated as made on the day it reaches the Benefits Agency office.[15] This applies even if it is a day on which the office is closed.[16] (See p101 if your initial claim was incomplete or made on the wrong form.)

You can claim up to three months before you qualify,[17] thus giving the Benefits Agency time to ensure you receive benefit as soon as you are entitled. This can be useful if you know you are going to qualify – eg, you are due to come out of hospital or prison. Otherwise, you must usually claim on the first day you want benefit to start.[18] However, the Secretary of State can decide to accept a claim up to one month late.[19]

Your claim can be backdated if you can show that throughout the time between the date by which you should have claimed, and the date you actually claimed you had 'good cause' for failing to claim. If you can show 'good cause' for part but not all of this period you can be paid from that date.[20] Even if you show 'good cause', IS cannot be paid for more than 12 months before the date on which you actually claim.[21] You may be paid less than 12 months arrears if your claim arose because of a new interpretation of the law[22] (see p104). If you want a claim to be backdated you must ask for this to happen – the Benefits Agency will not consider it unless you do.[23]

It has been held that **good cause** means 'some fact which, having regard to all the circumstances (including the claimant's state of health and the information which he had received and that which he might have obtained), would probably have caused a reasonable person of his age and experience to act (or fail to act) as the claimant did'.[24] So, there is a general duty to find out your rights, but your age and experience are taken into account in deciding whether you have acted 'reasonably'. If you claim late because you were ignorant of your rights, the first thing you need to explain is *why*.[25] You are expected to make enquiries by looking at the relevant Benefits Agency leaflets[26] or asking the Benefits Agency[27], a solicitor[28] or a citizens advice bureau[29]. Relying solely upon the advice of friends,[30] or even a doctor[31], is not enough.

If you *have* made enquiries, you will have good cause for a late claim if you were misinformed, or insufficiently informed of your rights or were accidentally mis-led. [32] The enquiries need not necessarily have been in connection with that particular claim, and people have succeeded in proving good cause where they have simply misunderstood the system. So, a person who had once made enquiries about the rights of the self-employed to unemployment benefit and who had thought that the answers applied equally to sickness benefit succeeded in showing good cause. [33]

While language difficulties, illiteracy and unfamiliarity with technical documents do not in themselves amount to good cause for not claiming, they obviously increase the likelihood of confusion and are important matters to be taken into consideration. [34]

Ill health, whether physical or mental, may also amount to good cause in other cases. [35]

If you have made no enquiries at all it is more difficult to show good cause. You must show that your ignorance was due to a mistaken belief *reasonably* held, so you must explain exactly how you came to be under the wrong impression. [36] The general rule is that you cannot be expected to claim something if you have no reason to suspect you have a right to claim it. You are likely to be excused ignorance of detailed changes in the law which give you new rights. [37]

If a person has been formally appointed by a court or the Secretary of State to act on your behalf, the question is whether the appointee has good cause for any late claim – not whether you have had. [38] If someone is *informally* acting on your behalf, the question is whether *you* have good cause and you must show that the delegation of the claim was reasonable, and that reasonable supervision was exercised. [39]

The good cause must continue up to the date of claim. Although the odd day may be overlooked, a substantial break in the good cause for not claiming will result in only the later period counting. [40]

If you are prevented from receiving benefit because your claim was more than 12 months late due to an error on the part of the Benefits Agency, you should try to persuade the Benefits Agency to meet its moral obligation and make an *ex gratia* payment to you. The intervention of an MP or the Ombudsman (see p117) may help in these circumstances. You should also ask the Benefits Agency for compensation for having underpaid your benefit. To do this, simply write to your Benefits Agency office and ask.

2 DECISIONS AND REVIEWS

(i) Who decides your claim

It is important to know who makes the decision on any particular question in your claim because that determines how you challenge the decision.

Most decisions are made by an adjudication officer at the Benefits Agency office where you claimed IS. [41] Some questions may be referred to an adjudication officer at the unemployment benefit office:

☐ whether you are involved in a trade dispute (see p58);
☐ whether it was your fault you lost your last job or left a training course (see p45);
☐ whether you are available for and/or actively seeking work (see p39);

☐   whether you have refused a suitable offer of a job without good reason (see p41).
An adjudication officer at the child benefit centre may advise:
☐   whether you are in full-time non-advanced education (see p12).
While an adjudication officer elsewhere is being consulted on your case, it will count
as decided against you in the meantime. [42]

Some decisions are made by the **Secretary of State** rather than an adjudication
officer. These are:
☐   whether to accept a claim made other than on the approved form;
☐   whether a claim for one benefit can be treated instead of, or in addition to, a
claim for another benefit;
☐   whether to demand recovery of an overpayment, and the amount of weekly
deductions (subject to the maximum, see p115);
☐   the suspension of benefit pending determination of a question on review or
appeal;
☐   whether IS should be awarded to a 16 or 17-year-old on grounds of severe hardship;
☐   whether a person living in a residential care or nursing home should receive a
higher allowance to prevent hardship;
☐   whether to take action against persons liable to maintain, including those
responsible for maintaining a person under the Immigration Act 1971;
☐   appointment of appointees;
☐   who should be treated as the claimant when a couple are unable to decide;
☐   issue and replacement of giros and order books and how IS should be paid;
☐   whether to pay an interim payment;
☐   whether a school or college is a 'recognised educational establishment';
☐   circumstances in which a claim is to be treated as withdrawn;
☐   how often you have to sign on.
You should be notified in writing of the decision on your claim unless the decision
is to pay you in cash, or your benefit is being stopped and it is reasonable not to give
you a written decision. [43] Sometimes the decision is unclear or difficult to understand. To get an explanation, write to the appropriate office within three months of
that decision. [44] If you appeal (see Chapter 8) the papers you receive will give the
full background to the decision made by the adjudication officer.

You should automatically receive Form A14N showing how your benefit has been
worked out. [45] You can ask for a more detailed breakdown (Form A124). Check the
details on this form.

(ii)   Delays

It is very unlikely that you will get an immediate decision on your claim because the
facts will need to be checked and your benefit calculated.

An adjudication officer should decide a claim for IS within 14 days 'so far as
practicable'. [46] Your claim should be passed on to an adjudication officer as soon as
the basic information required to decide it is available (which could well be as soon
as your claim form containing the necessary information reaches the Benefits
Agency). [47]

If you have been waiting more than 14 days for a decision contact the benefit
office. First, check that your claim has been received. If it has not, let the office have

a copy of your claim or fill out a new form and refer them to the claim form you sent in earlier.

If your claim has been received but not dealt with, ask for an explanation. If you are not satisfied with the explanation for the delay, make a complaint (see p116).

In addition to taking the steps already described, you should ask the office to make interim payments to you while you wait for the decision (see p107). You may also be able to obtain a crisis loan (see p314).

(iii) Reviews

An adjudication officer can review any decision of an adjudication officer, social security appeal tribunal, or Social Security Commissioner. Following the review, the decision may be revised either to increase or decrease the amount of your IS. You can ask for a review (in writing to your local Benefits Agency) or the adjudication officer may decide that one is necessary. A review can be done at any time, even if it is several years since the decision was made.

A decision may only be reviewed if: [48]

☐ **There was a mistake about the facts of your case or it was made in ignorance of relevant facts.** If a decision is reviewed on this ground, any revision will take effect from the beginning of the period covered by the original decision. If it is in your favour, you will receive arrears. If not you may have been overpaid and the adjudication officer will decide whether or not you should pay it back (see p112).

☐ The original decision was made by an adjudication officer (not a tribunal or Commissioner) and was **wrong in law.**

☐ **Your circumstances have changed since the original decision** or it is anticipated that they will do so. If a decision is reviewed on this ground it takes effect from the first day of the week in which it occurs if you are paid in arrears, or the week following the change if you are paid in advance (unless the change occurs on the first day of your benefit week in which case it is that day). [49] Some situations never count as a change of circumstance: staying in temporary accommodation for seven days or less while on an employment course; the repayment of a student loan, and your absence from a nursing or residential care home for less than a week. [50]

An adjudication officer may review your benefit but still not change the decision. Alternatively, s/he may decide that there are no grounds for a review. In either case, you can appeal against the decision, but in the latter you must show why there are grounds for review as well as giving your reasons for disputing the decision.

A review can be a quicker and simpler way of getting a decision changed than an appeal. It can also be a way of getting round the three-month time-limit for appeals.

If the adjudication officer agrees to change the decision, you can usually get arrears of benefit going back a year before the date of your request for a review, or if you did not request a review, from the date the review took place. [51] It is important to make it clear that you want payment for the past period.

You can get more than a year's backdating if [52] the ground for review was ignorance of, or mistake about the facts and you can show that the decision is being revised because:

☐   there is specific evidence which was before the adjudication officer (or SSAT) who originally decided the claim, but which they failed to take into account even though it was relevant. You should argue that this applies even if the evidence does not conclusively prove your entitlement. So long as it raised a strong possibility that you were entitled to (more) benefit, it should have been taken into account; [53]

☐   there is documentary or other written evidence of your entitlement which the DSS, DHSS or Department of Employment had, but failed to give to the adjudication officer (SSAT or Commissioner), at the time of the earlier decision;

☐   new evidence has come to light which did not exist earlier and could not have been obtained. This will only apply if you provide this evidence as soon as possible after it is available to you.

If the ground for review was that the decision was wrong in law you can get more than 12 months backdating if:

☐   the adjudication officer overlooked or misinterpreted part of an Act, Order, regulation or decision of a Commissioner or court when deciding your claim.

You may get less than a year's backdating if your entitlement is reviewed following a new interpretation of the law by a Social Security Commissioner or court. In this case you only get arrears back to the date of the decision by the Commissioner or court. [54]

If you were underpaid benefit because of a clear error by the DSS/Benefits Agency you could apply for compensation as well as getting arrears owed to you (see p109).

3   PAYMENTS OF BENEFIT

(i)   How and when you should be paid

The Secretary of State decides how benefit is paid to you. [55] You will be paid either by giro or benefit order book. It may be possible to be paid cash in certain circumstances. [56] From May 1992 if your IS includes mortgage costs these will be paid direct to your lender rather than to you (see p109).

Once you have been awarded benefit you must cash it within a year of it being due. [57] This period can be extended if you can show good cause for the delay. [58] However, a giro or order is only valid for three months – if you don't cash it within this period you will have to try and get a replacement.

If you are entitled to less than 10 pence a week you will not be paid IS at all, unless you are receiving another social security benefit which IS can be paid with. If you have just returned to work after a trade dispute, the same rule applies if your IS entitlement is less than £5. [59] If you are entitled to less than £1 a week the Secretary of State can decide to pay you quarterly in arrears. [60] If your IS includes a fraction of a penny it will be rounded-up to a full penny if it is more than a halfpence. Otherwise the fraction will be ignored. [61]

The date your payments start depends upon whether you are to be paid in advance or in arrears.

You will be paid in advance if you are: [62]

☐   receiving retirement pension; *or*

☐   over pension age (60 for a woman, 65 for a man) *and* not receiving unemployment or sickness benefit, invalidity pension or severe disablement allowance nor involved in a trade dispute (unless you were receiving IS immediately before the dispute began); *or*

☐ receiving widows' benefits (but only if you are not required to sign on, nor signing on voluntarily nor providing or required to provide medical evidence of incapacity for work); *or*

☐ returning to work after a trade dispute.

If you are paid in advance, your entitlement will begin on the first pay day of any other social security benefit to which you are entitled (or would be entitled if you had sufficient contributions) following the date of your claim for IS. For example, retirement pension is paid on a Monday. If you claim IS on a Wednesday you will be entitled to IS in advance from the following Monday. But if you claim on a Monday you will be able to get it from that day.

You will be paid in arrears, if you are not in one of the above groups. [63] Your entitlement to IS starts from the date of your claim. [64]

Once your entitlement has been worked out, the Secretary of State will decide how often and on which day of the week you will be paid [65] *unless* you are entitled to unemployment benefit; sickness benefit; invalidity pension; severe disablement allowance; retirement pension; and widows' benefits.

If you are entitled to one of these (or would be if you satisfied the contribution conditions), you will be paid IS on the same day of the week as that other benefit and at the same intervals. [66]

This means that if you are unemployed and signing on you will be paid fortnightly in arrears. When you first claim, you will therefore have to wait two weeks before you get your first payment of IS. You may have to wait longer if you receive certain payments at the end of a job – see p253. You may be able to get a crisis loan if you would suffer severe hardship before your first payment of IS is due (see p314).

(ii) Interim payments

If payment of your IS is delayed you may be in urgent need of money. If this is the case, you can ask for what are known as 'interim payments'. Interim payments are provisional payments and can be deducted from any later IS payment. [67]

An interim payment can be made where it seems that you are or may be entitled to IS and where: [68]

☐ you have claimed IS but not in the correct way (eg, you have filled in the wrong form, or filled in the right form incorrectly or incompletely) and you cannot put in a correct claim immediately (eg, because the Benefits Agency office is closed); *or*

☐ you have claimed IS correctly, but it is not possible for the claim or for a review or appeal which relates to it to be dealt with immediately; *or*

☐ you have been awarded benefit, but it is not possible to pay you immediately other than by means of an interim payment.

Whether to award an interim payment is a Secretary of State's decision and therefore cannot be appealed to a tribunal (see p118). If you are refused an interim payment contact your MP and see Chapter 23 for whether you can get a crisis loan.

If your interim payment is more than your actual entitlement, the overpayment can be recovered. [69]

(iii)   Suspension of payments

The Secretary of State can order that your IS be suspended if: [70]

☐ **A question has arisen about your entitlement to benefit:** In this case, all or part of what is due to you is suspended pending a decision on a review or appeal concerning your entitlement. For example, if you are being paid IS but it is thought that you are in full-time work, your benefit may be suspended while information is gathered about the true situation.

☐ It looks as though your IS award should be revised.

☐ **You are awarded benefit by an appeal tribunal but the Benefits Agency wants to appeal:** If this happens, your award can only be suspended for a month after the adjudication officer receives the decision unless the Benefits Agency decides to seek leave to appeal, in which case you will have to wait until the case is resolved.

☐ **You are due to be paid arrears of a benefit but you may have been overpaid some benefit yourself:** Your arrears may be withheld in whole or in part while the possible overpayment is investigated.

☐ The Benefits Agency is appealing to the Commissioners or courts about some-one else's claim, and the issue under appeal affects your claim. Your benefit can be suspended in whole or in part until the appeal is decided.

The decision to suspend benefit is made by the Secretary of State and you cannot therefore appeal against it to a tribunal. You must negotiate to get your benefit reinstated.

(iv)   Lost and missing payments

If you lose a benefit giro or order book after you have received it, report the loss immediately to the relevant benefit office by telephone or by a personal visit and confirm the loss in writing, requesting a replacement at the same time. If your giro is lost or stolen before you have had a chance to cash it, the Secretary of State has a duty to replace it. This applies even if the giro is subsequently cashed by someone else. [71] You should also report the matter to the police, and note the investigating officer's name and number.

If you have lost your order book, the benefit office will issue you with a replace-ment, but will probably want to make some enquiries to see how many payments had been cashed and how many were left.

If the benefit office refuses to issue a replacement, or takes too long considering your request, you can take legal action to get the benefit due to you.

Before taking legal action, you should write to the local Benefits Agency request-ing them to replace the giro within a reasonable time, say seven days. Explain that court action will be taken if they do not respond. Keep a copy of the letter.

If the Benefits Agency does not replace your giro, you will need to begin proceed-ings in the local county court. The forms to do this are available from the county court. Complete these and return them to the court. You will have to pay a court fee, calculated as a percentage of your unpaid giro. The fee is refundable if you win. The Benefits Agency is allowed time to respond to your summons, but you will almost certainly find that the local Benefits Agency office will replace your giro without the need to proceed to a court hearing. Your court fee will be repaid separately by the Bene-fits Agency Solicitors (see Appendix 1 for address), and you should not withdraw the summons until you have received both a replacement giro, and your court fee.

(v) Extra-statutory payments

Sometimes the Benefits Agency makes mistakes about the amount of your benefit. Where possible they will correct the mistake by carrying out a review and awarding you the correct benefit (see p105).

If the procedure for review does not apply or does not properly compensate you for the effects of the mistake that has occurred, you may claim a compensatory payment. This is called an **extra-statutory payment** because it is made outside the normal benefit rules. Another name for it is an 'ex gratia' or 'concessionary' payment. An agreement between the Benefits Agency and the Treasury means that you are entitled to compensation if you are underpaid benefit and:

☐ the underpayment was solely due to Benefits Agency error; *and*

☐ the underpayment was more than £50; *and*

☐ the delay in payment must have been more than a year. Delays in the normal adjudication process do not count.

You will not automatically be awarded compensation. You must write to your local Benefits Agency office and ask.

(vi) Payments to other people

Payment will usually be made direct to you but there are some circumstances in which payments can be made to other people or organisations on your behalf.

☐ If you are unable to manage your own money, your benefit will be paid to a person appointed to act on your behalf (see p101). [72]

☐ If it is in the interests of you, your partner or your children, the Secretary of State can pay your benefit to someone else. [73] For example, if you are neglecting your children even though benefit is being paid for them, it might be paid to another person to help look after them (eg, a grandparent or other relative). If your partner is refusing to support you, all or part of her/his benefit can be paid to you.

Amounts can also be deducted from your IS for housing, fuel and other costs and paid over for you (see 'direct deductions' below). [74]

Deductions can also be made from your IS for the recovery of social fund loans (see p319) and overpayments (see p115). You should argue that these take a lower priority than the deductions covered below.

Deductions are made at the Benefits Agency office before you receive your regular benefit payment, so you will have less money to live on while they are being made. If you want to have deductions made to help you clear any arrears or debts you owe, ask at the Benefits Agency office dealing with your IS claim. If you disagree with a decision about deductions, you can appeal (see p118).

From May 1992 it is intended that IS for mortgage interest payments should be made direct to your lender rather than to you as claimant once you have qualified for 100% interest (see p25). Full details are not yet known but look out for these changes.

When can direct deductions be made? [75]

☐ **Rent arrears** [76] **(and any inclusive water, fuel and service charges):** If you are on IS you should be getting regular housing benefit to help pay any rent. If you are in debt with your rent while on benefit, an amount for arrears can be deducted from your IS and paid direct to your landlord.

'Rent arrears' do not include non-dependant deductions.[77] However, deductions can cover any water charges or service charges payable with your rent and not covered by housing benefit.[78] Fuel charges cannot be covered by direct deductions if they change more than twice a year.[79]

To qualify for direct deductions for rent arrears you must owe the equivalent of four times your full weekly rent.[80] Deductions will be made if it is in the 'overriding interests' of your family to do so – eg, where you are threatened with eviction if you do not pay and you have not paid your full rent for a period of less than eight weeks.[81] If you have not paid your full rent for more than eight weeks, direct deductions can be made automatically if your landlord asks the Benefits Agency to make them.[82]

☐ **Mortgage arrears**[83] **(and other housing costs):** If your current IS includes money for housing costs (see p19) and you are in debt for these costs (excluding payments for a tent, but including other loans to buy your house[84]), direct deductions can be made from your benefit both to clear the debt and to meet current payments. Deductions will be made if it would be 'in the interests' of you or your family to do so – eg, where you would face repossession proceedings or the prospect of even higher interest.

In the case of mortgage payments, you must have paid less than eight weeks' worth of full payments in the last 12 weeks. For other housing costs, you can only qualify for direct deductions if you owe more than half of the annual total of the relevant housing cost. Even these conditions can be waived if it is in the 'overriding interests' of you or your family that deductions start as soon as possible – eg, repossession is imminent.[85]

☐ **Accommodation charges:**[86] If you receive IS, the amount you are paid should cover charges for your accommodation if you live in a residential care or nursing home, or local authority residential accommodation.

These charges can be met by direct deductions from your benefit if you have (a) failed to budget for the charges from your benefit and (b) it is in your own interests that deductions should be made. If you are in a home run by a voluntary organisation for alcoholics or drug addicts, direct payments can be made even if these conditions do not apply.[87]

☐ **Water charges:**[88] Your weekly IS is assumed to include money to pay any water charges you have to pay. If you get into debt with water charges direct deductions might be made – 'debt' includes any reconnection charges. 'Water charges' means water rates and charges (except in Scotland) for sewerage and allied environmental services.[89] If you pay your water rates to your landlord with your rent, deductions will be made under the arrangements for rent arrears (see above).[90]

Deductions can be made if you owe at least half the annual water charges. If you have a water meter the Benefits Agency must estimate your annual charge and then decide if your arrears add up to at least half of this amount. If you owe less, it must be in the interests of your family to make deductions.[91] If you get into debt with water charges you should consider making an agreement for direct deductions because the water authority can cut off your water supply if you do not meet your debts and current charges. If you are in debt to two water companies you can only have a deduction for arrears made to one of them at a time. Your debts for water charges should be cleared before your debts for sewerage costs, but the amount paid for current consumption can include both water and sewerage charges.[92]

☐ **Fuel debts:**[93] Your weekly IS is supposed to cover gas and electricity bills. If you are in debt, an amount can be deducted from your benefit each week and paid over to the fuel board in instalments – usually once a quarter. In return, the fuel board will agree not to disconnect you. Deductions can be made where[94] the amount you owe is more than £42.45 (including reconnection charges if you have been disconnected); *and* you will continue to need the fuel supply; *and* it is in your interest to have deductions – known as 'fuel direct'.

The amount deducted for current consumption will be whatever is necessary to meet your current weekly fuel costs. This will be adjusted if the cost increases or decreases and deductions for current payments can be continued after the debt has been cleared.[95]

☐ **Community charge arrears:**[96] Deductions can be made from IS if the local authority gets a liability order from a magistrates' court (in Scotland, a summary warrant or decree from a sheriff's court) and applies to the Benefits Agency for recovery to be made in this way. If they want to recover arrears from both partners in a couple the order must be against both of them. Deductions can be made for arrears, recoverable overpayments and any unpaid costs or penalties imposed by the Community Charge Registration Officer. If further arrears arise while deductions are being made, these will not be dealt with until the first debt is cleared.

☐ **Hostel payments:**[97] If you (or your partner) live in a hostel *and* you have claimed HB to meet your accommodation costs *and* your payments to the hostel cover fuel, meals, water charges, laundry and/or cleaning of your room, part of your benefit can be paid direct to the hostel. You do not have to be in arrears for this to apply. These costs are all items which cannot be covered by HB (see p158) and which you must meet for your IS. Fuel costs are not paid direct if the charge varies according to actual consumption, unless the charge is altered less than three times a year.

How much can be deducted?

Deductions are made to pay off the debt or to cover current weekly costs or both. The amount that can be deducted for **rent arrears** is £2.15 per week.[98] For **housing costs covered by IS** it is £2.15 per week for arrears plus the current weekly cost. If you have more than one debt for housing costs covered by IS they can only deduct for three of them at any one time (ie, three lots of £2.15).[99] For **fuel arrears** they will deduct £2.15 per week, for each fuel debt plus an estimated amount for current consumption. But they cannot deduct more than £4.30 altogether for arrears.[100] The deduction for **community charge arrears** is £2.15 for a single person or £3.35 for a couple.[101] If a couple separate the lower deduction will normally apply. For **water charges** the deduction is £2.15 for arrrears plus an amount for current costs. If you pay by meter this is estimated. Where the estimate proves to be too high or too low it should be adjusted over a period of 26 weeks. If a debt is paid off, deductions for current charges can continue.[102]

If you have debts for several items, the total deducted for all your arrears, excluding community charge arrears, cannot be more than £6.40 per week (plus current liabilities). [103]

In the case of fuel, rent arrears and water charges, if the combined cost of deductions for arrears and current consumption is more than 25 per cent of your total applicable amount (excluding any amount for housing costs) the deductions cannot be made without your consent. [104]

The deduction made to meet **accommodation charges** in a residential care or nursing home is your IS accommodation allowance (see p75) but no amount for arrears. [105] For **hostel charges** the local authority should have assessed how much of your accommodation charge covers these costs when assessing your HB and this is the amount which is deducted from your benefit and paid direct. If the HB section have not yet decided the amounts, the Benefits Agency must estimate the cost. [106]

Deductions are made from your IS and from any unemployment, sickness, invalidity benefit, retirement pension or severe disablement allowance paid with it in the same giro or order book. [107] You must be left with at least 10 pence. Community charge arrears can be deducted from IS only. [108]

Priority between debts

If you have more debts or charges than can be met within the limits for direct deductions, they will be paid in the following order of priority: [109]

1st   housing costs (and within these mortgage payments have highest priority)
2nd   rent arrears (and related charges)
3rd   fuel charges
4th   water charges
5th   community charge arrears

If you owe both gas and electricity, the Benefits Agency will choose which one to pay first, depending on your circumstances. If you have been overpaid benefit or given a social fund loan, you may have to repay by having deductions from your IS. [110] You should argue that these deductions should take a lower priority.

4   OVERPAYMENT AND FRAUD

(i)   Overpayments

Duplication

Sometimes you receive too much IS because money which is owing to you does not arrive on time. For example, if you claim child benefit but it is not paid for several weeks, your IS will continue at the same rate while you are not actually receiving child benefit. However, if child benefit had been promptly paid, your IS would have been reduced (see p259).

You must repay the IS which you would not have received if the other income had been paid on time even though it is not your fault that the income was paid late. The rule applies to all types of income which affect the amount of your IS, including other social security benefits. It also applies to benefits paid by other EC states[111] (see Chapter 18). You will always have to pay the money back, even though it was not your fault that the income was paid late.[112]

Other overpayments

For all other overpayments, repayment can only be required if you have misrepresented or failed to disclose a material fact and too much benefit has been paid as a result.[113] You may have to repay even if you innocently misrepresented your situation or you failed to tell the local office certain facts because you did not understand how the benefit scheme works.

If you have been (or are being) overpaid, your benefit entitlement will be reviewed.[114] If the adjudication officer does not conduct a proper review before asking you to repay any money, the decision that you have been overpaid is invalid and you can avoid having to repay.[115] However, it is likely that your entitlement will then be reviewed and benefit may be recoverable (see below). Pending this review, some or all of your current benefit can be suspended (see p108).

Even if they decide you have been overpaid, you will not have to repay if you told the Benefits Agency all about your circumstances, and the overpayment was due to their error.

If you do not agree that you owe the Benefits Agency money, you can appeal (see p118). Do not pay back any of the money until your appeal has been decided, as they may keep any money you voluntarily repay, even if you later win your case![116]

There are three questions to consider when deciding whether you have to repay benefit and, if so, how much. For all three of the following questions, the burden of proving the case lies with the adjudication officer.

(a)   Did you misrepresent or fail to disclose a material fact?

The first thing to check is whether you have been accused of misrepresenting your circumstances or of failing to disclose a material fact. **Misrepresentation** can be completely innocent.[117] Thus, if you misrepresent your circumstances because you yourself were unaware of the true situation, it still counts – eg, where you did not know that your partner's earnings had changed. You would not be guilty of misrepresentation if you add the phrase 'not to my knowledge' to your statement.[118] It is what you do or say on your current claim that is important. If you have declared a fact on a previous claim but inadvertently give incorrect information on a later claim, you will have to repay. The Benefits Agency are not required to check back for you.[119] **Failure to disclose** is different. You cannot be said to have failed to disclose a fact you did not know about. Also, it must be reasonable to have expected you to notify the office of the particular facts.[120] So if you were told that such facts were not relevant you could say it was not reasonable for you to disclose them.

You cannot assume that changes in your social security benefits, paid by one section of the Benefits Agency, will be known to the other sections. You should give the IS section *any* information which might affect your IS. [121]

It is not necessary for you to show that you told the office in writing about your situation. It will do just as well if you give the information over the telephone, or in an office interview, either verbally or by presenting the relevant documents. [122] If you filled in a form while giving information, a tribunal should look at what you said in the form, but also consider whether you gave the necessary information in another way. [123] A claimant who fails to fill in a form correctly, but who nevertheless gives the relevant information in the wrong place, has told the Benefits Agency the material facts. [124]

If there is no record of a verbal statement a claimant only has a case to answer once the adjudication officer has shown, 'on the balance of probabilities', that there would be a record of the conversation at the local office if it had taken place. In order to do this, the adjudication officer must give a tribunal information on [125]:

☐ the instructions for recording information which should have applied in the case, and the instructions for attaching the information to the claimant's file;

☐ whether there were the appropriate administrative arrangements to enable these instructions to be carried out;

☐ to what extent *in practice* these instructions are carried out, or not carried out. Where there is no record of what happened, other than the claimant's own statement, the Benefits Agency will be unable to prove that there has been a recoverable overpayment. [126] However, an admission by you that you did not tell the Benefits Agency relevant facts may be used as grounds for saying there has been an overpayment, even if there is no other evidence. You need not report a change direct to the Benefits Agency if you give the information in another way which might reasonably be expected to reach the relevant local office – eg, you tell the pensions section and ask them to inform the IS section too. However, if a claimant realises or should have realised that the information has not reached the IS section, s/he is under an obligation to take further steps to inform them. [127] Some time, if only a short time, may elapse before you can reasonably be expected to realise that the original information has not been acted on. [128] You could argue that the unemployment benefit office acts as 'agent' for the Benefits Agency in connection with IS for the unemployed. This would mean that information disclosed to the unemployment benefit office counts as though it had been disclosed to the Benefits Agency. [129] However, it is not good enough if the information is given to the unemployment benefit office in the course of a different transaction.

(b) Did an overpayment result?

Even if you admit that there is information you failed to give the Benefits Agency or that you did misrepresent your circumstances, you can still argue that this was not the cause of the overpayment. However, if it was a contributory factor you will have to repay. If the Benefits Agency have been given the correct information to decide your claim by someone else, but fail to act upon it, you could argue that any overpayment did not arise because of your failure. [130]

(c) How much is repayable?

It is always worth checking how the overpayment has been calculated as you may be asked to repay too much by mistake. Do not be afraid to ask the office for more information if you need it.

The amount of the overpayment is the difference between what *was* paid and what *should have* been paid. [131] The Benefits Agency works out the latter using the information that you originally gave the office, *plus* any facts which you misrepresented or did not declare. [132] No other facts are used. If, when looking again at your claim, you discover you have also been underpaid during the same period, you cannot offset this against the overpayment if new facts and evidence are needed to prove the underpayment. [133]

However, if other facts come to light which suggest that you have also been underpaid you can ask the Benefits Agency to review your claim and pay you any arrears. They could then withhold any arrears owed to you and thus reduce the overpayment. [134]

If you were overpaid because you had too much capital they should calculate the overpayment taking account of the fact that had you received no benefit, you would have had to use your capital to meet everyday expenses. For each 13-week period, the Benefits Agency assumes that your capital is reduced by the amount of overpaid benefit. [135] This is known as the 'diminishing capital rule'.

(ii) Recovery of overpayments

If an overpayment must be repaid, it can be done through deductions from [136] any National Insurance benefit; family credit; disability working allowance or IS.

No deduction can be made from guardian's allowance, child benefit, housing benefit, or community charge benefit.

If the overpayment is due to late payment of another social security benefit, the Benefits Agency normally deducts any overpaid IS from the arrears owing to you. [137]

Other overpayments can also be recovered from arrears you are owed, except arrears where benefit has previously been suspended. [138]

When it comes to your current weekly benefit, the following are the maximum amounts which can be deducted: [139]

☐ £8.50 if you have admitted fraud or been found guilty of fraud; *or*
☐ £6.40 in any other case.

If you have any earnings or income subject to the £5 or £15 disregard, the deduction may be increased by half this amount. [140] Remember, the above are maximum amounts. The Benefits Agency might be persuaded to deduct less, especially if you have other direct deductions made from your benefit. As long as a couple are married or living together as husband and wife (see p229), the amount of overpaid benefit can be recovered from either partner's IS or FC. [141]

If a claimant has died by the time the overpayment is discovered, the money can be recovered from the estate. [142]

It is important to note that a tribunal cannot 'write off' part of the overpayment even if there are mitigating circumstances. It can only decide how much is repayable. In a case where you acted in all innocence and hardship is likely to be caused, the best tactic is to apply to the Secretary of State who has the discretion to decide whether or not to recover the overpayment.

(iii) Fraud

If you deliberately make a statement which you know is false while you are claiming benefit, you may be guilty of a criminal offence. [143] The Benefits Agency only takes action in a small number of cases where benefit has been overpaid as a result.

If the Benefits Agency suspects you of fraud, it may well suspend your benefit (see p108). Benefit cannot be stopped for fraud itself, but only because you fail to satisfy one of the general conditions for benefit – eg, you are working full-time while on IS, or living with a man as his wife but claiming as a single person.

You may be interviewed by the Benefits Agency. Often the evidence against you is very flimsy – eg, an anonymous telephone call – and the officer may need your admission of guilt to prove the case. If possible, have someone with you at the interview. If in doubt about how to answer a question, it is best to refuse to answer until you have sought advice.

If your benefit is stopped, you can do three things:

☐ **You can make a fresh claim for benefit.** Benefit should be paid regardless of what the situation was in the past, if the local office is satisfied your circumstances are now different. If you were suspected of full-time working while on IS, you should be prepared to sign a statement saying you are not working full-time at present.

☐ **You can also appeal to a tribunal** (see p118). Check the calculation of the overpayment – adjudication officers often forget the normal rules about earnings disregards, etc, when calculating the figure. It is best to appeal before any criminal proceedings have been decided.

☐ **You can also apply for a social fund payment** (see p314, Crisis loans).

In some cases of fraud, the Benefits Agency may decide to prosecute. [144] If this happens, you should seek help from a solicitor. You may qualify for help with the legal costs. Should the court find you guilty, it could fine you, or in extreme cases send you to prison. It could also impose a probation order, a conditional discharge or a community service order.

Any fine or prison sentence imposed by the court is completely separate from the right of the Benefits Agency to recover an overpayment of benefit. The court may also order you to pay compensation to the Benefits Agency for the overpaid benefit. This will be in addition to any fine. Often this will not cover all of the overpayment and the Benefits Agency will try to recover the rest in the normal way. You should check that it is not asking you to repay twice over.

5 COMPLAINTS ABOUT ADMINISTRATION

The procedures for appeal and review allow you to challenge decisions about your benefit (including the refusal of benefit). If you simply want to make a complaint about the way in which your benefit claim was handled there are other procedures you can follow. The things you might want to complain about could include:

☐ delay in dealing with your claim;

☐ poor administration in the benefit office (eg, they keep losing your papers, or you can never get through on the telephone);

☐ the behaviour of members of staff. Most benefit staff do a good job and try to be helpful, but you should certainly complain about staff rudeness or any sexist or racist remarks;

☐ the general inadequacy of the benefits.

The Benefits Agency produces a form (BAL1 'Have your say') which explains your rights and contains a form which you can use to explain your complaint.

Complaining to the Benefits Agency

As a first step contact the supervisor or assistant manager. Alternatively, you can contact the customer services manager for your branch office. S/he will investigate your complaint. If this does not solve the problem you should write to the manager of your district office with details of the complaint. (Keep a copy of your letter.)

Complaining to your MP

If you are not satisfied with the reply from the officers to whom you have written, the next step is to take up the matter with your MP.

Most MPs have 'surgeries' in their areas where they meet constituents to discuss problems. You can get the details from your local library or citizens advice bureau. You can either go to the surgery or write to them with details of your complaint.

Your MP will probably want to write to the benefit authorities for an explanation about what has happened. If you or they are not satisfied with the reply, the next stage is to complain to the ombudsman, via your MP.

The Parliamentary Commissioner for Administration (commonly called the 'ombudsman' – see Appendix I) investigates complaints made by MPs against government departments. The Ombudsman's office will send you a leaflet providing further information. Many of the complaints are about benefits. If s/he investigates your case, your MP will be sent a full report. If the ombudsman finds you were badly treated, s/he will recommend an apology and possibly compensation.

Chapter 8

Appeals

This chapter explains what you can do if you disagree with the Benefits Agency decision on your IS claim. It covers:

1 Social security appeal tribunals (see below)
2 How to prepare an appeal (p121)
3 Appealing to the Social Security Commissioner (p124)
4 Appealing to the courts (p126)

1 SOCIAL SECURITY APPEAL TRIBUNALS

(i) When you can appeal

You can appeal to an independent social security appeal tribunal (SSAT) against any decision taken by an adjudication officer. Decisions made by the Secretary of State cannot be appealed (see p104); thus, if you are awarded IS but do not receive payments, you cannot appeal but must go to court to seek payment. [1] If you wish to challenge a decision taken by the Secretary of State you write to the manager of the local office asking for it to be looked at again. You could also ask your MP to intervene. The only legal remedy available to you is to apply to the High Court for judicial review (see p127).

Sometimes, benefit is refused on the grounds that you have not provided all the information required to decide your claim (see p101). If correct, this argument would prevent you from having the right to appeal. But an adjudication officer must make a decision on every claim, even those where, having allowed a reasonable amount of time, the information demanded by the Benefits Agency has not been provided. [2] It is then up to the tribunal to decide whether the decision is correct.

(ii) How to appeal

Before challenging a decision, it is useful to know why it was decided against you. You have a right to a written statement of reasons if you apply for it within three months of being given the decision in writing. [3] In practice, you will need to ask for this before the three months is up because you only have three months from the date of the adjudication officer's original decision in which to appeal. On receiving the statement of reasons, you may decide it is worth asking for a review of the decision rather than appealing straightaway (see p105).

You appeal by writing to the adjudication officer explaining which decision you wish to appeal against and giving the reasons why. The appeal letter must arrive within three months of the written decision being sent to you.[4] If your appeal is late you should explain why. The chairperson of the appeal tribunal can accept a late appeal for 'special reasons'[5] – eg, if the adjudication officer delayed sending you the reasons for her/his original decision, or where sickness or a domestic crisis prevented you from making your appeal.

You cannot appeal against the refusal of the chairperson to hear a late appeal,[6] but you may be able to apply to the High Court for **judicial review** (see p127).

Your appeal letter must give some reason why you wish to appeal. It would be helpful if you provided references to the law. If you do not have access to these, put in your appeal and provide more details after you have taken further advice. It should refer the tribunal to the law and any Commissioners' decisions which apply to your case. This *Handbook* explains the legal rules – see p123 for where to find the relevant law.

Include any evidence you can produce to support your case. Are there any documents it would be useful to show the tribunal? Are there any witnesses who could give helpful information? All correspondence with the Benefits Agency which is relevant to your appeal should be considered by a tribunal.[7]

Your appeal letter will appear in the documents which go before the appeal tribunal, along with a submission from the adjudication officer. The tribunal members receive these documents beforehand so they will have some idea of your arguments.

If you want the tribunal to hear your appeal quickly, make this plain in your letter, explaining why. About a week after you send in your appeal, you could telephone the clerk at the Independent Tribunal Service office (see Appendix 1 for address) to check they have received your letter and to ask her/him to deal with the matter quickly.

If you change your mind you can withdraw your appeal. You can only do this with the written consent of the adjudication officer. Once the appeal tribunal hearing has begun, you can withdraw the appeal only with the consent of the chairperson and provided the tribunal has not yet made a decision.[8]

(iii) The tribunal hearing

After your appeal is received at the local office, you should receive an acknowledgement from the clerk of the Independent Tribunal Service. It can take several weeks before the appeal is actually heard. During this period, the local office is supposed to look again at the decision to see if it ought to be revised.

Consider asking your local advice centre or citizens advice bureau to help you prepare your appeal. They may be able to send someone to represent you at the hearing. If you take someone with you to a tribunal your chances of winning are much higher. You can take a friend, relative, adviser or representative with you[9] – you can only have more than one person if the chairperson of the tribunal agrees.[10]

You have to be given at least 10 days' notice of the hearing. If not, the tribunal can only go ahead if you agree.[11] Make sure that you return the form to say whether you will be attending. If the hearing date is inconvenient or you want more time to prepare your case, you can ask for it to be put off until a later date. Telephone the clerk's office as soon as you decide that you want a postponement and confirm the request by letter the same day. If you do not attend and have not asked for a postponement, the tribunal can hear the case without you, and you are less likely to succeed.

Along with the letter telling you the date of the hearing, there will be a copy of the papers which have been sent to the tribunal members. Read these papers carefully, and check for any mistakes.

Hearings before a social security appeal tribunal are in public unless you request a private hearing, or the chairperson thinks it should be in private. In practice, it is extremely rare for members of the public to turn up. However, the rule does mean that you could sit in on the case before yours, or see what tribunals are like before you actually represent someone. [12]

The tribunal members

A tribunal usually consists of three people. There is a chairperson, who is a lawyer, and two 'wing members', who sit on either side of the chairperson. They are supposed to be people who have knowledge or experience of conditions in your area, and who are representative of people living or working there. Wherever possible, at least one member of the tribunal should be the same sex as the claimant. [13] Tribunals can sit with only one wing member, but only if you agree. In this case, the chairperson has the casting vote. [14] The chairperson has to record the tribunal's decision, and write down its findings on the relevant facts of the case and the grounds for its decision. If the decision is not unanimous, s/he has to note the reasons why a tribunal member disagreed with the decision. [15]

The standards of tribunals are the responsibility of the President of Social Security Appeal Tribunals. The President is in charge of training, monitoring and ensuring that tribunals have all the materials they need. The President is helped by six regional chairpersons and eight full-time chairpersons, all appointed by the Lord Chancellor and all of whom are legally qualified. There is also a President of Appeal Tribunals in Northern Ireland. If you have a complaint about a tribunal member, or the way a hearing was conducted, write to your regional chairperson or the President (see Appendix 1 for the addresses).

Other people present at the hearing

The clerk to the tribunal is there in an administrative capacity. S/he will meet you when you arrive and pay your expenses. You, your representative, an interpreter if needed – and any witnesses may be able to get travel expenses paid. You can also claim for meals and loss of earnings. [16] S/he will also take you into the tribunal room when they are ready to hear your case. During the hearing s/he will take notes of what is said. The clerk should not express any views on the case.

The presenting officer represents the adjudication officer. S/he will explain the reasons for the decision you are appealing about.

Procedure at the hearing

When the tribunal is ready to hear your case, you are taken into their room with the presenting officer.

The three members of the tribunal sit on one side of a large table. The clerk sits either at one end or at a separate table to one side. You are shown where to sit. Usually you and the presenting officer both sit directly opposite the tribunal.

There are no strict rules of procedure. Usually the chairperson starts by introducing the members of the tribunal and everyone else who is present. The presenting officer then summarises the adjudication officer's written submission and you are asked to explain your reasons for disagreeing with it. You can call any witnesses and can ask questions of the presenting officer or any witnesses called by her/him, and the tribunal members ask questions.

Your case may be adjourned unfinished to be heard on another day because, for instance, more evidence is required. If this happens, the new tribunal must rehear your case from the beginning unless it has the same three members as before or you agree to it being heard by two members of the previous tribunal without the third. [17]

(iv)　The tribunal decision

Often you are told of the tribunal's decision at the hearing and then written notice of the decision is sent to you later by the clerk. It is on a standard form and should include relevant findings of fact and reasons for the tribunal's decision. [18]

If you have won, the Benefits Agency ought to carry out the tribunal's decision straightaway. However, they have three months in which to appeal against the tribunal's decision to a Social Security Commissioner. If considering an appeal, you will not be paid for a month while they decide what to do. If they decide to appeal, you will not be paid until the Commissioner hears the case. If you are left without any money meanwhile, you might be able to get a crisis loan (see p314).

A tribunal decision can be overturned in a number of ways: it can be **reviewed** in the normal way (see p105) *except* where the tribunal made a mistake about the law in which case you must **appeal to the Social Security Commissioners** (see p124). It may be quicker to apply to the chairperson of the tribunal to have the decision 'set aside'. This is appropriate where: [19]

☐ you or your representative did not receive the appeal papers, or did not receive them in sufficient time before the hearing; *or*

☐ you or your representative were not present at the hearing; *or*

☐ 'the interests of justice so require'. This applies where there has been a procedural irregularity. [20]

An adjudication officer may also ask for a decision to be set aside. 'Setting aside' means cancelling the decision and hearing the case again. You must apply within three months of the decision being sent to you. A late application will only be accepted if there are special reasons. Applications are normally decided without a hearing, so make sure you give a full explanation of your reasons when you apply. [21]

If the written decision contains an accidental error this can be corrected by the tribunal. [22]

2　HOW TO PREPARE AN APPEAL

Your case may concern a dispute about the **facts** or the **law**, or both. Always try, if possible, to link the facts of your case and your arguments to the rules laid down in the benefit regulations.

Sorting out the facts

The tribunal will have to decide your appeal on the evidence given by you and the Benefits Agency. Check through the appeal papers carefully to work out where there are disagreements between you. This will help you decide what evidence you need to win your case. Evidence consists of what you (and any witnesses) actually say at the hearing and any documents which you produce to support your case. Written evidence would include letters of support, medical reports, wage slips, bank statements, birth certificates and anything else which helps to prove the facts. If, for example, the Benefits Agency say that you failed to disclose an increase in your earnings and you have been overpaid, you could explain to the tribunal how and when you told them, but you may also be able to produce a copy of the letter which you sent informing them of the change.

Proving your case with additional evidence is useful but not essential. A tribunal cannot dismiss your verbal evidence without a proper explanation of why it has done so. [23]

The presenting officer puts the adjudication officer's case at the tribunal but is not usually the person who actually made the decision in your case. The presenting officer's submissions are not evidence, [24] nor are comments made by another AO if s/he did not decide your claim. [25] The presenting officer can report what other people have said. This is called hearsay evidence. Tribunals can accept hearsay evidence but they should carefully weigh up its value as proof, given that the person who originally made the statement is not present at the hearing. Most evidence relied on by adjudication officers is written and you can point out that you have not had the opportunity of cross-examining the witnesses. You are not entitled to insist on the presence of any particular witness, [26] but you should argue that the tribunal should not place any weight on the written evidence of, say, an interviewing officer if you are disputing the interview.

Both you and the Benefits Agency can ask witnesses to come and give information to support your case. Chairpersons do have the power to refuse to hear witnesses who are not relevant, but they should always be fair to claimants and generally allow witnesses to speak, even if it looks as if they may have nothing useful to say. [27]

When presenting your case to the tribunal, it is therefore important to correct any mistakes in the appeal papers and bring up new facts or arguments which the adjudication officer did not know about when s/he took the original decision. There may be facts which have arisen since the officer's decision, which you consider relevant. Present the true facts as clearly as you can and use any written evidence or witnesses to back up what you are saying.

A tribunal hearing is a complete re-hearing of your case, so fresh facts and arguments can be put by either side. [28] You or the presenting officer can also ask for an adjournment if you think you need time to prepare your response to the new evidence, or arguments. It is up to the tribunal whether to grant an adjournment or not. [29]

Checking the law

The adjudication officer often gets the law wrong so it is worth checking the benefit rules to see if they have been incorrectly applied in your case. This *Handbook* explains what the law says and also gives you the legal references if you want to look them up for yourself. The adjudication officer will also have quoted certain bits of the law which support their decision and you should check these.

The law relating to IS, DWA and FC consists of Acts of Parliament and Regulations. You can ask to see the law concerning IS, DWA and FC at the local Benefits Agency office. It should be available for public inspection at all reasonable hours and without payment.[30] Benefit laws are collected together in a large looseleaf book called the *Law Relating to Social Security*. It is in several volumes and is known as the 'Blue Book'. It is kept up-to-date with regular supplements. You can look at a copy of the 'Blue Book' at your nearest major library as well as at the Benefits Agency. Most of the law you need is contained in *CPAG's Income support, the social fund and family credit: The legislation* edited by John Mesher. As well as giving the law it gives explanations of what each bit means and tells you about relevant case law (see below).

Law relating to benefit is complicated and the staff who administer benefits are issued with guidance manuals. The *Adjudication Officer's Guide* covers benefits administered by the Benefits Agency. It is written by the Chief Adjudication Officer (CAO) who is responsible for advising local adjudication officers about the law.[31] The CAO also issues regular circulars to staff.

This manual is only guidance and not law but sometimes provides information which may help clarify any difficulty you have with the benefit office. The adjudicating authorities are bound by the regulations but not by the guidance.

Case law is made by the **Social Security Commissioners** who are part of the appeal system (see p124).[32] Rulings they make about the meaning of benefit law are binding and must be applied in similar cases by adjudication officers and tribunals. The most important Commissioners' decisions are published by HMSO and are called 'reported decisions'. They are prefixed by the letter R. Thus, R(IS) 1/90 was the first Commissioner's decision on IS to be reported in 1990. IS decisions are reported as R(IS) and family credit as R(FC). Sometimes you will be referred to supplementary benefit decisions which are R(SB), and to decisions on other benefits. Only the most important decisions are reported. Decisions which are not reported are prefixed by the letter 'C', and the year is written out in full – for example, CIS/13/1989. They are available for £1 each from the Office of the Social Security Commissioners (see Appendix 1 for the address).

This *Handbook* gives references to Commissioners' decisions and you can keep up-to-date with the latest Commissioners' decisions by reading CPAG's bi-monthly *Welfare Rights Bulletin*. The main library in your area may have copies of reported Commissioners' decisions or you can ask to see them at any Benefits Agency office.

Always check the decisions referred to by the adjudication officer to see if they really go against you. Then see if you can find others which help your case. If you want to refer to an unreported Commissioner's decision, it is best to circulate it to the SSAT and Benefits Agency in advance. If this is not possible take enough copies for them, to the hearing. Sometimes Commissioners' decisions conflict. If so, the tribunal must follow a reported decision in preference to an unreported one, and a

Tribunal of Commissioners' decision to that of a single Commissioner. [33] If there is a decision on the same point by the High Court on judicial review, the Court of Appeal or the House of Lords, it must be followed in preference to a Commissioner's decision.

3 APPEALING TO THE SOCIAL SECURITY COMMISSIONER

Both you and the Benefits Agency have a further right of appeal to a Social Security Commissioner, but only if the tribunal has made an error of law. [34]

The Social Security Commissioners are lawyers with at least 10 years' experience. Their offices are in London for England and Wales; Edinburgh for Scotland; and Belfast for Northern Ireland (see Appendix 1 for addresses). Their job is to interpret the law. The decisions they make must be followed by adjudication officers and tribunals in all future cases.

(i) An error of law

There will have been an error of law if: [35]

☐ The tribunal got the law wrong – eg, it misunderstood the particular benefit regulation concerned.

☐ There is no evidence to support the tribunal's decision.

☐ The facts found by the tribunal are such that, had it acted reasonably, and interpreted the law correctly, it could not have made the decision it did. This argument would be used where the facts are inconsistent with the decision – eg, a tribunal finds that a man and a woman live in separate households, but decides they are living together as husband and wife.

☐ There is a breach of the rules of natural justice. This is where the procedure followed by the tribunal leads to unfairness (eg, you are not allowed to call witnesses to support you or the tribunal refuses a postponement, even though you cannot attend for a good reason and have told it so), and the result is that you lost without having a chance to put your case properly.

☐ The tribunal does not give proper findings of fact or provide adequate reasons for its decision. This is a very common fault of tribunals. The tribunal must not simply announce its conclusion. It must put down sufficient reasons so that you can see why, on the evidence, it reached the conclusion it did.

(ii) How to appeal

You must first obtain leave to appeal. [36] This means that you have to show that there has *possibly* been an error of law and that you have the beginnings of a case.

If you wish to appeal, you should first apply to the chairperson of the tribunal. [37] You may do this orally at the end of the hearing when you are told the decision, or by writing to the clerk of the tribunal at the Regional Office within three months of being sent the decision of the tribunal. The chairperson is usually the one who heard your case originally. [38]

If the chairperson refuses leave to appeal, you may make a fresh application for leave to appeal direct to a Commissioner within six weeks of being sent the decision refusing you leave. [39]

If you miss the time-limit, you may still apply for leave to appeal but any application must be made direct to a Commissioner who will give you leave only if there are 'special reasons'. [40]

Once you have been given leave to appeal, you have six weeks in which to send in notice of the appeal itself. [41] You are sent a form on which to do this. The time may, again, be extended for 'special reasons'. You may have been told that your notice of application for leave has been treated as a notice of appeal, in which case you do not have to send in another. [42]

(iii)   The written procedure

All cases are taken over by adjudication officers at the Office of the Chief Adjudication Officer (see Appendix 1 for the address). A bundle of documents is prepared by that office or by the Secretary of State's representative and is sent to the Commissioners' office who add it to any submissions from you. The Commissioners' office then sends copies of the bundle to each party.

You are given 30 days in which to reply to the submission of the adjudication officer or the Secretary of State although the Commissioner may extend the time-limit. There is a right of reply, if required, within 30 days. [43] If you have nothing to add and do not want to reply at any stage, tell the Commissioners' office. A Commissioner has the power to strike out an appeal that appears to have been abandoned, although you can apply for it to be reinstated. [44]

When the Commissioner has all the written submissions, s/he decides whether or not there should be an oral hearing of the appeal. If you ask for an oral hearing, the Commissioner will hold one unless s/he feels that the case can properly be dealt with without one. [45] It is not usual for a Commissioner to refuse a claimant's request for an oral hearing unless s/he is going to decide the case in the claimant's favour. Occasionally, the Commissioner decides to hold an oral hearing even if you have not asked for one.

If there is no oral hearing, the Commissioner reaches a decision on the basis of written submissions and other documents.

Because of the length of time you have to wait before your case is dealt with, you should consider making a fresh claim for benefit.

(iv)   The hearing

If there is an oral hearing, it will be at the Commissioners' offices in London, Edinburgh or Belfast, or at the Law Courts in Cardiff, Leeds or Liverpool. You are told the date in good time and your fares are paid in advance if you want to attend. At least half a day is set aside for each case.

Usually, one Commissioner hears your case but, if there is a 'question of law of special difficulty', the hearing may be before a Tribunal of Commissioners. [46] The procedure is still the same.

The hearing is more formal than those before social security appeal tribunals but the Commissioner will let you say everything you want. Commissioners usually intervene a lot and ask questions so you need to be prepared to argue your case without your script. A full set of Commissioners' decisions and the 'Blue Books' (see p123) are available for your use. The adjudication officer is usually represented by a lawyer, so you should consider trying to obtain representation as well. The Commissioner may exclude members of the public if intimate personal or financial circumstances or matters of public security are involved.[47] This is not usually necessary because it is rare for anyone not involved in the case to attend.

(v) The decision

The decision is always given in writing[48] – often at some length – and it may be a few weeks before it is sent to you.

After a successful appeal the case is usually sent back to a differently constituted social security appeal tribunal with directions as to how the tribunal should go about reconsidering the issues.[49] However, if the Commissioner feels that the record of the decision of the original tribunal contains all the material facts, or s/he feels that it is 'expedient' to make findings on any extra factual issues necessary to the decisions, the Commissioner will make the final decision.[50] It is unusual for a Commissioner not to send a case back to a tribunal if there is a dispute about facts not determined by the original tribunal, unless all the evidence points in one direction.[51]

A Commissioner may correct or set aside a decision in the same way as a tribunal (see p121).[52]

In certain circumstances, an adjudication officer may review a Commissioner's decision (see p105).

Decisions of Commissioners establish precedents and so may affect many cases other than your own (see p123).

4 APPEALING TO THE COURTS

(i) Appeals from Social Security Commissioners

You may appeal against a decision of a Commissioner to the Court of Appeal (in Scotland, the Court of Session). Again, the appeal is only on a point of law and you must first obtain leave to appeal.[53] If you want to appeal you should seek help from a solicitor, but check that you qualify for help with legal costs.

The application for leave to appeal must first be made to a Commissioner, in writing, within three months of the date when you were sent the Commissioner's decision. The Commissioner may extend the time-limit for 'special reasons'.[54] If you do not apply to the Commissioner within the time-limit and the Commissioner refuses to extend it, the Court of Appeal (or Court of Session) cannot hear your appeal and you can only proceed by applying to the High Court (in Scotland, the Court of Session) for judicial review of the refusal to extend the time allowed for the appeal (see below).[55]

Applications to a Commissioner for leave to appeal are almost invariably considered without an oral hearing. If the Commissioner refuses, you can apply to the court for leave.[56] Your notice of application should be lodged with the Civil Appeals Office within six weeks of notification of the Commissioner's refusal being sent to you.[57] The court may extend the time but you must explain the reasons for your delay and file an affidavit in support of an application for an extension of time.[58] Generally, the Court of Appeal will first consider your application without an oral hearing. If leave is refused, you may renew your application in open court within seven days. Similarly, if leave is granted, the Chief Adjudication Officer or the Secretary of State has seven days in which to ask for an oral hearing.[59]

If leave to appeal was granted by a Commissioner, you must serve a notice of appeal on the relevant parties within six weeks of being sent notification of the Commissioner's grant of leave.[60] If leave was granted by the Court of Appeal, the notice of appeal must be served within the same six-week period or within seven days of the grant of leave whichever is later (unless your notice of application for leave was lodged outside the six-week time-limit, in which case a time-limit for lodging the notice of appeal should be contained in the court's order).[61] The solicitor to the Benefits Agency will accept service on behalf of the Chief Adjudication Officer (see Appendix 1 for address).

You cannot appeal to the Court of Appeal against a decision of a Commissioner refusing you leave to appeal to a Commissioner (against a decision of a tribunal), but you can apply to the High Court for judicial review of such a decision.[62]

The procedures in Scotland are similar.

The Chief Adjudication Officer or the Secretary of State has the same rights of appeal as you.

(ii)   Applying for judicial review

Occasionally it is possible to challenge the Benefits Agency by going to court for a **judicial review**. You will need the services of a solicitor, law centre or legal advice centre.

You can apply for judicial review of a decision made by the Secretary of State or of a tribunal chairperson or a Social Security Commissioner who refuses to grant you leave to appeal. However, this procedure cannot be used if you have an independent right of appeal such as against the decision of an adjudication officer or a social security appeal tribunal.

Legal aid is available for cases in the Court of Appeal, the High Court and the Court of Session and you should certainly obtain legal advice and representation (see Appendix 2). In the past, the legal aid authorities have taken the view that an application to a Commissioner for leave to appeal to the Court of Appeal cannot be covered by legal aid. However, it is arguable that such an application is a step 'preliminary to' proceedings in the Court of Appeal and is thus work for which legal aid is available.[63]

PART III
Family credit

Chapter 9

Family credit

This chapter covers all the rules about family credit (FC). It contains:

1 Introduction (below)
2 The basic rules (p130)
3 The amount of benefit (p133)
4 Special rules for special groups (p134)
5 Claiming and getting paid (p135)
6 Challenging a family credit decision (p138)

1 INTRODUCTION

Family credit is a tax-free benefit for low-paid workers with children. It tops-up your wages if you are in full-time work (see p131). If you have a disability, you may be able to claim DWA instead and this is likely to give you more money than FC (see p139). Part-time workers should claim IS instead of FC. If you pay rent and/or community charge you may get housing benefit (HB) (see p151) and community charge benefit (CCB) (see p213) as well but your FC will count as income for these benefits. FC also helps you to qualify for certain health service benefits (see Chapter 25), and some education benefits – but not free school meals (see Chapter 26). You may also qualify for some social fund payments (see Chapter 20). Under the Home Insulation Scheme you will qualify for a grant towards the cost of insulating your loft (ask at your town hall about this).

FC is a weekly payment which normally continues at the same rate for 26 weeks, regardless of any changes in your circumstances.

You qualify for FC if:
☐ your savings and capital are not worth over £8,000. Some of your capital may

be ignored, but you may also be treated as having capital you do not really possess (see p272);

☐ your income is low enough. This depends on your circumstances. Some of your income may be ignored, but you may be treated as having income which you do not possess (see p246);

☐ you are in Great Britain (see below);

☐ you work full-time (usually for 16 hours or more per week);

☐ you have at least one dependent child (see p132);

☐ you have made a proper claim (see p135);

☐ neither you nor your partner is entitled to DWA (see p132).

You can claim for your 'family' which consists of

☐ you;

☐ your partner (if any) who is

either   your husband or wife if you are living together (see p229);

or   a person of the opposite sex to whom you are not married, but with whom you are living together as husband and wife (see p229);

☐ any children for whom you are responsible (see p233).

You must claim in writing on the form in leaflet FC1 which you can get from your local post office or Benefits Agency office. The claim must be made by the woman in a couple unless the Secretary of State decides that it is reasonable to accept a claim from the man. Both members of the couple have to sign the claim form.

For more details about claims, see p135.

2   THE BASIC RULES

(i)   Residence in Great Britain

To be entitled you must be in Great Britain.[1] This means England, Scotland and Wales. You will be treated as being in Great Britain if:[2]

☐ you are present and ordinarily resident in Great Britain; *and*

☐ your partner (if any) is ordinarily resident in the United Kingdom (UK); *and*

☐ at least part of your earnings (or your partner's earnings) are derived from paid work in the UK; *and*

☐ your earnings (or those of your partner) do not come wholly from paid work done outside the UK.

You will be **ordinarily resident** here if you normally live in Great Britain (or, if relevant, the UK).[3] The **United Kingdom** includes Northern Ireland as well as Great Britain. If your husband or wife is living abroad and has never lived in this country, s/he will *not* be counted as a partner under social security law because s/he cannot be treated as a member of your household. If your spouse was living with you in this country and is now living abroad, s/he may continue to be treated as a member of your household and therefore count as your partner (see p228).

If you cannot meet these conditions you could argue that you are actually in Great Britain, and do not have to satisfy the test for being treated as being in Great Britain.

You cannot be treated as being in Great Britain if you or your partner are entitled to FC or DWA in Northern Ireland.[4]

There is no requirement for a child who is a member of your household to be present in Great Britain.[5]

If you or your partner are 'persons from abroad', see p134.

(ii) Full-time work

To be entitled to FC, you or your partner must be 'engaged and normally engaged in remunerative work'.[6]

You count as **engaged in remunerative work** *only* if all the following apply:[7]

☐ you work for not less than 16 hours, or, if your hours fluctuate, 16 hours on average, a week; *and*

☐ your work is paid, or done in the expectation that you will be paid (eg, on a commission basis). This includes work where the payment is in kind (eg, where a farm worker is provided with free produce and accommodation[8]). Work done as a volunteer or for a charity or voluntary body will not count if only your expenses are paid.[9]

☐ you are employed at the date of claim. In addition[10] you must:

☐ actually work for 16 hours or more in either the week in which you claim or one of the two or preceding weeks;

☐ be expected by your employers (or yourself if you are self-employed) to work for 16 hours or more in the week after you claim (this applies if you have just started work); *or*

☐ you are on holiday from work and thus not working – so long as you are expected to work 16 hours or more in the week after you return.

The work you are doing in any of the weeks referred to above must be work you normally do and you are likely to continue in that job for at least five weeks after your claim.[11] What is 'normal' depends on your individual circumstances.[12] They should consider the likely future pattern of work, the past pattern and all other relevant circumstances.[13] If your job is likely to end in the near future you will not qualify. However, if you have only just started work, but are likely to continue working, this should be sufficient to enable you to qualify.[14]

If you do not do at least 16 hours work in any of these weeks, your claim will be disallowed even if the reason you have not been working the necessary hours is because of sickness,[15] maternity leave, suspension, short-time working, lay-off or because you are only on call.[16] However, you should be treated as working if you are on duty and required to be available during a part of the day and/or night – eg, if you are a warden in sheltered housing.

If your claim is refused, claim again in the first week in which you will be working 16 or more hours. It often takes the Benefits Agency a long time to send you a decision on your claim. If this happens make sure that you ask for your new claim to be backdated to the first week in which you actually worked for 16 hours or more.

If you fulfil all these rules you will be treated as being 'normally engaged in remunerative work'.[17]

Work includes self-employment, but not a training course[18] nor a course of education as a student.[19] If you are studying and working you can claim FC as long as you can show that you normally work for 16 hours or more a week. People who work at home (eg, childminders, writers or carers) will be eligible for FC if they are paid and work at least 16 hours on average a week. [20] If you are getting Enterprise Allowance you should qualify, even if you do not yet have other income from your work. [21]

In calculating the number of your hours you may include all the hours you are expected or contracted to work (ie, all the hours for which you are paid). Lunch-breaks should be included in the total if they are paid. [22] Your total hours can be made up from more than one job. [23] If you are self-employed, you can count not only the hours spent on services for which you are paid, but also other time which is essential to your business (eg, preparation time). [24]

If you are employed and you have not got a normal pattern of working hours (eg, because you have just started a new job), you will qualify if it is expected that you will work 16 or more hours on average each week. [25] If you are self-employed and have not yet worked for five weeks, the average hours that you expect to work are used. [26]

If, when you claim, you have a normal cycle of work, the average weekly hours over one complete cycle are used, including periods when no work is done but excluding other absences, such as holidays. [27] Thus if you work two weeks on and one week off your hours are averaged over three weeks but if you have a week's holiday during your cycle this week is disregarded when working out the average. [28]

If you have no recognisable cycle of work, the average over the five-week period immediately before the week in which you claim is used, or over another period if this would more accurately reflect your average working hours. [29]

Sometimes it is difficult to show that you normally work over 16 hours per week and the distinction between FC and IS is not absolute. You may be excluded from both FC and IS. There are often difficulties with school workers who work regular hours during term-time but not at all in school holidays.

You may fall within *both* schemes and therefore have to choose which benefit to claim. If you are a childminder working for 16 hours or more a week, you will not be treated as in full-time work for the purposes of IS (see p10), and so may be entitled to claim either IS or FC.

(iii)　Responsibility for a child

To get FC, you or your partner must be responsible for at least one child who is a member of your household. [30] You do not have to be their parent. (For when you are responsible for a child, see p233.)

(iv)　Overlap with disability working allowance

You cannot get FC if you or your partner have been awarded DWA. This does not apply if your DWA is due to expire within six weeks of the date you claim FC, *and* you fulfil all the other conditions of entitlement to FC *and* you are claiming FC for the period immediately after your DWA ends.[31] In all other cases you will have to wait until your DWA award comes to an end before claiming FC (see p136).

3   THE AMOUNT OF BENEFIT

You cannot get FC if your capital is more than £8,000 (see p272). Your FC is calculated by taking account of the number and ages of your children and the income you and your family possess. If you are a single parent, you will receive the same amount of FC as a two-parent family.

To work out your FC, you first of all calculate the **maximum FC** for your family. Then you compare your income (see pp246-71) with a set figure of £66.60 (called the **applicable amount**).[32] If your income is £66.60 or less you will receive the maximum FC for your family.[33] If it is more than £66.60 you will get the maximum FC reduced by 70 per cent of the difference between your income and applicable amount.[34] Some people with disabilities may be able to choose among FC, IS or DWA

(i)   Maximum family credit

The maximum family credit is made up of an adult credit and a credit for each child.[35] The adult credit is the same whether you are a single parent or a couple. The credit for each child depends on her/his age. The current rates are as follows:[36]

Credit for adult (single parent or couple)	£41.00
Credit for child aged	
0-10	£10.40
11-15	£17.25
16-17	£21.45
18	£29.90

Example of maximum FC
For a couple and three children aged 5, 7 and 13 the maximum is:

£41.00	for the couple
£20.80	for the two children under 11 (2 × £10.40)
£17.25	for the eldest child
£79.05	is the total maximum FC for this family.

You will not receive a credit for any child who:[37]
☐   has more than £3,000 capital (savings etc) of their own (see p272); *or*
☐   has a higher weekly income (other than disregarded income or that from maintenance) than the appropriate credit for a child of that age; *or*
☐   has been in hospital or residential accommodation because of illness or disability for 52 weeks before the date of claim.
If you have more than one husband or wife (ie, you are polygamously married), and

they are all members of your household, you get an extra credit in addition to the usual £41.00 for a couple and the appropriate amounts for children.[38] The additional credit for each additional spouse is:

☐ £21.45 if they are under 18;
☐ £29.90 if they are 18 or over.

(ii)　The family credit calculation

You now compare your income (see pp246-71) with the applicable amount of £66.60.

Example 1: Income below applicable amount
Mary is a single parent with two children aged 10 and 14. She works 10am-3pm five days a week (25 hours) as a school-helper. Her total weekly income taken into account for the purposes of FC is £57. Her savings are less than £3,000.

Her maximum FC is £41 for herself and £10.40 for the younger, and £17.25 for the older of the children. This totals £68.65.

She will receive the full maximum FC of £68.65 a week, as her income is less than the applicable amount (£66.60).

Example 2: Income higher than applicable amount
Shahida has a partner and two children aged 3 and 5. Her partner works 35 hours a week and the total family income taken into account for the purposes of FC is £107.60. Family savings are less than £3,000. The maximum FC in her case is £61.80 (£41.00 for the couple and £10.40 for each child).

Her income exceeds the applicable amount by £41 (£107.60 less £66.60). 70 per cent of the excess is £28.70 (£41 × 70%).

Maximum FC	£61.80
less	£28.70 (70% of excess)
equals	£33.10 weekly FC.

Shahida will therefore receive £33.10 each week in FC. For every £10 by which her weekly income increases on any future claim, her FC will reduce by £7.

Any fractions produced at the end of the FC calculation are rounded up to a penny if they are more than a half-penny, and are ignored if less than a half-penny.[39] The minimum amount of FC that will be paid is 50 pence a week.[40]

4　SPECIAL RULES FOR SPECIAL GROUPS

(i)　People from abroad

If you are a 'person from abroad' you can claim FC as long as your immigration status does not debar you from working. Check that you fulfil the residence conditions (see p130). Capital abroad which you own will affect your entitlement to FC (see p284). However, claiming FC counts as having **recourse to public funds** (see p63). You should get immigration advice before claiming if you have been allowed to stay in the UK on condition that you do not have recourse to public funds.

If you have a partner and children who are British, or have settled status, they should be able to claim FC without jeopardising your immigration status. Technically, the amount awarded will cover your needs, but because the adult credit is the same for a single person or a couple you could argue that you are not *personally* having recourse to public funds.

(ii) People involved in a trade dispute

If you are involved in a trade dispute, you can still claim FC but your normal weekly earnings will be taken as those prior to the dispute[41] and so will not reflect your actual income during the dispute. If you are already getting FC when you become involved in a trade dispute you will continue to receive it at the same rate for the rest of the 26 weeks of your award.[42] However, you will not be entitled to FC if, because of the dispute, you were not at work in any of the three set weeks around the date of your claim (see p131).

Since there are no other special rules under FC for the assessment of your capital and income if you or your partner are involved in a trade dispute, the normal rules will apply.

5 CLAIMING AND GETTING PAID

(i) Claims

Your claim should be on form FC1 and is usually considered to have been made on the day it reaches the Family Credit Unit (see Appendix 1 for address).[43] If you do not use the right form or fill it in incorrectly, the Benefits Agency will ask you to correct this. If you then return the form within one month, the date of your first claim will count. This time-limit can be extended.[44] If you are just starting work after being unemployed you can ask a claimant adviser at the Unemployment Benefit Office to give you the form. Alternatively you can get it from your local Benefits Agency. Both will help you fill it in and, in either case, your claim is likely to be dealt with more speedily as the UBO/Benefits Agency should mark the FC1 to ensure that you get a quick decision. If you prefer, you can get the form from a post office or advice centre.

A claim for FC can be backdated,[45] but only for a maximum of one year. To get your claim backdated you must have 'good cause' for not having claimed earlier (see p102). A claim can be backdated for a month without good cause but this is at the Secretary of State's discretion. On renewal claims, the month is in addition to the 14 days after your last claim ran out (see below).

If you have made a claim but then your circumstances change (eg, your income suddenly drops), you can amend or withdraw your claim (see below). But you must act quickly. A claim can only be withdrawn or amended before a decision is made by the adjudication officer (AO).[46]

If you are **renewing your claim**[47] after a period on FC you should be reminded that it is about to run out and invited to make a fresh claim. You can put your claim in up to 28 days before the current award expires or within 14 days of it running out. Your new claim will then follow on immediately from your previous award. If you are changing from DWA to FC you can claim up to 42 days before your DWA award expires or 14 days afterwards and FC will be paid from the date the DWA ends.

(ii)   When to claim

It is worth thinking carefully about which day and week you should make your claim bearing in mind the following points:

☐   Awards of FC run from a Tuesday so you should try to get your claim to the Benefits Agency on a Tuesday or on the day before. If your claim arrives on a Wednesday, your entitlement will not start until the following Tuesday and you will lose benefit for that week.[48]

☐   Make sure your claim is made during a week in which you are eligible to claim – see p131.

☐   If you are thinking about making a claim in late February or March it might be to your advantage to consider delaying the claim until April. This is because the amounts for FC are uprated in April but only those claiming after the increase get the higher amounts. If you claim before April, you will only get the benefit of the increase when you come to renew your claim six months later.[49] However, if you claim no more than 28 days before benefits are increased and you do not qualify for FC at the old rates but would under the new ones, you can be treated as entitled and paid from the date the increases take effect.[50]

A claim for DWA can be treated as a claim for FC. If you are refused DWA, you could ask for this to happen and thus have FC paid from the date of your DWA claim. If you are entitled to both you must choose which one to claim *before* a decision is made. Once you have been awarded FC you cannot change to DWA until 26 weeks have elapsed and vice versa.

☐   Consider whether your family circumstances are about to change in a way which might affect your FC. For example, if you are about to take a drop in income or have another child, it might be worth delaying your claim.

☐   If you are making a renewal claim after your 26 weeks' FC has ended, your claim can be made 28 days before or 14 days after the FC finishes (see above).

Once you have made a decision about when to claim, apply as soon as possible. If you do not claim quickly you might lose money. Send off the form even if you cannot complete absolutely all the details. You can send those on later. Keep a copy of your claim in case queries arise later on.

(iii)   How your claim is dealt with

When your claim is received by the Family Credit Unit, the information you have provided will be checked and details will be obtained from your employer about your wages or salary.[51] You could ask your employer to reply promptly. If you have claimed through a claimant adviser or local Benefits Agency, your wages will be checked by telephone which speeds up your claim. On a renewal claim, if you are still working for the same employer, the Benefits Agency should accept your wage slips as evidence of your earnings and do not usually contact your employer again. [52]

Then your claim is referred to an AO for decision. It should be dealt with within 14 days 'so far as practicable'. [53]

If you have been waiting more than two weeks for the result of your claim, contact the Family Credit Unit. Always keep a copy of your letter or make a note of the date of your call, who you spoke to and what was said. Check that the Family Credit Unit has received your claim. If they have not, send them a copy or fill out a new form and ask them to pay from the date you sent in the first one.

If your claim has been received and you are not satisfied with the explanation for the delay, complain to the Manager, and/or go and see your MP (see p117). If the delay is unreasonable, you could take legal action.

You should also ask for **interim payments** to be made to you while you wait for the decision on your claim. The rules are the same as for IS (see p107). The Family Credit Unit have a policy of not making such payments and you may need to ask your MP to help you get one.

(iv)   Family credit decisions – getting paid

You are given the decision on your claim in writing. The letter from the Family Credit Unit gives the reasons for the decision and tells you about your right to appeal. [54] If you have been awarded FC you should be sent an order book 'as soon as reasonably practicable'. [55] You can choose to be paid by direct credit transfer into a bank or other account if you prefer. [56]

You can cash an FC order book at your local post office. The book will last for 26 weeks starting on the Tuesday of the week following that in which your claim was treated as made (see p135). Payments by order book are made weekly in arrears. [57] Credit transfer payments are credited to your account every four weeks in arrears.

If your order book is lost or stolen or your FC is suspended, see p108 (the rules are the same as for IS).

(v)   Change of circumstances

If your circumstances change during the 26 weeks (eg, your capital or income go up or down or you have another child), this will not usually affect the amount you are being paid. [58] However,

☐   if a child or young person leaves your household while FC is being paid and IS, DWA or FC is awarded to them or for them in a different household, your FC will stop from the first day of any overlap. [59] This may happen, for example, if your family splits up;

☐   if a claimant dies during the 26-week period, FC will stop if s/he was single. If s/he was one of a couple (see p229), the partner can take over the rest of the award provided that s/he was the partner when FC was claimed; [60]

☐   if a new award of FC is made on review or appeal, any award of FC with which it overlaps will be reviewed. [61]

(vi)   Overpayments and fraud

The rules on overpayments and fraud are the same as for IS (see p112). However, the IS rules limiting the maximum amount that can be recovered from your weekly benefit do not apply to FC. [62]

6   CHALLENGING A FAMILY CREDIT DECISION

It is always possible to apply for a review of the decision on your FC claim on the grounds that the Benefits Agency: [63]
- [ ]   did not know or made a mistake about facts relevant to your claim;
- [ ]   got the law wrong.

For instance, your employer may have provided incorrect information or a mistake may have been made in working out your FC. You cannot get a review because your circumstances have changed except in the situations described on pp137. [64]

   When an FC decision is reviewed, payment of arrears is not restricted *unless* the review was because of ignorance of, or a mistake about, the facts, and you were aware of these facts but failed to tell the Benefits Agency. In this case you can only get up to 12 months arrears. [65]

   If you feel that you have been wrongly refused FC or that your entitlement has been miscalculated, you can appeal to a social security appeal tribunal. [66] Chapter 8 explains how to appeal. The rules are the same as for IS. See also Chapter 8 for information about judicial review, and Chapter 7 if you want to complain about how your claim has been handled.

PART IV
Disability working allowance

Chapter 10

Disability working allowance

This chapter deals with the rules about disability working allowance (DWA). It covers:

1 Introduction (below)
2 The basic rules (p140)
3 The amount of benefit (p144)
4 Claims, reviews and getting paid (p145)
5 Appeals (p148)
6 Giving up work because of sickness (p149)

1 INTRODUCTION

Disability working alowance is a tax-free benefit for low-paid workers with a disability. It tops up your wages if you are in full-time work (see p141). Part-time workers can claim income support (IS) instead. If you are in low-paid work but do not have a disability you could claim family credit (FC) (see p129). If you pay rent and/or community charge you may get housing benefit (HB) (see p151) or community charge benefit (CCB) (see p213) as well. Receipt of DWA helps you to qualify for a disability premium with IS/HB/CCB. You may qualify for certain health service benefits if your income is low enough (see Chapter 25). You may also qualify for some social fund payments (see Chapter 20). Disability working allowance is a weekly payment which normally continues at the same rate for 26 weeks regardless of changes in your circumstances. If your earnings are too low to pay National Insurance you will get a credit for each week on DWA. [1]

(i) Who can claim

You qualify for DWA if:
- [ ] you are 16 or over;
- [ ] your savings and capital are not worth more than £16,000. Some of your capital may be ignored but you may also be treated as having capital you do not really possess (see p272);
- [ ] your income is low enough. This depends on your circumstances. Some of your income is ignored but you may be treated as having income which you do not possess (see p246);
- [ ] you are in Great Britain (see below);
- [ ] you work full-time (usually for 16 hours or more per week) (see p141);
- [ ] you have a physical or mental disability which puts you at a disadvantage in getting a job (see p141);
- [ ] you are, or have recently been getting, a sickness or disability benefit (see p143);
- [ ] you have made a proper claim (see p145);
- [ ] you are not getting FC (see p143).

(ii) Who you claim for

You claim for your 'family' which consists of:
- [ ] you;
- [ ] your partner (if any) who is
  either your husband or wife if you are living together (see p229);
  or a person of the opposite sex to whom you are not married, but with whom you are living together as husband and wife (see p229);
- [ ] any children for whom you are responsible (see p233).

(iii) How to claim

You claim in writing using the DWA claim pack which you can get from your local post office, Benefits Agency office or JobCentre (see p145). Alternatively, you can ring the Benefits Enquiry Line and speak to someone who will complete a claim form for you (see p145).

(iv) If you become sick while on DWA

There are special rules to protect your entitlement to the incapacity benefits which you were claiming before you took up work (see p149). If your disability prevents you from continuing in work you should not lose benefit because you tried to work.

2 THE BASIC RULES

(i) Residence in Great Britain[2]

The rules are the same as for FC, *except* that the condition that says that at least part of your earnings are from paid work in the United Kingdom *only applies to you the claimant and not to your partner*[3] (see p130).

(ii)   Full-time work

To be entitled to DWA you must be 'engaged and normally engaged in full-time work'.[4] This applies if you:[5]
☐   work for at least 16 hours per week; *and*
☐   are paid, or expect to be paid; *and*
☐   are employed at the date of your claim.

In addition to this you must
☐   have actually worked for 16 hours or more in the week you claim, or either of the two preceding weeks; *or*
☐   be expected by your employer to work for 16 hours or more in the week after the week you claim (this applies if you have just started work); *or*
☐   be prevented from meeting these conditions because you are on holiday from work. This only applies where your employer expects you to work 16 hours or more in the week after you return to work.
The work must be your normal job and you are expected to continue working for at least five weeks from when you claim. The week of the claim is included in this.

When working out how many hours you work, include paid meal breaks and paid time off to attend a hospital or clinic in relation to your disability. If within the last five weeks you have changed your hours, returned to work after a break of 13 weeks or more, or just started a new job, your hours are estimated.

Otherwise they are calculated by looking at your normal cycle of work and assessing your weekly hours. If you always work the same number of hours per week this is straightforward. If your work pattern is different – eg, you work one week on and one week off – your hours are averaged out. Periods when you do not work normally (eg, the 'week off') are included when working out the average but other absences (ie, for sickness) do not.

If you do not have an obvious pattern of working, the average hours worked over the five weeks prior to the week in which you claim are used. You can use a shorter or longer period if this gives a more accurate picture.

(iii)   The disability and disadvantage test

To qualify for DWA you must have a disability which puts you at a disadvantage in getting a job. Both physical and mental disability count.[6] If you are claiming for the first time, or after a period of two years when you were not getting DWA, you simply have to sign a declaration that this applies to you. This will be accepted *unless* the information given on your claim form is contradictory, *or* the adjudication officer has other evidence about you which indicates that you do not fulfil that condition.[7] For all other claims, you fulfil this condition if one of the following applies:[8]
☐   you are paid one of the following benefits (or its Northern Ireland equivalent):
    –   the highest or middle-rate care component or the higher rate mobility component of the disability living allowance;
    –   attendance allowance;

- industrial disablement benefit or a war pension, where you are at least 80 per cent disabled;
- mobility supplement;

☐ you have an invalid 'trike' or similar vehicle;

☐ you were paid severe disablement allowance (or Northern Ireland equivalent) for at least one day in the eight weeks prior to your 'initial claim'. **Initial claim** means your first successful claim for DWA, or a new claim where you have not been getting DWA during the last two years;

☐ you cannot keep your balance without holding on to something when standing;

☐ you cannot walk 100 metres on level ground without stopping or suffering severe pain. You are expected to use walking aids such as crutches, a stick, a frame or an artificial limb if you normally use these;

☐ you cannot use your hands behind your back (as you would when putting on a jacket or tucking your shirt in);

☐ you cannot extend your hands forwards in order to shake hands with someone without difficulty;

☐ you cannot put your hands up to your head without difficulty (as when putting on a hat);

☐ you cannot pick up a coin of 2½ cm diameter because you lack normal dexterity in both hands;

☐ you cannot pick up a full one litre jug and pour into a cup from it without difficulty;

☐ you cannot turn either of your hands sideways through 180 degrees;

☐ you are registered blind or partially-sighted;

☐ you cannot read 16-point print from more than 20 cm distance, even when wearing your normal glasses, if any;

☐ you cannot hear a telephone ring when in the same room, even with your hearing aid, if any;

☐ you cannot hear someone talking in a loud voice when the room is quiet and they are only two metres away from you;

☐ people who know you well have difficulty understanding what you say;

☐ you have difficulty understanding a person you know well;

☐ you lose consciousness during a fit, or go into a coma at least once a year;

☐ you are mentally ill and are receiving regular medical treatment;

☐ you are often confused or forgetful due to mental disability;

☐ you cannot do simple addition and subtraction;

☐ you hit people, or damage property or cannot socialise because of your mental disability;

☐ you cannot manage an 8-hour working day or a 5-day week because of your medical condition or because you suffer from severe pain;

☐ following illness or accident you are undergoing rehabilitation. You can only use this condition to qualify on an initial claim (see above).

If you fulfil the disability test for DWA because you were paid one of the specified benefits, or have an invalid trike, you will nevertheless be refused DWA if there is evidence that none of the other disability conditions are fulfilled.[9]

(iv) Receipt of a sickness or disability benefit

To qualify for DWA you must also be, or have been receiving, a sickness or disability benefit. [10] You are entitled if, *when you claim*, you are receiving:
- [ ] disability living allowance;
- [ ] attendance allowance, or an increase of your industrial disablement benefit or war pension for attendance needs;
- [ ] a corresponding benefit from Northern Ireland;
- [ ] mobility allowance.

Alternatively, you qualify if, for at least one day in the eight weeks prior to your claim, you were getting:
- [ ] invalidity benefit or severe disablement allowance;
- [ ] income support, housing benefit or community charge benefit, but only if your applicable amount included the disability or higher pensioner premium (see pp240 and 242);
- [ ] a corresponding benefit from Northern Ireland.

You can also meet this condition if you have an invalid trike or similar vehicle when you claim DWA.

If you are renewing your DWA claim within eight weeks of a previous award running out, you are deemed to be receiving invalidity benefit, severe disablement allowance or a disability or higher pensioner premium paid with IS, HB or CCB (or a Northern Ireland equivalent) where your previous award was made on this basis. [11]

Some people have difficulty meeting the benefit condition and thus may not qualify for DWA. For example:
- [ ] people with disabilities who are already in low-paid employment at the point that DWA is introduced;
- [ ] people who are temporarily off sick and getting statutory sick pay and whose DWA award ends while they are still sick. If they do not return to work within eight weeks they will not requalify for DWA *unless* they are getting DLA or AA, *or* they complete 28 weeks on statutory sick pay and go back on to invalidity benefit/severe disablement alowance prior to reclaiming DWA;
- [ ] people who do not receive invalidity benefit/severe disablement allowance because they get another social security benefit instead – eg, widow's benefit.

Contact your MP if you do not qualify because of this rule and press for it to be less restrictive.

(v) Entitlement to family credit

You are not entitled to DWA if, when you claim, you (or your partner) are entitled to FC. [12] However, this does not apply if: [13]
- [ ] your FC claim runs out within 28 days of your DWA claim;
- [ ] you are otherwise entitled to DWA;
- [ ] your DWA claim is for the period immediately after your FC runs out.

It is important to check whether you are better off claiming FC or DWA. If you make the wrong choice you could lose money. DWA is usually paid at a higher rate but this may reduce your HB/CCB entitlement. Remember also that DWA is not a 'passport benefit' for NHS charges, whereas FC is (see Chapter 26).

3   THE AMOUNT OF BENEFIT

You cannot get DWA if your capital is worth more than £16,000 [14] (see p272). Your DWA is calculated by first working out your **maximum disability working allowance**. You then compare your **income** (see pp246-71) with your **applicable amount** which is a set figure of

> £39.95 (single claimants)
> *or*   £66.60 (couples or lone parents).

If your income is less than your applicable amount you receive maximum DWA. If it is more, you get the maximum DWA minus 70 per cent of the difference between your income and the applicable amount. [15]

(i)   Maximum DWA

This is made up of allowances for each member of your family (see p227). These are as follows: [16]

single claimant	£42.40
couple/lone parent	£58.80
child aged:	
0-10	£10.40
11-15	£17.25
16-17	£21.45
18	£29.90
additional partners in a polygamous marriage	
under 18	£21.45
18 or over	£29.90

No allowance is given for a child who has:
☐   capital of over £3,000;
☐   weekly income (excluding maintenance) which is greater than their allowance;
☐   been in hospital or local authority residential accommodation for the 52 weeks prior to your claim because of physical or mental illness/handicap.

(ii)   Calculating DWA

Make sure that you have properly worked out your income (see pp246-71). Now compare this to your applicable amount.

Example
Winston is 19 and single. He works 25 hours per week. His income for DWA is £65. He has no savings.

His maximum DWA is £42.40.

His income exceeds the applicable amount of £39.95 by £25.05. Thus his maximum DWA is reduced by £17.54 (70% × £25.05) and he is paid £24.86 per week.

If his income had been below £39.95 he would have received the maximum DWA.

---

4 CLAIMS, REVIEWS AND GETTING PAID

(i) Claims

Disability working allowance came into force on 7 April 1992. Claims were allowed from 10 March 1992 to allow payments to be made from April.

You claim DWA using the claim pack[17] which you can get from the Benefits Agency, a post office or JobCentre. This consists of information about DWA and two forms. Form DWA1 is for basic information about yourself, your family and your earnings. There is also a form EEF 200 on which your employer must confirm your hours/earnings if you have not yet worked for nine weeks. If you have already worked for this long you simply need to send in payslips.

If you prefer, you can ring the Benefits Enquiry Line free of charge on 0800-882200. Benefits Agency staff will discuss your claim and complete the appropriate forms for you. These will then be sent to you to sign and post.

Your claim goes to the DWA unit in Preston (see Appendix 1). Do not delay in sending the DWA1 just because you do not yet have your payslips or a completed form EEF 200 – these can be sent later.

If you are one of a couple the disabled partner should claim. If both of you are disabled you can choose who should be the claimant, but if you cannot agree the Benefits Agency decides for you. [18]

If you do not use the proper form, but nevertheless claim in writing you will be sent the form and so long as you return it within a month, you will be paid from the date your original letter was received. This also applies **if you do not properly fill in the form** – it will be returned to you to correct, or provide additional information and if you do this within a month, you will not lose benefit. This period can be extended if you have a good reason but it is best to act promptly. [19] If you want to amend or withdraw your claim, write to the Benefits Agency immediately. Your letter must arrive before the adjudication officer has decided your claim. [20]

If you claim FC, this can be treated as a claim for DWA if you would be better off. [21] However, you must let both the FC and DWA units know that you want them to do this *before* your FC claim is assessed.

Your claim is normally treated as made on the date it is received at the DWA unit. [22] However, if you start work on a Monday or Tuesday and claim DWA in the same week your claim is treated as made on the Tuesday of that week. [23]

If you are claiming within three months of being turned down on an earlier claim, your second claim can be treated as a review request[24] (see p147) though your claim date is still treated as that of your later claim. [25]

A claim can be backdated for up to 52 weeks[26] but only if you have good cause for a late claim[27] (see p102 – the rules are the same as for IS).

Renewal claims

If you are currently getting DWA, you should be sent a claim form eight weeks before your payments end. You can reclaim from six weeks before your award runs out and up to two weeks afterwards. It is best to claim as early as possible to ensure that your payments are not interrupted. On your renewal claim you have to fill in a fresh DWA1 and you will also be sent form DWA2 which asks you questions about the extent of your disability and how it affects you.

If you are currently getting FC, you can claim DWA up to four weeks before your FC expires or two weeks afterwards. [28]

In both cases this period can be extended by a month, but claim as soon as you can. [29]

For practical advice on when to claim, see p136.

(ii)   How your claim is dealt with

When your claim is received in Preston, the information in it is checked to see if further details are needed. If so, you will be asked to provide extra information or documents. You are obliged to provide this if requested and should do so *within a month*. [30] If there is a good reason this time limit can be extended, but if you reply quickly your DWA will be paid sooner. The Benefits Agency can also approach your employer for confirmation of your earnings and s/he must reply. [31]

Your claim is then passed to an adjudication officer for decision, and this should be made within 14 days if possible. [32]

If this is your first claim for DWA or you are reclaiming after two years of not getting DWA, it is usually accepted that your disability puts you at a disadvantage in getting a job if you say it does in form DWA1. You do not have to fill in form DWA2 to prove this unless there is other evidence to suggest that you do not qualify, in which case the adjudication officer will ask you do so. In all other cases the adjudication officer will consider your answers to the disability questions to decide if you qualify. The DWA2 form asks you to give the names of two health professionals who know about your disability and the adjudication officer may contact them to confirm your answers to the quesetions. S/he can also ask for advice from DSS doctors about your condition and how it is likely to affect you but s/he must make the decision. [33] If necessary you can be asked to go for a medical, though this is unlikely.

You should be sent a written decision and informed that you can appeal if you disagree with it. [34]

(iii)   Payment of benefit

DWA is normally paid on a Tuesday. If you claim on a different day of the week you are paid from the following Tuesday [35] (but see p145 if you have just started a job). If you are currently getting DWA or FC and you reclaim within the time limits (see p145) you are paid from the day after your last award runs out. [36] If you claim up to 28 days before the annual benefit increases (which happens each April) and you are not entitled at the old benefit rates, you can be paid from the date the new ones come in. [37]

You will not be paid at all if your entitlement is less than 50 pence per week. [38]

If you are awarded DWA it is paid for 26 weeks. [39] You are normally paid by a book of orders which you cash each week at a post office but, if you choose, you can have the money paid into a bank or building society account. [40] To do this you should write to the Benefits Agency office giving details of your account number. There is a section on the DWA1 form on which you can ask for payment to be made in this way. Benefit is paid a week in arrears (by order book) or four-weekly in arrears (into a bank).

Payment is usually made to the claimant but it can be paid to a partner instead.[41] You could apply to the Benefits Agency for this to happen if it is more convenient. Payment of your DWA can be suspended (see p108). If your order book is lost or stolen, see p108. Changes of circumstances do not usually affect your DWA (but see below).

(iv) Change of circumstances

Disability working allowance is normally paid for 26 weeks. The amount remains the same even if your circumstances change during this period (eg, your earnings go up or down or the rate of allowances or applicable amounts are increased, as they are each April).[42] However, your entitlement ceases if:

☐ your DWA includes an amount for a child or young person (see p233), but s/he is no longer a member of your household and someone else is claiming for her/ him or a dependant in their DWA/FC/IS;[43]

☐ the claimant dies. However, if there is a surviving partner and s/he is included in the claim, DWA will continue to be paid for the remainder of the 26 weeks.[44]

In addition, if you are getting DWA and, on review or appeal, another award of DWA is made covering all or part of the same period, this will be treated as a change of circumstances and will replace the first award.[45]

(v) Reviews

If you are unhappy with the decision made by the adjudication officer you can ask for a review.[46] If you do, your claim will be looked at by a different adjudication officer who may give a more favourable decision. If you apply within three months of the date the decision was sent, you do not have to have special grounds for review,[47] you can simply say why you disagree with the decision. (If you apply within three months but because of an industrial dispute your application is received after this deadline, it will count as if made within three months.)

If you apply outside this period you must show that:

☐ there was a **mistake about or ignorance of facts** which are relevant to your claim;

☐ you have **claimed in advance and been awarded DWA**, but then do not fulfil the conditions on the date it is due to be paid. The review is to stop payment being made;

☐ the adjudication officer **got the law wrong**.

You cannot usually apply for a review because your **circumstances have changed**. Only the changes listed above will affect your right to DWA.

Decisions made by appeal tribunals and Social Security Commissioners can also be reviewed, but only where there was a mistake about, or ignorance of the facts, an award was made in advance or one of the limited changes of circumstances.[48] If a tribunal or Commissioner's decision is wrong in law you may have the right of appeal. The rules are the same as for IS (see p124 and p126).

The rules about review apply whether or not you are disputing the initial decision on your claim, or a decision which was itself made on review, including a refusal to review.[49] Thus you could have a series of reviews on your claim. However, once you have applied for a review on any grounds (ie, within three months of a decision) you then have a right to appeal to an independent tribunal if you are still dissatisfied (see below).

You can ask for a review by writing to your local Benefits Agency office.[50] If you are applying under the three-month rule you can simply say why you think you qualify. If you are applying for a review outside this time limit, you also have to explain your grounds for asking for a review.

If you were refused DWA and applied for a review within three months of the decision you are normally paid from the date you applied for the review. However, up to 12 months arrears of DWA can be paid if:

☐ you are applying for a review within three months *or* because there was a mistake about or ignorance of relevant facts; *and*

☐ the review arises because you provide some information which you knew (or should have known) but did not previously give to the Benefits Agency; *and*

☐ the review leads to an award of DWA or an increase in the amount you are getting.

The 12 months runs from the date you first provided the information.[51]

The rules for getting more than 12 months' arrears are the same as for IS (see p105).

(vi) Overpayments and fraud

The rules on overpayments and fraud are the same as for IS[52] (see p112) except that the maximum rate of recovery does not apply to DWA. Nevertheless, you should argue for realistic repayments.

5 APPEALS

(i) How to appeal

If you disagree with an adjudication officer's decision you must normally apply for a review (see p147). However, if you have applied for a review within three months on any grounds you then have a right to appeal to either a disability appeal tribunal (DAT) or a social security appeal tribunal (SSAT).[53] **Your appeal goes to a DAT if** it concerns whether or not you have a physical or mental disability which puts you at a disadvantage in getting a job. If you are appealing about *both* this disability question *and* the other conditions of entitlement, the DAT will hear the whole case.[54]. However, **the appeal goes to an SSAT if** you are appealing *only* about the other conditions. An SSAT cannot decide a question if there was a right of appeal to a DAT. The rules for appealing to both a DAT and an SSAT are the same as for IS (see pp118-24) but the DAT has a different membership (see below).

(ii) The tribunal hearing

A DAT is made up of a chairperson who is a lawyer, and two other members. One of these is a medical practitioner and the other is a person who has experience of dealing with people with disabilities, either in a professional or voluntary capacity or because they have a disability themselves. People with disabilities should be on the panels in preference to carers or professionals if at all possible. Ideally, at least one of the tribunal members should be the same sex as yourself.[55] The DAT is independent and the members must not have previously dealt with your claim.[56] The hearing cannot go ahead unless all three members are present. You have the right to attend to explain why you think you qualify for DWA. (See p121 for how to prepare your case.) The tribunal members cannot medically examine you but they can refer you to a doctor who will do an examination and prepare a report to help them decide your claim.[57] This should only happen in rare cases where the DAT do not feel able to make a decision without a medical report.

Once they have listened to all your points they will make their decision. (See p121 as the rules are the same for IS. The ways of overturning a DAT decision are also the same.)

6 GIVING UP WORK BECAUSE OF SICKNESS OR DISABILITY

Disability working allowance is intended to encourage disabled people to try and work. If you have to stop working and you are sick, there are special rules to ensure that you can go back on to the incapacity benefit which you were claiming before you took up a job and claimed DWA. The rules differ depending on whether you are temporarily off sick or whether you stop work altogether.

(i) Temporary sickness

If you are sick and off work but expect to return when you are well, you should claim statutory sick pay from your employer (unless you were getting sickness/invalidity benefit or severe disablement allowance within the last eight weeks, in which case you will go back on to that benefit). You may also be entitled to claim IS, HB and CCB if your income is low enough (see p7, 151 and 213 respectively).

(ii) Giving up work

If you were claiming invalidity benefit or severe disablement allowance prior to getting DWA and you stop working altogether within two years of your invalidity benefit/severe disablement allowance claim, you can go straight back on to that benefit from your first day of sickness.[58] This is because days on DWA count as days of incapacity for work (and also as days when you were disabled for severe disablement allowance purposes) and your two periods of sickness are linked together. As well as any basic invalidity benefit/severe disablement allowance you will be able to get increases for your partner or child (if any) under the rules which applied on your last claim.[59]

If your job ends after the two-year period but you are nevertheless incapable of work, claim sickness benefit when you stop working. If you give up work for reasons other than sickness or disability you must claim unemployment benefit instead. You can also claim IS/HB/CCB (see p7, 151 and 213 respectively).

For details about claiming sickness/invalidity/unemployment benefit and severe disablement allowance see the *Rights Guide to Non-Means-Tested Benefits*.

PART V
Housing benefit

Chapter 11

The basic rules

This chapter covers:

1 Introduction (below)
2 'Eligible rent' (p157)
3 'Unreasonably high' rents (p162)

1 INTRODUCTION

Housing benefit (HB) is paid to people who have a low income and who rent their homes. It is paid whether or not the claimant is in full-time work and may be paid as well as IS, FC or DWA, or just by itself.

HB is paid by local authorities and not by the Benefits Agency, although it is a national scheme and the rules are mainly determined by DSS regulations.

If you are a council tenant, your rent account is credited with your benefit. This is known as a **rent rebate**.

If you are a private tenant, you are paid a cash allowance (although it is sometimes paid direct to your landlord, especially if you have rent arrears). This is known as a **rent allowance**.

(i)   Who can claim?

You can claim HB if the following conditions are satisfied: [1]

☐   Your income is low enough. How low it has to be depends on your circumstances (see p168). Some of your income may be ignored, but you may also be treated as having income you do not actually receive (see p246).

☐   Your savings and other capital are not worth more than £16,000. Again, some of your capital may be ignored, but you may also be treated as having capital you do not actually possess (see p272).

☐ You or your partner are liable, or treated as liable, to pay rent for accommodation (see below). 'Rent' includes many payments not usually regarded as rent such as licensee payments. Payments for bed and breakfast accommodation and hostels may also count as rent.

☐ You normally occupy that accommodation as your home (see p153).

☐ You are not excluded under the rules explained on p155.

You can claim HB if you live in any type of accommodation – private, local authority, housing association, board and lodging, hostels, bed and breakfast, sheltered accommodation. You can claim if you are a sub-tenant or a lodger in someone else's home or if you share housing costs.

The amount of benefit you receive depends on your income (see pp66-71), the number of people in your 'family' (see below) and your 'eligible rent', which may be less than your actual rent (see p157). If there are people living in your home who are not members of your 'family', that, too, usually affects your entitlement (see p171). The full calculation is explained on p168.

(ii)   Who you claim for

As with IS, you claim for your 'family' which consists of:

☐ you; *and*

☐ your partner (if any) who is

either   your husband or wife, if you are living together (see p229),

or   a person of the opposite sex to whom you are not married but with whom you are living together as husband and wife (see p229); *and*

☐ any children for whom you are responsible (which may include children who have left school – see p233).

Income and capital belonging to your partner are treated as yours. There are special rules for dealing with income and capital belonging to your children (see pp247 and 272).

(iii)   How to claim

You must claim in writing from your local authority (see p185). If you are claiming IS, you should have been given an HB and CCB claim form with your IS form. You should return this to the Benefits Agency who will forward it to the local authority. Otherwise get a form from the local authority. See p184 for more detailed advice about claims. A claim may be backdated up to a year in certain circumstances (see p187).

(iv)   Liability to pay rent

To get HB, you must normally be either the person who is liable to pay the rent on your home, or the partner of the person who is liable. The partner of a student excluded from benefit can be treated as liable to pay rent. Even if you are not liable but are, in practice, paying the rent, you can get HB if you are the former partner of the person who is liable, or it is considered reasonable to pay you in the circumstances (eg, if the person who is liable may be away and you have taken over responsibility for the rent in order to continue living there).[2] So, your liability to pay rent does not have to be legally binding.

Joint liability

If you are a **married or unmarried couple** (see p229) and are jointly liable for the rent, only one of you can claim HB (see p184).[3]

If you are one of two or more **single people** who jointly occupy a home and are all responsible for the rent, the rent is apportioned and you can each claim benefit for your share.[4] If only one of you is responsible for the rent, s/he will be treated as the tenant or occupier and the other as a non-dependant (see p171). In most cases, you get more benefit by arguing you are joint tenants or occupiers who can each claim benefit on her/his share of the rent.

The definition of 'unmarried couple' does not apply to lesbian or gay couples, so if you are living with someone as part of a lesbian or gay relationship you are regarded as two single people sharing accommodation.

Special circumstances

If you have already paid your **rent in advance** before claiming HB, this will *not* affect whether you will be treated as liable for that payment – even though you have already met your liability.[5]

You can still get HB if your landlord has agreed to allow you a rent-free period as compensation for you undertaking reasonable repairs or redecoration which s/he would otherwise have had to carry out. However, this will only apply where you have actually carried out the work and then only for a maximum of eight benefit weeks in respect of any one single rent-free period.[6] As you will cease to be entitled to benefit once a particular rent-free period has lasted more than eight benefit weeks, you should arrange with your landlord to schedule the work in periods of eight weeks or less separated by at least one complete benefit week where you resume paying rent.

(v) Occupying accommodation as your home

HB can only be paid for accommodation which you normally occupy as your home.[7] In most cases, this means you will not be entitled to benefit until you have actually moved in and that benefit cannot be paid on more than one home at the same time.

In deciding whether accommodation can be regarded as 'normally occupied' as your home, the local authority must take into account any other accommodation which you or your immediate family occupy both within Great Britain and abroad. Where you or your family have more than one home, benefit will only be payable on the accommodation regarded as your main home – except in certain circumstances listed below. This rule cannot be used to exclude from entitlement people who have set up home in this country but whose family, who are no longer part of their household, remain living abroad.[8]

If your family is so large that the local authority have had to house you in two separate dwellings (whether adjacent or some way apart), you are treated as occupying both as your home and will be eligible for benefit on both. [9]

Temporary absences from home

If you are temporarily absent from home (even if abroad), for instance in hospital, in prison, working away or looking for work, you can get HB for up to 52 weeks. [10] You must intend to return to your home within 52 weeks, or, in exceptional circumstances, for not substantially longer (DSS guidance suggests that this means up to 15 months). While you are away, your accommodation must not be rented to anyone else. You will not get paid once it becomes clear that you do not intend to return. In all cases, the local authority has no power to pay you benefit for more than 52 weeks absence. People in prison will need to assess when they are likely to be able to return to their home. In practice, prisoners will not serve all of their sentence. With remission most prison sentences are reduced by a third. Therefore prisoners serving 18 months or less should get HB. Prisoners with longer sentences could qualify on the basis of their earliest date of release. If you do not claim HB, you may be able to claim HB backdated to cover the period in prison (see p187). If you are in hospital and are still entitled to HB under these rules, your benefit may be reduced after six weeks in hospital (see p175).

Students and trainees

If you are either a single person or single parent who is an eligible student (see p177) or a trainee on a government training course, and living away from home during your course, you are treated as follows:
☐ If you are only liable for payments (including mortgage interest) at one address, then that is treated as the one you occupy as your home, regardless of the proportion of time you actually live there. [11]
☐ If you are liable for payments at both addresses, you are only allowed to claim for the accommodation which is your *main* home. [12]
If one member of a **couple** is an eligible student or trainee who has unavoidably to live away from home in other accommodation during study-time, the claimant is regarded as occupying both dwellings as her/his home and can claim benefit for both. [13] Note that these rules only apply where the student is not excluded from benefit because of the full-time student restriction (see p176).

Domestic violence

If you have left your previous home, and remain absent from it, through fear of violence in that home or from a former member of your family outside the home, the local authority can pay you benefit on two homes for as long as it is reasonable to do so. [14] You should argue for double payments to continue if you are responsible for making payments on both homes and intend to return to your former home at some point in the future. You only have to show you left your former home through fear of, rather than actual, violence. 'Violence' can cover any kind of violence that could take place within or at the home, even though it may originate from outside it (eg, racial violence).

Temporary accommodation during repair work

If you have had to move into temporary accommodation to enable essential repairs to be carried out on your normal home and you are liable for payments on either (but not both) dwellings, you will be treated as occupying, as your 'home', the accommodation on which you are liable to make payments. [15] If you are a private tenant you should not be liable for payments on your normal home while you are unable to live there – in which case you should only be liable (and eligible for benefit) on your temporary accommodation during this period. However, it is common practice for many local authorities not to make any charge for the temporary accommodation, but to continue to levy the rent on the home address. In this case, you will be treated as still occupying your normal home and will remain eligible for benefit in respect of it, even though you are not actually living there. In any circumstances where you do have a liability for both your normal and temporary homes, you will only be regarded as occupying (and thus eligible for benefit on) the one you normally occupy.

Moving house

If you have moved into new accommodation and have no option but to pay rent on both your old and new home, you will receive HB for both homes for up to four weeks. Under this rule, you will only get HB for the new home once you have moved in and from the date that you move in. [16] However, in certain limited circumstances you can claim HB for a period of up to four weeks before moving into a new home, although you will not be paid until after the move. [17]

To qualify for this retrospective benefit you must have:
□ moved into your new home;
□ been liable to make payments before moving in;
□ claimed benefit before moving in and either your claim was not decided until after you moved in or it was refused (because you had not yet moved in) and you made a second claim within four weeks of moving in.

Furthermore, the delay in moving in to your new home must have been reasonable and:

either a member of your family is aged five or under, or your applicable amount includes one of the pensioner or disability premiums, and your move was delayed while the Benefits Agency decided on a claim for a social fund payment for a need connected with the move (eg, removal expenses or a household item or furniture). DSS guidance suggests that the delay should not be regarded as reasonable if you are waiting for a social fund payment but could manage, in the short-term, without the items for which you are waiting; [18]

or the delay was necessary in order to adapt your new home to the disability needs of either you or a family member;

or you became liable to make payments on your new home while you were a hospital patient or in other residential accommodation.

(vi) Who cannot claim?

There are some situations in which you cannot get HB even though you satisfy other conditions such as being liable for rent, having a low income or having less than £16,000 capital. You are not entitled to HB if:

- [ ] you have more than £16,000 capital or savings;
- [ ] you are a full-time student.[19] There are some exceptions (see p177);
- [ ] you live in a local authority residential care home, or a local authority hostel where board is provided[20] with a few exceptions (see p162)
- [ ] you own your accommodation or have a lease of more than 21 years – unless you are a 'shared owner' (ie, buying part of your house or flat and renting the rest from a housing authority or association), in which case you can get HB on the part you rent.[21] You are treated as the owner of the property if you have the right to sell it – even though you may not be able to do this without the consent of other joint owners;[22]
- [ ] you pay rent to someone you live with and either it is not a commercial arrangement or s/he is a close relative.[23] A close relative is a parent, son, daughter, step-parent, step-son, step-daughter, parent-in-law, son-in-law, daughter-in-law, brother, sister, and the partner of any of these.[24] You are regarded as living with your landlord if you share some accommodation with them other than a bathroom, toilet or hall/passageway – eg, you share a living-room or kitchen. However, it is possible to argue that you do not live with your landlord unless you also share living arrangements such as cooking and financial arrangements. DSS guidance suggests that local authorities should not assume you do not have a commercial arrangement just because you pay below a market rent or because the landlord does not rent for purely financial reasons, so long as s/he covers her/his expenses;[25]
- [ ] you have made an agreement to pay rent in order to take advantage of the HB scheme. The local authority must have reason to believe that the agreement to pay rent is 'contrived'. This rule cannot be used if you have been liable to pay rent for the accommodation at any time during the eight weeks before you made the agreement;[26]
- [ ] you became a joint tenant within eight weeks of having been a non-dependant of one of the other joint tenants, unless you can satisfy the local authority that you did not do this to take advantage of the HB scheme;[27]
- [ ] you are getting income support (IS) and housing costs are included in your IS applicable amount (see p22) – eg, rent for long leaseholders, charges for people in residential care. If you are now getting your housing costs met through IS but were previously getting HB for the same accommodation, your HB continues for your first four weeks on IS. This is deducted from your IS so you do not get any extra benefit; it is merely an administrative arrangement to help with the transfer of housing costs from HB to IS;[28]
- [ ] you are a Crown Tenant – there is a separate scheme for Crown Tenants;[29]
- [ ] you make payments under a co-ownership scheme under which you will receive a payment related to the value of the accommodation when you leave;[30]
- [ ] you make payments under a hire purchase, credit sale or conditional sale agreement for, say, the purchase of a mobile home;[31]
- [ ] you are a member of, and are fully maintained by, a religious order;[32]
- [ ] you are a student from abroad present in the UK to study – with some exceptions (see p179).

If you are excluded from benefit because of any of the rules above you may be treated as a non-dependant if someone else in your household claims HB (see p171).

People from abroad

If you are someone from abroad who has been admitted to the UK on the basis that you do not have recourse to public funds (see p63) you are not specifically excluded from HB – unless you are an overseas student (see p181). However, if you do claim you could jeopardise your stay in the UK because HB counts as **public funds**. You should seek independent immigration advice before claiming HB. If you discover it is safe for you to claim you should ask for your benefit to be backdated over the period you were sorting out your status on the grounds that you have 'good cause' for a late claim (see p187).

2 'ELIGIBLE RENT'

Your 'eligible rent' is the amount of your rent or other payments which are taken into account for the purpose of calculating your HB. It may be less than the actual amount of rent that you pay because your 'eligible rent' does not include payments such as water rates, charges for fuel or certain other services, or collective community charge contributions. If your rent is considered excessive, only part of it may be considered to be eligible for HB (see p162).

(i) What counts as 'eligible rent'

For HB purposes, most payments you make for the accommodation you occupy as your home (other than water rates and mortgage payments) can count as rent. The following charges are eligible rent for HB purposes: [33]
- Rent you pay in respect of a tenancy.
- Payments you make in respect of a licence or other permission to occupy premises.
- Mesne profits (in Scotland, violent profits) which include payments made if you remain in occupation when a tenancy has been ended.
- Other payments for use and occupation of premises.
- Payments of service charges required as a condition of occupation.
- Mooring charges for a houseboat.
- Site rent for a caravan or mobile home (but not a tent although that might be met through IS – see p22).
- Your eligible rent may include rent paid on a garage or land attached to your home. Either you must be making a reasonable effort to end your liability for it, or you must have been unable to rent your home without it. [34]
- Contributions made by a resident of a charity's almshouse.
- Payments made under a rental purchase agreement under which the purchase price is paid in more than one instalment and you will not finally own your home until all, or an agreed part of, the purchase price has been paid.

☐ In Scotland, payments in respect of croft land.
Deductions are made if your rent includes a collective community charge contribution (see below), fuel (see below), and certain other services (see p160) including meals (see p161).

Payments not counted as eligible rent

☐ Most fuel charges (see below).
☐ Some service charges (see p160).
☐ Meals (see p161).
☐ High rents (see p162).
☐ Water rates.[35]
☐ If you receive IS, any payment which can be met through IS[36] (see p22).
☐ Mortgage and other payments made by an owner-occupier.[37]
☐ Payments for any part of your accommodation which is used exclusively for business purposes.[38]
☐ Payments for most people living in registered residential care and nursing homes[39] (see p162).
☐ Payments made by a Crown Tenant[40] (because there is a separate rebate scheme for Crown Tenants).
☐ Payments made under a tenancy for over 21 years[41] (unless it is a shared ownership tenancy granted by a housing association or local authority under which you buy part of your home and rent the rest).
☐ Payments under a co-ownership scheme.[42]
☐ Payments under a hire purchase, credit sale or conditional sale agreement (eg, for the purchase of a mobile home).[43]
☐ Payments for living in local authority homes for elderly people (Part III accommodation) or other local authority accommodation (eg, a mother and baby home) where board is also provided.[44]
☐ Collective community charge contribution to your landlord. You may be entitled to community charge benefit (CCB) in respect of it (see p217).
☐ Rent supplements charged to clear your rent arrears.

(ii) Fuel charges

HB will not usually be paid for fuel charges that are included as part of rent, such as for heating, lighting, hot water or cooking.[45] As a rule of thumb, if the charge is specified this amount will be deducted from your rent. If the charge is not specified, a fixed amount will be deducted. People on IS may get help if they have very high charges.

☐ **If you are not on IS, and your fuel charge is specified on your rent book or is readily identifiable from your agreement with your landlord** – the full amount of the charge will be deducted in arriving at your eligible rent.[46] Where your fuel charge is specified but the local authority considers it to be unrealistically low in relation to the fuel provided, the charge will be treated as unspecified and a flat-rate deduction made instead (see below). This will also be the case where your total fuel charge is specified but contains an unknown amount for communal areas.

If you are a council tenant, the regulations assume your fuel charges will always be specified or readily identifiable since the local authority is also your landlord. [47]

☐ **If you are on IS and you pay a fixed fuel charge** – there is a maximum permitted deduction. This is the total amount of any deductions which apply to you using the figures in (a) below plus £7.50 [48] – however many rooms you occupy. So the maximum permitted deduction in all cases where heating and hot water are supplied will be £17.15 (£8.60 + £1.05 + £7.50). For all fuel it will be £18.90 (£11.40 + £7.50). In any case where your charge is less than the maximum permitted deduction, the amount you actually pay will be deducted.

The effect of this rule is that any amount of your fuel charge above the maximum permitted deduction will be covered by HB. In practice, few people have fuel charges as high as the maximum permitted deduction and so will not get help. These rules cannot be varied if you have an inadequate 'partial' heating system which you have to supplement. In April 1993 the limit on fixed fuel deductions will be abolished altogether. The objective is to phase out all help with fuel charges.

In this context, **a fixed fuel charge** is a set amount included in your rent which does not reflect the actual amount of fuel you have used. Where you pay a regular set charge supplemented by a periodic refund or surcharge based on your actual fuel consumption, the *full amount* of your fuel charge should be deducted. [49] In practice, the majority of claimants paying fixed fuel charges will be local authority tenants living in flats on estates and in tower blocks, although it will include some private tenants (eg, in private apartment blocks), particularly housing association tenants.

☐ **If your fuel charge is not readily identifiable, regardless of whether or not you get IS** – a flat-rate deduction will be made for fuel. [50] This will also apply where your fuel charge is specified but considered unrealistically low or where it contains an unknown amount for communal areas. [51] The flat-rate fuel deductions are:

(a) **Where you and your family occupy more than one room:**

– for heating (other than hot water)	£8.60
– for hot water	£1.05
– for lighting	£0.70
– for cooking	£1.05

(b) **Where you and your family occupy one room only:**

– for heating alone, or heating combined with either hot water or lighting or both	£5.18
– for cooking	£1.05

These amounts will be added together where fuel is supplied for more than one purpose. If you are a joint tenant, all the deductions will be apportioned according to your share of the rent. [52]

Where flat-rate fuel deductions have been made in calculating your HB, the local authority must notify you about this and explain that if you can produce evidence from which the actual or approximate amount of your fuel charge can be estimated, the flat-rate deductions may be varied accordingly. [53] This applies regardless of whether you occupy more than one room, or one room only. However, there is no point in providing such evidence unless it is likely to show that your charge is less than the flat-rate deductions (eg, where you live in a small bedsit).

Guidance suggests that the lower deduction for one room only should apply where you occupy one room exclusively – even if you share other rooms (such as a bathroom or kitchen, or communal lounge in a hotel). [54] You should also argue for the lower level of deductions to be made where you are forced to live in one room because the other room(s) in your accommodation are, in practice, unfit to live in (eg, because of severe mould/dampness etc).

Fuel for communal areas

If you pay a service charge for the use of fuel in communal areas, and that charge is *separately identified* from any other charge for fuel used within your accommodation, it may be included as part of your eligible rent. [55] Communal areas include access areas like halls and passageways, but *not* rooms in common use *except* those in sheltered accommodation (eg, a shared TV lounge or dining-room etc). [56] If you pay a charge for the provision of a heating system (eg, regular boiler maintenance etc), this will also be eligible where the amount is separately identified from any other fuel charge you pay. [57]

(iii)   Service charges

Most service charges are covered by HB but only if payment is a condition of occupying the accommodation. [58]

The following services are eligible for HB:

☐   Services for the provision of adequate accommodation including general management costs, gardens, children's play areas, lifts, entry phones, communal telephone costs, portering, rubbish removal, TV and radio relay (only relay for ordinary UK channels is covered – not satellite dishes or decoders. Cable TV is also excluded unless it is the only practicable way of providing you with ordinary domestic channels). [59]

☐   Laundry facilities (eg, a laundry room in an apartment block), but not charges for the provision of personal laundry. [60]

☐   Furniture and household equipment (as provided in a furnished tenancy), but not if there is an agreement in which the furniture will eventually become your property. [61]

☐   Cleaning of communal areas. [62]

☐   Cleaning within your own accommodation, but only if no one living in the household is able to do it. [63]

☐   Emergency alarm systems in accommodation designed or adapted for elderly, sick or disabled people, or which is otherwise suitable for them taking into account factors such as size, heating system or other facilities. In all other cases, emergency alarms are ineligible. [64]

☐   Counselling and support services, but only to the extent that they are necessary for the provision of adequate accommodation or are provided personally by the landlord or a warden or caretaker whose main duty is to provide eligible services. [65]

Deductions are made for the above charges only if the local authority regards the charges as excessive, in which case the authority will make an estimate of what it considers to be a reasonable amount given the cost of comparable services.[66]

The following services are not eligible for HB:[67]
- ☐ Food including prepared meals (see below).
- ☐ Sports facilities.
- ☐ TV rental and licence fees (but TV and radio relay charges are).
- ☐ Transport.
- ☐ Personal laundry service.
- ☐ Medical expenses.
- ☐ Nursing and personal care.
- ☐ Counselling and other support services not connected to the provision of adequate accommodation.
- ☐ Any other charge not connected with the provision of adequate accommodation and not specifically included in the list of eligible charges above.

Any ineligible service charge must be deducted in full from your rent. Where the ineligible charge is specified, this amount will be deducted from eligible rent. Authorities have the power to substitute their own estimate of the ineligible charge where the amount is considered by them to be unreasonably low for the services provided.[68] (Note: Although this is the intention of the regulations, the wording does not accurately reflect this.) Where the amount has not been specified in your rent agreement, the local authority must estimate how much is fairly attributable to the service, given the cost of comparable services.[69] There are special rules relating to charges for the provision of meals.

(iv) Charges for meals

Any charges for meals (including the preparation of meals or provision of unprepared food) cannot be covered by HB.[70] Where your housing costs include an amount for board, the local authority will make set deductions in arriving at your eligible rent. These standard deductions will always apply, regardless of the actual cost of your meals.[71]

Where at least three meals a day are provided:
☐ for the claimant and for each additional member of the family aged 16 or over	£15.20
☐ for each additional member of the family aged under 16	£ 7.65

Where breakfast only is provided:
☐ for the claimant and each additional member of the family, regardless of age	£ 1.85

In all other cases (part-board):
☐ for the claimant and for each additional member of the family aged 16 or over	£10.10
☐ for each additional member of the family aged under 16	£ 5.05

Where no meals are provided within the rent for either you, or a member of your family, no meals deduction should be made for that person. Otherwise, standard deductions will be made for everyone who has meals paid for by you – including meals for someone who is not part of your 'family' (eg, a non-dependant). [72]

(v)   Registered residential care or nursing homes

Payments made for residential care and nursing homes are not eligible for HB except in limited circumstances. [73] Prior to 1 January 1991, people paying for such accommodation and unable to claim IS could get HB for the rent element of their residential costs. In most cases, these people retain their entitlement to HB, unless they claimed after 30 October 1990 (when the change was announced).

You are still entitled to HB for the rent element of charges for residential care and nursing homes if: [74]

☐   you are in full-time work (see p172); *or*

☐   you make payments to a close relative with whom you do not reside and the tenancy or other agreement is on a commercial basis (see p156); *or*

☐   you were entitled to, or became entitled to, HB before 30 October 1990 for residential accommodation; *or*

☐   you are entitled to HB for residential accommodation on or after 30 October 1990 but only if your claim for HB was made before 30 October 1990.

Unless you are in full-time work or pay rent to a close relative, your entitlement to HB will be protected even if you move to another registered home, or return to such a home after a period in ordinary accommodation. [75]

Residential care and nursing homes are those registered or mentioned under the Registered Homes Act 1984 and, in Scotland, under the Social Work Act 1968 and Nursing Homes Registration Act 1938. [76] The exclusion from HB only applies to people living in registered residential care and nursing homes. If you live in a 'small home' (less than four people) you can still claim HB as long as you are not already getting help with these costs under IS. [77]

3   'UNREASONABLY HIGH' RENTS

The local authority must consider whether or not your accommodation is too large or expensive, and if so it must reduce your eligible rent.

Local authorities are assisted in assessing rents by the local Rent Officer Service and have been encouraged to restrict rents through the central government subsidy system which penalises authorities who pay rents above certain levels. The role of the rent officer and the subsidy scheme is described in more detail on p166. In deciding on rent levels for HB purposes, the authority is not bound by the decision of a rent officer and need not take into account the implications of subsidy arrangements. The local authority cannot automatically impose a blanket 'rent stop' without considering your individual circumstances. [78] A blanket policy can be challenged by way of a judicial review in court (see p210). A large number of local authorities appear to rely on illegal 'rent stops', rather than on a proper application of the law.

If the local authority decides to impose a rent restriction in your case, you should insist on a full explanation which gives you not only the reasons why this has been done, but also all the factors and evidence which the local authority took into account in arriving at that decision. If you suspect that the local authority has either failed to apply all the proper tests or has allowed itself to be influenced by irrelevant factors – such as administrative convenience – you should ask for a review (see p206). Advisers with evidence of persistent abuse by their local authorities should write to CPAG's Citizens' Rights Office for advice on further action.

The various steps which all local authorities must take in every case are set out in the following paragraphs.

(i) Is your accommodation unsuitable?

The local authority can only consider your accommodation unsuitable if either of the following apply:[79]

☐ it is larger than is reasonably needed for you and anyone who also occupies the accommodation (including non-dependants and sub-tenants) – taking into account the sort of accommodation occupied by other households of the same size; *or*

☐ your rent is unreasonably high compared with that for suitable alternative accommodation elsewhere.

The local authority can take account of any assessment made by a rent officer (see p166).

Is it too large?

The needs of everyone living in your accommodation must be considered. For example, if anyone needs additional space (eg, because of a disability), this should be taken into account. If you have a child in care, or an elderly or disabled relative who normally lives in a residential home but who regularly comes to stay with you, it is reasonable that you should have a spare room for this purpose. You should also argue that it is reasonable to remain in a home where you have lived for many years but which is now larger than you need because you are widowed, separated or divorced, or because your children have now grown up and live away.

Is it too expensive?

It is not sufficient for the local authority just to show that cheaper alternative accommodation exists. It must be regarded as 'suitable' for you personally.[80] If you currently have security of tenure, any suitable alternative accommodation should offer you a reasonably equivalent degree of security. The local authority must also bear in mind your age and state of health, and that of your family or relatives described under (iii) below.

Guidance suggests that your housing costs should only be compared with accommodation outside the local authority's own area if no valid comparisons exist locally. Local authorities should not 'make comparisons with other parts of the country where accommodation costs differ widely from those which apply locally'.[81]

Finally, it is not enough for the local authority to show that your rent is merely higher than that for suitable alternative accommodation. It must be 'unreasonably' higher. This means your rent must be shown to be more than might reasonably be expected for your dwelling in comparison with the alternative accommodation. In making this comparison, the local authority must consider the full spectrum of rents which could be paid for such accommodation and not just the cheapest.[82] Providing your rent falls somewhere within the band of rents one could reasonably expect to pay for such alternative accommodation, no restriction should be made – even though some cheaper accommodation may exist at the lower end of this rent band.

(ii) What are the personal circumstances of your household?

If the local authority has decided that your accommodation is unsuitable under (i), it must then consider the personal circumstances of your family and relatives living in your accommodation before deciding whether or not to restrict your eligible rent.[83]

Your family and relatives include:
☐ the claimant and any partner (see p229);
☐ any child or young person (see p233);
☐ any relative of the claimant or partner (including non-dependants, sub-tenants and joint occupiers), who have no separate right to occupy the accommodation.[84] Your relatives are a parent/son/daughter, step-parent/son/daughter, parent/son/daughter-in-law, brother or sister; or a partner of any of these people; or a grandparent, uncle, aunt, nephew or niece.[85]

If you or any of the above people living with you:
☐ are aged 60 or over; *or*
☐ satisfy any of the tests of being incapable of work for social security purposes (see p240); *or*
☐ have a child or young person living with you for whom you are responsible (see p233),
– the local authority must consider whether cheaper suitable alternative accommodation is actually available to you and whether it is reasonable to expect you to move (see below).

(iii) Is it reasonable to expect you to move to a cheaper alternative?

There are two separate tests involved.

Is there cheaper suitable alternative accommodation?

If a local authority considers that suitable alternative accommodation is available, it must identify the specific accommodation it has in mind and show that it is actually available to you and those who live with you. [86] In addition, the DSS guidance states quite clearly that 'authorities should regard accommodation as not available if, in practice, there is little or no possibility of the claimant being able to obtain it – eg, because it could only be obtained on payment of a large deposit'. [87] This means that it is not enough for the local authority to reach a conclusion on this issue based only on general evidence of the state of the local housing market and the likely chance of someone in your circumstances being able to obtain something suitable. You should insist on being told exactly what accommodation is being referred to, why it is considered 'suitable' for you and those who live with you, and on what evidence it is considered to actually be available to you. Where the local authority is unable to provide a satisfactory reply to any of these questions you should ask for a review (see p206).

Is it reasonable to expect you to move?

The regulations compel local authorities to consider the adverse effects of a move on your job and on the education of any child or young person living with you. [88] The authority can also take account of any other relevant factors which could have a bearing on whether or not such a move could be considered reasonable in your case. For example, you should press the local authority to consider the impact of a move on any of the following:
- [ ] if you are unemployed, your chances of getting a job;
- [ ] if you are a single parent, your access to family support and adequate childcare facilities;
- [ ] the care and support you give to an elderly or disabled friend or relative who does not live in your accommodation but who lives nearby;
- [ ] the effect on your health of the move;
- [ ] the increased likelihood that you will suffer domestic or racial violence if you move into the area where the alternative accommodation is situated;
- [ ] your finances, if you are in debt and cannot afford the cost of moving home;
- [ ] if you require special medical treatment or counselling, your access to the facilities you need.

It must be reasonable to expect you to move.

If the local authority refuses to consider any relevant factor which you bring to its attention, you should request a review (see p206).

If the local authority finally considers that suitable cheaper alternative accommodation does not exist or, where it does exist, it is not reasonable to expect you to move – your HB entitlement will be based on your *full* eligible rent.

(iv)   The amount of the eligible rent restriction

If you cannot satisfy the tests set out in (i) to (iii) above, the local authority must restrict your eligible rent to whatever amount it considers appropriate. However, the local authority must consider your individual circumstances and have regard to the cost of suitable alternative accommodation elsewhere. The reduction cannot reduce the eligible rent below that payable for suitable alternative accommodation. [89]

No restriction can be made within 12 months of the death of anyone who used to live in your accommodation and whose circumstances would have been taken into account in deciding whether or not to impose a restriction[90] (see p164). Also, if you or someone else in your household were able to meet your housing costs when you first moved in, no restriction will be made for the first 13 weeks of your benefit period[91] unless you were previously receiving HB within 52 weeks of the beginning of your current benefit period[92].

(v) The role of the rent officer and subsidies

Local authorities get a reduced subsidy from central government where HB is paid for rents above a fixed threshold, set by the Secretary of State, for each area. They also get a reduced subsidy on individual claims for private rents if the rent officer decides that the accommodation occupied is either too large for the claimant's reasonable needs or above a reasonable market rent. Where this happens, full subsidy will only be calculated on the basis of the lower rent figure considered by the rent officer to be reasonable in that particular case.[93]

To assess the market rate for subsidy purposes, the local authority will refer your case to the rent officer if you live in private accommodation and have a deregulated tenancy, licence or other agreement (including where you are a boarder). As a rule of thumb, this will probably apply to you if your tenancy etc was either created or renewed on or after 2 January 1989 in Scotland, or 15 January 1989 in England and Wales. In some cases, it will be necessary for the rent officer to visit you at home. While the rent officer has no right to demand entry into your home, if you refuse to co-operate with her/him the local authority can withhold your HB.[94]

The local authority cannot decide to restrict your eligible rent simply because the rent officer has decided that your rent is higher than what they consider is a market rent, or because reduced subsidy is payable in your case.[95] However, where the rent officer decides that your accommodation is either too large or expensive, the local authority can take the rent officer's view of these matters into account when assessing your eligible rent (see (i) to (iv) above). But the local authority is not bound by the rent officer's assessment. It can still pay HB on your full rent if it considers that your rent is not unreasonable or you are protected by the legislation, despite the rent officer's decision and the subsidy implications.

The authority must consider your case individually against the steps described above. In particular, the criteria that the authority must consider in assessing unreasonably high rents and suitable alternative accommodation is quite different from that adopted by the rent officer in deciding market rents. Decisions by the rent officer can be, therefore, only one source of information used by an authority to assess eligible rents under HB legislation. If an authority automatically imposes a restriction based solely on the rent officer's decision you should insist on a review (see p206).

(vi) Unreasonable rent increases

The starting point in the calculation of your rent rebate or allowance is 100 per cent of your eligible rent. Any increase in your rent will be reflected by a corresponding increase in your HB. However, the local authority has the power not to meet the full amount of a rent increase in your benefit if it thinks that:

☐ the increase is unreasonably high compared with the increases in suitable alternative accommodation;

□   the increase is unreasonable because a previous increase has occurred within the
preceding 12 months. [96]

Where the local authority considers a rent increase to have been unreasonable, it
may either refuse to meet all of that increase or only so much of it as it considers
appropriate in the circumstances. However, if your rent has been increased for the
second time in under 12 months but is still below the market level, or the increase
reflects improvements made to your accommodation, you should press for the full
amount to be allowed. [97] If the local authority refuses, you should ask for a review
(see p206).

Chapter 12

The amount of benefit

This chapter covers:

1   THE BASIC CALCULATION

(i)   How your benefit is worked out

This depends on:

☐   your 'applicable amount' – which represents your family's needs (see p236);
☐   your 'eligible rent' (see p157);
☐   whether any deductions are to be made for non-dependants who live in your home (see p171);
☐   your income (see p246).

Remember that no benefit is paid if your capital is over £16,000.

The most HB you can get is called your '**maximum housing benefit**'. This is your 'eligible rent' less any deductions for non-dependants.[1] In some exceptional cases you can get extra HB (see p174).

You are entitled to your maximum housing benefit if:

either   you are entitled to IS;
or   your income is the same as or less than your applicable amount (including no income at all).[2]

Because entitlement to IS acts as an automatic passport to maximum HB (once you have made a claim for HB), you and the local authority do not need to work out applicable amounts, income or capital. However, if you are not on IS, you do need to work them out (see below).

If your income is higher than your applicable amount, your HB is equal to your maximum HB *less* 65 per cent of the difference between your income and your applicable amount.[3]

No HB is payable if the amount would be less than 50 pence a week.[4]

A local authority may round any figure used in working out your entitlement to the nearest penny (with fractions of half a penny being rounded upwards).

The steps below will help you to calculate HB.

If you are on income support

Step 1 Work out your **weekly eligible rent** (see p157).
Step 2 Work out whether there should be any **non-dependant deductions** from your rent (see p171).
Step 3 Work out your **maximum HB** which is your eligible rent, *less* any non-dependant rent deduction.

The result in Step 3 is the amount of HB to which you are entitled.

If you are not on income support

Step 1 Work out your **capital** (see pp272-84). If you have more than £16,000 capital, you do not need to continue as you will *not* be entitled to any benefit.[5] If you have capital between £3,000 and £16,000, remember this will give you an assumed tariff income which will need to be included in Step 5 (see p266).
Step 2 Work out your weekly **eligible rent** (see p157).
Step 3 Work out whether there should be any **non-dependant deductions** from your rent (see p171).
Step 4 Work out your **maximum HB** which is your eligible rent, *less* any non-dependant deductions.
Step 5 – Work out your applicable amount (see pp236-45).
　　　　　– Work out your income (see pp246-71).
　　　　　– Compare your income with your applicable amount. *If your income is equal to, or less than, your applicable amount,* you are entitled to your maximum HB worked out in Step 4.[6] *If your income is more than your applicable amount,* work out the difference and carry on to Step 6.
Step 6 Work out your HB which is your maximum HB (worked out in Step 4) *less* 65 per cent of the difference between your income and applicable amount.

The percentage of 65 is known as a 'taper' because it determines the rate at which your HB is reduced (or tapers off) as your income rises above your applicable amount.[7] In practice, this means a reduction of 65 pence in your maximum HB for every pound of extra income.

Example 1
Mr and Mrs Finestein and their adult son live together in a flat. Mrs Finestein is the sole tenant and pays rent of £65 per week, which includes all their fuel. Mr Finestein receives IS for himself and his wife while they are looking for work. Their son earns £100 per week. Mr Finestein claims HB.

His eligible rent is £53.60 per week (ie, £65 – £11.40 deducted because of the fuel charges – see p159).

His son counts as a non-dependant and the appropriate deduction for him is £12.00 per week (see p172).

Therefore, his maximum HB is £41.60 per week (£53.60 – £12.00).

Because he receives IS, his HB is £41.60 per week. The amount is lower than his actual rent because his fuel charge is not covered by HB and because his son is expected to make a contribution to the rent.

Example 2
Mrs Finestein then finds a job for which she is paid £120 per week after deductions of tax and National Insurance contributions. There is no occupational pension scheme. Her husband ceases to be entitled to IS because of her earnings and he makes a new claim for HB.
  Mr Finestein's maximum HB is still £41.60 per week.
  His applicable amount is £66.60 (the standard rate for a couple – see p237).
  His income is £110 per week (because £10 of his wife's earnings is disregarded – see p256).
  The difference between his income and his applicable amount is therefore £43.40 per week.
  65 per cent of £43.40 per week is £28.21 per week.
  Mr Finestein's HB is therefore £41.60 – £28.21 = £13.39 per week.

(ii) Calculating a weekly amount of HB

Entitlement to HB is always paid for a specific benefit week, a period of seven consecutive days beginning with a Monday and ending on a Sunday.[8] So if you pay rent at different intervals (eg, monthly) the amount has to be converted to a weekly figure before the benefit can be calculated.[9]
  If your rent is paid in a multiple of weeks (eg, four-weekly), you simply divide the rent figure by the number of weeks it covers.[10]
  If the rent period is not a whole number of weeks, you divide the figure by the number of days in the period. This 'daily rent' is then multiplied by seven to give the equivalent weekly figure to be used in the calculation.[11]

Rent-free periods

If you have a regular rent-free period (eg, you pay rent on a 48-week rent year) you will get no benefit during your rent-free period, but instead slightly more benefit during the weeks you pay rent. This is achieved by adjusting all the relevant figures used so that they relate to the same period as your rent. The relevant figures are your applicable amount, your weekly income, non-dependant deductions, the set deductions for meals and fuel charges and the minimum amount payable.[12] The rules for doing this are as follows:
☐ **Where your rent is paid weekly or in a whole multiple of weeks**, you should multiply the figures to be converted by 52 (or 53 as appropriate) to give the annual amounts. These should then be divided by the number of weeks in the year in which you actually pay rent to give the converted amounts for use in the calculation. So, for a 48-week rent year, all the figures would need to be multiplied by 52 and the result divided by 48.[13]
☐ **Where your rent is paid on some other basis**, you should multiply all the

figures to be converted by 365 (or 366 as appropriate) and divide the result by the number of days in the rent year for which rent is actually payable. So, if you pay rent every calendar month except December (31 days), all the figures would need to be multiplied by 365 and the result divided by 334 (365 – 31). [14]
The intention is that the total amount of benefit you receive over the whole year should be the same as if your annual rent had been spread equally without any rent-free period. If your landlord has temporarily waived the rent in return for you doing repairs, see p153.

2 DEDUCTIONS FOR NON-DEPENDANTS

A deduction may be made from your HB where you live with someone who is not part of your family. [15] These people are called 'non-dependants'. The idea is that they must contribute towards the costs of the accommodation.

(i) Who is a non-dependant

A non-dependant is someone who normally lives in your household such as an adult son/daughter or other relative. If someone pays you to live in part of your accommodation s/he is not a non-dependant but a tenant, sub-tenant or boarder – unless s/he does not count as paying rent under the HB rules, in which case s/he is counted as a non-dependant – eg, someone paying rent to a close relative (see p156).

The definition of non-dependant is a negative one in that it includes everyone who 'resides' with you who does not fit into some other category. **The following people living with you will not be counted as non-dependants** in your benefit assessment: [16]

☐ any member of your 'family' (see p152);
☐ any child or young person who lives with you but who does not count as a member of your 'household' (eg, a foster child – see p233);
☐ anyone who jointly occupies your accommodation and shares liability for 'payments in respect of occupation' – eg, a joint tenant. The intention of this rule is to restrict the definition of a 'joint occupier' to people who share liability for mortgage or rent payments. However, the wording leaves open the possibility that 'payments in respect of occupation' could include joint responsibility for payments such as fuel costs and water rates;
☐ anyone who occupies part of your dwelling who is your tenant/sub-tenant, boarder or your landlord and their family;
☐ any carer engaged by a charitable or voluntary body to live in your home and look after you or your partner – but only where a charge is made for doing so.
A non-dependant will only be regarded as 'residing' with you if s/he is not separately liable for her/his own housing costs to the landlord and s/he shares some accommodation with you apart from a bathroom, lavatory, or a communal area such as a hall, passageway or a room in common use in sheltered accommodation. [17] For example, where part of your home has been converted to include a self-contained 'granny-flat', the person occupying it would not be a non-dependant even though s/he shares your bathroom and toilet. On the other hand, a grown-up son or daughter who lives in your home and shares the use of the kitchen as well as the bathroom and

toilet would be classed as your non-dependant – even though they may have another room to themselves. However, it is possible to argue that a person cannot be considered to be 'residing with' you unless s/he also shares living arrangements, such as cooking and paying the bills, as well as accommodation. Before advancing this argument it is important to check that you will be better off, because income from non-dependants is ignored but income from other people may be taken into account (see p265).

(ii)   Deductions from your eligible rent

When no deduction is made

☐   No non-dependant deductions are made if either you or your partner are registered blind or have regained your eyesight within the last 28 weeks; or receive attendance allowance, or the care component of the disability living allowance. This is regardless of the number of non-dependants or their circumstances. [18]

☐   No deduction is made in respect of any non-dependant who is: [19]
   – currently staying in your household but whose normal home is elsewhere;
   – receiving Youth Training allowance;
   – a full-time student. This only applies during the period of study (which includes the short vacations) and also during the summer vacation unless the student is in full-time work;
   – in hospital for more than six weeks;
   – in prison;
   – under 18 years old; [20]
   – aged under 25 and receiving IS. [21]

The amount of deductions

Unless you or your non-dependant(s) are exempt, a deduction will be made from your eligible rent for *every* non-dependant living in your household (except in the case of a couple – see below).
   The non-dependant deductions are as follows: [22]

Circumstances of the non-dependant	*Deduction*
Aged 18 or over and in full-time work with a weekly gross income of	
£65-£99.99	£ 8.00
£100-£129.99	£12.00
£130 or more	£18.00
Aged 25 or over on IS	£ 4.00
All others aged 18 or over (including those in part-time work, on	
pensions or other benefits but excluding those on IS between 18-24)	£ 4.00

Full-time work is paid employment of 16 hours or more each week. [23] In estimating the number of hours worked, any recognised holidays or leave will be ignored. The local authority will also ignore any absences from work which, in its opinion, are without good cause [24] (this will probably include days lost through strikes and lay-offs). Where the number of hours worked fluctuates, the average will be taken. [25] However, where a person is on IS for more than three days in any benefit week, they will not be treated as being in full-time work for that week. [26]

Generally, non-dependants involved in Employment Training will not be regarded as being in full-time work. [27]

DSS guidance suggests that a non-dependant on extended sick leave and getting statutory sick pay or on maternity leave and getting statutory maternity pay should not be counted as being in full-time work – ie, the lower deduction should apply, even if the employer is making up the non-dependant's full wages. [28]

The earnings amounts are gross figures (ie, in the case of wages it is the amount before tax and National Insurance are deducted). They relate to the total income of the non-dependant, apart from attendance allowance and disability living allowance, and not just income from employment. For example, where the non-dependant is a working single parent, any child benefit or maintenance received would be taken into account along with wages. In the case of a non-dependant couple, their joint income will count.

The earnings bands only apply to non-dependants in full-time work. A non-dependant who works less than 16 hours will not attract the higher levels of rent deduction even if their weekly gross income exceeds £65.

The DSS guidance stresses that local authorities are not expected to investigate the income of non-dependants in every case. [29]

Non-dependant couples

Only one deduction is made for a married or unmarried couple (or the members of a polygamous marriage) who are non-dependants. Where the individual circumstances of each partner are different, the highest deduction is made. [30]

Non-dependants of joint occupiers

Where joint occupiers share a non-dependant, the deduction is divided between them. This should be done taking into account the number of joint occupiers and the proportion of housing costs paid by each one. But no apportionment should be made between the members of a couple. [31]

(iii)   Capital and income of a non-dependant

Normally, the capital and income of any non-dependant living in your household is completely ignored when assessing your HB entitlement [32] (except for deciding which non-dependant deduction applies). However, if

☐   you are not on IS, *and*
☐   the capital and income of the non-dependant are both greater than yours, *and*
☐   the local authority is satisfied you have made an arrangement with the non-dependant to take advantage of the HB scheme,

your benefit entitlement is assessed on the basis of the non-dependant's capital and income rather than your own. [33] Any capital and income normally treated as belonging to you is completely ignored (but the rest of the calculation proceeds as normal – ie, the non-dependant deduction is based on the non-dependant's circumstances and the applicable amount will depend on the circumstances of you and your family). [34]

This would apply, for example, where a tenancy has been transferred to another household member with lower capital and income in order to qualify for, or increase the amount of, HB. In such cases, the local authority must notify both the claimant and non-dependant of what action it has taken and why, and must advise them of their right to ask for further information and a review of the decision.[35]

3 EXTRA BENEFIT IN EXCEPTIONAL CIRCUMSTANCES

If the local authority considers your circumstances to be 'exceptional', it can pay you extra HB over and above your normal entitlement.[36] The meaning of the term exceptional circumstances is not defined and it is for local authorities to decide how to use their discretion in any individual case. You should argue for this to be used wherever hardship would otherwise arise. Examples are where you have additional expenses due to disability but do not meet the strict criteria for a disability premium; where you are in serious financial difficulties because some unexpected event has led to a dramatic drop in your income, such as a family bereavement, illness or redundancy; where there is some temporary increase in your commitments, such as removal expenses and deposits etc on moving home; where you are threatened with eviction or fuel disconnection because of arrears.

The DSS guidance emphasises the individual nature of the power and suggests that it should not be used to pay extra benefit to whole groups on the basis of predefined conditions. In any case where additional benefit is paid, it can either be paid on a weekly basis for as long as the exceptional circumstances warrant it, or can be made as a 'one-off award'.[37]

You are unlikely to be considered for any additional benefit unless you specifically ask for it. Make sure you give clear reasons why you need the additional help. The local authority must consider your request on the merits of your individual case. If you are refused additional benefit, you should ask for a review.

The overall limit is your eligible rent[38] (see p157). This means additional benefit can compensate for any non-dependant deductions and the effect of the taper. If you need a lump sum you can ask for your additional benefit to be backdated or paid in advance. The local authority cannot use this power unless you are entitled to receive HB during the period of payment of the extra benefit. The power can only be used to pay benefit in addition to, and not as a substitute for, normal entitlement.[39]

The local authority also has the power to pay extra benefit to people getting either a war disablement pension or a war widow's pension including similar pensions paid by non-UK governments, by ignoring this as income in the HB calculation.[40] If the authority uses this power it must apply the income disregard to all people in receipt of these benefits. This arrangement is usually called a 'local scheme' because the authority must pay for the extra benefit. The authority also has to pay for extra benefit paid to individuals because of exceptional circumstances. The amount they can pay under both conditions is limited.[41]

4 PEOPLE IN HOSPITAL

If you or your partner go into hospital your HB is affected as follows:
☐ **up to six weeks** – there is no change to your HB;
☐ **after six weeks** – benefit is reduced for adults in hospital (see below);
☐ **after 52 weeks** – no HB is paid.
If you get IS the six-week rule does not apply to HB (but may to your IS) and your HB will be paid in full for up to 52 weeks, as long as you intend to return home within the year, or not much more than a year[42] (see p154).

After six weeks in hospital

If you are on IS these rules do not apply and your HB will be paid as normal. If you are not on IS, after six weeks your applicable amount (see p236) will be reduced as follows:
☐ **Single claimant** – Your applicable amount will be reduced to £13.55 personal allowance.[43]
☐ **Single parent** – Your applicable amount will be reduced to £13.55 personal allowance *plus* your children's personal allowances, *plus* the family, lone parent and disabled child premiums.[44]
☐ **Couple with one adult in hospital** – Your applicable amounts will be reduced by £10.85 (this also applies if you are both in hospital but only one of you has been there for over six weeks).[45]
☐ **Couple with both adults in hospital** – Your applicable amounts will be reduced to £27.10 personal allowance for you both, *plus* personal allowances for your children, if any, *plus* family and disabled child premiums, if any.[46]
☐ **Premiums** – Your applicable amount continues to include family, lone parent and disabled child premiums for up to 52 weeks, when HB will stop altogether – so long as your children continue to be treated as members of your family (see p233). The remaining premiums (pensioner and disability premiums) will stop after six weeks in hospital, unless you are a couple and one of you is at home or has not yet been in hospital for more than six weeks (see above).
The six weeks are calculated by adding together any separate stays in hospital less than 28 weeks apart. The reduction takes effect from the beginning of the benefit week (see p191) *after* you have been in hospital for six weeks.
There are no reductions to your benefit if a dependent child goes into hospital.

5 TRANSITIONAL PAYMENTS

In April 1988, HB was changed. Some people who were worse off under the new scheme were made payments to compensate for their losses.
For more information, see the 19th edition of the *Handbook*, p209.

Chapter 13

Special rules for students

This chapter covers:

1 General rules (below)
2 Students who are eligible (p177)
3 Students who are ineligible (p178)
4 Students from overseas (p179)
5 Calculating students' benefit (p182)
6 Payments (p183)

Most full-time students cannot claim housing benefit (HB) during their course, including the summer vacations falling within it. However, there are some exceptions to this rule (see p177). Students who remain eligible for HB are subject to additional rules. There are special rules for the treatment of students' income, including grants and top-up loans (see p183). For the position of students claiming CCB, see Chapter 15.

1 GENERAL RULES

(i) Who counts as a student

A **student** is someone attending a course of study at an educational establishment.[1] This covers any full-time, part-time or sandwich course, either advanced or non-advanced, whether or not you get a grant for attending it. The term educational establishment is not defined in law, but DSS guidance to local authorities suggests it should include private as well as state-funded institutions. Once you have started on your course you will, for HB purposes, be treated as a student attending a course throughout all your term and vacation periods, until you leave the course. If your course is part of an employment training programme you do not count as a student.

(ii) Full-time students

The law does not define 'full-time student', except to say that it includes someone on a sandwich course.[2] The local authority is expected to decide by looking at the nature of the course you are attending and, if in doubt, by consulting the educational establishment involved. Local authorities are advised that student grants are normally only payable for full-time courses. If you get a grant, and especially if the level of your grant seems appropriate to a full-time course, the local authority will probably decide to treat you as a full-time student.[3] If you disagree with a decision made by the local authority, you should request a review (see p206).

(iii) The period of study

If you are eligible, your entitlement in any week will depend on whether that week falls either inside or outside a period of study. Your period of study will be either:

(a) where your course is for one year or less – the period from the first to the last day of the course;

(b) where your course is for more than one year and a grant is paid, or would be paid, on the basis of you studying throughout the year (as in many post-graduate courses) – the period from the first day of the course until the last day of the course;

(c) in any other case (ie, in most cases), where your course is for more than one year – from the first day of each academic year until the day before the start of the recognised summer vacation.[4] In the final year the period of study ends with the last day of your final academic term.

In deciding whether or not your grant has been assessed on the basis of you studying throughout the whole year (as in (b) above), the local authority should ignore supplements to your grant (eg, dependant's allowances) which are paid for the full year, regardless of the length of the course.

Your period of study includes Christmas and Easter vacations and periods of practical experience outside the educational establishment for students on sandwich courses.[5]

2 STUDENTS WHO ARE ELIGIBLE

(i) Full-time students

There are a number of exceptions to the general rule that full-time students are not entitled to HB. You can claim HB as a full-time student if:[6]

☐ you are on IS;

☐ you are under 19 and not following a course of higher education. Higher education includes degree courses, teachers' training, HND, HNC, post-graduate courses;

☐ you and your partner are both full-time students and have dependent children;

☐ you are a lone parent who satisfies the conditions for a lone parent premium;

☐ you are a lone foster parent where the child has been formally placed with you by a local authority or voluntary agency;

☐ you have a disability and:

– meet the conditions for either the disability or severe disability premium, *or*

– were getting IS immediately before 1 September 1990 as a disabled student on the grounds that you would be unable to get a job within a reasonable period of time compared to other students, *or*

– claimed HB/IS after 1 September 1990 and for any period in the 18 months before you claimed HB/IS, were getting IS as a disabled student in both advanced or non-advanced education, *or*

– satisfy the conditions for a grant supplement in the form of a disabled student's allowance award because of deafness;

☐ you are a pensioner who satisfies the conditions for one of the pensioner premiums.

Full-time students who can claim HB will be subject to the special rules described in this chapter.

(ii)   Partners of ineligible students

Partners who are not themselves ineligible as students can claim HB.[7] Where a partner makes a claim, her/his benefit will be calculated according to the normal rules (ie, based on a couple's applicable amount and joint income/capital), except that the special rules for calculating a student's income (see p183) and for calculating eligible rent (see p182) will be applied.

(iii)   Part-time students

Part-time students can claim HB (see below).

3   STUDENTS WHO ARE INELIGIBLE

(i)   Full-time students

You cannot get HB for the duration of the whole of your course (including vacations) if you are a full-time student (but for exceptions, see p177).[8] Note that a different rule applies for CCB purposes (see p224). If you have a partner who is not a full-time student s/he may be able to get HB (see above). Part-time students can still claim HB.

(ii)   Being away from your accommodation

If you are a **full-time student** (see p176) who is eligible for HB and you are absent from your accommodation for the whole of any benefit week outside your period of study, you will still not be entitled to HB for your rent for that week unless:[9]

☐ your main purpose in occupying your accommodation is not because it makes it easier for you to attend your course – eg, it is where you normally live; *or*

☐ you have had to go into hospital for treatment – except where you would have been absent anyway, for some other reason.

Full-time students are affected by this during the long summer vacation. But it only applies where it is the *claimant* who is a full-time student. If you are claiming HB, and you are the partner of a full-time student, this restriction will not apply unless you are also a full-time student.[10] Thus, if you are not a full-time student you should ask the local authority to treat you as the claimant instead (see p184). Where this restriction does not apply, any temporary absences will be dealt with under the normal rules as for other claimants (see p154).[11]

(iii) Accommodation rented from an educational establishment

If you rent your accommodation from your educational establishment (ie, you live in a hall of residence), *regardless of whether you are a full-time student or not*, you will not be eligible to claim HB during your period of study (see p177). [12]

However, this only applies where you pay rent to the same educational establishment as the one you attend for your studies. It will not apply where your educational establishment itself rents the accommodation from a third party, unless this is on a long lease or where the third party is an education authority providing the accommodation as part of its functions. [13] So you will be eligible for benefit where your educational establishment has temporarily leased accommodation from a private landlord, housing association or housing authority and sub-lets it to students.

However, the local authority can still apply this rule if it decides that your educational establishment has arranged for your accommodation to be provided by a person or body other than itself in order to take advantage of the HB scheme. [14]

If you and your partner jointly occupy accommodation rented from your educational establishment, and your partner is not a student, the restriction which would have been applied to you will also apply to her/him if s/he is the claimant. [15]

Regardless of any restrictions which may apply during your period of study, you will be able to claim a rent allowance if you continue to rent your accommodation from your educational establishment outside that period. [16]

(iv) Living in different accommodation during term-time

The rules about claiming HB for two homes are explained on p154.

If you are a member of a couple and receive HB for two homes, the assessment of benefit for each home is based on your joint income, your couple's applicable amount and, in both cases, the rent deduction (see p182) and corresponding income 'disregard' (see p183) is applied.

4 STUDENTS FROM OVERSEAS

Some overseas students cannot claim HB. Under the immigration rules, students from abroad are frequently admitted into the UK on the basis that they must be able to support themselves and pay their accommodation costs 'without recourse to public funds' (see p63). A successful claim for HB could affect your right to stay in this country and it is best to get immigration advice before making a claim.

(i) Eligible overseas students

If you are a student from abroad in the UK for the purpose of study, you can get HB if:
- [ ] you are entitled to IS (see p63); [17]
- [ ] you have the right of abode in the UK or leave to stay here indefinitely. This

includes all British citizens and Eire nationals and anyone else who has been granted the right of abode or indefinite leave. Many people from Commonwealth countries are British nationals but not British citizens and do not automatically have the right of abode in the UK (eg, British Overseas citizens, British Dependant Territories citizens or British subjects);[18]

☐ you are an EC national (ie, from Belgium, Denmark, Eire, Germany, France, Greece, Italy, Luxemburg, the Netherlands, Spain and Portugal) or a national of Iceland, Malta, Norway, Sweden and Turkey;

☐ you do not come into any of the above categories but you have been granted leave to enter the UK without the restriction that you must not have recourse to public funds. This could apply, for example, if you have been granted refugee status or political asylum.

If you are present in the UK for a reason other than attending a course of education you will also be able to claim HB, even if you are a student. For example, if you come to the UK in order to join a partner or visit a relative and are studying.[19]

If you think you may be entitled to HB under the above rules, there are a number of points you should bear in mind both before and during your claim:

☐ If you are a British national and either you are unsure of whether or not you are also a British citizen or whether you have the right of abode in the UK, it may be wise to get independent advice about your status before making a claim for HB (see p63).

☐ If you are a student from the EC (or Iceland, Malta, Norway, Sweden or Turkey), your claim may result in a letter from the local authority telling you that receiving HB could affect your right to stay in the UK. However, if you are a student from one of these countries you have a legal right to claim HB – even if your entry has been made subject to the 'no recourse to public funds' condition. The local authority has no need to ask you about any restrictions on your stay in the UK in order to determine your entitlement to benefit. All that needs to be confirmed is your nationality and if this can be done without directly involving the immigration authorities you should have no problem. In any event, powers to refuse admission to the UK, or to deport, are very limited as far as anyone from one of the EC countries is concerned. If you are at all anxious, you should get *independent* advice (see p63).

☐ The local authority may advise you that, if you are uncertain about your status in the UK (particularly regarding the 'no recourse to public funds' restriction), you should check with the immigration authorities.[20] Any overseas student in doubt about her/his immigration status or entitlement to HB or having problems with a claim, should *always seek independent advice* first (see p63).

☐ If you are an eligible overseas student but you have delayed making a claim for HB while you were confirming your status in the UK, you should ask the local authority to backdate your application because you have 'good cause' for making a late claim. You can also argue 'good cause' if you have recently arrived in the UK and you did not know about your possible entitlement to benefit because you were unfamiliar with the British social security system (see p187).

(ii) Ineligible overseas students

If you are here as a student *and* have limited leave *and* cannot have recourse to public funds, you are not entitled to claim HB unless you come into one of the above categories (p179). Nor will you be entitled to claim if you have stayed beyond your period of leave, or are subject to a deportation order, or have been judged by the immigration authorities to be an illegal entrant into the UK. If you are not entitled, this will apply regardless of whether or not you are, for the time being, actually studying.[21]

If you are unsure of your immigration status and, hence, your right to claim HB, *try and get independent advice* (see p63). Where you subsequently discover you are entitled to claim, ask for your claim to be backdated (see above).

(iii) Partners of ineligible overseas students

Where you are not eligible, but there are no restrictions on your partner, s/he may be able to claim.[22] However, the local authority may tell your partner that if s/he receives HB this may affect your right to remain in the UK under the 'no recourse to public funds' rule.[23] This is because under the normal method of assessment for couples, a claim by one partner is a claim for both.

If an overseas student's partner makes a claim on behalf of the couple, there is absolutely no need for the local authority to concern itself with the student's immigration status since this is not relevant to the partner's right to claim benefit under the HB regulations. As the immigration authorities do not need to be involved in the assessment of the claim, it is unlikely they would find out about it anyway – unless, for some reason, the local authority makes a special point of giving them the information (see below).

(iv) Contact between the Home Office and local authorities

Local authorities are advised that it should be possible to identify most of the overseas students who are eligible for HB by including appropriate questions on the HB claim form.[24] They should only need confirmation of immigration status in cases where information provided by the student raises doubts about her/his eligibility which cannot be resolved in any other way. Students should not, therefore, be asked to produce their passports as a matter of course.[25] However, if such a doubt about your entitlement does arise, local authorities are advised to ask you to produce your passport or get a letter from the immigration authorities giving details of your immigration status.[26]

Local authorities are advised that they should not normally need to contact the immigration authorities.[27] The model leaflet which the DSS suggests local authorities should use states quite clearly: 'The information you give will be treated as confidential and not used for any purpose other than in connection with your claim for housing benefit.'[28] However, this may not always be true. DSS guidance also advises local authorities that it might be 'appropriate' to give out certain confidential information to other authorities without the claimant's agreement (eg, to a government department to safeguard public funds).[29] This would clearly apply to giving information to the Home Office. However, some local authorities have adopted policies which prohibit their staff requesting passports or passing information on to the Home Office, and you should check your local authority's policy on this issue.

5 CALCULATING STUDENTS' BENEFIT

If you or your partner get IS, the fact that you are a student does not affect how your HB is calculated and none of the rules which follow apply to you. In all other cases where you and/or your partner are students and eligible for HB, this is worked out in the same way as for other non-IS claimants (see p168), apart from some extra rules about assessing your income and eligible rent (see below).

(i) Assessing your rent

The student rent deduction

If you are a **full-time student**, your weekly eligible rent (ie, the rent figure used in working out your HB – see p157) will, in most cases, be reduced during your period of study by:

☐ £23.45 if you are attending a course in London; *or*

☐ £16.25 if you are studying elsewhere. [30]

Note that the level of deduction depends on the area where you study rather than the area where you live. When a deduction applies, it must be made every week during your period of study (see p177), even where a grant is not paid or is paid for term-time only. Where the deduction is more than your rent, your eligible rent is reduced to zero and you are not eligible for any HB regardless of your income level. However, you may be entitled to some HB outside your period of study when the rent deduction does not apply.

In any week in which your eligible rent is reduced, your income used for calculating your entitlement is reduced by the same amount (see p183). Nevertheless, the overall effect is to give you less benefit.

The rent deduction applies equally where it is the claimant's partner who is a full-time student, [31] but only one rent deduction and income disregard should be made where both partners are full-time students. Where several full-time students share accommodation as joint occupiers (see p153), the full rent deduction must be made from each individual student's share of the total rent.

When the student rent deduction does not apply

The student deduction is not made if: [32]

☐ you are only a part-time student;

☐ you or your partner are on IS;

☐ you or your partner receive an allowance paid by, or on behalf of, the Training Commission – either for your own maintenance or for that of your child;

☐ you are a student on a sandwich course during any period of work experience (industrial, professional or commercial);

☐ your income for HB purposes is less than the sum of your applicable amount and the amount of the rent deduction, and one of the following also applies:

– you are a single parent; *or*

– the disability premium applies; *or*

– you have a partner and only one of you is a full-time student.

If none of these apply to you and the deductions result in hardship, see p174.

(ii) Assessing your income

These extra rules apply equally where a student's partner is the claimant.

In any week when the student rent deduction applies (see p182), an equivalent amount is also deducted from your income.

For rules about the treatment of grants, top-up loans and covenant income, for the purpose of calculating your income, see pp260-3.

6 PAYMENTS

Students are covered by all the normal rules on the administration and payment of HB. However, there are two provisions which can apply specifically to students.

Firstly, the local authority has the discretion to decide how long your benefit period should last and, therefore, when you will need to renew your claim. For most eligible students, there will be two benefit periods a year – one during their period of study, and the other during the long summer vacation (see p191).

Secondly, the local authority may decide to pay a rent allowance once each term, subject to two conditions: [33]

☐ Rent allowance payments cannot be made more than two weeks before the end of the period to which they relate (this means that you would have to wait until two weeks before the end of term before being paid).

☐ Students have the same right as other claimants to insist on fortnightly payments if their rent allowance entitlement is more than £2 a week (see p192).

Chapter 14

Claims, payments and reviews

This chapter covers:

1 CLAIMS

(i) Who can make a claim

If you are a **single person**, (including a single parent or a member of a gay or lesbian couple), you make a claim on your own behalf.

If you are a **member of a couple**, or a **partner in a polygamous marriage**, you can decide between you who should claim for your family. In most cases, the choice of claimant will not affect the level of benefit you receive as your needs and resources are combined (but see p241 and p178 for some important exceptions). If you cannot agree who should be the claimant, the local authority can decide for you. [1]

If a person is either temporarily or permanently unable to manage her/his own affairs (eg, because of an accident or through mental or physical disability), the local authority must accept a claim made by someone formally appointed to act legally on that person's behalf – eg, someone appointed with power of attorney, a Receiver appointed by the Court of Protection, or, in Scotland, a tutor, curator or other guardian administering the person's estate. [2]

Otherwise the local authority can decide to make someone an **appointee** who can act on the claimant's behalf. This may be someone who is already the appointee for DSS benefits or some other suitable person aged 18 or over (such as a relative, friend, neighbour or social worker). [3] For the purpose of the HB claim, an appointee has the responsibility of exercising all the rights (to make a claim, receive payment, request reviews etc) and duties (to provide information, report changes in circumstances etc) as though s/he were the claimant. [4] You can write in to ask to be an appointee, and can resign after giving four weeks notice. The local authority may terminate any appointment it has made at any time. [5]

(ii) How to make a claim

All claims must be made in writing, either on an official claim form or otherwise in a way which is 'sufficient for the purpose' in your case, and accompanied by the information necessary to assess your claim.[6] Claim forms are available from your local authority – but if you are claiming IS you should find a special shortened HB and CCB claim form (NHB1) folded into your IS claim form.[7]

DSS guidance suggests that a letter stating that you wish to claim could be regarded as an acceptable alternative to a claim form.[8] So you should not delay making a claim just because you do not have an official claim form, or you could lose benefit. Where a claim by letter is not accepted as sufficient, you will be sent an official claim form to fill in. If you return this within four weeks (or longer at the local authority's discretion), it is treated as if it had been received on the date of your original claim.[9] Similarly, if you do not complete the claim form properly it is sent back to you and, if you return it properly completed within four weeks (or longer, if the local authority allows more time), it is treated as though you had completed it properly in the first place.[10] Send your claim form immediately, as other information and evidence such as pay slips can be sent later (see p186).

As a claim must always be in writing, you cannot claim by telephone. However, if you telephone to ask for a claim form, ask on the form to have your claim backdated to the date of your phone call (or longer, if appropriate) because you have **good cause for a late claim** (see p187).

You may **amend or withdraw your claim** in writing at any time before it has been assessed. Amendments must be made in writing and are treated as though they were part of your original claim.[11] A notice to withdraw your claim will take effect from the day it is received.[12]

Usually, you claim HB and CCB together but in Scotland some claimants have to make a separate claim for a rent rebate or allowance and for community charge benefit. This is because in Scotland District Councils are responsible for HB and Regional Councils are responsible for CCB. In most cases, however, District Councils agree to operate the CCB scheme for Regional Councils on an agency basis so that only one claim is necessary.

(iii) Where to make your claim

Unless you are claiming IS, you should always send your claim to the local authority[13] (the address will be on the claim form). If you pay rent to a New Town Corporation, the Development Board for Rural Wales or the Scottish Special Housing Association, you should apply to them for benefit.[14]

If you are claiming IS, you can either send your claim to your Benefits Agency office or to the local authority.[15] If you claim IS and send your HB/CCB claim to the Benefits Agency, it must be forwarded by the Benefits Agency to the local authority within two working days of either the date your IS claim was assessed, or the date your HB/CCB claim was received at the Benefits Agency, whichever is later, or as soon as possible after that.[16] One important implication of this is that a delay in assessing your IS claim will also cause a delay in processing your HB/CCB claim. So, if you know there are significant delays at your local Benefits Agency office, it may be wise to send your HB/CCB form directly to the local authority. If you

you do this the local authority will want to verify your entitlement to IS before assessing your HB and will usually do this by contacting the Benefits Agency direct, but should also accept a girobook as proof of IS. This may or may not speed up your HB/CCB claim.

(iv)　Information to support your claim

Your application for benefit should be accompanied by all the information and evidence needed to assess your claim, but you should not delay your claim just because you do not have all the evidence ready to send. [17] If you fail to do this the local authority can require you to provide any further information it reasonably needs, before it assesses your claim. You must supply any information requested in connection with your claim within four weeks – or longer if the local authority thinks you need more time. [18] If you fail, without good reason, to provide information which it is reasonable for them to request within the time allowed, your claim will not be dealt with. [19] Contact the local authority as soon as possible with the information requested and ask them to extend the four-week period. You will need to give a good reason for your delay – eg, you did not receive their letter requesting extra information, or the information was not available sooner. The local authority should not ask you to provide unnecessary proof or evidence which you cannot provide because it does not exist – eg, proof that you have no income. You do not need to declare receipt of payments from any of the MacFarlane Trusts, nor income in kind. [20]

The local authority must also remind you of your duty to report any relevant changes of circumstances which may take place both before and after your claim is assessed, and tell you exactly what sort of changes you must report[21] (see p195).

If you live in privately-rented accommodation and have a deregulated tenancy or licence your claim will usually be referred to the rent officer (see p166) and so you may be visited by the rent officer in connection with your claim for HB. The rent officer will want to know whether your accommodation could be considered too large for your reasonable needs or whether you are paying more than a reasonable market rent for it. The main reason for the visit is to decide whether your rent is 'unreasonably high' or your accommodation is 'unreasonably large' (see pp162-67). If you refuse to co-operate with the rent officer, the local authority has the power to withhold your HB until you do. [22] Payment of HB may be delayed pending a decision of the rent officer and local authority over the level of your rent. If this happens you should ask for a payment on account (see p192).

(v)　Your date of claim

Your date of claim is important because it affects the date from which your HB begins (see p191). Usually, your claim is treated as made on the day it reaches the local authority. [23] The only exceptions are if:

☐　you have successfully claimed IS and your HB claim reached the Benefits Agency within four weeks of the date you claimed IS – in which case the HB claim is treated as having been made on the first day of entitlement to IS; [24]

☐　you have unsuccessfully claimed IS – in which case your HB claim is treated as having been made on the day it reached either the Benefits Agency or the local authority, whichever is the earlier; [25]

☐ you have made an advance claim (see p188);
☐ you are on IS and have just become liable to pay rent, and you claim HB within
   four weeks of becoming responsible for the new rent – in which case the HB
   claim is treated as being made on the date that you first became liable for the
   new rent, so long as the authority or Benefits Agency office receives your claim
   within the four weeks.[26]

Your HB normally starts from the Monday after the date of your claim.[27] This is
called your **date of entitlement** (see p191). A claim may be backdated if you had
good cause for the delay.

(vi)   Backdating a claim

If you have been entitled to HB at some point over the past year, but failed to
claim, you can make a late claim and receive backdated benefit. However, the
local authority will accept a late claim only if you can prove you had continuous good cause for your failure to make that claim throughout the whole time
for which you want to claim.[28] The maximum period for which a claim can be
backdated is 52 weeks. Any backdated benefit will be calculated on both your
circumstances and the HB rules which applied over the backdating period. Once you
have established good cause for a late claim the local authority *must* backdate your
benefit.

What amounts to 'good cause' is not spelled out in the HB regulations. DSS
guidance to local authorities, based on IS rules, suggests that the general test is
where any reasonable person of your age, health and experience would probably
have failed to claim in the same way as you did. While none of the social security
case law is strictly binding on HB cases, the DSS guidance to local authorities
does refer to the rules for IS – for more information, see p102. Although ignorance of your rights cannot normally, in itself, be regarded as good cause for a
delay, the HB rules leave it open for you to argue your particular reasons for a late
claim.[29]

Your local authority may be reluctant to backdate your claim because backdated
benefit attracts a lower rate of government subsidy than would normally apply.
However, the subsidy arrangements are not part of the 'good cause' test. So if you
think your late claim has been turned down on any basis other than failure to prove
good cause, you should insist on a review (see p206).

If you are not currently entitled to any HB, the local authority may refuse to
backdate your claim because it mistakenly believes that it can only backdate an
existing entitlement. This is wrong. If you satisfy the 'good cause' test, it is not your
entitlement but the date from which you are treated as having made a claim which is
backdated – whether you are actually entitled to any benefit from that date will then
depend on what your circumstances were at that time, and not on your current
circumstances. Regardless of whether you have any current entitlement, therefore, it
is still possible to receive backdated HB in respect of an earlier period of entitlement
that both began and ended before the date on which your current claim was actually
made. You must, however, make a claim in order to have it backdated, even though
you know you have no current entitlement.

As your claim cannot be backdated for more than 52 weeks, you lose any
unclaimed HB in respect of any earlier period.[30] However, if you claimed late

because you were given wrong information, or misled by the local authority, you should press for an *ex gratia* payment outside the HB rules, as compensation. Alternatively, you could ask for additional weekly benefit on the grounds of exceptional circumstances (see p174). Both of these possibilities also apply if you did receive some benefit but were underpaid more than 52 weeks ago (see reviews, p206).

(vii)   Advance claims

If you have become liable for rent for the first time but will not be able to move into your new home until after your liability to make payments has started, it is important that you claim benefit *before* you move in (ie, as soon as you are due to pay). This is because, once you have moved in, you may be able to receive benefit retrospectively for up to four weeks prior to moving in (providing you satisfy the conditions set out on p155).[31]

If you are not entitled to HB in the benefit week immediately following your date of claim, but will become entitled within 13 weeks of claiming (eg, because of a reduction in income or because a birthday will increase your 'applicable amount'), the local authority can treat your claim as having been made in the benefit week immediately before you are first entitled.[32] If this happens, you will not need to make a further claim later on. The effect of this rule is to treat your advance claim in the same way as if you made a claim when you became entitled.

(viii)   Making a further claim when your HB runs out

Your HB will be paid to you for a period up to 60 weeks, after which you will have to reapply. The length of this **benefit period** (see p191) depends on the circumstances of your case[33] and you must be told how long it will last.[34] Provided you make a repeat claim not more than 13 weeks before, and not less than four weeks after, your current benefit period ends, your new benefit period starts immediately your old one finishes. If you have been granted benefit for more than 16 weeks and you have not made a further claim within eight weeks of when your existing benefit period is due to end, the local authority must send you an application form and remind you to reclaim.[35]

You also have to reapply for HB if your entitlement to IS ends because that causes your benefit period to end (see p192).[36] Make sure you tell the local authority if you stop getting IS. A repeat claim form must be sent to you and, providing you return this within four weeks of the end of your previous benefit period, your new benefit period will follow on without a break.[37]

If your partner or former partner was the original claimant but you are now making an HB claim for the same accommodation costs, the DSS guidance suggests that your claim will be treated as a repeat claim.[38]

2   DECISIONS

(i)   Delays

Once the local authority has received your claim, it must make a decision on that claim, tell you in writing what the decision is, and pay you any benefit you are entitled to within 14 days, or, if that is not reasonably practicable, as soon as possible after that. [39] However, the local authority is under no duty to deal with your claim if:

☐ your claim was not accepted because *either* you did not claim on an official application form, *or* your application form was not properly filled in and you did not re-submit your application within four weeks of being asked to do so (see p185); *or*

☐ you failed to provide information needed to assess your claim within four weeks of being asked to do so (see p186); *or*

☐ you have told the local authority you have withdrawn your claim (see p185); *or*

☐ you have reclaimed benefit more than 13 weeks before the end of your current benefit period (see p188). [40]

In practice, many local authorities take considerably longer than 14 days to deal with claims. If you are experiencing an unreasonably long delay in getting your HB sorted out, you should write to the HB manager and threaten a formal complaint of 'maladministration' to the Ombudsman (see p210), unless you are paid within 14 days. You should send a copy of the letter to your ward councillor and to the councillor who chairs the council committee responsible for HB, usually the Housing or Finance Committee, (you will be able to get their names and addresses from your local library). It might also be worth asking your local tenants' association for support. If this does not produce results, or if the delay is causing you severe hardship, you should consider court action.

If you are a private tenant and have not received your rent allowance within 14 days of your claim, you can get a payment on account (see p192).

(ii) Notification of the decision

Who should be notified

Written notification must be given to everyone affected by any decision taken on your HB, whose rights, duties or obligations are affected. [41] For example:

☐ the claimant;

☐ an appointee (see p184);

☐ your landlord, if your rent is paid direct (see p194);

☐ non-dependants whose capital and income are used instead of yours in calculating your benefit (see p173);

☐ your partner, if s/he is now the claimant and it is proposed to recover an overpayment made when you claimed (see p201).

Where a third party, such as a landlord, is notified as a 'person affected' it should *only* be about that particular aspect of your claim which affects her/him, such as a decision to pay rent direct. People taken into account in your benefit assessment but *not* directly involved in your claim, such as non-dependants (apart from the case mentioned above) will *not* be notified. Nor will the members of your family whose capital and income are automatically combined with yours. [42]

Information a notification should contain

When the local authority writes to tell you what decisions it has made about your entitlement it must include in its notification a minimum amount of information. [43] In addition to this, it may also include other relevant information. [44]

All notifications must tell you:

☐ of your right to ask for a further written explanation of the local authority's decision, how you must do this and the time-limit for doing so [45] (see below); *and*

☐ of your right to ask the local authority to reconsider its decision, how you can do this and the time-limit for doing so [46] (see p206).

Other information that the local authority must provide will vary with the particular circumstances of your case. All the following should be included where relevant: [47]

☐ the normal weekly amount of benefit you are entitled to;

☐ your weekly eligible rent;

☐ the amount of any notional fuel deductions, why they have been made, and that they can be varied if you can provide evidence of the actual amount involved;

☐ the amount and category of any non-dependant deductions;

☐ if you are a private tenant, the day your HB will be paid and whether payment will be made weekly, monthly etc;

☐ the date on which your entitlement starts and how long it will last (your benefit period);

☐ if you are not receiving IS, your applicable amount and how it is calculated;

☐ if you are not receiving IS, your assessed weekly earnings and other income;

☐ if your level of benefit is less than the minimum amount payable, that this is the reason why you have no entitlement;

☐ if your claim was successful, your duty to notify the local authority of any changes in circumstances which might affect your entitlement and say what kinds of changes should be reported;

☐ if your claim was unsuccessful, a statement explaining exactly why you are not entitled to benefit;

☐ if it has been decided to pay your rent allowance direct to your landlord, additional information saying how much is to be paid to your landlord and when payments will start. (This is the only information, apart from a statement on the right to obtain a further written explanation and request a review, which will be provided in a written notice to your landlord);

☐ if the capital and income of a non-dependant has been used instead of yours to calculate your HB (see p173), additional information saying that this has happened and why. (This is the only information, apart from a statement on the right to obtain a further written explanation and request a review, which will be provided to the non-dependant concerned);

☐ if the local authority decides you have been overpaid, it must also provide you with detailed notification about this (see p203).

In addition to this information you have a right to ask the local authority for a more detailed explanation of how your benefit has been worked out. This must be sent to you within 14 days, or, if that is not reasonably practicable, as soon as possible after that. [48] The local authority should also answer any further queries you have. [49] Local authorities have also been recommended to tell you, in non-IS cases, if they think you are likely to be entitled to IS. [50]

3 PAYMENT OF BENEFIT

(i) Benefit period

Your benefit period is the length of time for which your benefit will be paid before you need to reapply.[51]

When your entitlement starts

The date your entitlement starts will depend on your date of claim (see p186). Normally, your benefit starts on the Monday after your date of claim.[52] This is because your entitlement to HB starts in the benefit week following your date of claim.[53] A **benefit week** is a period of seven days running from Monday to Sunday.[54]

However, if you take on a new tenancy (or otherwise become liable for housing costs which can be met by HB), your HB entitlement starts in the same benefit week as your new liability – provided your date of claim for HB occurs in that same benefit week.[55] This means that:

☐ if your rent is due weekly or at intervals of a multiple of a week, your HB starts at the beginning of the week in which liability starts (ie, you will receive a full week's benefit for that first week – even if your tenancy did not start until part-way through that week);[56]

☐ if your rent is due at other intervals (eg, each calendar month) your HB starts on the same day your liability actually begins (ie, the benefit you receive in the first week will be equivalent to one-seventh of your normal weekly benefit multiplied by the number of days in that week for which rent is due).[57]

When your entitlement ends

Your benefit period could last any number of complete benefit weeks at the local authority's discretion, usually up to a maximum of 60.[58] In deciding how long your benefit should last before you must renew your claim, account is taken of any likely future changes which could affect your entitlement.[59] In particular, the benefit period is often limited to a few months for boarders, self-employed people and students.

Your first week of entitlement normally marks the beginning of your benefit period.[60] But if your date of claim has been backdated (see p187), your benefit period begins in the benefit week in which your claim was actually received.[61] Any backdated benefit does not, therefore, form part of your benefit period. This enables your benefit period to end on the future date originally fixed by the local authority, irrespective of any benefit you may receive for a past period.

If you reapply for benefit within four weeks after the end of your old benefit period, your new benefit period follows on immediately so that you continue to get benefit without a break.[62] If you have not renewed your claim by the last week of your current benefit period, and you are either on IS or your applicable amount includes the disability premium, severe disability premium or higher pensioner premium, the local authority can decide to extend your current benefit period by up to four weeks to give you a further reminder, and more time, to reapply.[63]

Your benefit period *will* end early if your entitlement ceases because of a change of circumstances[64] and *may* end early if your entitlement is altered because of a change of circumstances.[65] In particular, your benefit period ends when you cease to be entitled to IS[66] – although you should be invited to reapply and be reassessed.[67] In all cases, whatever the change in your situation, your benefit period ends with the last benefit week in which you have any entitlement.[68] This will be determined by the date on which the relevant change of circumstances takes effect (see p196).

If your benefit period ends it is important that you reapply within four weeks if you think you might still be entitled. If you delay you may lose benefit. If there is a gap between two benefit periods, you can ask for the second period to be backdated if you have a good reason for the delay in your claim (see p187).

(ii)   How your benefit is paid

If your landlord is the housing authority responsible for the payment of HB, you receive HB in the form of a reduction in your rent. This is called a **rent rebate**.[69]

If you are the sub-tenant of a council tenant, your landlord is the council tenant and not the council. Therefore, you will receive a rent allowance and not a rebate.

If you are a private tenant, you receive HB in the form of a **rent allowance** which is usually paid to you as a cash payment[70] although, in some cases, it may be paid direct to your landlord or to someone acting on your behalf (see p193).

If you are entitled to a rent allowance it can be paid either weekly, two-weekly, four-weekly, or monthly, depending on when your rent is normally due. It can also be paid at longer intervals if you agree.[71] If rent is paid in arrears, your rent allowance may be paid in arrears. Otherwise, if you are paid two-weekly, you are paid in advance.[72]

If your rent allowance is less than £1 a week, the local authority can choose to pay you your benefit up to six months in arrears.[73]

You can insist on two-weekly payments if your rent allowance is more than £2 a week.[74] The local authority can pay your rent allowance weekly either to avoid an overpayment or where you are liable to pay weekly and it is in your interests to be paid weekly.[75]

Although rent allowances are normally paid in cash, the local authority has the discretion to pay you by whatever method it chooses but, in doing so, it must have regard to your 'reasonable needs and convenience'.[76] It should not insist on payment into a bank account if you do not already have a bank or giro account, nor make you collect benefit if it involves a difficult journey.[77] If it does, you should ask for a review (see p206) and complain to your local councillor (see p210). If that has no effect, ask your MP to take the matter up with the local authority, and also complain to the Ombudsman (see p210).

(iii)   Interim payments on account

If you are a private tenant and the local authority has not been able formally to assess your rent allowance within 14 days of receiving your claim, you should receive a payment on account while your claim is being sorted out, whether or not you are also getting IS. Some local authorities treat these interim payments as though they were discretionary. However, the law says the local authority must pay you an amount which it considers reasonable, given what it knows about your circumstances, unless it is your fault your claim cannot be formally assessed because you failed, without good cause, to provide all the information needed and requested (see p186).[78] If you are not responsible for the delay, the only discretion the local authority has is in deciding how much it is reasonable to pay you – not whether or not you should be paid. If you are having difficulties obtaining any payment within 14 days, see p189.

If the local authority makes a payment on account, it should notify you of the amount and point out that it can recover any overpayment which occurs as a result.[79] This is because, when a formal decision on your claim is eventually made, your actual benefit entitlement may be different from the interim amount. If so, your future benefit payments are adjusted until the underpayment or overpayment has been put right.[80] If it is found that you are not entitled to any HB, the overpayment may be recovered from you by other methods (see p201).

(iv)   Lost and missing cheques and giros

The law says nothing specifically about the replacement of lost or missing giros. This is seen as an administrative matter. The DSS guidance advises that, before replacing a payment, local authorities must satisfy themselves that all reasonable steps have been taken to ensure the loss is genuine. Beyond that, the question of whether to replace a payment is left for local authorities to decide.[81] However, if the local authority refuses to replace a payment which has never arrived, you could either try appealing on the basis that the authority had not paid you[82] or you could threaten to sue them in the county court. The process is the same as for the Benefits Agency (see p108).

(v)   Payment of your benefit to someone else

The payment of any rent allowance should normally be made to you as the person entitled to benefit.[83] However, sometimes payment may be made to a third party such as an appointee, agent, your landlord or your next of kin.

Payment to a claimant's personal representative

Where an appointee, or some other person legally empowered to act for you, has claimed HB on your behalf, that person can also receive the payments[84] (see p184).

If you are able to claim benefit for yourself, you can still nominate an agent to receive, or collect, your benefit for you. To do this you must make a written request to the local authority. Anyone you nominate must be aged 18 or over.[85] This may be useful if you are temporarily away from home (eg, in hospital or prison) or you are housebound and need someone to collect your benefit from the post office etc (eg, a neighbour or home-help).

If a claimant dies, any unpaid benefit may be paid to their personal representative or, where there is none, to their next of kin aged 16 or over. For payment to be made, a written application must be received by the local authority within 12 months of the claimant's death. However, the time-limit can be extended at the local authority's discretion.[86]

Payment direct to a landlord

The local authority **must** pay your HB directly to your landlord:
□ if you or your partner are on IS and the Benefits Agency has decided to pay part of your benefit to your landlord for arrears; [87] *or*
□ if you have rent arrears equivalent to eight weeks' rent or more, unless the local authority considers it to be in your overriding interest not to make direct payments [88] – in which case, your benefit is withheld (see below). Once your arrears have been reduced to less than eight weeks' rent, compulsory direct payments will stop. The local authority can then choose to continue direct payments on a discretionary basis if it considers it to be in your best interests to do so (see below).

The local authority **may** pay your HB directly to your landlord:
□ if you have requested or agreed to direct payments; [89] *or*
□ without your agreement, if it decides that direct payments are in the best interests of yourself and your family; or
□ without your agreement, if you have left the address for which you were getting HB and there are rent arrears. In this case, direct payments of any unpaid benefit due in respect of that accommodation can be made, up to the total of the outstanding arrears.

If the local authority implements direct payments, both you and your landlord should be notified accordingly. If it is not in your interests to have benefit paid directly to your landlord (eg, because you are deliberately withholding rent to force your landlord to carry out repairs) it is worth trying to persuade the authority to withhold benefit rather than paying it to your landlord where there are more than eight weeks arrears. Landlords can sometimes place authorities under pressure to pay them direct and the authority may not use this alternative option as a result.

(vi)   Withholding benefit

Your rent allowance **must** be withheld if you have rent arrears equivalent to eight weeks' rent or more but the local authority has decided it is in your overriding interest not to make direct payments to your landlord [90] (see above).

HB should not be withheld if either you pay off your arrears or can satisfy the local authority that you will pay off your arrears once you have received your payments. [91] This could apply, for example, if you have recently been discharged from residential care and direct payments to your landlord could undermine a rehabilitation programme. In this case, the local authority could be asked to pay you your benefit if you can show you will be able to clear your rent arrears because you have regular support to get your finances under control (eg, through debt counselling).

If the local authority subsequently decides it is no longer in your overriding interest not to pay your landlord, the benefit withheld must be paid direct to your landlord unless your arrears have been reduced to less than eight weeks' rent (see above).

Your rent allowance **may** be withheld if:
□ the authority believes you are not paying your rent regularly to your landlord; [92]
□ you have claimed HB and have a de-regulated tenancy, licence or other agreement, but have refused to co-operate with the rent officer in her/his assessment of your rent level [93] (see p166);

☐ a query has arisen about your entitlement to, or the payment of, your benefit;[94]
☐ the local authority thinks you may have been overpaid and that the overpayment is recoverable[95] (see p197).

Any HB suspended because you are not paying your rent regularly is paid to you if you *either* pay off your rent arrears, *or* satisfy the local authority that you will pay off your rent arrears once you have received the amount withheld.[96] Otherwise, you can ask for your benefit to be paid direct to your landlord (see p181).

If your HB has been withheld pending a review of your entitlement, payment or possible overpayment, any benefit withheld and to which you are subsequently found to have been entitled, will be paid to you once the queries have been sorted out. If you have been overpaid HB, only those overpayments which are legally recoverable may be deducted from the benefit withheld (see p197).[97]

4   CHANGES IN YOUR CIRCUMSTANCES

(i)   Duty to report changes of circumstances

From the moment you claim HB, you have a duty to let the local authority know in writing of any changes in your circumstances which you might reasonably know are likely to affect your benefit in any way. If you do not, you may be overpaid benefit and might have to pay it back (see p197). This applies to changes which occur before your claim is assessed, as well as those which occur throughout your subsequent benefit period. If your benefit is paid to someone else on your behalf (eg, an appointee or landlord), the duty to report any relevant changes extends to her/him as well.[98] The local authority must tell you about the changes you have to report.[99]

You must always report the following changes, in writing, to the local authority:[100]
☐ any change to your rent if you are a private tenant;
☐ when entitlement to IS ends;
☐ any change in the number of, or circumstances of, any non-dependants that may affect the level of deductions made to your benefit (see p171).

If you do not receive IS you must also report:
☐ any change in family capital or income;
☐ any change in the number of boarders or sub-tenants or in the payments made by them;
☐ any change in your status (eg, marriage, cohabitation, separation or divorce).

Other changes

Whether or not you get IS, there may be other changes which the local authority requires you to report, depending on the particular circumstances of your case. The need to report these additional changes must be drawn to your attention at the time you are notified of your benefit entitlement[101] (see p190). This is important because you only have a duty to report changes which you 'might reasonably be expected to know' might affect your benefit. [102] This may affect whether or not you have to repay any overpayment resulting from your failure to report a change (see p199).

You do not have to report: [103]

☐ any changes in your rent if you are a local authority tenant;

☐ changes in the ages of members of your family, or of non-dependants, unless the change results in a young person ceasing to be a member of the family.

It is important that you should remember to report any changes to the right department. In theory, the Benefits Agency and the local authority should pass on information you give (eg, if you tell the Benefits Agency about a change regarding your non-dependants, it should be passed on to the local authority). But you must not rely on this; it is your responsibility to see that any changes relating to your rent, and non-dependants are reported by you in writing to the local authority. You also cannot assume that information you give to one part of the local authority, eg, a housing officer, will be passed to the HB section. Your duty to notify changes is to the HB Department not to the local authority as a whole. [104]

(ii)   When changes in circumstances take effect

If you have made an application for benefit and reported a change of circumstances before the local authority has assessed your claim, your application will be assessed on the basis of the revised information you have provided.

If a change of circumstances takes place within your benefit period, the local authority must establish the date on which that change actually occurred. [105] Where you have ceased to be entitled to some other benefit (including IS and FC), the date the change occurred must always be taken as the day after your last day of entitlement to that benefit. [106]

In most cases, the change takes effect from the start of the benefit week after the one in which the change actually occurred. [107] This means that, on whatever day of the week the change actually occurs, from Monday to Sunday, the change will be implemented as from the following Monday. This includes cases where IS stops and HB ends, except for the exceptions listed below.

☐ If IS ends because another benefit becomes payable, the HB benefit period will end at the end of the benefit week in which the **payment** of IS ceases (where IS ends in any other case, the HB benefit period ends at the end of the benefit week in which IS **entitlement** ceases – ie, the normal rule applies). [108]

☐ A change in rent is taken into account in the benefit week in which it actually occurs. If you pay your rent weekly, or in a multiple of weeks (ie, two-weekly, four-weekly etc), the change is taken into account for the whole of the week in which it occurs. This means that the change takes effect on the Monday, though your rent may not have changed until, say, the Thursday, of that week. If you pay rent monthly, the change is taken into account on the day it actually occurs. [109]

☐ A change in your income solely due to a change in tax and National Insurance contributions can be disregarded for up to 30 weeks (see p250). [110]

☐ A change in the HB regulations takes effect from the date the amendment occurs. [111] If the change is the annual uprating of benefits, it takes effect from the first Monday in April if you pay rent weekly (or in multiples of weeks). If you pay at other intervals it counts from 1 April.

☐ A change in the regulations affecting other social security benefits at uprating in April can be taken into account up to two weeks before the uprating date. [112]

If two or more changes occurring in the same benefit week would, according to the above rules, normally take effect in different benefit weeks, they are treated as taking effect in the same benefit week in which they occur and take effect from the beginning of that benefit week (unless one of the changes relates to monthly rent, in which case all the changes take effect on the same day as the rent changes). [113] If you pay rent weekly (or in multiples of weeks) and the annual uprating occurs at the same time as another change (excluding a change to your rent or the HB regulations) they all count from the first Monday in April.

(iii) Reassessment of your benefit

The local authority may deal with your change of circumstances by ending your benefit period early and inviting you to reclaim so that your entitlement can be completely reassessed. [114] This always happens if you have ceased to be entitled to IS (see p192). [115] Otherwise, it reviews your existing entitlement and either increases or reduces your existing benefit, as appropriate. [116] If you delay in reporting changes of circumstances, you could be underpaid or overpaid. If you have been underpaid, you can be paid the arrears, but *only* for up to one year (but see p206). [117] If you have been overpaid, the local authority can recover the overpayment. [118]

5 OVERPAYMENTS

If the information you give the local authority is wrong, or if you do not report a change in your circumstances (see p195), you could end up being paid too much benefit. You could also be overpaid as a result of an official error or delay which is not your fault. Not all overpayments are legally recoverable and have to be paid back.

(i) What is an overpayment?

An overpayment is any amount of HB (including a 'payment on account' – see p192) which has been paid to you but to which you were not entitled under the regulations. [119] A 'payment' includes both a direct payment of benefit to you and also benefit entitlement as a credit on your rent account. [120] The local authority must have actually *paid* you some benefit to which you were not entitled for an overpayment to have taken place. It does not matter whether you were overpaid by cash, a cheque, payment into your bank account, credits to your local authority rent account, or direct payment to your private landlord.

(ii) Dealing with overpayments

Local authorities should take the following steps in an overpayment case:

Step 1 Establish the cause, or causes, of the overpayment (see p198).

Step 2 Determine whether any of the overpayment is recoverable by the local authority under the regulations (see p199).

Step 3   Decide, where the overpayment is recoverable, whether or not recovery should be sought (see p199).

Step 4   Work out the amount of the overpayment and the period over which it occurred (see p200).

Step 5   Decide from whom recovery should be made, by what method and at what rate (see p201).

Step 6   Notify you of all the above decisions regarding the overpayment and give you an opportunity to request further information or a review (see p203).

The rules and procedures regarding overpayments apply equally to all cases regardless of whether or not you get IS.

(iii)   The cause of the overpayment

The reason why any overpayment has taken place determines whether, and from whom, it is legally recoverable. The local authority has a duty to tell you why it thinks the overpayment occurred (see p203). [121]

An overpayment may arise for a number of reasons. [122] These are:

☐ **Claimant error or fraud** if you or someone acting on your behalf (eg, an appointee) are responsible for the overpayment taking place. For example, perhaps you gave the wrong information on your application form or failed to report a change of circumstances. You may have caused the overpayment innocently (eg, through a genuine mistake, or forgetfulness) or fraudulently (eg, by knowingly making a false statement or deliberately not reporting a pay rise). If fraud has been committed, the local authority can prosecute you as well as recovering the overpayment (see p204). [123]

☐ **Official error** if the overpayment is due to something done, or not done, by the local authority or Benefits Agency (or the Department of Employment acting on behalf of the Benefits Agency). For example, the local authority may have delayed acting on information supplied by you, or miscalculated your weekly benefit, or the Benefits Agency may have mistakenly awarded you IS. However, if you or someone acting on your behalf (eg, an appointee), or someone to whom the payment was made (eg, an agent or landlord), contributed to the overpayment it will be classified as a *claimant error*. In particular, it is regarded as a claimant error if you report a change of circumstances to the Benefits Agency instead of the local authority and the information is not passed on or is forwarded late. This is because you have a duty to report changes, in writing, directly to the local authority (see p196).

☐ **Third party error** if the overpayment has been caused by someone other than you or the local authority or Benefits Agency. For example, your landlord or employer may have provided inaccurate information.

☐ A **'payment on account'** if a private tenant has received an interim payment at the beginning of a claim which is subsequently found to exceed her/his actual benefit entitlement (see p192).

☐ **Other errors** including other overpayments which may not be anyone's fault. For example, you may have received a backdated pay rise, or social security benefit.

An overpayment may have **more than one cause**, in which case the local authority must separately identify the amount of the overpayment which has arisen as a result of each particular cause. The two most usual causes of overpayments are delays in notifying and acting on changes of circumstances. For example, if you delay notifying the local authority of a change in circumstances for three weeks and then the local authority subsequently fails to take any action for a further two weeks, two kinds of overpayment have taken place – a 'claimant error' overpayment for the first three weeks and an 'official error' overpayment for the last two weeks.

(iv) Overpayments which are recoverable

Most overpayments, including all HB 'payments on account' (see p192), are legally recoverable which means that the local authority can make you pay them back. However, you do not have to pay back an overpayment if: [124]

☐ it was due to an official error (see p185); *and*

☐ it was paid for a past period; *and*

☐ you or someone acting on your behalf (eg, an appointee) or someone to whom the payment was made (eg, an agent or landlord), could not have reasonably been expected to know that an overpayment was being made at the time that the payment was notified or received.

This rule does not apply where benefit has been credited to your rent account for a future period. In this case the forward award of benefit can be withdrawn even if it arose due to official error. Benefit paid after the date your claim is reviewed is recoverable.

However, where too much benefit has been credited to your account for a *past* period you could argue that the overpayment cannot be recovered if you have not been notified of the credit. [125] This is because you cannot reasonably be expected to know that you have been overpaid until you have been told about your entitlement. For the same reason, if you are a private tenant you should argue that if official errors lead to the wrong payments being directly credited to your bank/giro account or that of your appointee, agent or landlord, the past overpayment is not recoverable unless you were notified of the payment.

The extent to which you can reasonably be expected to realise that an overpayment is being made to you depends on the extent to which the local authority has advised you about the scheme or your duties and obligations, particularly about your duty to notify changes of circumstances. It depends not on what you know, but on what you could have known at the time of the payment or the notification.

(v) Recovering overpayments

Any overpayment of a 'payment on account' **must** be recovered by the local authority in every case [126] (see p192). All other recoverable overpayments may be recovered at the local authority's discretion. [127] In practice, authorities operate a wide range of different policies towards the recovery of overpayments. Some recover all recoverable overpayments and others only recover those caused by claimant error.

The Benefits Agency guidance makes it clear that local authorities are expected to 'minimise overpayments' and to make recoveries 'wherever appropriate'. This is reinforced by the subsidy arrangements which have clearly been designed to offer local authorities a financial incentive to make recoveries, and which impose financial penalties where overpayments remain unrecovered. [128]

Nevertheless, local authorities have a legal duty to exercise their judgement on whether or not to make a recovery *on the merits of each and every individual case* (and the merits of the case do not include the subsidy arrangements!). While they may have general policy guidelines on how to approach the issue in a consistent manner, these must *not* be so rigid as to effectively decide the outcome of each case in advance. A policy of always recovering recoverable overpayments would, there- fore, amount to an unlawful 'fettering' of the local authority's discretion which could be challenged at a review.

If you have been overpaid and this was either not your fault or the result of a genuine mistake or oversight on your part, you should ask the local authority not to recover the overpayment, especially if recovery causes you hardship. You should tell the authority about any existing financial difficulties you have which will be aggravated by recovery action – eg, where you already have serious debts or have to repay a loan from the social fund. Any illness, disability or other family problems may also be relevant. If the local authority still insists on proceeding with recovery action, you should ask for a review. The rules allow you to ask for a review on both the recovery method and the rate of recovery. [129] This is not the same as IS rules where you cannot appeal these decisions. If the overpayment was caused by some- one else (eg, your landlord), you could suggest that recovery is made from her/him instead. You may be asked to repay an irrecoverable overpayment on a voluntary basis. You are under no legal obligation to do so.

(vi)   The amount of overpayment which is recoverable

If you have been overpaid HB and the local authority considers that it is recoverable, it must tell you how it worked out the amount of the overpayment. [130] This should be the difference between what you were paid and what you should have been paid during the period of the overpayment. [131] The authority should distinguish between those overpayments it regards as recoverable and those it does not. Complications can arise where some of the overpayment is caused by claimant error and some by official error. You should also check that the authority has offset certain payments against the overpayment. These are:

☐ if you have been getting a rent rebate over the overpayment period and, for some reason, have paid more into your rent account than you should have paid according to your original (incorrect) benefit assessment, any overpayment aris- ing over that period will be reduced by the amount of the excess payment; [132]

☐ a recoverable overpayment has occurred because your capital has been incor- rectly assessed – eg, because the local authority made a mistake, was misled, or not told, about how much capital you or your family have. If this overpayment is for a period of more than 13 benefit weeks, the local authority will apply the 'diminishing capital rule' when calculating the amount of the overpayment. [133]

The logic behind the **diminishing capital rule** is that, had your unassessed capital been taken into account in the first place, and your benefit consequently reduced or withdrawn, you would have drawn on your capital in order to help meet your housing costs. The rule works in the following way: [134]

☐ The amount overpaid during the overpayment period is first calculated in the normal way.

☐ At the *end* of the first 13 benefit weeks the claimant's assessed capital is reduced by the amount of the overpaid benefit which occurred over that period.

☐ This reduced capital is then used to recalculate the claimant's entitlement, and hence, overpayment, from the beginning of the 14th benefit week onwards.

☐ This procedure is then repeated for each subsequent block of 13 weeks until either the claimant's capital is reduced to below £3,000 (so it has no effect on entitlement) or there are less than 14 weeks left before the end of the overpayment period.

The reduction in capital only takes place at the end of each complete block of 13 weeks in the overpayment period. This means the rule has no effect until the beginning of the 14th week of the overpayment period. It also means that capital cannot be regarded as reducing over any period of less than 13 weeks. [135]

If you are making voluntary repayments following an official error, make sure the local authority has taken the diminishing capital rule into account when calculating the amount of the overpayment. The diminishing capital rule is only relevant for calculating overpayments. Your current entitlement will be based on your actual capital.

(vii) How overpayments are recovered

There are special rules that lay down who a local authority can recover an overpayment from and how they can recover it. There are no rules about how much can be recovered. Authorities have a lot of discretion in how they decide to recover an overpayment. You can challenge any decisions they take in recovering an overpayment from you (see p206).

From whom the overpayment is recovered

In all cases, the local authority has the power to recover a recoverable overpayment from either the claimant or the person to whom it was made (eg, a landlord). [136] However, where the overpayment arose as a result of a 'misrepresentation or failure to disclose a material fact' (either fraudulently or otherwise) by the claimant, someone acting on her/his behalf, or the person to whom benefit was paid, the local authority has the power to recover the overpaid HB from the person responsible. This could apply to an appointee, agent or landlord. [137] See p113 for information on what constitutes 'misrepresentation or failure to disclose a material fact'.

An overpayment may also be recovered from the partner of a claimant, but *only* where they were members of the same household both at the time of the overpayment, and when recovery is made. [138]

In the event of the death of the person from whom recovery is being sought, local authorities may consider recovering any outstanding overpayment from that person's estate. [139]

How the overpayment is recovered

If an overpayment is recoverable, the local authority has the discretion to decide both how it will recover the money and at what rate. [140] It can make deductions from any future HB or from any arrears of HB owing to you. If you are no longer entitled to HB, you can be asked to repay the money directly through instalments or by a lump sum. In some cases, the local authority can ask the Benefits Agency to undertake recovery by making deductions from other social security benefits you are getting (see below). As a last resort, the local authority can recover the money you owe through the county court if it thinks you could afford to make repayments. [141] You have six weeks to ask for a review of the decision that the overpayment is recoverable (see p206). This should be borne in mind when local authorities are deciding when to start proceedings.

If a local authority recovers overpaid HB by adjusting its own rent account, the overpayment should be separately identified and you should be informed that the amount being recovered does *not* represent rent arrears. Local authorities are reminded in the Benefits Agency guidance that overpayments of HB in respect of their own tenants are not rent arrears and should not be treated as such. [142] Unfortunately, this advice seems to have been frequently ignored. The practice of debiting overpayments to rent accounts to become rent 'arrears' can cause unnecessary difficulties for council tenants – such as being refused a housing transfer because they 'owe rent'. It can also lead to inappropriate methods of recovery, such as possession proceedings, because the local authority can no longer distinguish between the overpaid HB and genuine rent arrears. If you are a council tenant you should check that the authority has assessed the overpayment according to the steps outlined on p197.

The local authority cannot evict you for an overpayment of HB. If you are threatened with eviction for 'rent arrears', therefore, you should point out that the fact that these 'arrears' consist either solely or partly of overpaid HB will be a defence in court.

Recoveries of overpayments made to your partner (see p201) may be recovered by deductions from your HB (although the actual rate of recovery is not specified).

Overpayments arising as a result of a 'payment on account' (see p192) can only be recovered through deductions from HB unless you no longer have any current entitlement.

Overpayments of HB cannot be recovered by deductions from CCB (and vice versa). [143] Unpaid community charge *cannot* be recovered through HB payments (although some local authorities *do* attempt to do this). [144]

Recovery through the Benefits Agency

The primary responsibility for recovering overpaid HB lies with the local authority. However, it can ask the Benefits Agency to recover the overpayment through deductions from some other social security benefits if: [145]

☐   a recoverable overpayment has been made as a result of a misrepresentation or failure to disclose a material fact (whether innocently or fraudulently – see p113) by, or on behalf of, the claimant or some other person to whom HB has been paid; *and*

☐   the local authority are unable to recover that overpayment from any HB entitlement; *and*

☐ the person responsible for that overpayment is receiving at least one of the benefits from which a deduction can be made – providing that this benefit is payable at a sufficiently high rate for deductions to be possible. [146]

Benefits from which deductions can be made are IS, FC, DWA and other social security benefits except child benefit and guardian's allowance. Benefits paid by other EC states count [147] but CCB is not included. The amount deducted each week is limited in the case of IS (see p115).

Deductions continue until the overpayment has been recovered. If deductions stop because the person ceases to be entitled to that social security benefit, or entitlement drops below the minimum for deductions, the Benefits Agency notifies the local authority who, once again, becomes responsible for any further recovery action.

How much is recovered

A local authority can decide how much of a recoverable overpayment it will actually recover. It can ask for the whole amount at once or recover it by instalments.

The DSS guidance suggests that, if you are getting IS, the **rate of recovery** should be limited to the maximum that could be recovered from IS itself (see p115) unless you agree to more. However, if you are already having deductions made from your IS (eg, for fuel debts), you should ask the local authority to deduct less to avoid causing you hardship.

If you are not on IS but your income is below or not much above your applicable amount, you can argue for the same weekly maximum to apply. You should also ask the local authority to take into account any other debts or financial commitments you may have. If you complain to the local authority that the rate of recovery is causing you hardship, they should consider reducing the amount of the repayments. [148]

You should check that the methods used by the authority and the rates of recovery are consistent between groups of claimants. For example, council tenants should not be required to repay overpayments in a lump sum (ie, the whole overpayment is debited to their account) where private tenants can repay by instalment (ie, by weekly deductions made to their HB). If this is happening, you should ask for a review.

(viii) Notification of overpayments

If the local authority decides that a recoverable overpayment has occurred, it must write to the person from whom recovery is being sought (within 14 days, if possible) and notify them accordingly. [149] This notification must state: [150]

☐ the fact that there is an overpayment which is legally recoverable;
☐ the reason why there is a recoverable overpayment;
☐ the amount of the recoverable overpayment;
☐ how the amount of the overpayment was calculated;
☐ the benefit weeks to which the overpayment relates;
☐ if recovery is to be made from future benefit, how much the deduction will be;
☐ that you have a right to ask for a further written explanation of any of the decisions the local authority has made regarding the overpayment, how you can do this and the time-limit for doing so;

☐ that you have a right to ask the local authority to reconsider any of the decisions it has made regarding the overpayment, how you can do this and the time-limit for doing so.

It may also include any other relevant matters (eg, that you should tell the local authority about any hardship which will result from recovery action or, where recovery is to be made by a means other than deduction from your HB, what the recovery method will be).

If you write and ask the local authority for a more detailed written explanation of any of the decisions it has made regarding the overpayment, it must send you this within 14 days or, if this is not reasonably practicable, as soon as possible after that. [151] Notifications provided by many local authorities have been either inadequate or non-existent. Such authorities are in breach of their statutory duties. If your local authority does not give proper notification, you should write and point out that the decision to recover the overpayment is not valid until you are given proper notification. No recovery should be sought until you have had a chance to discuss your case or apply for a review. [152]

6   FRAUD

The two provisions under which people are usually prosecuted for HB frauds are s55 of the Social Security Act 1986 (s112 of the Social Security Administration Act) and s15 of the Theft Act 1968. Under s55 of the Social Security Act you commit an offence if: [153]

☐ you deliberately make or use false statements; *and*
☐ as a result you get benefit to which you are not entitled.

Under s15 of the Theft Act you commit an offence if: [154]

☐ you deliberately deceive the authority about something; *and*
☐ you do this to get benefit to which you are not entitled.

You only commit an offence if you do something dishonest. Local authorities often treat an innocent failure to notify a change of circumstances as fraud, and may stop benefit as a result. Even if there has been fraud in the past, that should not prevent you from obtaining HB now if you are entitled to it (although the local authority can recover any overpayment by deductions from your current HB – see p201).

To avoid confusion between ongoing entitlement, overpayments generally and fraud specifically, authorities should apply the following steps:

Step 1   Establishing the facts – the authority should advise you about the information they have that may affect your present entitlement and give you an opportunity to comment. The information should be capable of being used in court – eg, it should not be based on statements from people who cannot be identified so that they could not be brought to court as witnesses. You should ask for proof of any information they say they have. You should be able to have someone with you if you want – eg, a friend or adviser. While the authority is establishing the facts they can decide to withhold benefit [155] (see p194).

Step 2   Reassessment of benefit – on the basis of the facts of the case, and in the light of your comments, the local authority should take whatever action is necessary on the claim. This might involve no change in benefit, a change in the amount of benefit, or an end to benefit if the authority considers there is no longer entitlement. It must inform you of its decision and you can ask for a review if you disagree (see p206). If it decides that you are still entitled to benefit, it can no longer withhold benefit, even though it is still investigating a previous fraud.

Step 3 Is there an overpayment? – a change of benefit may have created an overpayment. This should be dealt with according to the normal rules (see p197).

Step 4 Is there fraud? – if, during the course of establishing the facts, the authority considers you have committed an offence (see above), they may take action against you, which includes prosecution. The powers of recovery of overpayments and prosecution are separate, so that any fine imposed by the court will have to be paid in addition to the repayment of the overpayment.

If you are on IS, the authority may liaise with, and pass information to, the local Benefits Agency. Conversely, the Benefits Agency can ask the authority for information about you if they are investigating IS fraud. [156]

7 REVIEWS

A review is the process by which a local authority or the housing benefit review board (see p206), looks again at a decision and decides whether it should be altered.

A decision may be reviewed by the local authority without any request from you to correct an error or to take account of a change of circumstances. Such a review may be in your favour or may reduce the amount of benefit you receive.

However, *you* also have the right to *ask* for a review. This is very important because there is no right of appeal to an independent tribunal in HB cases. If you wish to challenge a decision, you can do so only by asking for a review.

(i) Local authority reviews

The local authority can review any of its own decisions, and those of the review board, at any time if:

☐ there has been a change of circumstances (see p195); *or*

☐ it is satisfied the decision was made in ignorance of, or based on a mistake as to, some material fact. In the case of a review board decision, this must be shown by fresh evidence that was not available to the board (and which could not have been put before the board at the time); *or*

☐ in the case of a local authority decision only, it is satisfied that it was based on a mistake as to the law. [157]

If a decision is amended on a review initiated by a local authority, this counts as a fresh decision requiring notification in the normal way, so you can ask for yet another review (see below) if it is unfavourable to you. [158] When notifying you of the review decision, the local authority need give details only of the part of your claim being reviewed, the reasons for the review and your right to ask for the new decision to be reviewed.

If, as a result of the review you get more benefit, any arrears due to you can only be paid for a maximum of 52 weeks, unless the review concerns a decision to backdate your claim, in which case any arrears will be paid from the date your claim is treated as being made. [159]

(ii)   *Your* right to a review

You can always ask a local authority to review its decision under the powers described above. This may be done at any time.

You can ask for a review of any decision (including a local authority review decision) simply on the ground that you disagree with it. The right to a review also applies to other people affected by the decision – eg, a landlord. [160] Such an application must be received by the local authority within six weeks of the decision being notified to you, [161] although the local authority can allow a late application if there are special reasons. [162] The local authority *must* tell you of your right to apply for a review every time you are notified of a decision. [163] If it fails to do so, that will be a special reason for allowing a late application.

If you want a written explanation from the local authority (see p190) so that you can state your case more effectively, the period between your request reaching the local authority and the explanation being posted to you is ignored when calculating the six-week limit. [164] It is often worth asking the local authority for a written explanation before formally requesting a review, because the law is complicated and you will then know the basis on which the decision was taken. However, if the reasons for the decision are clear or your situation is urgent, you should not delay asking for a review. You can ask for a further written explanation at any time. [165] The local authority has the discretion to extend the six-week limit if there are good reasons for doing so. An application for an extension must be made in writing, and, if it is refused, the local authority's decision is final [166] (although, in an exceptional case, it might be challenged by judicial review – see p210).

Any written comments or observations you have made in support of your request for a review must be considered. There is no time-limit laid down within which the authority must carry out the review. Some local authorities have a policy of carrying out the review within 14 days of receiving a request for a review.

You must be notified in writing of the outcome of the review. The information given to you following the review must conform to the normal rules about the notification of decisions (see p190). This means it should be sent to you within 14 days, if possible, and that it must include an explanation of your right to request a further written statement of reasons for the review decision. [167] It must also inform you of your right to ask for a further review by a review board (see below). [168]

If a decision is altered on review, the revised decision takes effect from the date of the original decision. [169] However, if the review results in an increase in your benefit, arrears cannot normally be paid for more than 52 weeks before the date the local authority first received your request for the review. The only exception is where the local authority has reversed a decision not to backdate your claim under the 'good cause for a late claim' provisions – in which case any arrears may be paid from the date your claim is now treated as having been made [170] (see p187).

(iii) The housing benefit review board

A hearing before a housing benefit review board is the nearest thing there is to an independent appeal for HB cases. Although review boards are not really independent, they must act as if they were independent. The review board is made up of local authority councillors.

Applying for a hearing

If you have exercised your right to a review (see p206), and remain dissatisfied with the local authority's decision, you can write and ask for a **further review**. It is this 'further review' that is carried out by a housing benefit review board.

When you apply, you must give your reasons. These need not be detailed or technical as long as it is clear what it is you disagree with. The request for the further review must reach the local authority within 28 days of the notification of the internal review being posted to you. [171] The review board may extend the deadline if there are special reasons for doing so. An application for an extension must be made to the local authority in writing, and, if it is refused, the review board's decision is final (although, in an exceptional case, it might be challenged by judicial review – see p210). [172]

The hearing

A hearing before a review board should take place within six weeks of your request reaching the local authority or, if that is not reasonably practicable, as soon as possible after that. [173] However, if you are challenging a decision to restrict your eligible rent (see p157) and the local authority has asked the rent officer to reconsider your case as a result, the review board may decide to defer your hearing pending the outcome. [174] You must be given at least 10 days notice of the time of the hearing and the place where it will be held, otherwise you have the right to insist on another date being set. [175] If you have been given adequate notice but would like the hearing to be postponed, or if you wish to withdraw your request for a hearing altogether, you must write to the review board chairperson who will decide whether the hearing should still proceed. [176]

The review board consists of at least three local authority councillors (or members of the New Town Corporation, Development Board for Rural Wales or Scottish Special Housing Association) one of whom will act as chairperson. [177] But if there are only two members of the board present when you attend, the hearing can go ahead provided all parties consent. [178] DSS guidance suggests that the board should not consist of anyone who has had a previous involvement in your case. [179] If the issue to be considered by the review board affects both your claim for HB and CCB (eg, the assessment of your income), the same review board can consider your claim for both benefits at the same time, provided everyone concerned in the case agrees. [180]

The board chairperson will decide how the hearing should be conducted. [181] If you want to provide a written statement to the review board, it must consider all the points you make. [182] You also have the right to attend the hearing and to present your case, call witnesses and question the local authority's witnesses. You can be accompanied to the hearing or be represented. During the hearing your representative has the same rights as you in presenting your case. [183] The local authority should pay your travelling expenses and those of one other person who accompanies or represents you, also anyone else affected (eg, witnesses). [184] The tactics for presenting a case before the review board are similar to those for social security appeal tribunals (see p121).

The review board has the right to ask people to give evidence, but it cannot compel anyone to appear before them who does not wish to. [185] If you fail to attend a hearing, the review board can proceed in your absence. [186] If you were unable to attend through circumstances beyond your control, and the review board has given an unfavourable decision, you may be able to have the decision 'set aside' (see p209).

You may apply to the chairperson in writing for the hearing to be adjourned, or for the case to be completely withdrawn, at any time before the review board has come to a decision (even during the hearing itself).

If the review board decides to adjourn a hearing and the case is subsequently heard by a board composed of any different members, the second board should hear your whole case again. [187]

The decision

After hearing your case, the review board either confirms or alters the decision of the local authority. [188] If the board is not unanimous, a majority decision is taken. If there are an even number of members, the chairperson has a second or casting vote if necessary. [189] The chairperson must record the board's decision and its finding on any material question of fact. [190]

In arriving at its decision, the review board is bound only by the law and not by any local authority or DSS policy. It may exercise any discretion open to the local authority under the regulations. [191] It is not bound by any of its own previous decisions, nor by any of the decisions made by social security appeal tribunals or Social Security Commissioners on similar cases and issues in other areas of the social security system, although it can take them into account. In particular, it should be slow to disagree with a Commissioner's decision as Commissioners are judges with considerable experience of this sort of law.

A copy of the decision must be sent to you within seven days or, if that is not practicable, as soon as possible after that, together with the reasons for the decision and the board's findings of fact. [192] These should give a clear explanation of why you have won or lost. [193] If the review board has altered the local authority's decision in any way, the local authority must implement the board's decision with effect from the date the original decision was made. [194] However, decisions of a review board are binding on the local authority only in the particular case in question.

If the board has awarded additional benefit, arrears may only be paid for up to 52 weeks before the date on which the local authority completed its initial internal review. The only exception is where the review board have overturned a previous local authority decision not to backdate a claim under the 'good cause for a late claim' provisions – in which case any arrears may be paid from the date your claim is now treated as having been made (see p187). [195]

A decision of a review board may be reviewed by a local authority in certain circumstances – see p205.

There is no right of appeal from a review board's decision but, if the decision was wrong in law, you can apply for judicial review (see p210).

(iv) Correcting a decision

Both local authorities and review boards can correct any accidental errors which have occurred in their decisions.[196] An accidental error is where the decision actually made is not the one recorded or notified because of a slip of the pen, a misprint, a mathematical error, or the omission of a word etc. Corrections may be made at any time and will take effect as though they were part of the original decision, or record of a decision, being corrected. Every person affected must be informed of the correction. You cannot seek a review against the correction of a decision, but you can ask for a review of the decision itself.[197]

(v) Setting aside a decision

Both local authorities and review boards also have the power to set aside their own decisions if the interests of justice warrant it.[198] 'Setting aside' means deleting the decision as though it had never been made in the first place. A new decision is then made.

The law allows a decision to be set aside if it appears just to do so because:[199]

☐ you, your representative, or some other person affected by the decision, were not sent, or did not receive, a document relating to the matters concerned in that decision, or the document arrived too late;

☐ in the case of a hearing before a review board, you, your representative, or some other person affected by the decision were not present;

☐ for some other reason, the interests of justice require it.

Any person affected by a decision may apply to have that decision set aside.[200] Applications must be in writing and must reach the local authority or review board concerned within 13 weeks of the notification of that decision being posted to the applicant.[201] The 13-week limit cannot be extended but does not include any period before the correction of (or refusal to correct) that decision, or the setting aside of a previous decision.[202] The local authority or review board must send copies of the application to any other persons affected by the decision and give them a reasonable opportunity to comment.[203]

The outcome of an application to have a decision set aside must be notified in writing to every person affected as soon as possible, and this must contain a statement explaining the reasons for meeting or rejecting that request.[204]

If your request to have a decision set aside is rejected, this cannot be challenged by means of a review,[205] but you may still request a review of the original decision itself. In applying the time-limits for requesting a review, no account will be taken of any period between the date when the notification of the decision, and the notification of the refusal to set it aside, were each posted to you.[206] If you have been denied a fair hearing before the review board and your request to have the board's decision set aside is turned down, you may be able to challenge this by way of a judicial review (see p210).

(vi) Judicial review

Judicial review is a method of challenging a decision of any form of tribunal, government department or local authority.

Applications are made to the High Court (in Scotland, the Court of Session).

In practice, it is not a procedure that can be used very much in social security cases except in HB and CCB cases against decisions of review boards. That is because there are two major restrictions on the power of the Court to intervene. Firstly, the court will very seldom intervene if there is an alternative right of appeal. Secondly, the court can only intervene to correct an error of law. For these purposes, error of law has the same meaning as for appeals to a Social Security Commissioner in IS cases (see p124). In nearly all social security cases where there is no right of appeal to a tribunal, the person or authority making a decision is using a purely discretionary power and it is very difficult to show that an error of law has been made in such cases. Judicial review can, however, be used to compel a person or body to make a decision if there is excessive delay.

Review boards quite often make errors of law. If you consider that one has been made in your case, you should consult a solicitor. Legal aid is available in judicial review cases. CPAG's solicitors may be able to advise if you go through an advice agency.

8 COMPLAINTS

(i) Complaints to councillors

If you are not satisfied with the treatment of your case by the local authority you can complain to a local councillor. A councillor will not be able to do anything about a decision made on a particular case, but they can take up issues around local authority policy and procedure where the authority has discretion in the way it implements the HB scheme. A councillor can also take up complaints about the way the authority has handled your case – eg, delays, discrimination and other ways in which the service is provided such as opening hours, getting hold of someone to talk to. Before you do take up a complaint with a councillor you should try and sort out the problem with the HB section. Ask to speak to the Principal Officer in charge. If you are dissatisfied with a decision on your case you should ask for a review/further review (see p206). To complain to a councillor you can either contact your local ward councillor, the Chair of the Committee that is responsible for HB – usually Housing or Finance Committees, or you can go straight to the Leader of the Council. The names of councillors are kept by local libraries.

(ii) The local government Ombudsman

If there is maladministration in the way the local authority has handled your case, you should complain to the local government Ombudsman. An example of maladministration would be a long delay in dealing with your case.

However, if you are dissatisfied with the decision of the local authority you should ask for a review (see p206). The Ombudsman will not investigate the decision of an authority, only the administration by an authority. You must show that there has been maladministration.

While it can often take a long time for a case to be investigated by the Ombudsman, the mere fact that you have made a complaint (or have threatened to) can prompt the local authority into sorting the problem out.

If you want to complain to the Ombudsman (whose full title is the Commissioner for Local Administration), you must first of all ask your local authority to look at your complaint. If you are dissatisfied with its response, or it does nothing, you can approach the Ombudsman directly by writing to the relevant local office (see Appendix 1).

PART VI
Community charge benefit

Chapter 15

Community charge benefit

This chapter covers:

1   THE BASIC RULES

The community charge is what is popularly known as the poll tax. Community charge benefit (CCB) is what is popularly known as a poll tax rebate.

CCB is paid by local authorities and not by the Benefits Agency, although it is a national scheme and the rules are mainly determined by DSS regulations.

If you are liable to pay a personal community charge, your liability is simply reduced. If you are liable to pay a collective community charge contribution, you are paid a cash allowance (although it is sometimes paid direct to your landlord, especially if you are in arrears).

People with entry restrictions placed on their stay in the UK, **can** claim CCB if they are liable to pay the charge because CCB is **not** treated as public funds (see p63).

The rules for CCB are very similar to the rules for HB. This chapter looks at the rules that are different from HB and makes references to the HB sections where the rules are the same.

(i) Who can claim

To claim CCB, you must be paying either the personal community charge or collective community charge contributions (see p215).

You can claim CCB if:

☐ your income is low enough. How low it has to be depends on your circumstances (see p218). Remember that some of your income may be ignored but that you may also be treated as having income you do not really receive (see p246);

☐ your savings and other capital are not worth more than £16,000. Again, some of your capital may be ignored but you may also be treated as having capital you do not really possess (see p272);

☐ you are shown in the community charge register as liable to pay a personal community charge (see p215); *or* you are liable to pay a collective community charge contribution (see p215).

The amount of benefit you receive depends on your income (see pp246-71), the number of people in your 'family' (see below) and your 'eligible community charge' (see p217). The full calculation is explained on p218.

(ii) Who you claim for

As with IS, you claim for your 'family' which consists of:

☐ you; *and*

☐ your partner (if any) who is

either your husband or wife, if you are living together (see p229),

or a person of the opposite sex to whom you are not married but with whom you are living together as husband and wife (see p229); *and*

☐ any children for whom you are responsible (which may include children who have left school – see p233).

Income and capital belonging to your partner are treated as yours. There are special rules for dealing with income and capital belonging to your children (see pp247 and 272).

(iii) Claiming benefit

The rules for claiming benefit and payment of benefit are very similar to those for HB (see p184). If you get IS you can claim through your local Benefits Agency office by filling out a combined HB/CCB form. Other people should get a claim form from their local authority. You may be able to claim CCB on the same form as for HB. In most cases benefit is paid directly into your community charge account, reducing the amount of community charge you have to pay. Couples have to make a joint claim, but are paid separately.

2 LIABILITY TO PAY A COMMUNITY CHARGE

There are several kinds of community charge, but only the personal community charge and collective community charge contributions may be considered for a rebate in the form of CCB. Some full-time students are not entitled to CCB because they already pay a reduced community charge (see below). Certain other groups are exempt from paying community charge altogether (see p216). Some people may be able to get a reduced charge as well as CCB (see p216).

(i) The personal community charge

If you are 18 or over and solely or mainly resident in a local authority area you have to pay the personal community charge unless you fall into one of the groups who are exempt (see p216). Your liability is assessed on a daily basis. If you live in an area for part of the year only, you will have to pay a corresponding proportion of the annual personal community charge in that area. The level of the personal community charge is set by the local authority and is the same amount for every liable person within that local authority's area, regardless of personal circumstances. If you are a couple, you are each individually liable for your own separate personal community charge but in the event of your partner not paying, you are also liable for your partner's personal community charge.

Students

Full-time students only have to pay 20 per cent of the personal community charge. These students, called 'registered students', cannot claim CCB for their 20 per cent liability since everyone must pay at least 20 per cent of their community charge. See p224 for the definition of a registered student, and those students who can and cannot claim CCB. Registered students do not pay the collective community charge contribution.

(ii) Collective community charge contribution

You may have to pay a collective community charge contribution instead of the personal community charge. You pay this if you are 18 or over and living in accommodation where the majority of residents are likely to stay only for a short time – eg, houses in multiple occupation, some lodging houses and hostels. The Community Charge Registration Officer decides which accommodation should be 'designated' for a collective community charge, which the owner of the property has to pay. If you live in this type of accommodation, your landlord collects from you collective community charge contributions towards the collective charge that s/he must pay. The landlord must issue you with receipts. The collective community charge contribution is calculated as a daily equivalent of the local personal community charge. You do not have to pay it if you are a full-time student (see above) or are exempt from paying a community charge (see p216).

(iii) Other kinds of community charge

You cannot get CCB for the standard community charge (payable on second homes), the collective community charge (payable by landlords of certain short-stay premises but recoverable by them from their residents in the form of collective community charge contributions), or the national business rate (payable on non-domestic properties). In Scotland, CCB also cannot be paid on standard community charge contributions or on community water charges.

(iv)   People who are exempt

Certain groups are exempt from paying the personal community charge and collective community charge contribution. These are set out below:

☐ people under 18;

☐ people over 18 who are still at, or have just left, school and for whom child benefit is (or could be) paid;

☐ students under 20 at technical colleges, etc;

☐ students whose term-time address is in Northern Ireland;

☐ homeless people sleeping rough;

☐ people staying in some short-stay hostels and night shelters;

☐ residents in women's refuges (Scotland only);

☐ people detained in prison, hospital or detention centres as a result of a court order, warrant, sentence or direction (*including* prisoners on remand but *excluding*, in England and Wales, those imprisoned or ordered to pay a fine for non-payment of the community charge);

☐ patients who are solely or mainly resident in hospital or in residential care homes, nursing homes, mental nursing homes or hostels where personal care or treatment is provided (but there is no exemption during a temporary stay);

☐ care workers (eg, community service volunteers) who work for charitable bodies, either voluntarily or for nominal wages, providing residential care to members of the community;

☐ people living in religious communities on which they are dependent for their support;

☐ foreign military personnel in Britain under treaty obligations and foreign members of NATO and other international organisations;

☐ residents of designated Crown property who either live there for short periods only or who should not be registered for reasons of national security;

☐ people with a severe mental disability and who are entitled to invalidity pension, disability living allowance at the higher or middle rate, DWA following the receipt of invalidity benefit or severe disablement allowance, attendance allowance or constant attendance allowance, severe disablement allowance or unemployability supplement or allowance or, in Scotland only, who are over 65 (men) or 60 (women). There is no exemption for anyone with a severe physical disability, unless they happen to come into one of the other exempt categories above.

(v)   Reductions to your community charge

From April 1992, if the community charge you are paying is £52 more than a notional amount which you would have paid under the rates system (including rates paid as part of rent) prior to April 1990, you may be able to get a reduction to your community charge. The reduction is worked out by the local authority and CCB is calculated on the amount payable after the reduction has been made. Prior to April

1991, the reduction scheme was called transitional relief and had slightly different rules. However, the effect on CCB is the same. There is also another scheme for elderly and disabled people who were not ratepayers prior to April 1990 and who pay more than £52 community charge. Under this scheme, the local authority will not automatically make the reduction – you must make an application first.

3 YOUR 'ELIGIBLE COMMUNITY CHARGE'

Your eligible community charge is the whole of your personal community charge or your collective community charge contribution, although the maximum CCB you are entitled to is 80 per cent of your eligible community charge.

(i) Shared accommodation

Any single person liable to pay the personal community charge or the collective community charge contribution may be eligible for CCB in her/his own right. This means that many people excluded from getting HB for housing costs (eg, grown-up sons and daughters treated as non-dependants, or people with 'contrived tenancies' etc) may still be able to get help in the form of a rebate on their community charge but they must claim for themselves.

In the case of single people sharing accommodation, each of you can claim a separate rebate on your own individual community charge. In calculating your CCB, no account will be taken of any other person living in your accommodation, apart from your dependants, or income you receive from commercial arrangements – eg, sub-tenants/boarders. Unlike HB there are no 'non-dependant deductions'.

(ii) Couples

If you are a member of a married or unmarried couple (or of a polygamous marriage), only one of you is able to claim CCB on behalf of you and your partner(s)[1] (see p229 for the definition of 'couple'). The CCB calculation is based on your combined community charge liability, your joint capital and income and the couple's applicable amount (plus an amount for dependants where appropriate). However, any benefit is divided between you and your partner in proportion to the community charge you each are due to pay.[2] So you are each paid CCB separately.

In most cases, couples have to pay the same and so any CCB divided equally between them. However, if one partner is exempt from paying the community charge, the calculation is based solely on what the other partner has to pay, but still takes into account the couple's joint capital, income and applicable amount. The full CCB entitlement is then paid to the partner who is liable for community charge.[3] Exactly the same process applies where one partner is a student with reduced liability (see p224). Note that, in this case, however, the student's 20 per cent liability is completely ignored in the calculation and any benefit is paid to the non-student partner.[4]

(iii) Absence from home

If you are away from your normal home and liable for both the personal community charge and a collective community charge contribution at the same time (this cannot happen in Scotland) the two charges cannot be added together in one claim. You can get help with both charges but must make separate claims for each – even where both are due in the same local authority area.[5] Absence from home does not affect your entitlement to CCB, so long as you are still liable to pay the community charge and you are still treated as part of your household (see p228).

(iv)　Discounts and reductions

If you receive a discount on your community charge bill because you paid it promptly, this is ignored for CCB purposes and does not reduce your benefit entitlement.[6]

However, if your community charge bill has been reduced because you have received a community charge reduction to limit your losses as a result of the change-over from the rates in April 1990, your CCB entitlement is based on the net amount of community charge you pay after any reductions (see p216).[7]

4　THE AMOUNT OF BENEFIT

(i)　The basic calculation

The rules for calculating CCB are similar to those for HB (see p168). The local authority must calculate HB and CCB separately. The calculation depends on:
☐　your 'applicable amount' which represents your family's needs (see p236);
☐　your 'eligible community charge' (see p217);
☐　your income (see pp246-71).
There are *no* deductions for other people living in your household.

The most you can be paid (your **maximum CCB**) is 80 per cent of your 'eligible community charge' - ie, what you are liable to pay.[8]

If *either* you are entitled to IS, *or* your income is less than your applicable amount, your benefit is your maximum CCB.[9]

If your income is higher than your applicable amount, your CCB is your maximum CCB *less* 15 per cent of the difference between your income and your applicable amount.[10]

A local authority may increase the amount of CCB up to the maximum CCB in exceptional circumstances (see p174). This extra payment may be credited to your community charge account or paid directly to you.[11]

Unlike HB, there is no minimum payment rule for CCB.

The local authority may round any figure used in working out your entitlement to the nearest penny with fractions of half a penny being rounded upwards.

Example

Ms Zaman pays a personal community charge of £417.15 a year (£8 a week). She is a pensioner aged 62. She has a retirement and occupational pension of £58.50.

Income

State retirement and occupational pension	£58.50

Applicable amount

Personal allowance	£42.45
Pensioner premium	£14.70
	£57.15

Her income exceeds her applicable amounts by £1.35.

Ms Zaman pays £8 per week community charge:	
Maximum benefit is 80% of £8 =	£ 6.40
Less 15% of £1.35	
ie, excess income =	£ 0.20
CCB =	£ 6.20

She has to pay the difference between her community charge and her benefit, ie, £8 – £6.20 = £1.80 per week.

(ii) Calculating a weekly amount of community charge

Entitlement to CCB is calculated in respect of a HB/CCB benefit week, a period of seven days beginning on a Monday (see p191), so your community charge is converted into a weekly figure. An annual personal community charge is divided by 365 (or 366) and multiplied by 7. Similarly, if a collective community charge contribution is payable other than weekly, a weekly figure is obtained by dividing the figure by the number of days it covers and multiplying by 7. You are entitled to CCB for any day on which you are liable to pay a personal charge or collective contribution. You cannot get CCB for any day for which you are not liable to pay these charges.

5 CLAIMS, PAYMENTS AND REVIEWS

(i) How to claim and date of claim

You must claim in writing from the local authority which levies the community charge.[12] If you are claiming IS, you should have been given an HB and CCB claim form with your IS form. Otherwise, get a form from the local authority. If you get the form by telephoning or writing to the local authority your claim is normally treated as having been made when you asked the local authority for the form (see p185).

Except in the cases mentioned below, the rules for claiming CCB, and for establishing your date of claim, are the same as for HB, so see pp184-88 for more detailed advice. (The notes at the back of the book to Chapter 14 contain the relevant references to CCB legislation.) Note that a claim may be backdated up to a year in certain circumstances (see p187). Note also that CCB is paid for a period of up to 60 weeks and that you must make a new claim at the end of the period (see p188).

There are five cases when the date of claim for CCB is not the same as for HB:

☐ If you already get CCB and subsequently acquire a new partner, or your partner becomes liable for a community charge, or your partner ceases to be a registered student, the effective date of your new joint claim for CCB is the date on which notification of your change of circumstances is received by the local authority (or Benefits Agency, in IS cases). This means that if you delay telling the local authority about your new partner, or existing partner's change of circumstances, there is likely to be a period during which your partner will have to pay the full community charge without being entitled to any CCB – whereas your CCB over the same period is modified to take into account your joint income and the couple's applicable amount (but not your partner's community charge). [13]

☐ If you claim CCB up to 13 weeks before you expect to become entitled to it (because, for instance, you are about to become liable for the full community charge on becoming 18 or on ceasing to be a registered student), the local authority has the discretion to treat your claim as having been made in the benefit week before your expected entitlement. Advance claims may be accepted in this way, even if you have not yet been entered on the community charge register. [14] This is similar to the rule for HB (see p188).

☐ If you have:
  – been registered for the personal community charge by two or more local authorities for the same period; *and*
  – appealed against one or more register entries; *and*
  – claimed CCB within 14 days of the appeal decision confirming to which local authority the personal community charge must be paid; *and*
  – the local authority concerned is satisfied that you would have been entitled to CCB for any of the days for which the personal community charge is now due;
  the local authority must treat your claim as having been made on the first day on which CCB entitlement could have arisen. [15]

☐ If you are not yet listed on the register for the community charge but are liable to pay, you can claim in advance of registration and the date of claiming is treated as the date the claim is made, or the date of registration, whichever is later. [16]

☐ If you have recently moved into the local authority area and get IS, you are allowed four weeks from the date of moving into the area to claim CCB, so long as the authority or the Benefits Agency office from which you claim IS receives your claim within the four weeks. Claims made within this time are effective from the date of moving into the area. [17] This is similar to the rule for HB (see p188).

(ii) Decisions

The basic rules about the way decisions are made are the same as for HB (see p188). The notes to Chapter 13 include CCB legislation where appropriate.) However, there are two important differences:

☐ Notification of a CCB decision should be given to your partner as well as you, although the DSS guidance suggests that a joint notification is sufficient provided it deals with the entitlement of both of you. [18]

☐ The local authority does not have to notify you of an overpayment caused by a change in the amount of its community charge or an adjustment because you qualify for a reduction (see p216). [19]

(iii)　Your benefit period

This is the length of time your entitlement lasts before you have to make a new claim. The rules on benefit periods are the same as for HB (see p191). However, the rules on when your CCB begins are different from HB.

Your benefit usually begins:

☐ if you are liable for a personal community charge, on the Monday after your date of claim; [20]

☐ if you are liable for a collective community charge contribution, on the day of your date of claim. [21]

For your date of claim, see p186.

However, if you or your partner have only just become liable for a personal community charge (because you have just moved or ceased to be exempt or because you, or your partner, have ceased to be a registered student, or you have acquired a partner), your CCB starts on the first day of your liability, provided that you claim during the same benefit week as your entitlement starts. [22] A benefit week runs from Monday to Sunday.

If you have just become liable for collective community charge contributions, or have ceased to be a registered student and must now pay the contributions, your CCB starts on the first day of your liability so long as you claim in the same benefit week that your liability started. [23] Otherwise it starts on the date of your claim.

Your benefit period ends at a date chosen by the local authority. The period must not exceed 60 weeks. See p191 for the HB rules which are the same as those for CCB.

(iv)　Payment methods

Your weekly CCB entitlement in respect of the **personal community charge** is converted into a daily amount and multiplied by the number of days between the day that entitlement starts and the following 31 March. This amount is, wherever possible, then deducted from your outstanding personal community charge liability for the period. [24] The balance of any personal community charge left for you to pay is then divided by the number of instalment periods remaining up to 31 March. Any such CCB deduction must be specified on the bill. [25] If you have already paid your personal community charge bill in full, or if the amount you still have to pay is less than your rebate, your rebate can be paid to you in cash, by cheque or giro, or by making deductions from your future liability. [26] The DSS guidance reminds local authorities that if benefit is to be carried over and deducted from your next community charge bill, this rebate must be paid off as quickly as possible at the beginning and not spread out evenly over the whole period covered by that bill. If you cease to be liable for the community charge, any outstanding rebate entitlement must be paid to you in cash, cheque or giro within 14 days of it becoming due or, if that is not reasonably practicable, as soon as possible after that. [27]

CCB in respect of a **collective community charge contribution** must be paid to you within seven days of receipt of the claim – in cash, or by cheque or giro, or by issuing you with a special voucher.[28] Your landlord must accept the voucher as part-payment of your collective community charge contribution and the local authority must, in turn, accept the voucher as part-payment of the landlord's collective community charge liability.[29] The local authority must take account of the times and frequency with which your collective community charge contributions are due in deciding how often to pay you.[30] In many cases, your collective community charge contribution is paid at the same time as your rent – in which case your CCB payments should match your rent cycle. If a cheque or giro is lost, see p193.

Payment to a landlord

If a collective community charge contribution is due to your landlord, the local authority may pay your CCB directly to her/him:
- [ ] if you have requested or agreed to direct payments;[31] *or*
- [ ] without your agreement, if you are owed arrears of CCB in respect of any unpaid contributions, and you no longer live at the accommodation in respect of which the contributions are payable, and the authority considers it impractical to pay the CCB to you.[32]

Both you and your landlord should be notified of any direct payments. If these are to be made against your wishes, you can ask for the decision to be reviewed (see p206).

Withholding payment

CCB may be withheld if a query has arisen as to your entitlement or it is thought that you have been overpaid and that the overpayment is recoverable. The arrears will be paid when the query has been resolved.[33] An overpayment cannot be deducted from any arrears unless it is legally recoverable (see below).

Any benefit withheld and then paid at a later date should either be credited to your community charge account in order to reduce your liability or, if that is not possible, or if you request it, paid directly to you.[34] If you pay collective community charge contributions, your permission is needed before any withheld CCB can be paid directly to your landlord.[35]

(v) Overpayments

An overpayment of CCB is usually described as 'excess benefit' but the rules and methods of recovery are broadly the same as for HB (see p197 – the notes to Chapter 14 contain CCB legislation where appropriate). The differences are noted here.

As with HB, only certain overpayments may be recovered from you. Unlike HB, they may be recovered only from the claimant or the person to whom they were paid – eg, landlord/appointee; they cannot be recovered from other people who caused the overpayment.[36] A recoverable overpayment made to you may be recovered by deductions from your partner's CCB if, at the time the overpayment was both made and recovered, you were a couple.[37]

If both HB and CCB have been overpaid, they must be recovered separately. CCB overpayments cannot be recovered from HB.[38]

Any overpayments of CCB caused by a reduction of the community charge under the transitional relief and reduction schemes (see p216) may be recovered. Similarly, overpayments caused because of charge-capping may also be recovered.[39]

If you pay a personal community charge, the overpayment may be added to your community charge account.[40] It can then be recovered as though you were in arrears with your community charge. For a collective community charge contribution, overpaid CCB cannot be recovered by increasing the collective community charge to the landlord, and expecting the landlord to recover it from you.[41]

Overpaid CCB cannot be recovered by court action until at least 21 days after you have been notified of the amount due.[42]

If the local authority decides that a recoverable overpayment has been made, you must be told what method of recovery will be used – whether by demanding payment in 21 days, adding it to a community charge account or making deductions from future payments of CCB or from social security benefits paid by the Benefits Agency.[43]

(vi) Reviews and change of circumstances

The rules for CCB reviews and change of circumstances are the same as those for HB (see p205 and p195 – the notes to Chapter 14 include CCB legislation).

Changes in the amount of your personal community charge or collective community charge contribution take effect from the day of the change.[44] This is also true where the change is the death of your partner or an amendment to the CCB regulations. If you separate from your partner and s/he ceases to be liable for that authority's community charge during the same benefit week, the change takes place on the date her/his liability ended.

If your circumstances need to be reviewed because you, or your partner, have become liable for the charge, any changes to your joint CCB take effect from the date of the change so long as you report the change in the same benefit week as your new liability starts. If you delay reporting the changes, any changes to *your* benefit take effect from the next benefit week following the change (eg, joint income etc) and any change to your *partner's* benefit (eg, her/his liability) takes effect from the next benefit week following the notification about your partner's benefit.[45] The dates that other changes take effect are the same as for HB (see p196).

You must notify any change in your collective community charge contribution or of any new liability for a personal community charge. You do not need to notify the local authority of any change in the rate of your personal community charge if you have not moved.[46] Your duty to report other changes in your circumstances are the same as for HB (see p195).

(vii) The community charge benefit review board

This is the same as a housing benefit review board (see p206 – notes to Chapter 14 include CCB legislation where appropriate). It is the only sort of appeal body there is for CCB cases. It is not independent, being composed of councillors from the local authority (or members of the Scottish Development Board or Scottish Homes if appropriate). Nevertheless, review boards do not always agree with council officers, so apply for a further review by a review board if you have not succeeded with an internal review. If the same issue affects both your HB and your CCB and the same local authority is concerned with both, one review board can be convened to deal with both claims if everyone agrees.

A decision of a review board can be challenged by judicial review (see p210).

(viii)   Making complaints

The same avenues are open in CCB cases as in HB cases (see p210).

6 STUDENTS

Registered students cannot claim CCB.[47] A registered student is someone in advanced or further education, who studies for an average of 21 hours a week or more, and for at least 24 weeks in the academic year. Student nurses are not registered (unless they are on Project 2000) because they spend more than 50 per cent of their study-time on work experience.

Registered students cannot claim CCB because they already receive maximum help through the community charge scheme – ie, they only pay 20 per cent of their charge (see p215). In practice, then, most full-time students cannot claim CCB.

Any other student who is not registered can claim CCB (eg, part-time students), but s/he will be subject to special income rules similar to those that apply for HB. Partners of registered students (who are not themselves registered students) can claim CCB for their own community charge liability, but there are specific rules that apply to the calculation of their benefit (see below). People who are studying under the Employment Training Scheme do not count as students.

(i)   Special rules for eligible students

Claims for CCB from eligible students are calculated according to the rules that apply for other claims. However, there are special rules that apply to the treatment of your income[48] (see p260). These rules are the same as for HB. If you, or your partner, get IS, the income rules on students do not apply and your CCB will be calculated in the normal way (see p218).[49] If you are not on IS, you will be subject to the student income rules and will need to check that you are counted as a student for CCB purposes and the period of time that you are considered to be a student[50] – this is the same as for HB (see p176). The student income rules apply to students and their partners.[51] Apart from the treatment of student income there are no other special rules that restrict CCB entitlement to students. This means that, unlike HB, students from abroad can claim CCB (CCB is not public funds – see p63) and absence from your accommodation during vacations does not affect your entitlement (so long as you remain liable for a charge).

7 PEOPLE IN HOSPITAL

If you, your partner or child go into hospital your benefit may be affected.[52] The rules are the same as for HB (see p175) *except:*

☐ CCB can be paid indefinitely despite your absence from your home – ie, for periods over 52 weeks. However, if the local authority decides you are no longer part of your family (ie, partner/children) they may reassess you as a single person (see p227);

☐ your CCB will stop if the community charge registration officer decides that you are now resident in the hospital. If this is the case, you will not be liable for the personal community charge (see p216). Registration officers have been advised by government guidelines to use the HB 52-week absence rule to assess whether someone has their permanent residence in hospital or whether they intend to return home (see p154).

PART VII
Calculating needs and resources

*Income support (IS), family credit (FC), disability working allowance (DWA), hous-ing benefit (HB) and community charge benefit (CCB) are all means-tested benefits. The amount you get depends on the **size of your family**, how much **capital** you have and how your **income** compares with your **needs** (called your applicable amount). The rules for all five benefits are the same or similar. This Part covers those rules which are common to all.*

Chapter 16

Who counts as your family

This chapter explains who is included in your benefit claim. It covers:

1 Introduction (below)
2 Claiming as a couple (p229)
3 Claiming for children (p233)

1 INTRODUCTION

(i) Who is a 'family'

You claim IS/FC/DWA/HB/CCB for yourself, your partner and any dependent children who are members of your household. This is your 'family' for benefit pur-poses.[1] A partner can include a wife, husband or cohabitee. When your benefit is worked out, the needs of your partner and any children are added to yours and so, usually, is their capital and income.

If one member of your family is claiming IS/FC/DWA/HB/CCB, no other member can claim the same benefit for the same period.[2] However, partners can choose which of them should be the claimant, except for FC when the woman must usually claim, and DWA when the disabled partner should claim (if both of you are disabled, you can choose which one of you should be the claimant.) For details about how to claim see p100 (IS), p129 (FC), p139 (DWA), p151 (HB) and p213 (CCB).

(ii)   Membership of the same household

The idea of sharing a household is central to whether you can include a child or a partner in your claim. Your right to claim benefit for either ends if you cease to be treated as a member of the same household. This also means that their income and capital is not added to yours when assessing your benefit.

However, the term 'household' is not defined. In many cases it will be obvious that you are members of the same household – eg, if you, your husband or wife and your children all live together in one house. There are also certain situations in which you will *not* be treated as members of the same household (see p231 for couples and p234 for children), though temporary absences from the home do not mean that you cease to share a household.[3]

There will be some occasions where you are regarded as members of the same household, when you think you should not be – eg, if you are two friends of the opposite sex sharing a house. If this arises you must try to show that although you both live in the same **house** you maintain separate **households**.

A separate household might exist if there are:
☐   independent arrangements for the storage and cooking of food;
☐   independent financial arrangements;
☐   separate eating arrangements;
☐   no evidence of family life;
☐   a separate commitment for housing costs.

If you can show that you maintain separate homes you cannot be part of the same household.[4] Even if you only have the right to occupy part of a room you may have your own household.[5] A separate liability for housing costs could also show that you are not in the same household.[6] Separated or estranged couples living under the same roof should not be treated as a couple.

You cannot be a member of more than one household at the same time; so if you are a member of one couple, you cannot also be treated as part of another. Note that being married to someone does not necessarily mean that you cannot be treated as part of a couple with someone else instead.[7]

Much of the case law on this issue relates to IS, but you should assume that it is also relevant for FC/DWA/HB/CCB.

A local authority and the Benefits Agency will look at the question of cohabiting separately, and may reach different conclusions. However, if the Benefits Agency has decided that you are not cohabiting, and has awarded income support, the local authority should not make a separate decision.[8]

Where a child lives for part of the week with each parent, only one parent can claim for the child, but s/he will be treated as a member of her/his household for the whole week (see p233).

2 CLAIMING AS A COUPLE

You claim as a couple if you and your partner are:[9]
- □ married, and living in the same household (see above for definition); *or*
- □ not married but 'living together as husband and wife'.

If you are lesbian or gay partners you do not count as a couple, and must claim as single people.

You count as polygamously married if you are married to more than one person and your marriages took place in a country which permits polygamy.[10]

(i) Living together as husband and wife

If it is decided that you are living together, only one of you will be able to claim benefit. Either partner (but see pp130 and 145 for special rules for FC and DWA) can be the claimant but s/he must claim for both partners. The amount of benefit for a couple is usually less than that for two single people, so it is important to dispute a decision that you are living together if you believe you are not. However, in some cases you may have to prove that you are living together to get benefit – eg, where you want to claim FC, you have children and you do not work, but your partner does. You must, of course, be consistent about your circumstances for each different benefit.

The following criteria are used to decide whether you are living together.[11] These are taken from IS law, but, as the rules for FC/DWA/HB/CCB are the same, you should argue that they apply to all benefits.

Do you live in the same household?

In all cases, you must be living and spending the major part of your free time not only under the same roof, but in the same **household** (see p228 for definition of 'household'). If one of you has a separate address where you usually live, the cohabitation rule should not be applied.

Even if you *do* share a 'household', you may not be cohabiting. It is essential to look at *why* two people are in the same household.[12] For example, where a couple were living in the same household for reasons of 'care, companionship and mutual convenience' (one of them was disabled) they were not living together as husband and wife.[13]

Is your relationship stable?

Marriage is expected to be stable and lasting. It follows that an occasional or brief association should not be regarded as 'living together as husband and wife'. However, the fact that a relationship is stable does not make it a 'husband/wife' relationship. You can have a stable landlord/lodger relationship but not be 'living together as husband and wife'.

What are your financial arrangements?

If one partner is supported by the other or household expenses are shared, this may be treated as evidence of a husband and wife relationship. However, it is important to consider how they are shared. There is a difference between, on the one hand, payment of a fixed weekly contribution or the rigid sharing of bills 50/50 and, on the other hand, a free common fund attributable to income and expenditure. The former does not imply 'living together as husband and wife', the latter might.

Do you have a sexual relationship?

Officers may not ask you about the existence of a sexual relationship, so they will only have the information if you volunteer it. If you do not have a sexual relationship, you should tell the officer yourself – and perhaps offer to show her/him the separate sleeping arrangements.

A sexual relationship is a normal part of a marriage and therefore of living together as husband and wife. But just having a sexual relationship is not sufficient by itself to prove you are 'living together as husband and wife'.

A couple who abstain from a sexual relationship before marriage on grounds of principle (eg, religious reasons) should not be counted as living together as husband and wife until they are formally married. [14]

Do you have children?

If you have had a child together, this is strong evidence of cohabitation.

How do you appear in public?

Officers may check the electoral roll and claims for National Insurance benefits to see if you present yourselves as husband and wife. If the woman has adopted the man's name, this will be considered strong evidence of cohabitation. On the other hand, many couples retain their identity publicly as unmarried people. This does not mean they cannot be regarded as living together as husband and wife.

Challenging a 'living together' decision

Sometimes benefit is stopped or adjusted because a boyfriend/girlfriend regularly stays overnight, even though you might have none of the long-term commitments generally associated with marriage. But couples with no sexual relationship who live together (eg, as landlord/lodger, tenant/housekeeper, or as flat-sharers) also sometimes fall foul of the rule. People who provide mutual support and share household expenses are not necessarily living together as husband and wife, as this also happens where people of the same sex or friends of different sexes share a home. [15]

However, it is difficult to challenge such a decision. You should appeal (see p118) or apply for a review (see p103 and p205) and carefully consider what evidence to put before the tribunal/review board in relation to each of the six questions above. Possibilities include evidence of the other person having another address, a rent book, receipts for board and lodging or statements from friends and relatives.

If the tribunal or review board does not wish to go into the question of whether or not there is a sexual relationship, you should argue that sex is an important part of marriage and that it is not possible to consider 'living together as husband and wife' properly in isolation from it. The burden of proof is on the Benefits Agency/local authority to prove that you are living together as husband and wife, because disqualification from benefit is involved.

If your benefit is withdrawn because you are living with someone as husband and wife, you should reapply immediately if your circumstances change. You should also apply immediately for any other benefits for which you might qualify. You should apply on the basis of low income for other benefits for which you previously qualified automatically if you were on IS – eg, health benefits (see Chapter 25).

If you are still entitled to benefit you should be paid as a couple.

If your IS stops and you have diverted a maintenance order to the Benefits Agency (see p91), contact the magistrates' court immediately to get payments sent direct to you.

If you have no money at all, you may possibly be able to get a social fund payment (see Part IX).

(ii) Couples living apart

If you separate *permanently* you can claim as single people immediately, but you will continue to be treated as a couple while you and your partner are *temporarily* apart. [16] There is no specified period of time after which an absence is considered to be no longer temporary, but each case will be decided according to its particular circumstances.

If your partner has never lived with you in GB, you are not treated as a couple because you are not members of the same household. [17]

For HB
You will no longer count as a couple if any of the following apply to either of you: [18]
☐ You do not intend to return to your home.
☐ You have been (or expect to be) away from home for more than 52 weeks.
☐ The part of your home where you usually live is being let out while you are away.

For CCB
You will continue to be eligible as a couple as long as you both remain liable for the community charge at your address. [19]

For FC/DWA
You will no longer count as a couple if you or your partner: [20]
☐ is living permanently in local authority Part III accommodation; *or*
☐ is detained in custody under a sentence of 52 weeks or more; *or*
☐ has been in hospital for over a year; *or*
☐ is a compulsory patient held there under the mental health provisions.

For IS

You will no longer count as a couple if any of the following apply to either of you: [21]

☐ You do not intend to return to your home.

☐ You have been (or expect to be) away from home for more than 52 weeks.

☐ The part of your home where you usually live is being let out while you are away.

☐ You are in custody.

☐ You are a compulsory patient in hospital held there under the mental health provisions.

☐ You are staying permanently in a local authority home, residential care or nursing home.

☐ You are temporarily resident in local authority residential accommodation and, if assessed as a couple, you are not entitled to IS and you cannot pay the local authority's minimum charge for the accommodation. (Residential accommodation here includes homes provided by social services under NHS legislation for care and aftercare – whether or not board is available – and homes for the rehabilitation of alcoholics and drug users.)

☐ The claimant is abroad and does not qualify for IS (see p18). Where your partner is temporarily abroad you continue to be treated as a couple, but after four weeks (eight if s/he has taken a child abroad for medical treatment – see p19) the amount of IS you receive is that for a single claimant or single parent. [22] You can get benefit without signing on if you have children under 16. [23] Your partner's income and capital will continue to be treated as yours.

If you are no longer treated as a couple for the purposes of calculating your IS, you may still be liable to maintain your partner (see p88).

However, **you will still be treated as a couple, and you can get more IS than usual**, if you are temporarily living apart and the following applies: one of you is at home or in hospital, or in local authority residential accommodation or in a residential care or nursing home, and the other is: [24]

☐ resident in a nursing home, but not counted as a patient; *or*

☐ staying in a residential care home; *or*

☐ in a home for the rehabilitation of alcoholics or drug addicts; *or*

☐ in Polish resettlement accommodation; *or*

☐ on a government training course and has to live away from home (see below for your right to housing costs for more than one home); *or*

☐ in a probation or bail hostel.

Although your income and capital will be calculated in the normal way for a couple, your applicable amount will be calculated as if each of you were single claimants, if this comes to more than your usual couple rate. If you have children, one of you will be treated as a single parent. [25] If you have housing costs, your applicable amount will include these as well as any costs of the temporary accommodation of the partner away from home. [26] If you are both away from home, the costs of both sets of temporary accommodation and the family home will be met. [27] If both homes are rented, see pp154-5 for when HB can be paid for more than one home at a time. If you own your home and your partner is staying in rented accommodation, board and lodging or a hostel you will get your housing costs met by IS and your partner will be able to claim HB.

(iii) Additional points

☐ See p23 and p154 if one of you lives away from home as a student or on a government training course and you have to pay for two homes.

☐ See p309 if your child is in hospital and you have to stay in lodgings to be nearby.

☐ See p80 if one or both of you are temporarily in a local authority home, and see above if you cannot pay the charge.

3 CLAIMING FOR CHILDREN

You do not have to be a *parent* to receive benefit for a child, but you must be 'responsible' for a child who is **living in your household**.[28] You claim for any child under 16; or under 19 if they are still in full-time 'relevant' education (up to and including A-level or its equivalent).[29] Full-time means more than 12 hours a week. (See p234 for when a child no longer counts as your dependant.)

(i) 'Responsibility' for a child

You claim IS, FC, DWA, HB or CCB for a child for whom you are responsible. For FC/DWA/HB/CCB this is a child who is *normally living* with you.[30] For IS, it is where you are the person who has the *sole or main responsibility* for them.[31] In either case, this will usually be obvious, but where it is not (eg, because the child spends an equal amount of time with two parents in different homes), then you are treated as having responsibility if:[32]

☐ you get child benefit for the child;

☐ no one gets child benefit, but you have applied for it;

☐ no one has applied for it, or both of you have applied, but you appear to have the most responsibility.

Receiving child benefit is important *only* where it is unclear whether the child is normally your responsibility.

If a child regularly spends part of the week with one parent, and the rest of the week with the other, only one parent can claim benefit for that child.[33] This could create problems if both parents are on benefit, but the parent who gets the extra benefit is unwilling to share it with the other.

If a child who normally lives with one parent comes to stay with the other for a fixed period (eg, two weeks in the summer holidays), that parent can be treated as responsible and receive IS for the child for that period.[34]

If your child is away from home temporarily (eg, staying with relatives) but you receive child benefit for the child and you are clearly the person usually responsible for her/him, you should receive benefit for your child while s/he is away.

(ii) Living in the same household[35]

If you are counted as responsible for a child, then that child is usually treated as a **member of your household** despite any temporary absence. (For the meaning of 'household', see p228.) However, s/he will not count as a member of your household if s/he:

IS/FC/DWA/HB/CCB

☐ is being fostered by you under a statutory provision. You can claim benefit for a child you are fostering privately;

☐ is living with you prior to adoption, and has been placed with you by social services or an adoption agency;

IS/HB/CCB

☐ is boarded out or has been placed with someone else prior to adoption;

☐ is in the care of, or being looked after by, the local authority and not living with you. You should receive IS for her/him when s/he comes home – eg, for the weekend or a holiday. [36] Make sure you tell the Benefits Agency in good time so they can pay you the extra money. The local authority can also increase your applicable amount to include the child for HB/CCB for all of that week whether the child returns for all or only part of it; [37]

IS/FC/DWA

☐ has been in hospital or a local authority home for more than 12 weeks, and you or other members of your household have not been in regular contact with them (for FC/DWA this means 12 weeks prior to the claim; for IS the 12 weeks run from the date they went into the hospital or home or from the date you claimed IS, if later).

   Note: If a child has been in hospital or a local authority home for 52 weeks or more because of illness or disability, your FC/DWA will not include a credit/allowance for her/him even if you are still in regular contact; [38]

☐ is in custody. (For FC/DWA, being in custody on remand does not count.) You should receive IS for any periods your child spends at home;

IS only

☐ has been abroad for more than four weeks (the four weeks run from the date they went abroad, or from the date you claimed IS, if later), or for more than eight weeks if the absence abroad is to get medical treatment for the child;

☐ is living with you and away from their parental or usual home in order to attend school. The child is not treated as a member of your family, but remains a member of her/his parent's household.

(iii) When you stop claiming for a child

For IS, HB and CCB

You claim for a child until s/he is 16, or 19 if s/he is in relevant education (see p12). Children count as in relevant education until the 'terminal date' (see p13), so you can claim for them until then, or until they get a full-time job if that is earlier.

   A 16/17-year-old who has left school or college may continue to be counted as part of your 'family' for a few months after the terminal date. You will get benefit for them during the **child benefit extension period** (see p53 for details and dates) provided the following apply: [39]

☐ you were entitled to child benefit for that child immediately before the child benefit extension period started; *and*

☐ you have made a fresh claim for child benefit in writing for the child benefit extension period; *and*

☐ they have registered for work/Youth Training (YT) at the JobCentre or Careers Office; *and*

☐ they are not in full-time work.

As soon as the child gets a full-time job or a YT place or becomes 18 s/he ceases to be your dependant. If s/he loses the job or leaves YT before the end of the child benefit extension period, s/he becomes your dependant again and you can claim for her/him as long as the above conditions are satisfied. You will have to claim child benefit *again* in writing, but you should receive benefit for the 16/17-year-old in full.

Some 16/17-year-olds can get IS in their own right before they are 18 (see pp52-3) and you will not be able to claim for them. [40]

An 18-year-old who has left school or college can claim IS in their own right and does not count as part of your family.

You cannot claim for any child in advanced education (above A-level) even if they are under 19. [41]

For FC/DWA

A child will only count as your dependant for the purposes of your FC/DWA claim where, at the date of the claim, s/he is actually undergoing full-time non-advanced education. [42] Children do not count as dependants once they have actually left school even if you are still getting child benefit for them up to the terminal date, or in the child benefit extension period. This could be important if a claim for FC/DWA is not made before a young person actually leaves school but is submitted shortly afterwards during the following school holidays. They are also not counted as dependants if they become entitled to IS in their own right, or if they are in advanced education. [43]

Chapter 17

Applicable amounts

This chapter covers:

1 INTRODUCTION

For IS, HB and CCB the 'applicable amount' is a figure representing your weekly needs for the purpose of calculating your benefit. For IS, your applicable amount is the amount you are expected to live on each week. For HB/CCB it is the amount used to see how much help you need with your rent or community charge. This chapter explains how you work out your applicable amount for those benefits. For the way the amount of benefit is then calculated, see p20 for IS, p168 for HB and p218 for CCB.

The applicable amount for FC is always £66.60, and for DWA is £39.95 for single people and £66.60 for couples. It does not vary according to your personal circumstances. For the way FC/DWA are calculated, see pp133 and 144 respectively.

For IS, HB and CCB, your applicable amount is made up of:
☐ **personal allowances:** this is the amount the law says you need for living expenses (see p237);
☐ **premiums:** this is the amount given for extra needs you or your family may have (see p238);
☐ for IS only, **housing costs:** not all housing costs are met by IS and the applicable amount for these is covered on p22.

For IS your applicable amount is different if you are in a residential care or nursing home (see p75) or in local authority residential accommodation (see p80), and it is reduced if you are:
☐ voluntarily unemployed (see p45) or getting IS on hardship grounds (see p18);
☐ receiving an urgent cases payment (see p35);
☐ in hospital (see p83);
☐ involved in a trade dispute (see p58);
☐ a 16/17-year-old (see p52);
☐ a couple, one of whom is a person from abroad (see p65);
☐ without accommodation (see p86);
☐ a prisoner (see p85).
Some IS claimants get an amount of transitional protection on top of their ordinary IS (see p31).

2 PERSONAL ALLOWANCES

For IS, your personal allowance is an amount which is supposed to cover all your weekly needs, including 20 per cent of your community charge, your water rates and also enable you to save for larger essential household items that need replacing, such as bedding, as well as pay for food, heating, clothing, etc.

The amount of your personal allowance for IS, HB and CCB depends on your age and whether you are claiming as a single person or a couple. You also get an allowance for each dependent child. Remember that you cannot get a personal allowance for a child who has £3,000 or more capital (see p272).

If you are polygamously married you receive an extra amount for each additional partner.[1] (See Chapter 15 for who is included in your claim.)

(i) Rates of personal allowances

Rates for children are the same for IS and HB/CCB. They are also the same for people over 18. However, your IS personal allowance is paid at a special rate if you, or your partner (if any), are under 18 (see p52). No CCB is payable for a couple where both are under 18 because they are not liable to pay the charge. Where one partner is 18 or over then they get the couple rate for over-18s. Otherwise the personal allowances are the same for IS/HB/CCB.

Single claimant:

Aged under 18 (some IS cases (see p56) and all HB cases)	£33.60
Aged under 18 (other IS cases only, see p56)	£25.55
Other claimants aged under 25	£33.60
Aged 25 or over	£42.45

Single parents:

Aged under 18 (some IS cases (see p56) and all HB cases)	£33.60
Aged under 18 (other IS cases (see p56))	£25.55
Aged 18 or over	£42.45

Couple:

Both aged under 18 (some IS cases (see p56) and all HB cases)		£50.60
Both aged under 18 (other IS cases (see p56))	*either*	£33.60
	or	£25.55
One aged under 18 (some IS cases (see p56) and all HB and CCB cases)		£66.60
One aged under 18 (other IS cases (see p56))	*either*	£42.45
	or	£33.60
Both aged 18 or over		£66.60

Polygamous marriages:

Each additional partner living in the same household[2]	£24.15

Children:

Under 11	£14.55
11-15	£21.40
16-17	£25.55
18	£33.60

3 PREMIUMS

(i) Introduction

Premiums are added to your basic personal allowances and are intended to help with extra expenses caused by age, disability or the cost of children.
The eight premiums are:

Family premium	£ 9.30	
Severe disability premium		These can be paid on top of
Single	£32.55	any other premiums (including
Couple	£65.10	disability or higher pensioner).
Disabled child premium	£17.80	The disabled child and carers' premiums can be paid for each
Carers premium		qualifying person in the
one partner	£11.55	family.
both partners	£23.10	
Lone parent premium		
IS	£ 4.75	
HB/CCB	£10.60	
Disability premium		
Single	£17.80	Only one of these can be paid:
Couple	£25.55	if you qualify for more than
Pensioner premium*		one you will get whichever is
(i) if aged 60-74		the highest[3]
Single	£14.70	
Couple	£22.35	
(ii) if aged 75-79		
Single	£16.65	
Couple	£25.00	
Higher pensioner premium*		
Single	£20.75	
Couple	£29.55	
* From 5 October 1992 these will be increased – see pv.		

If you live in a **residential care or nursing home** and you are not entitled to IS but you claim HB (now only allowed in special cases – see p162), you are entitled to premiums in the normal way. If you are on IS, see pp72-79.

If you go into **hospital** your premiums may be affected (see pp83 and 175).

Entitlement to some premiums depends on receipt of other benefits. Once you have qualified for a premium, if you or your partner are not getting one of these benefits (eg, invalidity benefit or severe disablement allowance) because of the overlapping benefit rules, or because you or your partner are on an employment training course, you will continue to receive the relevant premium for that time.[4]

(ii) Family premium[5]

You are entitled to this if your family includes a child (see p233), even if you do not receive a personal allowance for any child because they have capital over £3,000. However, only one family premium is payable regardless of the number of children you have. Where a child who is in the care of or being looked after by a local authority or who is in custody comes home for part of a week, your IS includes a proportion of the premium, according to the number of days the child is with you;[6] for HB and CCB you may be paid the full premium if your child who is in care or being looked after by a local authority is part of the household for any part of the week: how often the child visits will be taken into account in deciding whether they are or not.[7]

(iii) Disabled child premium[8]

You are entitled to a disabled child premium for each of your children who gets disability living allowance or who is blind.

A child will be treated as blind if s/he is registered as blind and for the first 28 weeks after s/he has been taken off the register on regaining her/his sight.[9] For how to qualify for disability living allowance, see *CPAG's Rights guide to non-means-tested benefits*.

If a child has over £3,000 capital, you will not get this premium.[10] If your child has gone into hospital, see pp83 and 175.

(iv) Carer's premium[11]

You will qualify for this if you or your partner are getting invalid care allowance, or would get it but for the overlapping benefit rule (because you are receiving another benefit paid at a higher rate). For example, a woman getting invalid care allowance who at 60 goes on to retirement pension instead of invalid care allowance, will continue to qualify for the premium. If you are not already actually getting invalid care allowance, you must claim it on or after 1 October 1990 to take advantage of the overlapping rule.

If you stop getting, or being treated as getting, invalid care allowance, your entitlement to a carer's premium continues for a further eight weeks, even if you first claim IS/HB/CCB in this time.

An extra-statutory payment to compensate for non-payment of invalid care allowance also qualifies you for this premium.[12]

A double premium will be awarded where both you and your partner satisfy the conditions for it.

(v) Lone parent premium[13]

You are entitled to this if you are a single parent. You can continue to get it for as long as a child is treated as your dependant, which in some cases can be until s/he reaches 19 (see p234). You do not have to be the *parent* of the child, but you must be *responsible* for the child and s/he must be a member of your household (see p233).

You may qualify for a lone parent premium even if you do have a partner if s/he does not count as a member of your household – eg, if your partner is living abroad and is not able to come to this country because of the immigration rules. A lone parent premium will be paid even if you do not get a personal allowance for any child because s/he has capital over £3,000. Only one lone parent premium will be payable regardless of the number of children you have.

(vi) Disability premium [14]

You can get a disability premium if you are under 60 and one of the following applies to you [15] (after you are 60 you may get the higher pensioner premium):

☐ You are entitled to a **qualifying benefit**. These are **attendance allowance** (or an equivalent benefit paid to meet attendance needs because of an injury at work or a war injury [16]), **disability living allowance, disability working allowance, mobility supplement, invalidity pension** or **severe disablement allowance**. Extra-statutory payments to compensate you for not getting one of these benefits also count. [17] You must be receiving and not merely entitled to these benefits. [18] See CPAG's *Rights guide to non-means-tested benefits* for who can claim them.

   If you go abroad for some time or do not have proper evidence of incapacity while away you can lose your right to these benefits. But you may be able to get the disability premium paid straightaway by providing medical evidence from abroad that you were incapable of work while away (see below).

   If your attendance allowance or disability living allowance has stopped because you have been in hospital for more than four weeks you will not lose your disability premium immediately (see pp83 and 175). [19]

☐ You are **registered as blind** with a local authority (England and Wales) or regional or Islands council (Scotland); if you regain your sight you still qualify for 28 weeks after you are taken off the register. [20]

☐ You have an **NHS invalid trike or private car allowance** because of disability. [21]

☐ You have been **incapable of work for at least 28 weeks**. To qualify under this rule you must have been getting statutory sick pay, or have claimed sickness benefit, severe disablement allowance or invalidity benefit and sent in medical certificates. [22] Note that, except for statutory sick pay, you do not have to be getting one of these benefits, as long as you have put in a claim for one of them and it is accepted that you are incapable of work (see below). In all cases you lose the disability premium as soon as you stop sending in medical certificates. But if you fall ill again within eight weeks you can get the disability premium again without having to wait 28 weeks. [23]

'**Incapable of work**' means incapable of any work which it is reasonable to expect you to do bearing in mind your age, health, education, experience and any other personal factors. [24] In practice, for the first six months of illness an adjudication officer is likely to take account only of your capacity to do your normal work. After that your capacity to do any type of work will be considered. You need to explain your disabilities – eg, that you cannot sit or stand for long periods or you get frequent serious headaches etc. 'Work' in this context means paid work (full- or part-time) for which an employer would be willing to pay a normal wage.

   Couples will get the disability premium at the couple rate (£25.55) provided either one of you qualifies under the above rules. But if you qualify because one of you has been incapable of work for 28 weeks, you will only get the premium if the person who qualifies is the claimant for the couple. [25] You may, therefore, need to swap the claimant role (see pp101 and 184).

If you go on an Employment Training or Youth Training course, or for any period you receive a training allowance, you will keep the disability premium even though you may cease to receive one of the 'qualifying benefits', or cease to be incapable of work during the course, as long as you continue to be entitled to IS, HB or CCB. After the course, the premium continues if you are still incapable of work, or getting a qualifying benefit. [26]

Backdating

☐ Your 'qualifying benefit' (see p240) is not usually awarded until some time after you claim it, but it is then backdated to the date of your claim, or sometimes even earlier. You should ask for your disability premium to be backdated either to the same day, or to when you first got IS, HB or CCB if that is later.

Example
You apply for disability living allowance in May 1992. Disability living allowance is awarded in November 1992 backdated to May 1992. You request a review of your IS, HB and CCB in December 1992. You have been getting IS from July 1992 and were getting HB and CCB throughout this period. The increase in your IS will be backdated to July 1992. You will anyway have received maximum HB and CCB between July and September because you were on IS during that period. However, your HB and CCB will be increased for the period May to July to take account of your entitlement to the premium.

☐ If as a result of getting a 'qualifying benefit' backdated you now qualify for IS, HB or CCB because your needs are greater with the disability premium included in your applicable amount, you should make a new claim and ask for it to be backdated (see pp102, 187 and 214).

☐ You may have been incapable of work for 28 weeks but not sending in medical certificates and therefore not getting invalidity pension or severe disablement allowance. You should immediately claim the premium and also ask for it to be backdated. You will have to ask your doctor for backdated medical certificates and claim an incapacity benefit for that period (even if you know you will not qualify for it). The test for getting the premium is that you have been incapable of work for 28 weeks, so if your claim for the incapacity benefit is refused because it is a late claim, this does not matter, as long as your medical certificate for the backdated period is accepted.

☐ If you are one of a couple where the person who is incapable of work is not the claimant, it may be possible to backdate the swapping of the claimant role (see pp101 and 184). The new claimant should get backdated medical certificates, put in a claim and argue that s/he had good cause (eg, illness) for claiming late. You can argue that ignorance of the need to swap roles is good cause because it is a technical requirement which is not publicised. In this way you get the disability premium backdated but only for up to 12 months.[27]

(vii)   Pensioner premium[28]

The pensioner premium is paid at two rates according to age:
- [ ] The lower rate is paid if you are aged 60-74 inclusive.
- [ ] The enhanced rate is paid if you are 75-79 inclusive. (This is not to be confused with the higher pensioner premium paid to certain disabled pensioners and those aged 80 or over.)

Couples get the enhanced rate of this premium as long as one of them is between 75 and 79. The couple rate for either is paid if one partner fulfils the condition. If you or your partner are **sick or disabled** check to see if you could get the higher pensioner premium described below.

(viii)   Higher pensioner premium

You can get this if one of the following applies:[29]
- [ ] You or your partner are 80 or over.
- [ ] You or your partner are aged 60-79 *and* either of you receive a qualifying benefit, are registered blind, or have an NHS trike or a private car allowance (see p240). If you or your partner stop getting invalidity pension because you change to retirement pension, you can still get the premium if you remain continuously entitled to IS, HB or CCB.[30] Periods of eight weeks off benefit do not count.[31]

If you get severe disablement allowance and go on claiming it until you reach 65 (woman) or 70 (man), you will then be entitled to it for life and therefore continue to qualify for the higher pensioner premium.[32] Alternatively, if it ceases to be paid only because you get a retirement pension, you also continue to qualify.[33] If you get attendance allowance or disability living allowance and you have been in hospital for more than four weeks, you will not lose your higher pensioner premium immediately (see p83).

If you were not on both invalidity benefit and IS before you retired, and you are still incapable of work, you can de-retire. After six months on sickness benefit, you will receive invalidity benefit and qualify for the premium. You will only be able to qualify for the premium in this way if you are more than six months under retirement age – ie, 65 (woman) and 70 (man). This discrimination against women has been challenged in the European Court of Justice in Luxembourg in a case involving housing benefit. But unfortunately the European Court held that the housing benefit scheme was not covered by the terms of the EC Directive on equal treatment for men and women in social security.[34] However, the discrimination as regards the maximum age for claiming invalidity benefit that results from the UK's different pensionable ages may still be found to be in breach of European law as a result of another case (*Secretary of State for Social Security v Thomas*). If you are affected by this discrimination, to make sure you can backdate if this case is successful, you should ask to de-retire and claim invalidity benefit and ask for a review of your IS/HB/CCB to include higher pensioner premium. Appeal any refusal and postpone the appeal until the result in the *Thomas* case is known (see p106 for problems with backdating).

☐ You were getting a **disability premium** as part of your IS, HB or CCB before you were 60 and you have continued to claim that benefit. You must have been getting a disability premium at some time during the eight weeks before you were 60, and have received that benefit continuously since you reached 60. (But you can have a period off that benefit of up to eight weeks and still qualify.[35]) For HB/CCB, this applies if you were getting disability premium for either benefit.[36] In the case of **couples**, the person who was the claimant for that benefit before s/he was 60 must continue to claim after that, but it is not necessary for the claimant to have been the person who qualified for the disability premium.[37]

(ix) Severe disability premium[38]

This gives additional help to severely disabled people who need care. The conditions for receipt are:

☐ You are receiving attendance allowance (or the equivalent war pension or industrial injury benefit), or the higher or middle rate care component of disability living allowance (or extra-statutory payments to compensate for not receiving any of these[39]). If you are a couple, you must both be getting one of these benefits. This applies to all the partners in a polygamous marriage.

☐ No non-dependant aged 18 or over is living with you.

☐ No one is getting invalid care allowance for you.

☐ A couple, where both are severely disabled, only get the single rate if someone is getting invalid care allowance in respect of one of them.

(Conditions other than being in receipt of attendance allowance are being challenged in the House of Lords. Keep a look out for developments in this area.[40])

Non-dependants over 18[41]

The following people living with you do not count:

☐ Your partner, but only if they are receiving attendance allowance or the higher or middle rate care component of disability living allowance (see above).

☐ Any child living with you (this includes a child who is not treated as part of your household – see p233).

☐ Anyone staying in your home who normally lives elsewhere.

☐ A person (or, for IS only, their partner) employed by a charitable or voluntary body as a resident carer for you or your partner if you pay for that service (even if the charge is only nominal).

☐ A person receiving attendance allowance or the higher or middle rate care component of disability living allowance.[42]

☐ For HB/CCB only, a boarder.[43]

☐ A person (or, for IS only, their partner) who jointly occupies your home and is either the co-owner with you or your partner, or jointly liable with you or your partner to make payments to a landlord in respect of occupying it. For IS only, if this person is a close relative, they *will* count unless the co-ownership or joint liability to make payments to a landlord existed either before 11 April 1988 or by the time you or your partner first moved in (but see below).

☐ A person, or any member of their household, who is liable to pay you or your partner on a commercial basis in respect of occupying the dwelling (eg, tenant or licensee), unless they are a close relative of you or your partner (but see below).

☐ A person, or any member of their household, to whom you or your partner make such payments on a commercial basis, unless they are a close relative of you or your partner (but see below).

☐ For IS only, in the last three cases, close relatives will *not* prevent you from continuing to get the premium if you fall within the transitional provisions set out below.

Close relative means parent, parent-in-law, son, son-in-law, daughter, daughter-in-law, step-parent, step-son, step-daughter, brother, sister, or partners of any of these. [44]

The following applies to income support only:
☐ If someone (other than those listed above) comes to live with you in order to look after you, or your partner, your severe disability premium will remain in payment for the first 12 weeks. [45] After that, you will lose the premium (or get a lower rate premium), although invalid care allowance may well be payable to the carer.

☐ In the case of a couple, a person will be treated as receiving attendance allowance – even though it has stopped because s/he has been in hospital for more than four weeks. Similarly, a person will be treated as receiving invalid care allowance – even if the attendance allowance of the person for whom s/he is caring has stopped because that person has been in hospital for more than four weeks. [46]

Transitional provisions

In order to receive transitional protection, you need to be able to satisfy the two qualifying conditions: [47]

The first condition:
☐ You are receiving IS with a severe disability premium; *or*
☐ You have made a claim which, when decided, will award you IS with a severe disability premium; *or*
☐ You asked in writing for a review of your IS before 21 October 1991 on the basis that you had become either a co-owner of, or jointly liable to make payments to a landlord in respect of, your home with a close relative and, if revised, your IS will include a severe disability premium for a period before 21 October 1991.

The second condition:
☐ You are the co-owner and joint occupier of your home with a close relative; *or*
☐ You are jointly liable to make payments to a landlord in respect of your home which you jointly occupy with a close relative.
The second condition is satisfied if you and a close relative who were joint owners become in future jointly liable instead to make payments to a landlord (and *vice*

versa). It does not have to be with the same close relative. It also remains satisfied if you move to a new dwelling where you are jointly liable or a joint owner with either the same or another close relative.

To take advantage of the transitional provisions, you have to have satisfied the two qualifying conditions: [48]

☐ in the week before 21 October 1991; *or*

☐ in one of the eight weeks before 21 October 1991, provided that you satisfied them again not more than eight weeks after that week; *or*

☐ in the weeks immediately before and after:
  – you stopped getting IS because you worked for a period of not more than twelve weeks* starting before 21 October 1991 and ending after that date; *or*
  – you went on a government training course or a course at an employment rehabilitation centre which started before 21 October 1991 and which you were still attending at that date.

* See below for when this period is reduced to eight weeks.

You will lose this transitional protection if, for longer than eight weeks, you: [49]

☐ fail to satisfy the second qualifying condition; *or*

☐ stop getting IS.

But in calculating this eight weeks, **the following will be ignored**:

☐ up to twelve weeks* when you or your partner are in full-time work; *and*

☐ any period when you or your partner are on a government training course or at an employment rehabilitation centre.

* See below for when this period is reduced to eight weeks.

The twelve weeks will be reduced to eight if: [50]

(a) your IS becomes subject to a voluntary unemployment deduction (see p45) because of leaving that employment; *or*

(b) you or your partner worked for less than six weeks; *or*

(c) at any time during the 26 weeks before starting work, you, or your partner, if it is s/he who has left the employment, was a student, in relevant education or in full-time work.

But, if *you* fall within (b) or (c), and you are exempt from disqualification from unemployment benefit because of the trial period provisions (see CPAG's *Rights guide to non-means-tested benefits*) the period will be twelve weeks.

Severe disability premium and carer's premium

Receipt of invalid care allowance in respect of a disabled person will automatically exclude them from the severe disability premium. In this situation, an overall better-off calculation, balancing the carer's benefits and the disabled person's benefits will be necessary.

But where invalid care allowance has been claimed but is not being paid because of the overlapping benefit rules, a carer's premium should be payable to the carer without affecting the disabled person's severe disability premium. Invalid care allowance is not, in this case, 'in payment' to the carer. The disabled person must continue to get attendance allowance or the higher or middle rate care component of disability living allowance. [51]

Chapter 18

Income

This chapter explains the rules for working out your weekly income for income support (IS), disability working allowance (DWA), housing benefit (HB), community charge benefit (CCB) and family credit (FC). It contains:

1 Introduction (see below)
2 Earnings of employed earners (p250)
3 Earnings from self-employment (p256)
4 Other income (p258)
5 Notional income (p270)

1 INTRODUCTION

Your entitlement to IS/FC/DWA/HB/CCB and the amount you receive depends on how much income you have. Note that if you get IS you do not need to work out your income again for HB/CCB purposes because you receive your maximum HB (see pp168-9) or CCB (see p218).

The rules for working out your income are very similar for each benefit. Where there are differences these are indicated. If you are claiming IS and receiving maintenance payments from a former partner for yourself or any children, there are special rules on how this money is treated (see p91).

When working out your IS/FC/DWA/HB/CCB your income may be completely ignored, *or* partially ignored, *or* counted in full.

(i) Whose income counts

Income of a partner

If you are a member of a couple (see p229), your partner's income is added to your income and counts as if it belongs to you. [1]

If you receive a reduction of the normal personal allowance for a couple because your partner is under 18 and not eligible for IS (see p52), an amount of her/his income equivalent to the reduction will be ignored. [2]

Example
Kalid is 19. His partner, Kate, is 17 and is not able to claim IS. Kalid's personal allowance is £33.60 (the rate for a single person aged 18-24, see

p52). If Kate was eligible for IS, their personal allowance would be £66.60. Up to £33 (£66.60 – £33.60) of any income that Kate has will be ignored.

Income of a dependent child

If your child has over £3,000 capital, you do not get benefit for her/him and their income is not counted as yours.

If your child has capital of £3,000 or less, any of their income (including earnings, see below) that is not disregarded is usually treated as yours.[3]

If that income comes to more than the personal allowance plus any disabled child premium for IS/HB/CCB, and the 'child credit/allowance' for FC/DWA, the extra will be ignored.[4] However, maintenance paid to or for a child counts in full.[5]

Your child's **earnings** while they are at school do not normally count,[6] but if you are on IS/HB/CCB (not FC/DWA), and your child gets a full-time* (16 hours or more) job after leaving school but while you are still claiming for them (eg, during the summer holiday), their earnings over £5 count as your income (subject to the overall limit set out above).[7] If the child qualifies for the disabled child premium (see p239), £15 is ignored together with any income that exceeds their personal allowance and disabled child premium.[8] However, part-time earnings are still completely disregarded.

School fees paid by someone other than you or your partner are dealt with differently for each benefit.

Your entitlement to IS will not be affected if someone is paying school fees directly to the school,[9] except that the payments for the child's maintenance at the school count as the child's income for the period that the child is there.[10] If your child comes home for part of the week, s/he is treated as having income sufficient to wipe out her/his IS for the days s/he is at school that week and you receive benefit for the child for the days s/he is at home.[11] If your child spends a night with you they do not count as at school on that day.[12]

If your child goes away to school and this is paid for by the local education authority, the child is treated as having income equal to the amount of their IS for the days they are at school.[13] You are entitled to benefit for the child for the days they spend at home.

There are no special rules about school fees for FC/DWA, but for HB and CCB the local authority is advised not to treat payments made to a third party (such as school fees) by a former partner as the income of the claimant.[14]

* Before 7 April 1992 full-time work used to be 24 hours a week. For IS there is a transitional provision that if in the week beginning 7-13 April 1992 you are claiming for a child working between 16 to 24 hours a week they will not count as in full-time work until you stop claiming for them. But this does not apply if the week beginning 7-13 April 1992 is your first benefit week.

(ii) Converting income into a weekly amount

IS, FC/DWA, HB and CCB are all calculated on a weekly basis so your income always has to be converted into a weekly amount if it is paid for a longer or shorter period. The following rules apply to income from employment (but not self-employment, except in the case of HB and CCB) and other income (see p258):[15]

- ☐ If the payment is for less than a week it is treated as the weekly amount.
- ☐ If the payment is for a month, multiply the amount by 12 and divide by 52.
- ☐ For IS, FC and DWA, multiply a payment for three months by four and divide by 52.
- ☐ For IS, FC and DWA, divide a payment for a year by 52.
- ☐ For all benefits, multiply payments for other periods by seven and divide by the number of days in the period.

For IS, where your income fluctuates or your earnings vary because you do not work every week, your weekly income may be averaged over the cycle, if there is an identifiable one; or, if there is not, over five weeks, or over another period if this would be more accurate.[16] If the cycle involves periods when you do no work, those periods will be included in the cycle, but not other absences (eg, holidays, sickness).

Example
Ahmed works a cycle of two weeks 'on' and one week 'off'. He works 30 hours a week in the weeks he works for which he is paid £60. In the third week he is paid a retainer of £30. He claims IS in the third week. His average weekly earnings will be £50 a week (£60 + £60 + £30 = £150 divided by 3 = £50) which will be taken into account in calculating his IS entitlement.

For IS, there are a number of rules about the calculation of income for part weeks. They are:
- ☐ Where income covering a period up to a week is paid before your first benefit week, and part of it is counted for that week; or, if, in any case, you are paid for a period of a week or more, and only part of it is counted in a particular benefit week: you multiply the whole payment by the number of days it covers in the benefit week, and then divide the result by the total number of days covered by the payment.[17]
- ☐ Any payment of unemployment benefit, maternity allowance, sickness benefit, invalidity benefit, or severe disablement allowance which falls partly into the benefit week: only the amount paid for those days will be taken into account. For any payment of IS, that amount is the weekly amount multiplied by the number of days in the part-week and divided by seven.[18] The period normally covered by benefits is the same as for all other income, see p258.

For IS, where you have regularly received a certain kind of payment of income from one source, and in a particular benefit week you receive that payment and another of the same kind from the same source, only the one paid first will be taken into account.[19]

This will not apply if the second payment was due to be taken into account in another week, but the overlapping week is the first in which it could practically be counted (see p249).

See p249 for definition of IS benefit week.

If you are **self-employed**, the same rules apply for HB/CCB. For IS, FC and DWA, see rules on averaging on p257.

(iii) The period covered by income for IS

If you are an employed earner, or getting 'other income' and claiming IS, your income counts for a future period. There are special rules for deciding the length of this period and the date from which payments count. This rule does not apply to self-employed earnings.

☐ Where a payment of income is made in respect of an identifiable period, it will be taken into account for a period of equal length.[20] For example, a week's part- time earnings will be taken into account for a week.

☐ If the payment does not relate to a particular period, the amount of the payment will be divided by the amount of the weekly IS to which you would otherwise be entitled. If part of the payment should be disregarded, the amount of IS will be increased by the appropriate disregard. The result of this calculation is the number of weeks that you will not be entitled to IS.[21]

Example
You receive £663.20 net earnings for work which cannot be attributed to any specific period of time. You are a single parent with one child aged 8, and your rent and 80 per cent of your poll tax are met by HB/CCB. Your applicable amount is £71.05. As a single parent you are entitled to a £15 earnings disregard.

$$£663.20 \div £71.05 + £15 = 7 \text{ with } £60.85 \text{ left over}$$

This means that you will not be entitled to IS for seven weeks and the remaining £60.85 (less a £15 earnings disregard) will be taken into account in calculating your benefit for the following week.

☐ Payments made on leaving a job are taken into account for a forward period (see p253).

The date from which a payment is counted

The date from which a payment counts depends on when it was due to be paid. If it was due to be paid before you claimed IS, it counts from the date on which it was due to be paid.[22] Otherwise it is treated as paid on the first day of the benefit week in which it is due, or on the first day of the first benefit week after that in which it is practical to take it into account.[23] Payments of IS, unemployment benefit, maternity allowance, sickness benefit, invalidity benefit or severe disablement allowance are treated as paid on the day they are officially due.[24]

The **benefit week** for IS is the seven days running from the day of the week on which benefit is paid. It will often overlap two calendar weeks.[25]

The date that a payment is due may well be different from the date of actual payment. Earnings are due on the employee's normal pay day as set out in her/his contract of employment. Only if the contract does not reveal the date of due payment and there is no evidence pointing in another direction should the date the payment was received be taken as the date it was due. [26] If your contract of employment is terminated without proper notice, outstanding wages, wages in hand, holiday pay and any pay in lieu of notice are due on the last day of employment and are treated as paid on that day, even if this does not happen. [27] (If income due to you has not been paid you may be entitled to an urgent cases payment, see p35.) If an employee leaves without giving proper notice, the employer is not usually obliged to pay any outstanding wages etc until the date stated in the contract of employment. (For treatment of payments at the end of a job and how they affect your right to claim IS, see p253.)

2   EARNINGS OF EMPLOYED EARNERS

(i)   Calculating net earnings from employment

Only certain deductions are allowed from your gross earnings. These are income tax and Class 1 National Insurance contributions, plus half of any contribution you make towards a personal or occupational pension scheme. [28] The resulting net income will not always be the same as your weekly take-home pay – since, for example, you may have to pay the remaining half of the payment towards an occupational pension scheme from your net weekly income. There is no provision for the deduction of any other work expenses (eg, fares and childcare costs).

If your earnings are estimated (as is sometimes necessary for FC/DWA or HB/CCB) the authorities estimate the amount of tax and National Insurance you would expect to pay on those earnings, and deduct this plus half of any pension contribution you are paying. [29]

For HB/CCB, the local authority has the discretion to ignore **changes in tax or National Insurance contributions** for up to 30 benefit weeks. This can be used, for example, where Budget changes are not reflected in your actual income until several months later. When the changes are eventually taken into account and your benefit entitlement is either increased or reduced accordingly, you are not treated as having been underpaid or overpaid benefit during the period of the delay. [30]

(ii)   What counts as earnings

Earnings means 'any remuneration or profit derived [31] from . . . employment'. [32] As well as your wages, this includes: [33]

□   Any bonus or commission (including tips).

□   Holiday pay. But if it is not payable until more than four weeks after your job ends or is interrupted, it will be treated as capital. [34] **Note:** For IS, this rule does not apply if you are involved in, or returning to work after, a trade dispute (see p58). For more detail on payments at the end of a job, see p253.

□   Except for IS, any sick pay or maternity pay. For IS this is treated as other income and is counted in full less any tax, Class 1 NI contributions and half of any pension contribution. [35] For FC/DWA, statutory sick pay is counted as earnings [36] but statutory maternity pay is ignored. [37]

□   Any payments made by your employer for expenses not 'wholly, exclusively and necessarily' incurred in carrying out your job.

☐ A retainer fee – eg, you may be paid this during the school holidays if you work for the school meals service.

☐ For DWA, any payment made by your employer towards your community charge.[38]

☐ Except in the case of FC/DWA,[39] payments in lieu of wages or in lieu of notice, but only insofar as they represent loss of income.[40]

☐ An award of compensation for unfair dismissal and certain other awards of pay made by an industrial tribunal, and payments made directly by your employer as compensation for loss of employment.

☐ Certain other payments from your employer – eg, arrears of wages (but see below for payments from an employer which do not count).

See (iv) below for definitions of the last three.

The following are not counted as earnings:

☐ Payments in kind (eg, petrol).[41] These will be ignored[42] unless you are on IS and involved in a trade dispute, (see pp58-62).

☐ An advance of earnings or a loan from your employer. This will be treated as capital[43] (it will still be treated as earnings for IS if you or your partner are involved in a trade dispute, or have been back at work after a dispute for no longer than 15 days).[44]

☐ A job start allowance paid under the Employment and Training Act 1973.[45]

☐ Payments towards expenses that are 'wholly, exclusively and necessarily' incurred, such as travelling expenses during the course of your work.[46]

☐ If you are a local councillor, travelling expenses to and from council offices or constituents etc and home, and subsistence payments are ignored as expenses 'wholly, exclusively and necessarily' incurred in your work. However, allowances for attending meetings etc will be counted as earnings.[47]

☐ Earnings payable abroad which cannot be brought into Britain (eg, because of exchange control regulations).[48] If your earnings are paid in another currency, any bank charges for converting them into sterling will be deducted before taking them into account.[49]

☐ Any occupational pension.[50] This will count as other income and the net amount will be taken into account in full.[51]

The value of any **accommodation provided as part of your job** will be ignored for IS.[52] For FC/DWA, if it is free, the authorities will take account of its value by adding £12 to the calculation of your weekly earnings. If your employer charges you less than £12 rent, the difference between that amount and £12 is added instead. If the accommodation is worthless to you – eg, it is provided but you never use it,[53] no amount will be added.

For CCB, and for HB where job-related accommodation is in addition to the normal home, argue that this is payment in kind and disregarded.

(iii) How earnings are assessed

All payments of earnings must be converted into a weekly amount (see p247). For IS it is also necessary to work out the period which these payments cover (see p248). However, for FC/DWA/HB/CCB a past period is used to assess your 'normal weekly earnings'.

For FC

The normal rule is to average your weekly earnings over an 'assessment period' of:

☐ six consecutive weeks or three consecutive fortnights in the last seven weeks if you are paid weekly or fortnightly; *or*

☐ three months or three four-week periods if you are paid monthly or four-weekly; *or*

☐ six consecutive pay periods if you are paid at another interval that is less than a month (eg, daily); *or*

☐ one year if your pay period is longer than a month;

immediately before the week of your claim. [54]

Any weeks/months in the assessment period in which your earnings were reduced because you were involved in a trade dispute, will be ignored and replaced by the next earliest 'normal' pay period. [55]

Any pay period in which your earnings are 20 per cent or more above or below your average earnings will be left out. If this applies to all the weeks/months in your assessment period, only those in which you received no pay or received pay for a longer period than usual (eg, two weeks' holiday pay in one week) will be left out. If this still results in all the weeks/months in your assessment period being left out, your employer will be required to provide an estimate (which should not be an overestimate – see below) of your likely earnings for the period for which you are normally paid. [56]

For DWA

The normal rule is to take your weekly earnings over an 'assessment period' of:

☐ five consecutive weeks in the last six weeks if you are paid weekly; *or*

☐ two months if you are paid monthly;

immediately before the week of the date of your claim. [57]

Any time in the assessment period during which your earnings were irregular or unusual does not count [58] – eg, any week in which you received, for instance, a one-off bonus or holiday pay, or in which large deductions were made from your wages.

If your earnings fluctuate, or your earnings in the five-week or two-month period before your claim do not represent your normal earnings (eg, because you are on unpaid maternity leave [59]), a different period can be used if this gives a more accurate picture of your normal weekly earnings. [60]

If there is a period of short-time working of not more than 13 weeks or a trade dispute at your place of work, your normal weekly earnings will be taken as those prior to the period of short-time working or dispute. Trade dispute includes a work-to-rule or overtime ban as well as a strike. [61]

For FC/DWA

A bonus or commission paid separately, or for a longer period than other earnings, and which is paid in the year prior to your claim, counts as income. [62]

If you have just started a job or have just returned to work after a break of more than, for FC four weeks, or, for DWA 13 weeks, or your hours have just changed, and the period since the start or resumption of your employment or the change in your hours is less than, for FC your assessment period, or, for DWA nine weeks, your employer will be required to provide an estimate of your likely earnings for the period for which you are normally paid. [63] If your actual earnings turn out to be lower than the estimate, this will not result in your FC/DWA being reviewed and increased, so it is important that your employer does not overestimate your earnings.

For HB/CCB
Earnings as an employee are usually averaged out over:
☐ the previous five weeks if you are paid weekly; *or*
☐ two months if you are paid monthly.[64]
Where your earnings vary, or if there is likely to be or has recently been a change (eg, you usually do overtime but have not done so recently, or you are about to get a pay rise), the local authority may average them over a different period where this is likely to give a more accurate picture of what you are going to earn during the benefit period.[65]

If you are on strike, the local authority should not take into account your pre-strike earnings and average them out over the strike period.[66]

If you have only just started work and your earnings cannot be averaged over the normal period (ie, five weeks/two months), an estimate is made based on any earnings you have been paid so far if these are likely to reflect your future average wage.[67] Where you have not yet been paid or your initial earnings do not represent what you will normally earn over the benefit period, your employer must provide an estimate of your average weekly earnings.[68] Where your earnings change during your benefit period, your new weekly average figure is estimated on the basis of what you are likely to earn over the remainder of the benefit period.[69]

(iv) Payments at the end of a job

Redundancy payments are normally treated as capital (see below). If your payment, together with other capital that is not ignored (see pp275-79), comes to more than £8,000 (IS/FC) or £16,000 (DWA/HB/CCB), you are not eligible for benefit;[70] if the total comes to more than £3,000 you are treated as having a certain amount of income from your capital[71] (see p266).

In spending any redundancy money, it is worth bearing in mind that if you deliberately get rid of money in order to get benefit, you are treated as still having it (see p280).

Some redundancy schemes make periodic payments after leaving work: these are treated as other income (see p258).[72]

Other payments can cause problems, and are dealt with separately for each benefit.

For IS
If you retire from your job and you are aged at least 60 (women) or 65 (men), any payments counted as earnings (eg, final wages, holiday pay, etc) that you receive are disregarded in full.[73] You are not treated as in full-time work for any period covered by those earnings after the end of your job.

In all other cases, only the following final earnings that you are paid when you leave a full-time job will affect your right to IS:[74]
☐ holiday pay which counts as earnings (see p250);
☐ pay in lieu of notice;
☐ pay in lieu of wages (eg, any part of a compensatory award which is for loss of earnings over a certain period of weeks);

☐   a compensation payment in respect of employment (eg, where the employer fails to pay lieu of notice, but pays a lump sum instead – ie, *ex gratia*). This is divided by the maximum payable under the statutory redundancy scheme (uprated yearly). The result is the number of weeks the payment will cover up to a maximum of your notice period whether statutory, contractual or customary. [75] If the amount is less than the statutory maximum for one week or if the calculation creates a fraction, these are treated as capital. [76] Compensation for part-time workers is taken into account for one week only. [77] If the *ex gratia* payment is not compensation but a gift – eg, a 'golden handshake', it will be treated as capital, not income.

You are treated as in full-time work for the number of weeks covered by these payments after your employment ended. [78] These payments will be taken into account consecutively and in the following order:

☐   firstly, any pay in lieu of wages or in lieu of notice;
☐   then payments of compensation for loss of employment;
☐   then holiday pay. [79]

The period for which you are treated as in full-time work starts on the earliest date that any of these payments are due to be paid. [80] If you are paid a **retainer**, this will be taken into account as earnings in calculating the amount of your IS. If you later receive an award of compensation for unfair dismissal or certain other awards of pay from an industrial tribunal, these are taken into account as earnings in calculating the amount of your IS from when the award is made.

Example
Mary leaves her job with a final week's wages, a week in hand and one week's holiday pay. All three amounts are due to be paid on 30 May. Only the holiday pay will be taken into account, starting from 30 May. Mary will not be entitled to IS for one week.

If your employment is interrupted (eg, you are laid off), any holiday pay that is paid to you will affect your right to IS; all other payments will be disregarded except that any retainer you are paid will be taken into account as earnings in calculating the amount of your IS. [81] If you have been suspended, any payment you receive will be taken into account and affect your right to IS.

If you were working **part-time** (less than 16 hours per week) before you claimed IS, any payments you receive when the job ends or is interrupted, except any retainer, are ignored and do not affect your IS (unless you have been suspended). [82] If, however, you were claiming IS while you were in part-time work, any payments made to you when that job ends are taken into account as earnings in the normal way. Your wages, including any final wages, are counted first, then any pay in lieu of wages or notice, then any compensation paid by your employer for loss of earnings (see p253) and then any holiday pay. [83]

Once the period covered by payments at the end of a job has ended, any money remaining will be treated as capital. [84]

For FC/DWA

There are no special FC/DWA rules for payments received at the end of a job. However, if, for example, your partner has just lost his job and you apply for FC because you are working full-time, any payments that s/he received at the end of the employment (and indeed the amount of previous wages) should not be included as part of your 'normal' weekly income, unless there is evidence that the job will resume while you are getting your current FC award.

For HB/CCB

Where you have been in full-time work (16 hours or more) and have reached the age of 65 (men) or 60 (women), any earnings paid to you at the end of your job will be disregarded. [85]

Where you have been in full-time work and you are not 60/65, any earnings paid to you at the end of your job will be disregarded *except* where they relate to any of the payments treated as earnings on p253, but not bonus and commission and any payments made by your employer for expenses not wholly exclusively and necessarily incurred in carrying out your job (eg, fares to work). [86] Compensation for loss of earnings will be counted, but the detailed rules for IS do not apply.

If your work is interrupted, your earnings are disregarded except for holiday pay which counts as earnings (see p250) and any retainer paid to you.

Where you have been in part-time work (ie, less than 16 hours a week) immediately before claiming HB/CCB, any earnings paid when your job ends or is interrupted should be disregarded, *except* where that payment is a retainer. [87]

(v)   Disregarded earnings

For FC/DWA, your earnings, worked out in the way described above, are taken into account in full.

For IS and HB/CCB, some of your earnings are disregarded and do not affect your benefit. The amount of the 'disregard' depends on your circumstances. There are three levels.

£25 disregard

Lone parents on HB/CCB but not receiving IS have £25 of their earnings ignored. [88] This does not apply to IS.

£15 disregard

£15 of your earnings (including those of your partner if any) is disregarded if:

☐ for IS, you qualify for a lone parent premium (see p239). You are treated as qualifying for the premium if you would do so but for getting a pensioner premium or for being in a local authority home, residential care or nursing home; [89]

☐ you or your partner (if any) qualifies for a disability premium (see p240). [90] For IS, you are treated as qualifying for the premium if you would do so but for being in hospital, a local authority home or a residential care or nursing home;

☐ for HB/CCB only, you or your partner (if any) qualifies for a severe disability premium (see p243); [91]

☐ you or your partner (if any) qualifies for the higher pensioner premium, you or your partner are over 60 and, immediately before reaching that age, you or your partner were in employment and you were entitled to a £15 disregard because of qualifying for a disability premium (see above). Since reaching 60, you or your partner must have continued in employment (although breaks of up to eight* weeks when you were not getting IS or in employment are ignored). Again, for

IS, you are treated as qualifying for the higher pensioner premium even if you are in hospital etc; [92]

☐ you are a member of a couple, your benefit would include a disability premium but for the fact that one of you qualifies for the higher pensioner premium or the enhanced rate of pensioner premium (see p242), one of you is under 60 and either of you are in employment.

For IS, you are treated as qualifying for the higher or enhanced pensioner premium if you would do so, but for being in hospital, etc (see above); [93]

☐ you are a member of a couple, one of you is aged 75-79 and the other over 60, and immediately before that person reached 60 either of you were in employment and you were entitled to a £15 disregard because of qualifying, or being treated as qualifying, for an enhanced pensioner premium (see above). Since then either of you must have continued in employment (although breaks of up to eight* weeks when you were not getting IS or in employment are ignored). [94]

☐ you or your partner (if any) are an auxiliary coastguard, part-time firefighter or a part-time member of a lifeboat crew, or a member of the Territorial Army. [95] If you earn less than £15 for doing any of these services you can use up to £5 (for HB/CCB up to £10 if you have a partner) of the disregard on another job [96] or a partner's earnings from another job; [97]

☐ for IS only, you are a couple both under 60 and you have been receiving IS continuously for the last two years. It is sufficient if, throughout this time, either you or your partner has been getting IS for you both, or one of you has been the claimant for a couple (though not necessarily the same couple). Neither you nor your present partner must have been in full-time work or in full-time education for periods of more than eight consecutive weeks in the last two years. Breaks of eight* weeks or less when you were not a member of a couple or getting IS are ignored. [98]

* For IS, this is increased to twelve weeks if you stopped getting IS because you or your partner started full-time work (see p34 under (iii) for the detailed rules on this). Any period when you were not entitled to IS because you or your partner went on a government training scheme is ignored. But it will count as a period that you were in receipt of IS if you qualify for the £15 disregard as a long-term claimant (see above). [99]

If you qualify under more than one category you still have a maximum of only £15 of your earnings disregarded.

Basic £10 or £5 disregard

If you do not qualify for a £25 or £15 disregard, the rules vary depending on the benefit you are claiming.

For IS, £5 of your earnings is disregarded and £5 of your partner's earnings. [100]

For HB/CCB, £5 of your earnings is disregarded if you are single. If you claim as a member of a couple, £10 of your total earnings is disregarded – whether or not you are both working. [101]

3 EARNINGS FROM SELF-EMPLOYMENT

(i) Calculating net earnings

Your 'net profit' over the period before your claim must be worked out. This consists of your self-employed earnings, including any enterprise allowance, [102] minus: [103]

☐ reasonable expenses (see below); *and*
☐ income tax and National Insurance contributions; *and*
☐ half of a 'qualifying premium' – ie, a premium or any other contribution payable in connection with a life annuity which is subject to tax relief. [104]

For FC/DWA, the enterprise allowance will not count if it already ended before you claimed – so it may be worthwhile delaying your claim. [105]

(ii)   Reasonable expenses

Expenses must be reasonable and 'wholly and exclusively' incurred for the purposes of your business. [106] Where a car, or telephone, for example, is used partly for business and partly for private purposes, the costs of it can be apportioned and the amount attributable to business use can be deducted. [107]

Reasonable expenses include: [108]
☐ repayments of capital on loans for replacing equipment and machinery;
☐ repayment of capital on loans for, and income spent on, the repair of a business asset except where this is covered by insurance;
☐ interest on a loan taken out for the purposes of the business;
☐ excess of VAT paid over VAT received.

Reasonable expenses do not include: [109]
☐ any capital expenditure;
☐ depreciation;
☐ money for setting up or expanding the business (eg, the cost of adapting the business premises);
☐ any loss incurred before the beginning of the current assessment period. If the business makes a loss, the net profit is nil. The losses of one business cannot be offset against the profit of any other business in which you are engaged; [110]
☐ capital repayments on loans taken out for business purposes;
☐ business entertainment expenses;
☐ unpaid liabilities, even if earnings are deposited with a trustee-in-bankruptcy to discharge; [111]
☐ for HB/CCB only, debts not proven to be bad debts.

(iii)   Working out your average

There are different rules for each benefit.

For IS

For IS, the weekly amount is the average of earnings: [112]
☐ over a period of 52 weeks (this does not have to be the 52-week period immediately before the claim – it will normally be the last year for which accounts are available);
☐ over a more appropriate period where you have recently taken up self-employment or there has been a change which will affect your business.

If your earnings are royalties or copyright payments, the amount of earnings is divided by the weekly amount of IS which would be payable if you had not received this income *plus* the amount which would be disregarded from those earnings. You will not be entitled to IS for the resulting number of weeks.

For FC/DWA

Your normal weekly earnings are worked out by looking at: [113]

☐ your profit and loss account (and your trading account and/or balance sheet if appropriate), if this covers a period of at least 6 but not more than 15 months, which ends within 12 months before the date of your claim; *or*

☐ if you do not provide such a profit and loss account, the 26 weeks immediately before the week of the date of your claim; *or*

☐ a different past period, if this represents your normal weekly earnings more accurately (eg, if there has been a recent change in the circumstances of your business).

Your weekly earnings are worked out by averaging your earnings over the assessment period or, where you have provided a profit and loss account, by averaging the earnings relevant to the period covered by that account. [114]

Any complete week(s) in the assessment period when you are not actually working (eg, because you are sick or on holiday) are ignored. [115]

If you have just started being self-employed (ie, within the last six months), for FC your normal weekly earnings are estimated by looking at the payments you have already received and the amount you can expect to earn during the first 26 weeks of your business or any other relevant evidence. [116] If your actual earnings turn out to be lower than the estimate, a Commissioner has held that your FC can be revised to take account of this on the basis that your actual earnings are 'other relevant evidence'. [117] For DWA an estimate will be made of your likely weekly earnings over the next 26 weeks from the date of your claim. [118]

For HB/CCB

The amount of your weekly earnings is averaged out over an 'appropriate' period (usually based on your last year's trading accounts) which must not be longer than 52 weeks. [119]

(iv) Childminders

Childminders are always treated as self-employed. Your net profit is deemed to be a third of your earnings less income tax, your National Insurance contributions and half of a qualifying premium[120] (see p256). The rest of your earnings are completely ignored.

(v) Disregarded earnings[121]

The rules are the same as for employed earners (see p255).

Earnings payable abroad which cannot be brought into Britain (eg, because of exchange control regulations) are not counted. If your earnings are paid in another currency, any bank charges for converting them into sterling will be deducted before taking them into account.

4 OTHER INCOME

All other types of income are taken into account less any tax due on them. For HB/CCB, changes in tax rates may be ignored for up to 30 weeks, as for earnings (see p250).

Payments from ET and YT schemes are covered separately (see p49).

All income is converted into a weekly amount (see p247). For IS, this amount is attributed to a forward period (see p248) and affects the benefit payable for that period.

For FC/DWA/HB/CCB, a past period is used where possible to assess normal weekly income, and this figure is used to calculate benefit.

For HB/CCB, an estimate of income is made by looking at an appropriate period (not exceeding 52 weeks). The period chosen must give an accurate assessment of your income. [122]

For FC/DWA, your income during the 26 weeks immediately before the week of your claim will be used, unless a different period immediately before your claim would produce a more accurate assessment [123] (see p260 for maintenance).

(i) Benefits

Benefits that count in full:
- [ ] unemployment benefit;
- [ ] sickness benefit, invalidity benefit and severe disablement allowance;
- [ ] maternity allowance;
- [ ] invalid care allowance;
- [ ] widows' benefits (including industrial death benefit);
- [ ] retirement pensions;
- [ ] industrial injuries benefits (except constant attendance allowance and exceptionally severe disablement allowance);
- [ ] except for FC/DWA, child benefit and one parent benefit;
- [ ] other family benefits: guardian's allowance, child's special allowance, war orphan's pension;
- [ ] FC/DWA (for IS and HB/CCB);
- [ ] for IS only, [124] statutory sick pay and statutory maternity pay – less any Class 1 National Insurance contribution and half of any pension contribution and any tax. For HB/CCB, statutory sick pay and statutory maternity pay are treated as earnings (see p250). For FC/DWA, statutory sick pay is counted as earnings but statutory maternity pay is ignored (see p250).

Benefits that are ignored completely:
- [ ] attendance allowance (or constant attendance allowance or exceptionally severe disablement allowance paid because of an injury at work or a war injury). For IS only, it will be taken into account in full if you live in a residential care or nursing home, up to a maximum of £43.35 per week; [125]
- [ ] any care component of disability living allowance. For IS only, it will count in full if you live in a residential care or nursing home; [126]
- [ ] pensioner's Christmas bonus; [127]
- [ ] mobility allowance or the mobility component of disability living allowance; [128]

☐ mobility supplement under the War Pensions Scheme; [129]
☐ any extra-statutory payment made to you to compensate for non-payment of IS, mobility allowance, attendance allowance or disability living allowance; [130]
☐ for FC, disability working allowance. [131] For DWA, family credit; [132]
☐ social fund payments [133] – these do not count as part of your 'normal weekly income' for FC/DWA;
☐ except for DWA, resettlement benefit paid to certain patients who are discharged from hospital and who had been in hospital for more than a year before 11 April 1988; [134]
☐ any transitional payment made to compensate you for loss of benefit due to the changes in benefit rules in April 1988; [135]
☐ HB and CCB and transitional relief on CCB; [136]
☐ IS is ignored for FC/DWA and HB/CCB. [137] But there are special HB/CCB rules for IS claimants (see pp168-9 and 213-14);
☐ educational maintenance allowances [138] (see p345);
☐ certain special war widows' payments. [139]

Benefits that have £10 ignored:
☐ war disablement pension;
☐ war widow's pension;
☐ an extra-statutory payment made instead of the above pensions;
☐ similar payments made by another country;
☐ a pension from Germany or Austria paid to the victims of Nazi persecution. [140]
Only £10 in all can be ignored, even if you have more than one payment which attracts a £10 disregard.

Local authorities are given very limited discretion to increase the £10 disregard on war disablement and war widows' pensions when assessing income for HB/CCB. [141] Check your local authority's policy on this issue.

Problems can arise where a local Benefits Agency office deducts a benefit you are not receiving, such as child benefit that has been delayed. In such a case, the benefit is not to be treated as income possessed by you. You should get your full benefit, and then repay the extra amount paid out from the arrears of the benefit when they come through. [142] HB/CCB guidance says the same; although their note is about FC, it would apply to other benefits too. [143]

(ii)   Maintenance payments

The rules for **IS** are covered on pp91-96.

If you claim **FC/DWA** and maintenance payments are being made regularly (eg, weekly or monthly) before you claim, the normal weekly/monthly amount will count as income. [144] If they are due to be paid regularly but are not being so, the average of the payments made in the 13 weeks up to your date of claim counts as income. [145] If your payments are irregular, they are treated as capital. [146] Periodical payments made to or for a child are treated as yours. [147]

There are no special rules about maintenance for **HB and CCB**; periodical payments simply count as income and lump sums as capital. [148]

If you are a single parent, or a couple with a child, for FC/DWA, HB and CCB, £15 of any maintenance payment made by your former partner, or your partner's former partner, or the parent of any child in your family will be disregarded. [149]

For HB and CCB, if you make maintenance payments to your former partner or for a child, an equal amount of any 'unearned' income you have is ignored. If your 'unearned' income will not cover the maintenance payment, the balance can be disregarded from your earnings. [150]

(iii) Grants and covenants to students

The term **grant** includes bursaries, scholarships and exhibitions as well as grants or awards from education authorities. [151] An educational award which is paid by way of a loan counts as a grant for IS. [152] You will be treated as having the parental or partner's contribution to your grant whether or not it has been paid to you. [153] However, if you are a single parent, a single foster parent or a disabled student, only the amount of any contribution that you actually receive will be counted for IS. [154] Grant income will be taken into account for the academic year, excluding the summer vacation, unless the grant expressly covers the whole year (eg, postgraduate students), or a different period. In each case, it is divided equally over the weeks in the period. [155] In the case of a sandwich course, grant income will be averaged out over the period of study excluding the periods of experience (ie, in industry or commerce). [156] Any grant income that is intended for the maintenance of a student's dependants or which is an allowance for mature students will be spread over 52 or 53 weeks. [157] (Benefit weeks and academic years sometimes run to 53 weeks, including part-weeks.)

The following grant income is ignored: [158]

☐ A fixed amount of £257 or whatever you get in your grant towards the cost of books and equipment.

☐ Any amount for travelling expenses. Where you are in receipt of a mandatory grant, and living away from home, this will usually be £133.

☐ Tuition and examination fees.

☐ Except for DWA, any allowance to meet the cost of special equipment for certain courses which began before 1 September 1986.

☐ Any allowance to meet extra expenses because you are a disabled student.

☐ Any allowance to meet the cost of attending a residential course away from your normal student accommodation during term-time.

☐ Any allowance for the costs of your normal home (away from college) but, for IS, only if your rent and rates are not met by HB/CCB.

☐ Any amount for a partner or children abroad is ignored for IS and HB/CCB, but not FC/DWA.

Covenant income means, for IS, the income net of basic rate tax payable to a student under a deed of covenant by a parent or partner whose income has been or is likely to be assessed in calculating the amount of the student's grant. [159] For FC/DWA and HB/CCB it is gross, but any tax refund is ignored for FC/DWA and treated as capital for HB/CCB. [160]

The special rules concerning the treatment of covenant income are as follows:

☐ If your parent or partner has been assessed for a contribution towards the student's grant:

(a) there will be deducted from the annual amount of the covenant the amount of the contribution (plus the tax deducted in respect of the covenant

income, for HB/CCB) and the difference, if any, between the amount
allowed for travelling costs in the student's grant and the allowance for this
in the standard maintenance grant under the Education (Mandatory
Awards) Regulations 1991;

(b) the income from the covenant will then be taken into account with a £5
weekly disregard over a 52- or 53-week period. [161]

☐ If you do not receive a grant:

(a) there will be disregarded from the covenant income any sums intended to
cover expenses (except for travel expenses in the case of DWA) referred
to on p261 (plus the tax deducted in respect of the covenant income, for
HB/CCB). In the case of travel costs the disregard is equal to the amount in
the standard maintenance grant (this will depend on the individual grant);

(b) the covenant income up to the amount of the standard maintenance grant
will then be spread over your period of study;

(c) the balance of the covenant income, if any, will be taken into account over
a 52- or 53-week period with a £5 weekly disregard. [162]

☐ If you do have a grant, but no parental or partner's contribution has been
assessed, the same rules as for when you do not get a grant will apply except that:

(a) under (a) above, the amount to be disregarded from the covenant income
will only be the difference, if any, between the amount in the student's
grant for books and travel and the amount in the standard maintenance
grant (for books only in the case of DWA); *and*

(b) under (b) above, the amount of the covenant income to be spread over your
period of study will be the difference between the student's grant (less any
part that is disregarded – see p261) and the standard maintenance grant. [163]

The result this rule is intended to achieve is that the total amount of your grant and
covenant income attributed to your period of study should not exceed the amount of
the standard maintenance grant, with the remainder, if any, of your covenant income
being spread over the whole year.

General points about grant and covenant income

☐ If you have other income (eg, a regular charitable or voluntary payment) that
attracts a £10 disregard, only £10 per week in total can be ignored. [164]

☐ Any tax refund on a student's income is treated as capital for IS and HB/
CCB. [165] For FC/DWA, a tax refund on covenant income is ignored as capital
and income. [166]

☐ There is no tax relief available on covenants made after April 1988.

☐ Any payments you receive to help you with expenses referred to on p261, which
exceed the amounts for these purposes included in your grant or disregarded
from your covenant income, are ignored. [167]

☐ In the case of a couple, the amount of any contribution that one member has
been assessed to pay to her/his partner who is a student, does not count as her/
his income for IS/FC/DWA/HB or CCB purposes. [168]

☐ If you make a claim during the summer vacation and the income from the
covenant starts after the beginning of that vacation, it is ignored as income for IS
during that vacation. [169]

☐ For HB only, if your eligible rent is subject to a flat-rate deduction (see p182), the same amount is disregarded from your income. If your income does not cover the deduction, the balance is ignored from your partner's income.[170] For information about student grants, contact your Student Welfare Officer.

Student loans[171] under the statutory scheme are treated as income. Weekly income is calculated by dividing the loan over the 52 (or 53) weeks of the academic year. In the final year of the course, or for a one-year course, the loan is divided by the number of weeks from the start of the academic year to when the course ends. The end of the course is the last day of the last term.[172]

There is a £10 disregard on loan income, but it will overlap with any other £10 disregard on other income.[173]

If you give up your course before it finishes, your loan continues to be counted in the same way, but without any disregard.[174]

If you fail to apply for a loan to which you are entitled, the maximum amount payable to you is counted as weekly income, calculated as if you actually received it.[175] This does not apply if you have given up your course early (see above), since you are no longer a 'student'.

Access Fund payments[176] made to students by educational establishments to prevent hardship will be treated as voluntary or charitable payments (see below).

(iv) Adoption, fostering and residence order (in Scotland custody) payments

An **adoption allowance** counts in full for IS and HB/CCB up to the amount of the adopted child's personal allowance and disabled child premium, if any. Above that level it is ignored completely.[177]

For FC/DWA, anything above the level of the child's credit/allowance is ignored.[178]

If the child has capital over £3,000, you will not be entitled to any benefit for the child[179] and the entire adoption allowance will be ignored.[180]

The way that a **fostering allowance** is treated depends on whether the arrangement is an official one or a private one. If a child is placed or boarded out with you by the local authority or a voluntary organisation under legal provisions, any fostering allowances you receive will be ignored altogether.[181]

If the fostering arrangement is a private one, any money you receive from the child's parents will be counted as maintenance (see p260). If the money you receive is not from the child's parents, you should probably be treated as a childminder (see p258).

If you are paid a **residence order allowance** (in Scotland custody allowance)[182] by the local authority, this will be treated in the same way as an adoption allowance (see above). Arrears of residence order (in Scotland custody) allowances are treated as capital for IS.[183] Any payments made by the natural parents will be counted as maintenance (see p260).

If the local authority makes a lump-sum payment to enable you to make adaptations to your home for a handicapped child, this will be treated as capital and ignored (see p276).[184]

(v) Charitable and voluntary payments

Any payments including payments in kind from the MacFarlane Trust, the Macfarlane

(Special Payments) Trust and the MacFarlane (Special Payments) (No. 2) Trust or the Independent Living Fund (see p352) are disregarded in full. [185]

The MacFarlane (Special Payments) (No. 2) Trust is set up principally for haemophiliacs.

If you are, or were, a haemophiliac, the following payments from money that originally came from any of the three MacFarlane Trusts are also disregarded in full: [186]

☐ any payment made by you, or on your behalf, to, or for the benefit of:
   - your partner, or former partner from whom you are not estranged or divorced;
   - any child (see p233) who is a member of your family, or who was but is now a member of another family; *or*

☐ if you have no partner or former partner (other than one from whom you are estranged or divorced), or children, any payment made by you, or from your estate if you have died, to:
   - your parent or step-parent; *or*
   - your guardian if you have no parent or step-parent and were a child (see p233) or student at the date of the payment, or, if you have died, at the date of your death.

In the case of a payment to a parent, step-parent or guardian, this is only disregarded until two years after your death.

☐ any payment made by your partner, or former partner from whom you are not estranged or divorced, or on her/his behalf, to, or for the benefit of:
   - you;
   - any child who is a member of your family, or who was and is now a member of another family.

Any income or capital that derives from any such payment is also disregarded.

Any other charitable or voluntary payment that is made irregularly and is intended to be made irregularly will be treated as capital. [187] However, if you are on IS it will count as income:

☐ if you are involved in a trade dispute and for the first 15 days following your return to work after a dispute [188] (see pp58-62); *or*

☐ where payments made to a child's boarding school are treated as the child's notional income [189] (see p247).

An irregular charitable or voluntary payment will therefore normally only affect your benefit if the payment takes your capital over £3,000 or over £8,000 or £16,000 (see p272).

If you receive a capital payment from a charity to repair or improve your home, this should be disregarded in full [190] (see p276). Any capital payment in kind made by a charity will be ignored. [191]

Charitable or voluntary payments made, or due to be made regularly, will be completely ignored if: [192]

☐ for IS/HB/CCB, they are intended, and used for, anything *except* food, ordinary clothing or footwear, household fuel, rent for which HB is payable, community charge (but not standard community charge) and water rates, and for IS only, housing costs met under IS and residential or nursing home charges met under IS;

☐ for FC/DWA, they are intended and used for anything *except* food, ordinary clothing or footwear, household fuel, community charge (but not standard community charge) or any housing costs.

School uniform and sportswear are examples of clothing and footwear that is not ordinary.

If not ignored altogether, charitable or voluntary payments have a £10 disregard. This is subject to the maximum of £10 in all on any payments made in the same week as other income which attracts the £10 disregard.

These rules do not apply, for IS, where you are involved in a trade dispute, and for the first 15 days following your return to work after a trade dispute; for IS/FC/DWA/ HB/CCB, payments from a former partner, or the parent of your child will be dealt with as maintenance (see p260).

(See also, payments made to someone else on your behalf, p271, and payments disregarded under miscellaneous income, p268.)

(vi) Income from tenants and lodgers

Lettings without board

If you let out room(s) in your home to tenants/sub-tenants/licensees, £4 of your weekly charge per tenant will be ignored, and an extra £8.60 per tenant if the charge covers heating costs. [193] The balance will count as income.

Boarders

If you have a boarder(s) on a commercial basis, the first £20 of each boarder's weekly charge is ignored and half of any balance remaining is then taken into account as your income. [194]

If another member of your household makes payments to you which includes something for meals, but *not* on a commercial basis, they will be treated as a non-dependant rather than as a boarder (see pp27 and 171). Payments from non-dependants are ignored altogether. [195]

(vii) Income from capital

Actual income generated from capital (eg, interest on savings) of £8,000 or less (£16,000 for DWA/HB/CCB) is ignored as income [196] but will be counted as *capital* [197] from the date you are due to receive it, except income derived from the following items of *disregarded* capital [198] (see p275):

☐ your home;

☐ your former home if you are estranged or divorced;

☐ property which you have acquired for occupation as your home but which you have not yet been able to move into;

☐ property which you intend to occupy as your home but which needs essential repairs or alterations;

☐ property occupied wholly or partly by a partner or relative of any member of your family who is 60 or over or incapacitated;

☐ property occupied by your former partner, but not if you are estranged or divorced – unless (for HB/CCB) s/he is a single parent;

☐ property up for sale;

☐ property which you are taking legal steps to obtain to occupy as your home;
☐ your business assets;
☐ a trust of personal injury compensation.

Except in the case of your current home, income up to the amount of the total mortgage repayments (capital and interest) payable in respect of such property (and for CCB up to the amount of the standard community charge or community water charge) for the same period as you receive the income[199] is ignored.

Tariff income from capital over £3,000[200]

If your capital is over £3,000, you are treated as having an assumed income from it, called your **tariff income**. You are assumed to have an income of £1 for every £250, or part of £250, by which your capital exceeds £3,000 but does not exceed £8,000 (IS and FC) or £16,000 (DWA/HB/CCB). If your capital does exceed £8,000 (IS and FC) or £16,000 (DWA/HB/CCB), no benefit is payable at all (see p272).

The following is the full table for tariff income:

Capital	Tariff income
£3000.01 to £3250	£1
£3250.01 to £3500	£2
£3500.01 to £3750	£3
£3750.01 to £4000	£4
£4000.01 to £4250	£5
£4250.01 to £4500	£6
£4500.01 to £4750	£7
£4750.01 to £5000	£8
£5000.01 to £5250	£9
£5250.01 to £5500	£10
£5500.01 to £5750	£11
£5750.01 to £6000	£12
£6000.01 to £6250	£13
£6250.01 to £6500	£14
£6500.01 to £6750	£15
£6750.01 to £7000	£16
£7000.01 to £7250	£17
£7250.01 to £7500	£18
£7500.01 to £7750	£19
£7750.01 to £8000	£20

(Capital limit cut-off for IS and FC)

Capital	Tariff income
£8000.01 to £8250	£21
£8250.01 to £8500	£22
£8500.01 to £8750	£23
£8750.01 to £9000	£24
£9000.01 to £9250	£25
£9250.01 to £9500	£26
£9500.01 to £9750	£27
£9750.01 to £10000	£28
£10000.01 to £10250	£29
£10250.01 to £10500	£30
£10500.01 to £10750	£31
£10750.01 to £11000	£32

Capital	Tariff income
£11000.01 to £11250	£33
£11250.01 to £11500	£34
£11500.01 to £11750	£35
£11750.01 to £12000	£36
£12000.01 to £12250	£37
£12250.01 to £12500	£38
£12500.01 to £12750	£39
£12750.01 to £13000	£40
£13000.01 to £13250	£41
£13250.01 to £13500	£42
£13500.01 to £13750	£43
£13750.01 to £14000	£44
£14000.01 to £14250	£45
£14250.01 to £14500	£46
£14500.01 to £14750	£47
£14750.01 to £15000	£48
£15000.01 to £15250	£49
£15250.01 to £15500	£50
£15500.01 to £15750	£51
£15750.01 to £16000	£52

(Capital limit cut-off for HB and CCB)

If you are underpaid because of a change in your capital affecting your tariff income, you should ask for a review (see p103 for IS, p147 for DWA, p138 for FC, p205 for HB and p223 for CCB). If there is a change in your capital increasing the amount of your tariff income as a result of which you are overpaid, see pp112-16 for IS/FC/ DWA, and pp187-204 for HB and pp222-23 for CCB on recovery of overpayments.

(viii) Capital which counts as income

The following will count as income:
- [ ] Instalments of capital outstanding when you claim benefit if they would bring your capital over the limit (ie, £8,000 or £16,000 – see p272). For IS, the instalments to be counted are any outstanding either when your benefit claim is decided, or when you are first due to be paid benefit, whichever is earlier, or the date of any subsequent review.[201] For FC/DWA it is any instalments outstanding at the date of your claim.[202] For HB/CCB it is any instalments outstanding when your claim is made or treated as made, or when your benefit is reviewed.[203] Any balance over the capital limit will be counted as income, by spreading it over the number of weeks between each instalment.[204]

For IS, FC, and DWA, if instalments are outstanding in this way on your child's capital, a similar rule applies. If the total of these instalments and your child's existing savings come to more than £3,000, the outstanding instalments will count as your child's income, and be spread over the period between each instalment.[205] There is no equivalent rule for HB/CCB, so each instalment will count as the child's capital when they receive it.[206]

☐ Any payment from an annuity[207] (see below for when this is disregarded).
☐ For IS, a tax refund if you or your partner are involved in or have returned to work after a trade dispute[208] (see pp58-62).
☐ For IS, a payment under 'Section 17' (which broadly replaces local authorities' previous powers under Section 1) or 'Section 12' from your local social services department, or payments from social services to young people who have previously been in care or been looked after by them, if you or your partner are involved in or have returned to work after a trade dispute (see p58-62).[209]
☐ For HB/CCB, a local authority will sometimes treat withdrawals from a capital sum as income.[210] This is most likely where a sum was intended to provide regular maintenance over a particular period – eg, a bank loan taken out by a mature student. If this is not the intended use of any capital sum, you should dispute the decision.

Even where the sum is intended for maintenance, you should argue that unless it is actually paid in instalments it should be treated as capital.[211]

Any payments of capital, or any irregular withdrawals from a capital sum, which are clearly for one-off items of expenditure and not regular living expenses, should be treated as capital. Further, whatever the intention behind the sum, if no withdrawals are in fact made, it should be treated as capital.[212]

Capital which is counted as income cannot also be treated as producing a tariff income (see p266).[213]

(ix)   Income tax refunds

PAYE income tax refunds are not payable to unemployed people receiving unemployment benefit or IS until the end of the tax year, or until they obtain a job, whichever comes first. Strikers can only get a tax refund on return to work. Other people who are not counted as unemployed (eg, the sick or retired), or who are not entitled to unemployment benefit or IS (eg, married women who pay a reduced 'stamp'), can still get tax refunds when they fall due.
☐ Tax refunds under Schedule D (self-employed people) are treated as capital.[214]
☐ PAYE refunds are treated as capital.[215]
☐ For IS only, if you or your partner have been involved in or have returned to work after a trade dispute (see pp58-62), tax refunds will be treated as income and will be taken into account in full.[216]
For treatment of income tax refunds on mortgage interest or loans for repairs and improvements, see below; and on covenant income in the case of students, see pp260-63.

(x)   Miscellaneous income

Count in full:
☐ An occupational pension except any discretionary payment from a hardship fund.[217]
☐ Payments from an annuity. *Except* that in the case of 'home income plans', income from the annuity equal to the interest payable on the loan with which the annuity was bought will be ignored if the following conditions are met:
   – you used at least 90 per cent of the loan made to you to buy the annuity; *and*

- the annuity will end when you and your partner die; *and*
- you or your partner are responsible for paying the interest on the loan; *and*
- you, or both your partner and yourself, were at least 65 at the time the loan was made; *and*
- the loan is secured on a property which you or your partner owns or has an interest in, and the property on which the loan is secured is your home, or that of your partner.

If the interest on the loan is payable after income tax has been deducted, it is an amount equal to the net interest payment that will be disregarded, otherwise it will be the gross amount of the interest payment. [218]

The following are ignored:

☐ For IS only, payments you receive under a mortgage protection policy which you use to pay 50 per cent of the interest on your mortgage or loan for repairs and improvements to your home while the Benefits Agency is meeting only 50 per cent of your payments. Insurance payments which you use to repay the capital due on your mortgage or loan and the premiums on the policy are also ignored, [219] but not those intended to cover your endowment policy, or your other mortgage or loan interest.

☐ For IS only, and as long as you have not already used insurance payments for the same purpose, any money you receive which is given and used to pay:
- 50 per cent of the interest on your mortgage, or loan for repairs and improvements while the Benefits Agency is only meeting part of the interest on such mortgage or loan; [220]
- the capital repayments; [221]
- any of your other eligible housing costs which are not being met by IS [222] (see pp27-31) – eg, your house is considered too expensive and the Benefits Agency is not, therefore, paying the whole of your mortgage interest payments;
- any rent that is not covered by HB [223] (see pp157-67);
- the part of your accommodation charge that is above the maximum allowed if you live in a nursing home or residential care home [224] (see p72).

☐ For HB/CCB, payments you receive under a mortgage protection policy will be ignored up to the level of your repayments. [225]

☐ Educational maintenance allowances [226] (see p345).

☐ Any payment to cover expenses if you are working as a volunteer – eg, for a charity or voluntary organisation. [227]

☐ Payments in kind (if you or your partner are involved in a trade dispute, see p60). [228]

☐ A job start allowance paid under the Employment and Training Act 1973 and a payment (other than a training allowance) to a disabled person under that Act or the Disabled Persons (Employment) Act 1944 to assist them to obtain or retain employment. [229]

☐ Any payments, other than for loss of earnings or of a benefit, made to jurors or witnesses for attending at court. [230]

☐ A 'Section 17' payment (which broadly replaces local authorities' previous powers under Section 1) from the social services department, or a 'Section 12' payment from the social work department (in Scotland), of your local authority,

and payments from social services to young people who have been in care or been looked after by them. [231] For IS, such payments will not be ignored if you or your partner are involved in or have returned to work after a trade dispute (see pp58-62)
☐ Any payment you receive from a health authority, local council or voluntary organisation for looking after a person temporarily in your care. [232]
☐ Victoria Cross or George Cross payments or similar awards. [233]
☐ Income paid outside the UK which cannot be transferred here. [234]
☐ If income is paid in another currency, any bank charges for converting the payment into sterling. [235]
☐ Fares to hospital. [236]
☐ Payments instead of milk tokens and vitamins. [237]
☐ Payments to assist prison visits. [238]

5 NOTIONAL INCOME

In certain circumstances you will be treated as having income although you do not possess it, or have used it up.

(i) Deprivation of income in order to claim or increase benefit

If you deliberately get rid of income in order to claim or increase your benefit, you are treated as though you are still in receipt of the income. [239] The basic issues involved are the same as those for the deprivation of capital (see p280).

(ii) Failing to apply for income [240]

If you fail to apply for income to which you are entitled without having to fulfil further conditions – eg, statutory sick pay – you will be deemed to have received it.

This does not include income from a discretionary trust or trust set up from money paid as a result of a personal injury. For IS only, one parent benefit, unemployment benefit (if you do not have to be available for work) FC and DWA are also exempted.

You will be treated as having such income from the date you could have obtained it.

DSS guidance for HB/CCB now says FC (and presumably other benefits as well) should only count as notional income if you have not applied for it, but would stand a good chance of getting it. If you have applied for FC/DWA but have not yet been paid, it does not count as notional income and should be ignored until you actually receive it. [241] Remember that arrears of IS/FC/DWA/HB/CCB are treated as capital and not income (see p277). [242]

(iii) Income due to you that has not been paid

This applies to IS only. [243] You will be treated as possessing any income owing to you. Examples could be wages legally due but not paid, or an occupational pension payment that is due but has not been received. This rule does not apply if any social security benefit has been delayed, or you are waiting for a late payment of a pension under the Job Release Scheme, a government training allowance or a benefit from a Common Market country. Nor does it apply in the case of money due to you from a discretionary trust, or a trust set up from money paid as a result of a personal injury.

If this rule is applied, an urgent cases payment should be considered (see pp35-37). [244]

(iv) Unpaid wages

This applies to IS only: if you have wages due to you, but you do not yet know the exact amount or you have no proof of what they will be, you are treated as having a wage similar to that normally given for that type of work in that area. [245] If your wages cannot be estimated you might qualify for an interim payment [246] (see p107).

(v) Income payments made to someone else on your behalf [247]

If money is paid to someone on your behalf – eg, the landlord for your rent – this can count as notional income. The rules are the same as for notional capital (see p282). For IS, payments in kind are ignored, unless you or your partner are involved in a trade dispute (but even then they are ignored if they are from the Macfarlane Trusts or Independent Living Fund, see p351). [248]

(vi) Income payments paid to you for someone else [249]

If you or a member of your family get a payment for somebody not in the 'family' (see p227) – eg, a relative living with you – it will count as your income if you keep any of it yourself or spend it on your family. This does not apply if the payment is from the Macfarlane Trusts or the Independent Living Fund. Note that the same exception for payments in kind applies for IS as in (v) above.

(vii) Cheap or unpaid labour

If you are helping another person or an organisation by doing work of a kind which would normally command a wage, or a higher wage, you are deemed to receive a wage similar to that normally paid for that kind of job in that area. [250] The burden of proving that the kind of work you do is something for which an employer would pay, and what the comparable wages are, lies with the adjudication officer. [251]

The rule does not apply if:

either you can show that the person ('person' in this context includes a limited company [252]) cannot, in fact, afford to pay, or pay more;

or you are doing voluntary work and it is accepted that it is reasonable for you to give your services free of charge. [253]

If you are caring for a sick or disabled person it may be reasonable for them to pay you from their benefits, unless you can bring yourself within these exceptions. [254] It may, for example, be more reasonable for a close relative to provide services free of charge. [255]

Chapter 19

Capital

In this chapter we cover:

1 Introduction (see below)
2 What counts as capital (see below)
3 Disregarded capital (p275)
4 Notional capital (p280)
5 How capital is valued (p283)

1 INTRODUCTION

(i) The capital limit

This chapter explains how capital affects your entitlement to means-tested benefits and what counts as capital for IS, FC, DWA, HB and CCB. If you get IS, you do not need to work out your capital again for HB/CCB purposes because you receive your maximum rent rebate or allowance (see pp168-69) (less any non-dependant deductions) or your maximum CCB (see p218).[1]

If you have over £8,000 (IS and FC)[2] or £16,000 (DWA, HB and CCB)[3] you are not entitled to benefit. Some capital is ignored (see p275), but you may also be treated as having some capital which you do not actually possess (see p280). If you have up to £3,000 it will be completely ignored and will not affect your weekly benefit at all.[4] If you have between £3,000.01 and £8,000 (IS and FC)/£16,000 (DWA, HB and CCB) you are entitled to claim but some income will be assumed[5] (see p266).

(ii) Whose capital counts

Your partner's capital is added to yours.[6] Your child's capital does not count as belonging to you,[7] but if it is over £3,000 you will not get benefit for that child,[8] in which case any income of the child will not be counted as yours either.[9] The rules used to work out your child's capital are the same ones that apply to you[10] (see p267 for instalments of capital).

2 WHAT COUNTS AS CAPITAL

The term 'capital' is not defined. In general, it is used to apply to a lump sum or one-off payment rather than a series of payments.[11] It includes savings, property and lump-sum payments like redundancy payments.

A payment of capital can normally be distinguished from income because it is made without being tied to a period; it is not related to a past payment; and not intended to form part of a series of payments. [12]

Some capital is treated as income (see p267).

(i) Savings

Your savings generally count as capital, and include, for instance, cash you have at home, premium bonds, stocks and shares, unit trusts, money in a bank account, building society and the like.

Your savings from past earnings can only be treated as capital when all relevant debts, including tax liabilities, have been deducted. [13] Savings from other past income (including social security benefits) will be treated as capital. There is no provision for disregarding money put aside to pay bills. If you have savings just below the capital limit, it may be best to pay bills for gas, electricity, telephone etc by monthly standing order, or by use of a budget account to prevent your capital going above this limit.

(ii) Fixed-term investments

Capital held in fixed-term investments counts unless you can show that the money is unobtainable. If you can convert the investment into a realisable form or sell your interest, or even raise a loan through a reputable bank using the asset as security, its value counts. If it takes time to produce evidence about the nature and value of the investment, you may be able to get an interim payment for IS, FC or HB [14] (see pp107, 137 and 192) or, if you would be without any money immediately, a crisis loan from the social fund (see p314).

(iii) Property and land

Any property or land which you own counts as capital and you are not entitled to benefit if it is worth more than £8,000 (IS and FC)/£16,000 (DWA/HB and CCB). Many types of property are disregarded (see p275). See also proprietary estoppel – p274.

(iv) Loans

A loan usually counts as money you possess. However, a loan granted on condition that you only use the interest but do not touch the capital should not be counted as part of your capital because the capital element has never been at your disposal. [15] Where you have been paid money to be used for a particular purpose (eg, a holiday in India) on condition that the money must be returned if not used in that way, it should not be treated as part of your capital. [16] Where you have bought a property on behalf of someone else who is paying the mortgage; [17] or where you are holding money in your bank account on behalf of another person which is to be returned to them at a future date, [18] the capital should not count as yours.

For HB/CCB some loans might be treated as income even though paid as a lump sum (see p267).

(v) Trusts

A trust is a way of owning an asset. In theory, the asset is split into two notional parts: the legal title owned by the trustee, and the beneficial use owned by the beneficiary. A trustee can never have the use of the asset. For instance, if a sum of money is held on trust, the beneficiary can ask for it and use it, but the trustee has no right to do this, only the responsibility of looking after it. Anything can be held on trust – eg, money, houses, shares etc.

If you are the beneficiary of:

☐ **a non-discretionary trust** you can obtain the asset from the trustee at any time. You effectively own the asset, and so it will always count in full as capital;

☐ **a discretionary trust** you can usually only receive payments from the trust. These are made under the terms of the trust, or at the discretion of the trustee. Any payments made will be treated in full as income or capital depending on the nature of the payment. The trust would not normally count as capital because you have no control over the capital asset, and cannot normally command payment either. The only capital asset you have is the future right to receive payments under the trust. This is disregarded if the right is for life (see p278);

☐ **a trust in the future** (eg, on reaching 21), this is a right that has a present capital value (see p284), unless disregarded (see p278).

If you hold an asset as a trustee, it is not part of your capital. You are only a trustee either if someone gives you an asset on the express condition that you hold it for someone else (or use it for their benefit), or if you have expressed the clearest intention that your own asset is for someone else's benefit, and renounced its use for yourself (assets other than money may need to be transferred in a particular way to the trust). [19]

It is not enough to only *intend* to give someone an asset. However, in the case of property and land, **proprietary estoppel** may apply. This means that if you lead someone to believe that you are transferring your interest in some property to them, but fail to do so (eg, it was never properly conveyed), and they act on the belief that they have ownership (eg, improve, repair, or take on a mortgage), it would then be unfair on them were they to lose out if you insisted that you were still the owner. [20] In this case, you can argue the capital asset has been transferred to them, and you are like a trustee. Thus you can insist that it is not your capital asset, but theirs, when claiming benefit.

Trusts of personal injury compensation are always disregarded (see p278).

(vi) Income treated as capital

Certain payments which appear to be income are nevertheless treated as capital. These are: [21]

☐ an advance of earnings or loan from your employer;*

☐ holiday pay which is not payable until more than four weeks after your employment ends or is interrupted;*

☐ income tax refunds;*

☐ income from capital (eg, interest on a building society account) *but not* income from certain disregarded property, business assets and trusts of personal injury compensation (see p266);

☐ for IS/HB/CCB, a lump sum or 'bounty' paid to you not more than once a year as a part-time firefighter or part-time member of a lifeboat crew, or as an auxiliary coastguard or member of the Territorial Army – for FC/DWA this counts as earnings;[22]
☐ irregular (one-off) charitable payments;*
☐ for FC/DWA only, irregular maintenance payments (see p260);[23]
☐ for IS only, payments of compensation for loss of employment by an employer, not otherwise treated as earnings (see p253);
☐ for IS only, a discharge grant paid on release from prison;
☐ for IS only, arrears of residence order (in Scotland custody) payments from a local authority (see p263).

* Except, for IS, in the case of people involved in, or returning to work after, a trade dispute – see pp58-62.

Any income treated as capital is disregarded as income.[24]

3   DISREGARDED CAPITAL

(i)   Your home

If you own the home you normally live in, its value is ignored altogether when calculating your benefit.[25] Your home includes any garage, garden and outbuildings together with any premises (including land) that you do not occupy as your home but which it is impractical or unreasonable to sell separately (eg, croft land).[26] If you own more than one property, only the value of the one normally occupied is disregarded under this rule.[27] A holiday home would not be disregarded, as it is not your normal home.[28]

The value of other property can be disregarded even if you do not live in it, in the following circumstances:

☐ **If you have left your former home following a marriage or relationship breakdown,** the value of the property is ignored for six months from the date you left. It is also disregarded for longer if any of the steps below are taken. For HB/CCB, if it is occupied by your former partner who is a single parent its value is ignored as long as s/he lives there.[29]

☐ **If you have sought legal advice or have started legal proceedings in order to occupy property** as your home, its value is ignored for six months from the date you first took either of these steps.[30] The six months can be extended, if it is reasonable to do so, where you need longer to move into the property.

☐ **If you are taking reasonable steps to dispose of any property,** its value is ignored for six months from the date you first took such steps.[31] If you need longer to dispose of the property, the disregard can continue if it is reasonable – eg, where a husband or wife attempts to realise their share in a former matrimonial home but the court orders that it should not be sold until the youngest child reaches a certain age.[32] Putting the property in the hands of an estate agent or getting in touch with a prospective purchaser should constitute 'reasonable steps'.[33]

☐ **If you are carrying out essential repairs or alterations** which are needed so that you can occupy a property as your home (eg, the installation of a bathroom on the ground floor for a person unable to climb stairs), the value of the property is ignored for six months from the date you first began to carry them out. [34] If you cannot finish the work and move into the property within that period, its value can be disregarded for as long as is reasonable.

☐ **If you sell your home** and intend to use the proceeds of sale to buy another home, the capital is ignored for six months from the date of the sale. [35] If you need longer to complete the purchase, the authorities can continue to ignore the capital if it is reasonable to do so. If you intend to use only part of the proceeds of sale to buy another home, only that part is disregarded even if, for example, you have put the rest of the money aside to renovate your new home. [36] If you sell up and move to rented property with no intention of purchasing another home, all the capital from the sale of your former home is taken into account.

☐ **If you have acquired a house or flat for occupation** as your home but have not yet moved in, its value is ignored if you intend to live there within six months. [37] If you cannot move in by then the value of the property can be ignored for as long as seems reasonable.

☐ **If your home is damaged or you lose it altogether**, any payment, including compensation, which you intend to use for its repair, or for acquiring another home, is ignored for a period of six months, or longer if it is reasonable to do so. [38]

☐ **If you have taken out a loan or been given money for the express purpose of essential repairs and improvements** to your home, it is ignored for six months, or longer if it is reasonable to do so. [39]

☐ **If you have deposited money with a housing association as a condition of occupying your home**, this is ignored indefinitely. [40] If money which was deposited for this purpose is now to be used to buy another home, this is ignored for six months, or longer if reasonable, in order to allow you to complete the purchase. [41]

☐ **Grants made to local authority tenants to buy a home or do repairs/alterations** to it can be ignored for up to 26 weeks, or longer if reasonable, to allow completion. [42]

When considering whether to increase the period of any disregard, all the relevant circumstances must be considered – particularly your and your family's personal circumstances, any efforts made by you to use or dispose of the asset (if relevant) and the general state of the market (if relevant). [43]

It is possible for property to be ignored under more than one of the above paragraphs in succession.

Some income generated from property which is disregarded will be ignored (see p265).

(ii)   The home of a partner or relative

The value of a house will also be ignored if it is occupied wholly or partly as their home by: [44]

☐ your partner, or former partner from whom you are not estranged or divorced, but who is no longer treated as a member of your household (eg, because you have been away for more than 52 weeks); *or*

☐ for HB/CCB only, your former partner from whom you are estranged or divorced if s/he is a single parent. [45] Otherwise, see (i) above for rules; *or*

☐ a relative of yours, or of any member of your family who is 60 or over, or incapacitated.

A person should be accepted as 'incapacitated' if s/he is in receipt of a sickness or disability benefit, or if s/he is sufficiently incapacitated to qualify for one of those benefits.[46] For FC/DWA, the relative must have been incapacitated throughout the 13 weeks before you claim.[47] Relative includes: a parent, son, daughter, step-parent/son/daughter, or parent/son/daughter-in-law; brother or sister; or a partner of any of these people; or a grandparent or child, uncle, aunt, nephew or niece.[48] It also includes half-brothers and sisters and adopted children.[49]

(iii) Personal possessions

All personal possessions, including items such as jewellery, furniture, or a car are ignored unless you have bought them in order to be able to claim or get more benefit.[50]

Compensation for damage to, or the loss of, any personal possessions, which is to be used for their repair or replacement is ignored for six months, or longer if reasonable.[51]

(iv) Business assets

If you are self-employed, your business assets are ignored for as long as you continue to work in that business. For IS and FC, as little as half an hour's work a week will be sufficient.[52] If you cannot work because of physical or mental illness, but intend to work in the business when you are able, the disregard operates for 26 weeks, or for longer if reasonable in the circumstances.[53] If you stop working in the business, you are allowed a reasonable time to sell these assets without their value affecting your benefit. For FC/DWA, if you have sold a business asset but intend to reinvest the proceeds in that business within 13 weeks (or longer if reasonable) the money is ignored.[54]

(v) Tax rebates and arrears of benefits

Tax rebates for the tax relief on interest on a mortgage or loan obtained for buying your home or carrying out repairs or improvements are ignored.[55]

Arrears of certain benefits are ignored for a year after they are paid.[56] These are mobility allowance, attendance allowance (or an equivalent benefit paid because of a war or work injury), mobility supplement, disability living allowance, IS, supplementary benefit, FC, family income supplement, HB/CCB, certain war widows' payments,[57] refunds on community charge because you qualify for transitional relief,[58] or concessionary payments made instead of any of these, and for FC only, DWA.

Compensation for loss of housing benefit supplement, IS or HB at the changeover to IS in April 1988 will be completely ignored.[59]

(vi) Insurance policies and annuities

The surrender value of any life assurance or endowment policy is ignored.[60] So also is the surrender value of any annuity.[61] Any payment under the annuity counts as income[62] (but see p268 for when this is disregarded).

(vii) A reversionary interest

A reversionary interest – which is an interest in property that will only become yours when some event occurs – is ignored.[63] An example of a reversionary interest is where someone else has a life interest in a fund and you are only entitled after that person has died.

(viii) Trust funds from personal injury compensation

Where a trust fund has been set up out of money paid because of a personal injury to you, your partner or a child, the value of the trust fund is ignored.[64]

In this context, 'personal injury' includes a disease and injury suffered as a result of a disease. Thus a trust fund for a child who had both legs amputated following meningitis and septicaemia could be disregarded for the purposes of the parent's claim.[65]

Any payments actually made from these trusts count in full as income or capital depending on the nature of the payment.[66]

If there is no trust, the whole of the compensation payment counts as capital even if the money is held by your solicitor.[67]

(ix) The right to receive a payment in the future

If you know you will receive a payment in the future from, say, a trust fund or a pension scheme, you could sell that future right at any time so it has a market value and thus constitutes an actual capital resource. The regulations provide that the value of this will be disregarded where it is a right to receive:

- [ ] income under a life interest or, in Scotland, a liferent.[68] When the income is actually paid, it will count in full (see p274);
- [ ] any earnings or income which are ignored because they are frozen abroad[69] (see pp258 and 268);
- [ ] any outstanding instalments where capital is being paid by instalments[70] (see p267);
- [ ] an occupational pension;[71]
- [ ] a personal pension;[72]
- [ ] any rent;[73]
- [ ] any payment under an annuity (see p268);[74]
- [ ] any payment under a trust fund that is disregarded[75] (see above).

(x) Payments by social services, government departments and the social fund

A 'Section 17' payment (which broadly replaces local authorities' previous powers under Section 1) or a 'Section 12' payment from the social services department of your local council is ignored. Payments made by local authorities to young people who have previously been in care or been looked after by social services are also ignored. But if you or your partner are involved in a trade dispute or it is paid during the first 15 days following your return to work after the dispute,[76] it counts as income for IS.

The following payments are ignored for 52 weeks from receipt:

☐ Fares to hospital.[77]
☐ Payments in place of milk tokens or vitamins.[78]
☐ Payments to assist prison visits.[79]
Social fund payments are also ignored.[80]

A payment to a disabled person under the Disabled Persons (Employment) Act 1944 or the Employment and Training Act 1973 (other than a training allowance or training bonus) to assist with employment, or a local authority payment to assist blind homeworkers will be ignored.[81]

(xi)   Charitable payments

Any payment in kind by a charity is ignored.[82] All payments from the Macfarlane Trusts and Independent Living Fund (see p351) are ignored.[83] Payments from the Macfarlane Trusts do not have to be declared for HB/CCB at all, or to the Benefits Agency, if they are kept separately from the claimant's other capital and income.[84] Certain payments from money that originally came from any of the three MacFarlane Trusts are also ignored if you are, or were, a haemophiliac – the rules are the same as for income (see p263).

(xii)   Payments to jurors and witnesses

Any payments made to jurors or witnesses for attending at court are ignored, except for payments for loss of earnings or of benefit.[85]

(xiii)   Training bonus

A training bonus of not more than £200 is disregarded,[86] but only for a year for HB/CCB, FC and DWA.

(xiv)   Payments in other currencies

Any payment in a currency other than sterling will only be taken into account less banking charges or commission payable on conversion to sterling.[87]

(xv)   Capital treated as income

Some payments which appear to be capital are treated as income. These are:
☐ certain instalments of capital which you are owed;
☐ payments from annuities;
☐ for strikers, tax refunds or certain local authority payments;
☐ some lump sums from liable relatives (see p95);
☐ for HB/CCB certain lump-sum loans may be treated as income.
See p267 for the detailed rules.

Any capital treated as income is disregarded as capital.[88]

4   NOTIONAL CAPITAL

In certain circumstances, you are treated as having capital which you do not, in fact, possess. This is called 'notional capital' and it counts in the same way as capital you actually possess.[89] There is a similar rule for notional income, see p270.

(i)   Deprivation of capital in order to claim or increase benefit

If you deliberately get rid of capital in order to claim or increase your benefit, you are treated as still possessing it.[90] You are likely to be affected by this rule if, at the time of using up your money, you know that you may qualify for benefit as a result, or qualify more quickly. It should not be used if you know nothing about the effect of using up your capital (eg, you do not know about the capital limit for claiming benefit),[91] or if you have been using up your capital at a rate which is reasonable in the circumstances. Knowledge of capital limits can be inferred from a reasonable familiarity with the benefit system as a claimant,[92] but if you fail to make enquiries about the capital limit, this does not constitute an intention to secure benefit.[93] Even if you do know about the capital limits (see p272), it still has to be shown that you intended to obtain, retain or increase your benefit.[94] The longer the period that has elapsed since the disposal of the capital, the less likely it will be that it was for the purpose of obtaining benefit.[95]

A person who uses up her/his resources may have more than one motive for doing so. Even where qualifying for benefit as a result is only a subsidiary motive for actions, and the predominant motive is something quite different (eg, ensuring your home is in good condition by spending capital to do necessary repairs and improvements) you are still counted as having deprived yourself of a resource in order to gain benefit.[96] Local authorities tend to apply this test less stringently in the case of HB and CCB. Examples of the kinds of expenditure that could be caught by the rule are an expensive holiday and putting money in trust.[97] (Putting money in trust for yourself does not constitute deprivation if the capital being put in trust came from compensation paid for any personal injury.[98]) But the essential test is not the kind of item that the money has been spent on but the *intention* behind the expenditure.

In practice, arguing successfully that you have not deprived yourself of capital to get or increase benefit may boil down to whether you can show that you would have spent the money in the way you did (eg, to pay off debts or reduce your mortgage), regardless of the effect on your benefit entitlement. Where this is unclear, the burden of proving that you did it in order to get benefit lies with the Benefits Agency (IS, FC and DWA) or local authority (HB/CCB).

For IS, FC and DWA, you can only be treated as having notional capital under this rule if the capital of which you have deprived yourself is *actual* capital.[99] So if you are counted as owning half a joint bank account under the rule about jointly held capital (see p284), but your real share is only a quarter, you are not caught by the deprivation rule if you dispose of the other quarter. This is not spelt out in HB/CCB law, but you should try arguing that the same principle applies.

If you are treated as possessing notional capital, it is calculated in the same way as if it were actual capital.[100] Since 1 October 1990, there has been a 'diminishing capital rule' which provides a calculation for working out how notional capital is 'spent'.[101]

The rule is:

☐ Where your IS/FC/DWA/HB/CCB is reduced by the tariff income from your notional capital, that capital is diminished by the amount of that reduction each week (or part-week). For example, if your notional capital is £3,750, giving a tariff income of £3 a week, the reduction is £3 a week until it reaches £3,500 when it will be £2 and so on. The diminishing capital rule starts from the week after the decision is made to reduce benefit. If you are on HB and you have claimed CCB/IS/FC, or on CCB and have claimed HB/IS/FC, or on FC/DWA and claimed HB/CCB, but this was refused or reduced because of your notional capital, the weekly reduction includes the amount of any, or the additional amount of any, of these benefits you would have received.

☐ Where you are knocked off benefit altogether solely because of your notional capital, the capital is diminished by the aggregate of any of the other income-related benefits that you are otherwise entitled to and would have received, if not for the notional capital rule. If you receive some HB/CCB, then the capital is diminished by the difference between what you actually receive, and what you would have otherwise received. The calculation is done on a weekly basis, and the aggregated weekly amount is fixed for 26 weeks. If the amount you would have been entitled to increases during this period, there is no change in the amount by which the capital is reduced. It will only change if you make a further claim at the end of the 26 weeks. The aggregate of your benefit entitlements will then be recalculated and increased if it is more than before, but it will stay the same as in the prior 26-week period if it is unchanged or less. It is necessary to reclaim after each 26-week period. The 26-week period begins after the week of claim or reclaim.

Before 1 October 1990 this rule did not apply. Instead, a Tribunal of Commissioners' decision[102] held that notional capital could be diminished by reasonable expenditure on living and other sensible expenses. This could come to more than your weekly benefit entitlement, and was more generous than the new rule. It may still be possible to rely on this decision rather than being tied to the new rule, but this is very unclear. The decision still applies to other forms of notional capital, apart from deprivation of capital. It can also be used to calculate the reduction in capital where there has been deprivation for the period before 1 October 1990. Backdating this before 17 August 1990, the date of the decision, may be difficult because of the restriction on basing late claims and reviews on test cases for IS, FC and DWA (see pp102 and 106) although it may be possible to get round this by means of a late appeal against the decision on your original claim for benefit. As there was confusion as to the situation before the change in rules and the Commissioners' decision, this should be sufficient grounds for a late appeal (see p119).

Alternatively, write to the Secretary of State via your MP asking for a favourable decision or *ex gratia* payment on the grounds that the government never intended to remove the diminishing capital rule.[103]

The HB/CCB position before 1 October 1990 is less clear, although DSS guidance did suggest in the case of HB that notional capital could be diminished by any HB lost.[104] However, it may be possible to argue that the more generous approach adopted by the Commissioners should also apply to HB and CCB for this period since the law was essentially the same.

The restriction of basing late claims or reviews on test cases for IS/FC/DWA does not apply to HB/CCB, so the normal 52-week limit still holds.

(ii) Failing to apply for capital[105]

Examples of failure to apply could be where money is held in court which would be released on application or even an unclaimed Premium Bond win! It does not include capital from a discretionary trust or a trust set up from money paid as a result of a personal injury or a loan which you could only get if you gave your home or other disregarded capital (see pp275-79), as security. For IS, HB and CCB, you are only treated as having such capital from the date you could obtain it.

(iii) Capital payments made to a 'third party' on your behalf

If someone else pays an amount to a 'third party' – eg, the electricity board or building society – for you, this may count as your capital. [106] It counts if the payment is to cover your family's food, household fuel, community charge (but not any standard community charge) or ordinary clothing or footwear. (School uniforms and sportswear are not ordinary clothing; nor are, for example, special shoes because of a disability.)

It also counts if it is to cover:
- □ **for IS, HB and CCB**, any rent covered by HB, or water charges;
- □ **for IS alone**, any housing costs or accommodation charge for a nursing home or residential care home covered by IS;
- □ **for FC/DWA**, any housing costs at all.

If the payment is for other kinds of expenses – eg, a TV licence, accommodation charges above the IS limit, mortgage capital repayment or children's school fees – it does not count. Also remember that payments from the Macfarlane Trusts or Independent Living Fund do not count, whatever they are for.

Payments made for the food etc, of any member of the family, count as the capital of the member of the family in respect of whom they are paid. Since a child's capital is not counted as belonging to the claimant, a payment to, for example, a clothes shop for your child, should count as the child's notional capital and not yours.

For IS, there are different rules if you could be liable to pay maintenance as a liable relative (see p91).

(iv) Capital payments paid to you for a 'third party'[107]

If you or a member of your family get a payment for someone not in your family – eg, a relative who does not have a bank account – it only counts as yours if it is kept or used by you. Payments from the MacFarlane Trusts or Independent Living Fund do not count at all.

(v) Companies run by sole traders or a few partners

This applies if, as a sole trader or a small partnership, you have registered your business as a limited company. The value of your shareholding is ignored but you are treated as possessing a proportionate share of the capital of the company. [108]

This does not apply while you are working for the company.[109] DSS guidance says that for IS and FC, even if you only work for half an hour a week for the company this will suffice.[110]

5 HOW CAPITAL IS VALUED

(i) Market value

Apart from national savings certificates (see below), your capital is valued at its current market or surrender value.[111] This means the amount of money you could raise by selling it, raising a loan against it etc. So if an asset is difficult, or impossible, to realise, its market value should be very heavily discounted or even nil.[112]

In the case of a house, an estate agent's figure for a quick sale is a more appropriate valuation than the District Valuer's figure for a sale within three months.[113]

If you own part of an asset (eg, half of a house), it is your interest in the property that has to be valued, as this may be quite different from (and a lot less than) your proportionate share of the overall value.[114]

Appeal if you disagree with the valuation of your capital (see p118).

(ii) Debts

Deductions are made from the 'gross' value of your capital for any debt or mortgage secured on it.[115] Where a single mortgage is secured on a house and land and the value of the house is disregarded for benefit purposes, the whole of the mortgage can be deducted when calculating the value of the land.[116]

If you have debts which are not secured against your capital (eg, tax liabilities), these cannot be offset against the value of your capital.[117] However, once you have paid off your debts, your capital may well be reduced. You can be penalised if you deliberately get rid of capital in order to get benefit (see p280), but that should not happen if you are paying off genuine debts.[118]

(iii) Expenses of sale

If there would be expenses involved in selling your capital, 10 per cent is deducted from its value for the cost of sale.[119]

(iv) National savings

For IS, a certificate bought from an issue which ceased before the 1st July before your claim is decided, or your benefit is first payable (whichever is earlier), or the date of any subsequent review, has the value it would have had on that 1st July if purchased on the last day of the issue. For FC/DWA, it is the 1st July before the date of your claim; for HB/CCB, it is the 1st July before your claim is made or treated as made or when your benefit is reviewed. In any other case, the value is the purchase price.[120] DSS guidance contains a convenient valuation table for each issue.[121]

(v) Capital that is jointly owned with someone other than your partner

This is treated as being shared equally between you.[122] For example, if you own 70 per cent of an asset, and your brother 30 per cent, each of you will be treated as having a 50 per cent share. The value of the remaining 20 per cent that you actually own does not count as your capital.

(vi) Shares

Shares are valued at their current market value less 10 per cent for the cost of sale.[123] Fluctuations in price between routine reviews of your case are normally ignored. Where a claimant has a minority holding of shares in a company, the value of the shares should be based on what the claimant could realise on them, and not by valuing the entire share capital of the company and attributing to the claimant an amount calculated according to the proportion of shares held.[124]

(vii) Unit trusts

These are valued on the basis of the 'bid' price quoted in newspapers. No deduction is allowed for the cost of sale because, unlike shares, this is already included in the 'bid' price.[125]

(viii) The right to receive a payment in the future

The value of any such right that is not disregarded (see p278) is its market value: what a willing buyer will pay to a willing seller.[126] This may be very small.

(ix) Overseas assets

If you have assets abroad, and there are no exchange controls or other prohibitions that would prevent you transferring your capital to this country, your assets are valued at their current market or surrender value in that country.[127] If, as a result of this rule, there are problems and delays in getting benefit because it is difficult to get the assets valued, you may be able to get an interim payment of IS (see p107), or FC, or a 'payment on account' of HB/CCB (see p192).

If you are not allowed to transfer the full value of your capital to this country, you are treated as having capital equal to the amount that a willing buyer in this country, would give for those assets.[128] It seems likely that the price such a person (if there is one) would be willing to pay may bear little relation to the actual value of the assets.

The same deductions for any debts or mortgage secured on the assets abroad are made together with 10 per cent if there are expenses of sale. If the capital is realised in a currency other than sterling, charges payable for converting the payment into sterling are also deducted.[129]

PART VIII
The regulated social fund

Chapter 20

The regulated social fund

This chapter covers:

1 Maternity expenses payments (see below)
2 Funeral expenses payments (p287)
3 Cold weather payments (p288)
4 Reviews and appeals (p289)

There are two types of payments available from the social fund (SF).

☐ **Discretionary grants and loans** to meet a variety of needs. These are covered in Part IX – see p291.

☐ **Non-discretionary grants** for maternity expenses, funeral expenses and periods of cold weather. Unlike the discretionary payments, you are *legally entitled* to these grants if you satisfy the eligibility conditions.

1 MATERNITY EXPENSES PAYMENTS

(i) The basic rules

You are entitled to a payment for help with maternity expenses if:

☐ you (or a member of your family – see p227) are expecting a child within the next 11 weeks or have recently given birth (or have adopted a child – see p286); *and*

☐ you or your partner have been awarded income support (IS), family credit (FC) or disability working allowance (DWA) at the date of your claim; *and*

☐ you do not have too much capital (see p286); *and*

☐ you claim within the time-limits (see p286).

You cannot claim FC until your first child is born. Even if your FC claim has not been decided, you should claim a maternity expenses payment within the time-limits. You will be paid when your FC is awarded.

If you are under 19 and not able to claim IS or FC in your own right, an adult getting IS or FC can claim a maternity expenses payment for you if you count as a member of their family (see p227).

If you or your partner are involved in a trade dispute (see p58), and either one of you is getting IS, you will qualify for the payment if the dispute has been going on for six weeks or more at the date of claim. If either of you is getting FC, you will qualify for a payment if the claim for FC was made before the beginning of the dispute. [2]

(ii) The amount of the payment

The maternity expenses payment is £100 for each child. [3]

This sum is reduced by the amount of any capital you have in excess of £500 (£1,000 if you or your partner is 60 or over). [4] Capital is calculated in the same way as for IS, [5] except that lump-sum widow's payment (£1,000 – see CPAG's *Rights guide to non-means-tested benefits*) is ignored for 12 months from the date of your husband's death. [6]

(iii) Stillbirths

You are entitled to a payment for a stillborn child if your pregnancy has lasted 28 weeks. [7]

(iv) Adopted babies

You are entitled to a payment for a baby adopted by you or your partner if the baby is no more than 12 months old at the date of claim. [8] You will receive a payment even if one has already been made to the natural mother or a member of her family. [9]

(v) Claiming and getting paid

You should claim on form SF100 which you can get from your local Benefits Agency. The date of claim is the date the form is received by the Benefits Agency. If you make a written claim in some other way, you should be sent the form to complete. If you return it within a month, the date of claim will be the date the Benefits Agency received your initial application. [10] The Benefits Agency can treat an initial claim by letter as sufficient and will then not ask you to complete a form as well.

You can claim at any time from the eleventh week before your expected week of confinement (your twenty-ninth week of pregnancy) until 3 months after your actual date of confinement. If you adopt a baby, you can claim up to 3 months following the date of the adoption order. If you claim late, you will only be paid if you can show 'good cause' for not claiming in time (see p102). However, you cannot be paid if you claim more than 12 months after the date of confinement or adoption. [11]

If you claim before confinement, you will need to submit a maternity certificate (form MAT B1) or note from your doctor or midwife. If you claim after the child is born, you will usually be asked for a maternity, birth or adoption certificate.

The rules for getting paid and the recovery of overpayments are the same as for IS (see pp106 and 112).

2 FUNERAL EXPENSES PAYMENTS

(i) The basic rules [12]

You are entitled to a funeral expenses payment if:

☐ you or a member of your family (see p227) takes responsibility for the costs of a funeral; *and*

☐ the funeral (ie, burial or cremation) takes place in the UK; *and*

☐ you or your partner have been awarded IS, FC, DWA, HB or CCB at the date of your claim; *and*

☐ you do not have too much capital (see p288); *and*

☐ you claim within the time-limits (see p288).

The Benefits Agency should accept that you are responsible for the costs of a funeral if you have obtained a funeral director's estimate or bill. [13] You do not have to be a relative of the deceased or have arranged the funeral.

If you have claimed any of the qualifying benefits (IS, FC, DWA, HB or CCB) but not yet received a decision, you should claim a funeral payment within the time-limits and you will be paid when the qualifying benefit has been awarded.

Involvement in a trade dispute has no effect on a claim.

(ii) The amount of the payment

The payment is calculated by first adding up the costs of the following items: [14]

☐ any necessary documentation (eg, death and cremation certificates);

☐ an ordinary coffin;

☐ transport for the coffin and bearers, and one additional car;

☐ the reasonable cost of flowers from you;

☐ undertaker's fees and gratuities for a simple funeral;

☐ chaplain's, organist's and cemetery or crematorium fees for a simple funeral;

☐ any additional expenses arising from the religious faith of the deceased but not in excess of £75;

☐ where the death occurred away from the deceased's normal home, the costs of transporting the body within the UK to that home, or to an undertaker's premises or a chapel of rest;

☐ your reasonable travelling costs of one return journey within the UK in connection with the arrangement of, or attendance at, the funeral. Others, who are relatives of the deceased may be eligible for a community care grant for travelling costs – see p310.

The following amounts are then deducted to arrive at the amount payable: [15]

☐ the value of the deceased person's assets which are available to you without a grant of probate or letters of administration;

☐ any payment legally due to you, or a member of your family, from an insurance policy, occupational pension scheme, burial club or similar source on the death of the deceased;

☐ any contribution from a charity or a relative of your family (see p127) or the deceased's family, after offsetting any funeral expenses other than those specified above;

☐ a funeral grant paid by the government to a war- disablement pensioner.

The funeral expenses payment is also reduced by the amount of any capital you have in excess of £500 (£1,000 if you or your partner is 60 or over).[16] Capital is calculated in the same way as for IS[17] except that the lump-sum widow's payment (£1,000) is ignored for 12 months from the date of your husband's death.[18]

Any money you have been given or borrowed on the express condition that it be used to meet the costs of the funeral does not count as your capital.[19] However, if you have used any of your own capital (apart from disregarded capital) to pay for the funeral you are treated as though you still possessed it.[20]

(iii) Claiming and getting paid

You should claim on form SF200 which you can get from your local Benefits Agency. The date of claim is the date the form is received by the Benefits Agency. If you make a written claim in some other way, you should be sent the form to complete. If you return it within a month, the date of claim will be the date the Benefits Agency received your first claim.[21] The Benefits Agency can treat an initial claim by letter as sufficient and will then not ask you to complete a form as well.

You must claim within 3 months of the funeral. If you claim late you will only be paid if you can show 'good cause' for not claiming in time (see p102). You cannot be paid, however, if you claim more than 12 months after the funeral.[22]

The Benefits Agency can pay the funeral expenses payment direct to the funeral director, if the bill has not been paid.[23] Other than this, the rules for getting paid and the recovery of overpayments are the same as for IS (see pp106 and 112).

(iv) Recovery from the deceased's estate

The Secretary of State is entitled to recover funeral expenses payments from the deceased's estate and will normally seek to do so.[24] Funeral expenses are legally a first charge on the estate although there may, of course, be insufficient assets to meet full repayment.[25]

3   COLD WEATHER PAYMENTS

(i)   The basic rules

You are entitled to a cold weather payment if:

☐ a 'period of cold weather' has been forecasted or recorded for the area in which your normal home is situated (see p289);[26] *and*

☐ you have been awarded IS for at least one day during the period of cold weather; *and*

☐ *either* your IS includes one or more of the following premiums – pensioner; disability; higher pensioner; severe disability; disabled child (see p238);

☐ *or* you have a child under five. [27]

Note: The amount of capital you have does not affect the payment.

(ii)   A 'period of cold weather'

This is a period of seven consecutive days during which the average of the mean daily temperature forecasted or recorded for that period is equal to or below 0° Celsius. The 'mean daily temperature' is the average of the maximum and minimum temperatures recorded for that day. [28] The regulations divide the country into 63 areas, each covered by a weather station at which temperatures are forecasted or recorded. [29] The area your home is in is determined by your postcode.

(iii)   The amount of the payment

The sum of £6 is paid for each week of cold weather. [30]

(iv)   Claiming and getting paid

You do *not* need to make a claim for a cold weather payment. The Benefits Agency should automatically send you a giro if you qualify. [31] Your district Benefits Agency should publicise when there are periods of cold weather in your area by placing advertisements in local newspapers, by radio broadcasts, and by distributing posters and leaflets – eg, to doctors' surgeries and local advice centres. [32] If you do not receive a giro and you think you are entitled, contact your local Benefits Agency. If you do not receive a payment or are told you are not entitled, submit a written claim and ask for a written decision. You can then appeal against an unfavourable decision. [33]

The rules for getting paid and the recovery of overpayments are the same as for IS.

4   REVIEWS AND APPEALS

The rules relating to reviews and appeals are the same as for IS – see pp105 and 118. Decisions are made by adjudication officers and you can appeal against the refusal of a payment (see above).

PART IX
The discretionary social fund

Chapter 21

General principles

This chapter covers:

1   INTRODUCTION

In addition to the non-discretionary grants for maternity expenses, funeral expenses and periods of cold weather described in Part VIII, the social fund (SF) also provides **discretionary grants and loans** to meet a variety of other needs. This part of the SF is very different in character to all other social security provision:

☐   It is strictly **budget-limited**. Each district office of the Benefits Agency is given an annual allocation of money to spend.

☐   Payments are **discretionary**. There is no legal entitlement to a payment. The rules are only concerned with eligibility and how discretion is to be exercised.

☐   Many payments are in the form of **loans**. These have to be repaid to the Benefits Agency, usually by deductions from weekly benefit.

☐   Decisions are made by **social fund officers** (SFOs).

☐   There is **no right of appeal** to an independent tribunal. Instead there is a system of **review by SFOs** and further review by quasi-independent **social fund inspectors** (SFIs).

Despite the unpopularity and inherent problems of the discretionary SF, its wide remit makes it an important and valuable source of help and you should *always apply if you have a need which can be met by the fund.*

2 THE LAW AND THE GUIDANCE

(i) The law

Primary legislation

The SF was established by an Act of Parliament.[1] The Act empowers SFOs to make payments from the fund. In deciding whether to make a discretionary payment, the Act requires SFOs to take into account all the circumstances of each case and, in particular:[2]
☐ the nature, extent and urgency of the need;
☐ the existence of resources which could meet the need;
☐ whether any other person or body could meet the need;
☐ whether a loan is likely to be repaid;
☐ the amount of the Benefits Agency district office budget (see p293).
The Act also empowers the Secretary of State to issue directions to SFOs which are legally binding.[3]

The directions

The directions establish three types of discretionary payment available from the SF:
☐ **community care grants (CCGs)** (see p300);
☐ **budgeting loans** (see p312);
☐ **crisis loans** (see p314).
The directions set out the eligibility conditions for each type of payment. They also exclude payments for certain expenses (see p297) and cover reviews (see p325).

The regulations[4]

These deal with procedures. They cover:
☐ applications for grants and loans;
☐ applications for reviews; *and*
☐ the acceptance and recovery of loans.
The Act, directions and regulations are included in CPAG's *Income support, the social fund and family credit: the legislation* (see Appendix 3).

(ii) The guidance

National guidance

The Secretary of State issues guidance on how to interpret the directions and administer the SF. The guidance and directions are published in the *Social Fund Officer's Guide and Administration Guide* (see Appendix 3). The guidance suggests the circumstances in which a payment should be made, for what items and services and which applications should be given priority.

SFOs must take account of the guidance,[5] but it is *not* legally binding. The guidance repeatedly reminds SFOs that they must exercise discretion according to the individual circumstances of each case.[6] *The absence of guidance* about a particular situation or expense *does not mean that help should be refused.*

Local guidance

In addition to the national guidance, SFOs must also take account of guidance issued by SF managers in Benefits Agency district offices.[7] Copies of this guidance should be available from the local office. It suggests which groups of clients and which items should normally be regarded as priority for awards. The local guidance must not conflict with the principles laid down in the directions and the national guidance.[8]

It must also not impinge on the duty of SFOs to exercise individual discretion. In particular, local guidance which lists client groups in strict order of priority or suggests that certain groups or items should always be accorded low priority is likely to be unlawful.

Social fund inspectors' decisions

SFI decisions can be useful because they indicate how discretion should be exercised by SFOs. However, they apply only to the case under review and do not create precedents.

SFIs have consistently criticised SFOs for failing to exercise their discretion properly and, in particular, for sticking too rigidly to national and local guidance.

SFIs have also stressed that most of the terms in the directions and guidance are not defined. Where terms are not given special definitions, SFIs have said they should be given their normal everyday meaning.

3 THE BUDGET AND PRIORITIES

(i) Budget allocations

The government sets the total budget for the discretionary SF each year (£302m for 1992/93). Each Benefits Agency district office is then allocated a fixed sum for grants and another for loans.[9] The amount allocated to each district is based on their previous levels of expenditure and refusals on priority grounds (see below), and their income support caseloads.[10]

The district SF manager is responsible for planning and monitoring expenditure on a monthly basis. Any under or overspend in a particular month should lead to a revision of planned monthly expenditure for the rest of the year.[11] However, there is no monthly limit on expenditure and it would be unlawful to refuse a payment solely because planned expenditure for a particular month had been exceeded.[12] SFOs are instructed not to postpone decisions until subsequent months on budgetary grounds – ie, not to establish 'a waiting list of needs'.[13] However, they are advised to postpone decisions on 'borderline applications' to 'assist better decision-making'.[14]

The only limit on district expenditure is the total budget allocated for the year. The directions prohibit SFOs from spending more than their annual district budget.[15] Nevertheless, it is possible for the Secretary of State to allocate additional funds to a district in the course of the year.[16] The guidance suggests this could apply in an emergency or disaster or other 'exceptional circumstances',[17] but there is nothing to stop a district manager asking for more funds if the budget is being overspent to meet genuine need. Last year the government allocated an additional £49m to district offices (see also p295 – Tactics).

SFOs must have regard to the budget when deciding whether to make a payment and how much to award.[18] They do this by referring to up-to-date information about planned levels of monthly expenditure and to budget balances in their district. However, the state of the budget is only one factor they must take into account when making decisions (see p296). Refusal of an application on budgetary grounds alone is unlawful, unless the budget is exhausted. Always ask for a review if an application is refused on budgetary grounds.

Details of national and district office budgets are publicly available, including planned and actual levels of monthly expenditure.

(ii)   Priorities

The directions require SFOs to manage the budget so as to give priority to high priority needs throughout the year.[19] There is no definition of what constitutes a high priority need. SFOs must decide what priority to give each application by considering all the circumstances of the case concerned.

The national guidance gives suggestions and examples of priority claimant groups and circumstances. These are referred to in the chapters which follow about grants and loans.

Local guidance will also list priority groups and indicate which levels of priority can be met at any particular time. SFOs are told to try and meet a broadly similar level of need throughout the year.[20] SF managers must review their guidance on priorities at least once a month.[21]

The key point to remember is that the guidance about priorities is not legally binding. If an application is refused solely on the basis of the guidance, it should always be challenged by review (see p324).

4 HOW DECISIONS ARE MADE

(i) The theory

The demands placed on SFOs when making decisions are onerous and, in some respects, contradictory.

☐ They must carefully consider all the circumstances of each case including the nature, extent and urgency of the need and use their discretion and judgement to decide whether to award a payment.

☐ They must follow the law and the directions – see p292.

☐ They must take account of the Secretary of State's guidance and their district manager's local guidance (see p293), but must not be rigidly bound by either.

☐ They must have regard to the budget – see p293.

☐ They must give priority to high-priority needs – see p294.

☐ They are expected to exercise discretion flexibly but consistently so that all applicants are treated fairly and equally.[22]

☐ They must ensure their decisions are not in any way affected by bias or prejudice on such grounds as the race, colour, religion, gender or sexual orientation of applicants.[23]

☐ They are encouraged to liaise with local social services departments and other welfare rights and voluntary bodies about general matters (such as priority groups) and about individual applications, subject to normal confidentiality rules.[24]

(ii) The practice

Not surprisingly, the practice rarely matches the theory. Many people would argue that there is a basic conflict between meeting need and having regard to the budget; or between exercising discretion flexibly and taking account of the guidance. Also, most SFOs have neither the training nor the time to achieve the standard of decision-making imposed by all the above requirements.

The poor standard actually achieved is illustrated by the fact that only 18 per cent of cases which went to the SFI in 1990/1 were confirmed as correctly decided. In practice, your chances of success can depend on such factors as when you apply (ie, the state of the budget at that particular time), where you live (there is little consistency between offices) and which SFO deals with your case.

By far the most common deficiency in decision-making is the tendency of SFOs to rigidly follow local and national guidance, and automatically refuse payments to applicants who do not fall within the priority groups or circumstances covered by the guidance. This approach should always be challenged by asking for a review – see p324.

Refusal of payments on budgetary grounds, regardless of need, is also common practice which should always be challenged by review.

5 TACTICS

Despite the inherent problems of the SF, its wide remit makes it an important and valuable source of help. Perseverance is the key to getting a payment. The following general tactical points may help.

(i)   Applying for a payment

☐   Remember, you can apply as long as you meet the basic eligibility rules – see pp300, 312, 314. You can apply for help with anything other than excluded items – see p297. Do not be put off by what the Benefits Agency or their leaflets say.

☐   Always ask for a grant, rather than a loan, if you satisfy the conditions on p300.

☐   Tips on completing the application forms are on p323. Always give full details of your needs and circumstances and explain how you fit the eligibility conditions for a grant or a loan. It is usually best to submit a covering letter with the application form.

☐   Obtain a copy of the local guidance from your district office. If you fall into a suggested priority group, state this in your application. If the national guidance outlined in the following chapters is helpful to your case, you could also refer to it. Always explain why it is important for you to get a payment and argue that your needs are high priority.

☐   Send any supporting evidence you can get including, if appropriate, a letter from your doctor, social worker, housing officer, probation officer, advice worker etc.

(ii)   Challenging decisions

If you are unhappy about a decision, *always ask for a review and, if necessary, a further review by the SFI* – see p324. This could apply if you have been refused a payment, been given less than you asked for, or been offered a loan rather than a grant.

SFO decisions are often flawed. In particular, their tendency to rigidly follow local and national guidance rather than fully consider the circumstances of each application on its own merits is the commonest ground for review. SFIs regularly overturn SFO decisions on this basis. Thus, it is important to pursue the review process to the SFI stage and, if necessary to ask for a second review by the SFI – see p330.

(iii)   Getting the local budget increased

If applications are consistently being refused on budgetary grounds, it is important for individuals and groups to come together to pressurise the district SF manager to ask the government for more money. SF managers can, and should, ask for more money if they are unable to meet basic needs because of lack of funds. They may be reluctant to do so because of the stigma of 'bad management'. Nevertheless, a local campaign involving MPs, councillors, advice agencies and the local press could pressurise a manager to take action. Many offices received additional allocations last year on the basis of need.

If additional funds are secured, the District Office should reconsider all the applications refused on budgetary grounds earlier in the year – see p326.

6 EXCLUDED ITEMS

Help with the items listed below is excluded by the directions. [25] If you ask for help for an excluded item you will be refused.

(i) The general list of exclusions

☐ A need which occurs outside the UK.

☐ An educational or training need, including clothing and tools.

☐ 'Distinctive' school uniform, sports clothes or equipment (see p345 for clothing grants from local education authorities).

☐ Travelling expenses to and from school (but see p346).

☐ School meals and meals taken during the holidays by children on IS.

☐ Expenses in connection with court proceedings (including a community service order) – eg, legal fees, court fees, fines, costs, damages, travelling and other expenses.

☐ Removal charges where you are permanently rehoused following a compulsory purchase order, a redevelopment or closing order, or where there is a compulsory exchange of tenancies or you are permanently rehoused as homeless under the Housing Act 1985. (In all these circumstances your local authority *may* help you.)

☐ The cost of domestic assistance or respite care. Domestic assistance includes local authority home-helps. Respite care could include a short-term break in residential care. [26]

☐ Repairs to property owned by public sector housing bodies including Councils, most housing associations, housing co-operatives and housing trusts. [27]

☐ Medical, surgical, optical, aural or dental items or services. A medical item does not include an ordinary everyday item needed because of a medical condition – eg, cotton sheets when a person is allergic to synthetics. [28] SFOs are told to find out if there is help available from the NHS. [29]

☐ Work-related expenses. The guidance says this includes fares when seeking work and the cost of work clothes. [30]

☐ Debts to government departments. These could include National Insurance arrears, income tax liabilities and customs charges. [31]

☐ Investments.

☐ Community charges (including collective community charge contributions) and community water charges.

☐ Most housing costs, including deposits to secure accommodation, mortgage payments, water rates, rent, service charges, hostel charges and board and lodging charges. You can get a *loan*, however, for rent in advance where the landlord is not a local authority (see pp314-15); for hostel or board and lodging charges payable in advance (see pp314-15); and for minor repairs. [32] The guidance also says that owner-occupiers can get a budgeting loan for essential repairs and maintenance [33] (see p313). The guidance says you can get a grant for minor structural repairs, maintenance costs and internal redecoration and refurbishment for which you are responsible [34] (see p306). You can also get a grant for accommodation costs if you are visiting a child away from home[35] (see p310).

(ii) Additional items excluded from community care grants[36]

☐ Telephone costs, including installation, call and rental charges (see p350 if you are chronically sick or disabled and need a telephone).
☐ Any expenses which the local authority has a *statutory duty* to meet.
☐ The cost of *any* fuel and standing charges.

(iii) Additional item excluded from budgeting loans[37]

☐ The cost of 'mains' fuel and standing charges. This exclusion does not apply to help with liquid gas, paraffin and coal.

(iv) Additional items excluded from crisis loans[38]

☐ Telephone costs including installation, call and rental charges (see p350 if you are chronically sick or disabled and need a telephone).
☐ Mobility needs.
☐ Holidays.
☐ Television or radio, TV licence, aerial, TV rental.
☐ Garaging, parking, purchase and running costs of any motor vehicle – except where payment is being considered for emergency travel expenses.

(v) Maternity and funeral expenses

The discretionary SF covers needs other than maternity and funeral expenses, which are catered for by the regulated SF (see p285).[39]

Payments for items such as clothes, a cot, a pram and bedding for a young child can be distinguished from 'maternity expenses' and are not excluded from the discretionary SF.

Payments for ceremonies or religious services on death should not be excluded as they are not funeral (ie, burial or cremation) expenses.[40] CCGs are available for travelling expenses to attend a relative's funeral[41] (see p310).

7   PEOPLE INVOLVED IN TRADE DISPUTES

There are special rules affecting people involved in trade disputes (see p58).

(i) Community care grants

If you or your partner are involved in a trade dispute you are not eligible for a grant other than for travelling expenses to visit somebody who is ill and then only in the following circumstances.[42]

☐ **You are involved in a trade dispute and are visiting:**
  - your partner in hospital or a similar institution;
  - a dependant in hospital or similar institution, but only if you have no partner living with you who could get a grant, or your partner is also in hospital or a similar institution;
  - a close relative or member of your household who is critically ill (whether or not in hospital or a similar institution).

☐ **You are not involved in a trade dispute but you are the partner or dependant of somebody who is, and you are visiting:**
  - a close relative or member of your household who is a patient in a hospital or similar institution or who is critically ill (whether or not in hospital or a similar institution).

To get a CCG you must be receiving IS or would be but for the trade dispute.

You will normally be paid public transport fares (excluding air fares), the cost of petrol or taxi fares if necessary.[43] Overnight accommodation costs can be met if necessary.[44] You can get fares for an escort if you cannot travel alone, even if the escort is the person involved in the trade dispute. However, the guidance says that the person involved in the trade dispute should not normally get fares for an escort.[45]

(ii) Budgeting loans

You are not eligible for a budgeting loan if you or your partner are involved in a trade dispute.[46]

(iii) Crisis loans

If you or your partner are involved in a trade dispute, you are only entitled to a crisis loan for:[47]

☐ expenses arising from a disaster (see p314);

☐ the cost of items needed for cooking or space heating (including fireguards). This could include cooking utensils as well as a cooker.

Chapter 22

Community care grants

This chapter covers:

1 Introduction (see below)
2 Moving out of institutional or residential care (p302)
3 Staying out of institutional or residential care (p305)
4 Easing exceptional pressures on families (p307)
5 Travelling expenses (p309)

1 INTRODUCTION

Community care grants (CCGs) are intended to promote community care by helping people to move out of, or stay out of, institutional or residential care and by assisting families under stress.

There is no legal entitlement to a CCG. Payments are discretionary. However, you can ask for a review if you are not paid what you ask for – see p325. Chapter 21 covers how decisions are made by social fund officers (SFOs) and what tactics will help you get a payment. CCGs are a particularly valuable source of help because, unlike loans, they do not have to be paid back. [1]

(i) The basic rules

You must satisfy *all* the following rules in order to be considered for a CCG. The rules are laid down in directions issued by the Secretary of State, which are legally binding. None of the words used are defined.

☐ You must be in receipt of IS when you apply for a CCG. [2] The only exception to this rule is if you are due to leave institutional or residential care (see p303) within six weeks of your application for a CCG and you are likely to get IS when you leave. [3]

☐ You must not have too much capital. Capital of £500 or less (£1,000 if you or your partner is 60 or over) has no effect. Any CCG awarded is reduced by £1 for every £1 of capital you have in excess of these amounts. [4] Capital is calculated as for IS (see p272) except that any payments from the Family Fund (see p351) are disregarded. [5] Capital held by you and your partner count. Capital held by your children should be disregarded. [6]

☐ You or your partner must not be involved in a trade dispute unless your claim is for travelling expenses to visit a sick person (see p298).

☐ You cannot get a CCG for an excluded item (see p297).

☐ You must need a CCG of at least £30 (unless you are applying for travelling expenses or living expenses for a prisoner on home leave – see pp305 and 309). [7]

☐ You must need a CCG for one or more of the following purposes: [8]
- to help you, or a member of your family, re-establish yourselves in the community following a stay in institutional or residential care – see p302;
- to help you, or a member of your family, remain in the community rather than enter institutional or residential care – see p305;
- to ease exceptional pressures on you and your family – see p307;
- to allow you, or your partner, to care for a prisoner or young offender on home leave – see p305;
- to help you, or a member of your family, with travel expenses within the UK in certain circumstances – see p309.

Although at least one of the above purposes must apply you may be able to argue that a CCG will help in more than one way – eg, a grant will help you to stay in the community *and* ease exceptional pressures on your family.

(ii) The guidance

Introduction

The Secretary of State issues guidance to SFOs to help them decide who should get a CCG. Guidance is also issued by district office managers about local priority groups. This is discussed in Chapter 21. The guidance used to give greater emphasis to the importance of CCGs for people leaving institutional care and those needing help to remain in the community. This was reflected in local priority lists drawn up by SF managers. Local priority lists should now reflect the equal weight given to all types of CCGs in the national guidance.

The important point about the guidance is that it is *not legally binding*. SFOs are told to use their discretion flexibly, sensitively and imaginatively, avoiding a rigid interpretation of the guidance. [9] They are particularly reminded that the object of the scheme is to promote community care and that the absence of guidance applying to a particular circumstance, item or service does not mean that help should be refused. [10] They must take into account the nature, extent and urgency of the need in each case.

In spite of this, SFOs tend to rigidly follow national and local guidance and routinely refuse CCGs to applicants who do not fall within the suggested priority groups or circumstances. (See pp294-95 for a fuller discussion on priorities and how decisions are made.) You should always ask for a review if this happens and you are dissatisfied with a decision – see p324. If the guidance is helpful to your case (eg, it suggests you are in a high priority group), you should, of course, refer to it. If it is not, ignore it. Remember, the only legal requirements you must satisfy to be considered for a grant are the basic rules set out above. The guidance on CCGs is covered in the rest of this chapter.

Priority groups

The guidance lists priority groups for each of the circumstances it covers. It also gives a general list of priority groups. It stresses, however, that *none of the lists are exhaustive or given in any order of priority.* [11] The general list is as follows: [12]

(a)   elderly people, particularly those with restricted mobility or those who have difficulty performing personal care tasks;
(b)   mentally handicapped people;
(c)   mentally ill people;
(d)   physically disabled (including sensorily impaired) people;
(e)   chronically sick people, especially the terminally ill;
(f)   people who have 'misused' alcohol or drugs;
(g)   ex-offenders requiring resettlement;
(h)   people without a settled way of life undergoing resettlement;
(i)   families under stress;
(j)   young people leaving care.

Local guidance often lists the above groups in priority order. If you are not in a local high priority category but fall within the above list, you should point out that the national guidance regards you as priority. Local guidance which contradicts national guidance may be unlawful.

Do not be put off from making an application if you are not in any suggested priority group, including the general list above.

Always give *your* reasons why your situation should be seen as high priority.

Items and amounts

The guidance suggests what items or services to award a CCG for – see p304. Remember, however, that you can ask for anything which is not excluded by law – see p297.

There are no longer any suggested amounts for items. The minimum that can be awarded in most cases is £30 – see p301. [13] There is no legal maximum. The guidance states that the amount requested should normally be allowed unless it is unreasonable. [14] You should always cost the items you need and give a list with prices to the SFO. It is not generally necessary to provide written estimates from suppliers.

2   MOVING OUT OF INSTITUTIONAL OR RESIDENTIAL CARE

(i)   Interpretation

A CCG can be paid to help you or a member of your family to re-establish yourselves in the community following a stay in institutional or residential care. [15] There is no legal definition of 'family', 're-establish', 'the community', 'stay' or 'institutional and residential care'. SFOs are instructed to adopt a flexible approach and avoid rigid interpretations. [16]

Re-establishment in the community

Although the term 're-establish' is used, people moving out of care for the first time should be covered, including refugees moving from refugee camps abroad or from detention centres, hostels or temporary accommodation in the UK. The guidance says you should not be given a CCG if you are moving from one kind of care to another – eg, hospital to nursing home.[17] It seems you must be actually or imminently in the community.[18] 'The community' could be anywhere which is not care.

'A stay in' care

The guidance suggests that 'a stay in' care should normally mean at least three months, or a pattern of frequent or regular admission. However, the High Court has ruled that undue importance should not be attached to the reference to 3 months.[19] The word 'stay' is not defined in the law and could refer to any length of time, depending on the circumstances of the case.

'Institutional or residential care'

This is not defined in the law. It can be interpreted widely to include, for example, people living in hostels or temporary accommodation with support from social workers or other care workers. The guidance gives the following examples of institutional or residential care but stresses that the list is not exhaustive.[20]

- ☐ hospitals;
- ☐ residential care homes;
- ☐ nursing homes;
- ☐ staffed group homes;
- ☐ resettlement units;
- ☐ hostels for homeless people, ex-offenders or alcohol/drug misusers;
- ☐ hostels or other forms of accommodation for refugees;
- ☐ supported lodgings – eg, landlady schemes used by social services departments, social work departments, health or voluntary organisations as part of a programme of rehabilitation;
- ☐ staff-intensive sheltered housing providing a major level of personal care;
- ☐ prison;
- ☐ youth custody or detention centres;
- ☐ youth treatment centres;
- ☐ other custodial centres;
- ☐ local authority care;
- ☐ special residential schools.

SFIs have suggested that, to decide whether there is institutional care, SFOs should look at the extent of the care provided and the extent of the person's responsibilities and independence while living in the accommodation concerned.

(ii) What to claim for

You can claim for help with any expenses which are necessary to help re-establish yourself or your family in the community. The guidance gives the following examples:

Furniture, household equipment, bedding etc [21]

The guidance says you can be awarded a CCG for specific items or be given a lump sum. You should supply a costed list of everything you need. This could include a cooker, beds, mattresses, bedding, kitchen and cleaning equipment, fridge, floor-covering, curtains, storage units, tables, chairs etc. You should be paid the amount you ask for unless it is unreasonable. [22] SFOs often restrict an award to cover 'essential' or 'priority' items such as a cooker, bed and bedding. However, there is no restriction in the law and if you are given less than you need, you should ask for a review (see p325), and explain why you need all the items you listed.

Clothing and footwear [23]

The guidance says you can be awarded a CCG if you have few suitable clothes, including protective clothing. You should supply a costed list of what you need. You should be paid the amount you ask for unless it is unreasonable. [24]

Moving expenses [25]

The guidance says you should normally be asked to supply two estimates of removal costs. If you use a self-hire van and require funds for a refundable deposit, you could be given a budgeting loan – see p312. A CCG could be paid to meet furniture storage charges and fares when moving home. You can get a crisis loan for rent in advance – see p318. You should apply to the office which covers the area from which you are moving, if you are only asking for removal costs and fares. If you are also asking for a CCG to furnish a new home, your whole application becomes the responsibility of the office which covers the area into which you are moving. [26]

(iii) Circumstances covered by guidance

Discharge from hospital or nursing homes [27]

Suggested priority groups are groups (a)-(f) listed on p302. Suggested awards are for furniture etc, clothing and moving expenses – see above.

People leaving homes and hostels [28]

Suggested priority groups are (a)-(h) (see p302) where you are being resettled in the community as part of a planned programme of rehabilitation or resettlement. Suggested awards are for furniture etc, clothing and moving expenses – see p304.

Children and young people leaving care[29]

The guidance says it is reasonable to award a CCG for furniture and household items, and fares for moving, if a young person over 16 has left care in the last 12 months (including women leaving mother and baby homes) to set up home independently. The young person may have to get IS on a discretionary basis to qualify for a CCG – see p55. The guidance also suggests you should be given a CCG for essential furniture and clothing for a dependant under 19 who is rejoining your household after a period (normally 4 months or more) in care or in a special residential school.

Moving house to look after somebody[30]

Suggested priority groups are people moving to more suitable accommodation to look after somebody in groups (a)-(h) (see p303), who has been discharged from institutional or residential care and who will be living in your household. The guidance says the person could be a relative, close friend or former neighbour. Suggested awards are for moving expenses and furniture etc if needed – see p304.

Prisoners and young offenders[31]

The guidance covers people being resettled after discharge from prison or youth detention. Suggested priority groups are groups (a)-(f) (see p302), and young people unable to live with their parents because of moral or physical danger, broken relationships, unavoidable separation or unsuitable accommodation. The law says you can be awarded a CCG to care for a prisoner or young offender on home leave.[32] The guidance suggests you are paid one-seventh of the IS personal allowance (one-seventh of the difference between the single and couple rate if the prisoner is your partner) for each day of leave. A prisoner does not have to be in a priority group but should be somebody who would normally live in your household.[33] (In this situation the normal minimum £30 rule does not apply.)

3 STAYING OUT OF INSTITUTIONAL OR RESIDENTIAL CARE

(i) Interpretation

A CCG can be paid to help you or a member of your family to remain in the community, rather than enter institutional or residential care.[34] None of these terms are defined and SFOs are instructed to adopt a flexible and imaginative approach.[35] See p303 for the meaning of 'institutional or residential care'.

The sole legal test is whether a CCG will help somebody remain in the community rather than enter care. There is no requirement that a CCG must be able to 'prevent' entry into care. Nor does the threat of care have to be immediate.[36] SFOs are told to consider whether a CCG, 'would improve the applicant's independent life in the community and therefore lessen the risk of admission into care.'[37] Actual or potential risk to physical or mental health because of the lack of such items as basic furniture and cooking facilities, protective clothing, bedding and heating can be used to argue for a CCG on the basis that an award will lessen the risk of entry into hospital or other care. Special needs such as an orthopaedic mattress or firm upright armchair could be covered on the same basis.

The guidance is written as though the law only applies to you and your partner.[38] In fact, the possibility of a *child* having to go into hospital or care because of inadequate facilities, clothing etc, is a strong argument for the award of a CCG.

(ii)　Circumstances covered by guidance

The guidance suggests people in priority groups (a)-(e) (see p302) should be awarded a CCG in the following circumstances.[39]

Improving living conditions[40]

CCGs for the following are suggested if they will help a person remain in their home and lessen the risk of care:

☐ **Minor structural repairs and maintenance costs**[41] for which you are responsible, where your home is not Council, housing association etc owned. You will normally have to supply an estimate, which should be met unless it is unreasonable.[42] The interest on a loan to pay for major structural repairs can be paid for by IS – see p26. A CCG can be awarded for any survey fee incurred.

☐ **Internal redecoration and refurbishment**[43] for which you are responsible including, for example, worn out floor-covering. SFOs are reminded that 'although furnishings may be serviceable they might still need replacing'.[44] Items damaged by behavioural disturbances could be replaced (the guidance fails to mention damage by children, but there is no reason why this should not also apply). Single rooms could be redecorated if you are mainly confined to one room during the day. The award should cover the cost of materials and labour costs if the work cannot be done by relatives, friends, neighbours, charities or employment trainees.[45]

☐ **Bedding**[46] if you have an exceptional need because you or your partner is bedridden or incontinent. This guidance is unduly restrictive. There is no reason why you should not get a CCG for bedding whatever your circumstances if you can show that a grant will improve your living conditions and reduce any health risk and admission to care.

☐ **Fuel costs and heaters:**[47] You cannot get a CCG for fuel bills (see p298), but you could get a CCG for reconnection charges if you are going onto fuel direct (see p111); for re-siting meters for easier access; for installation of a pre-payment meter; *and* for heaters.

☐ **Laundry needs:**[48] If you are bedridden, incontinent or disabled and no one else can do your washing, you should be given a CCG for a washing machine and/or tumble dryer. There is no reason why this should not also apply if you have an incontinent child.

Moving to more suitable accommodation[49]

A CCG should be awarded if a move from unsuitable accommodation would help a person remain in the community. Accommodation could be unsuitable because of its size, structural defects, insanitary condition, difficult access or because your housing costs are not being met in full. Suggested awards are for moving expenses and furniture etc (see p304) but only for items you cannot transfer from your previous accommodation.

Moving to provide or obtain support

The guidance says you can get a CCG if you are moving nearer to or into the house of a person in priority groups (a)-(e) (see p302) to provide daily attention or supervision.[50] Alternatively, if *you* are in groups (a)-(e), you can get a CCG to help you move nearer relatives or close friends who will provide support for you.[51] Suggested awards are for moving expenses and any furniture etc you need – see p304.

Setting-up home for the first time[52]

This covers CCGs for setting-up home if you have been living with relatives or in lodgings, cannot continue to do so and might otherwise end up in care. If you would be homeless, you could argue you might end up in a hostel or hospital. Suggested awards are for moving expenses and furniture etc – see p304.

4 EASING EXCEPTIONAL PRESSURES ON FAMILIES

(i) Interpretation

You can get a CCG to ease exceptional pressures on you and your family.[53] The scope for applications is very wide. The term 'exceptional pressures' is not defined. Nor is 'family'. SFOs are instructed to use their discretion flexibly, sensitively and imaginatively.[54]

Despite this, families under exceptional stress tend to be classified as 'low or medium priority' in local office guidance. Refusal of help solely on this basis is unlawful and should be challenged by review – see p325. The national guidance suggests families under stress are a priority group (see p202) and SFOs must decide each application on its own merits. You should always fully explain your needs and circumstances when you make an application, giving details of the exceptional pressures you are experiencing and arguing that your needs are high priority (see p295 for general tactics).

'Exceptional pressures'

The guidance says that all families, especially those on low incomes, face stress at times, so that in itself is not a reason to award a CCG. [55] However, a CCG may be appropriate where circumstances put a family under greater stress than is normally associated with low income or lone parenthood. [56]

SFIs have made some useful comments in their decisions regarding exceptional pressures. These and some of our own comments are noted below:

☐ The cumulative impact of pressures should be considered. (You should always, therefore, list all the different pressures which are affecting your family.)
☐ Whether the pressures are foreseeable, expected or common is irrelevant.
☐ Low income, particularly reduced benefits, can add to pressures as can single parenthood.
☐ Pressures that arise from a sudden event (eg, a disaster) can be exceptional and traumatic. Pressures which have existed for a long time do not necessarily become easier to handle.
☐ There does not have to be any risk of a person going into care for exceptional pressures to exist.
☐ Mental stress, anxiety, depression, illness etc are all sources and symptoms of exceptional pressures. The fact that an applicant does not appear stressed at an interview does not mean that exceptional pressures do not exist.
☐ Exceptional pressures experienced by children are entirely valid – eg, shame, discomfort, health risk from lack of clothes.

'Family'

The law refers to 'easing exceptional pressures on a person and his family'. This implies that people not living in a family are excluded. This interpretation was endorsed in a High Court case. [57] A Social Security Commissioner, however, recently decided that the identical language which appears in IS legislation means 'a person and his family (if he has one)'. [58] However, this interpretation is only binding on IS law.

The word 'family' is not defined. The guidance says it should generally be taken to mean couples with children or single parents. SFIs, however, have frequently rejected this narrow interpretation. 'Family' could include:

☐ a couple without children;
☐ a household with grown-up children;
☐ adult brothers and sisters or relatives living together;
☐ a parent living with children for part of the week only.

It may also be possible to argue that a pregnant woman constitutes a family, particularly in later pregnancy when the baby is increasingly capable of independent existence.

(ii) Circumstances covered by guidance

The guidance on families under stress is very limited and restrictive. *If it covers your circumstances, you could refer to it. Otherwise ignore it.* Always explain why *you* consider your family to be under exceptional pressure.

Breakdown of a relationship[59]

The guidance suggests a CCG should be awarded to help you move after the recent breakdown of a long-standing relationship (if you have no children) or a breakdown after you have been living with a partner for at least 3 months (if you have children). Priority should be given to domestic violence cases. Suggested awards are for moving expenses, furniture etc and clothing and footwear – see p302.

Reconciliation of a relationship[60]

The guidance suggests a CCG for removal expenses if you are returning to a shared home after a period of separation following the breakdown of an established relationship.

Moving house[61]

The guidance suggests a CCG for moving expenses and furniture etc (see p302) if you are moving house to ease exceptional pressures – eg, if your home was over-crowded.

Disabled and other children

The guidance only covers:
☐ a washing machine and dryer if there are high washing costs;[62]
☐ clothes and footwear needed due to excessive wear and tear of clothes or rapid weight change because of a child's condition;[63]
☐ minor structural repairs to keep the home safe and habitable for children;[64]
☐ repair/replacement of items damaged by behavioural problems;[65]
☐ short-term boarding-out fees pending adoption;[66]
☐ fuel reconnection charges if you are going on to 'fuel direct' (see p111), or the cost of installing a pre-payment meter, if you have a disabled child or child under five.[67]

5 TRAVELLING EXPENSES

Travelling expenses within the UK are specifically allowed for in SF directions.[68]

Listed below are the five situations covered, and the guidance on each one. For the amount of payments, see p311.

(i) Visiting someone who is ill

The law merely states that a CCG can be paid to assist you or a member of your family with travel expenses in the UK to visit someone who is ill. [69] The guidance is much more restrictive. [70] *Ignore it, if it does not apply to you.*

It suggests the person you are visiting should be a relative, partner or someone (a close friend if in hospital or care), who has no relatives or whose relatives have lost touch. The person could be at home, in hospital, in a care home or in staff-intensive, sheltered housing. SFOs are told to take account of any IS paid to the family for the patient which exceeds the hospital personal expenses allowance (see p82) and to off-set it against travel expenses. You should claim the costs of overnight accommodation if you need to stay with a child in hospital. [71]

(ii) Attending a relative's funeral

You, or a member of your family, can get a CCG to attend a relative's funeral in the UK. If you are responsible for arranging the funeral you may instead be eligible for a funeral expenses payment (see p287), which includes travel expenses.

(iii) Easing domestic crises

You can get a CCG for travel costs to ease a domestic crisis. [72] The guidance suggests that priority should be given to those 'whose needs are most acute' – eg, a single parent who is going into hospital or is too ill to look after her/his child. Fares will not normally be paid for a holiday or short break. However, you can argue that a short break may be very necessary for a parent of a disabled child who needs a rest. An SFI accepted that it would be reasonable to pay a grant for fares to enable a person to take regular advantage of respite care.

(iv) Visiting a child pending a court decision

You can get a CCG for travel costs to visit a child who is with the other parent pending a court decision on who is to have responsibility for the child. This is 'to ensure that neither parent is seen by the Court to be in a less advantageous position simply because s/he cannot afford the fares'. [73]

Where the child is staying some distance away, you may need to pay for accommodation as well and the guidance does say that the cost of reasonable overnight accommodation may be met as part of the grant where the distance is too far to make a return journey in one day. [74]

The guidance says you cannot get a CCG once responsibility has been decided.

(v) Fares when moving home

You can get a CCG for fares to move to suitable accommodation.

(vi)   The amount of the payment

The guidance suggests that grants for travelling expenses should be calculated as follows: [75]

☐   the cost of 'standard' rate public transport (excluding air fares); *or*

☐   the cost of petrol, either up to the cost of public transport if available or in full if public transport is not available; *or*

☐   taxi fares, if public transport is unavailable or you or your partner cannot use public transport because of physical disability or because you are frail or elderly and you cannot use private transport.

The reasonable cost of overnight accommodation may be paid if it is necessary, and the cost of an escort's fare if the person travelling is incapable of travelling alone – eg, they are a child, elderly, ill or disabled. CCGs for fares may be awarded in advance, or in instalments if the SFO considers it to be in your interest.

Chapter 23

Loans

This chapter covers:

1 Budgeting loans (see below)
2 Crisis loans (p314)
3 Repayments (p319)

The two types of loans covered in this chapter are very different from each other. Budgeting loans are intended to help people who have been receiving income support (IS) for at least 26 weeks to meet one-off expenses. They are not just for people with special problems. By contrast, crisis loans are not restricted to those receiving IS, but are only available to deal with special problems.

There is no legal entitlement to a loan. Payments are discretionary. You can, however, ask for a review if you are not paid what you ask for (see p324). Chapter 21 covers how decisions are made by social fund officers (SFOs) and which tactics will best help you get a payment.

Loans are obviously far less attractive than grants because they must be repaid to the Benefits Agency although they are, at least, interest free.[1] Another problem with loans is that they cannot exceed what you can afford to repay.

It is always better, therefore, to ask for a grant if you are eligible to do so (see Chapter 22). There is nothing to stop you asking for a grant and a loan for the same item at the same time (see p323).

1 BUDGETING LOANS

(i) The basic rules

You must satisfy all the following rules in order to be eligible for a budgeting loan. The rules are laid down in directions issued by the Secretary of State, which are legally binding. None of the words used are defined.

☐ you must be in receipt of IS when your application for a budgeting loan is decided by the Benefits Agency;[2] *and*
☐ you, or your partner, between you must have been receiving IS throughout the 26 weeks before the date on which your application is decided.[3] ('Partner' here can have its ordinary everyday meaning.) One break of 14 days or less when IS was not being paid can be included in the 26 weeks.[4] The guidance says that you can have had more than one partner during the 26 weeks;[5] *and*
☐ you must not have too much capital. The rules are the same as for CCGs (see p300 for details); *and*

☐ you, or your partner, must not be involved in a trade dispute (see p58); *and*
☐ the loan is to assist you to meet important intermittent expenses for which it may be difficult to budget;[6] *and*
☐ the loan is not for an excluded item (see p297); *and*
☐ the loan is at least £30; and at most £1,000 less any outstanding SF loan(s);[7] *and*
☐ the loan does not exceed an amount which you are likely to be able to repay[8] (see p314).

(ii) The guidance

Introduction

The Secretary of State issues guidance to SFOs to help them decide who should get a budgeting loan. Guidance is also issued by district office managers. This is discussed in Chapter 21.

The guidance is *not* legally binding, but if it is helpful to your case, you can, of course, refer to it. If it is not, ignore it. Remember, you only have to satisfy the basic rules above to be eligible for a loan.

SFOs must consider each application on its merits taking into account the nature, extent and urgency of the need. If you are refused a budgeting loan, and you satisfy the basic rules, you should always ask for a review (see p324).

Priorities

The guidance gives examples of high, medium and low priority expenses. It stresses, however, that the examples are not exhaustive and should only be used as a guide.[9] SFOs are reminded that '. . . the absence of directions or guidance applying to a particular item requested . . . does not mean that help should be refused'.[10] They are also told that the personal circumstances of the applicant could raise the priority normally given to particular items.[11] Within this framework, the following examples are covered.

High priority:[12]
☐ essential (unspecified) items of furniture and household equipment;
☐ bedding, if you do not have sufficient;
☐ essential home repairs and maintenance if you are an owner-occupier and you cannot get a bank loan or mortgage;
☐ removal charges if it is essential for you to move to more suitable accommodation;
☐ fuel meter installation and reconnection charges;
☐ non-mains fuel costs (eg, oil or bottled gas). Coal is not mentioned in the guidance but is a non-mains fuel cost.

Medium priority: [13]
- ☐ 'non-essential' items of furniture and household equipment;
- ☐ redecoration costs, if you are responsible for these;
- ☐ hire purchase and other debts;
- ☐ clothing, if you do not have sufficient.

Low priority: [14]
- ☐ rent in advance if you already have secure accommodation and a move is not necessary (SFOs are advised not to award rent for more than a month);
- ☐ removal charges if it is not essential for you to move;
- ☐ leisure items.

(iii)   The amount of the loan

The amount awarded must be between £30 and £1,000 (see p313). [15]

There is no guidance on how much should be paid for specific items or services. SFOs are told to accept your estimate of the cost if it is 'within the broad range of prices that would be considered reasonable for an item of serviceable quality'. [16] It is usually unnecessary to submit estimates from suppliers. [17] SFOs are told to consider whether an item could be repaired.

You cannot be awarded more than you can afford to repay. The amount you can afford to repay is usually calculated by multiplying your weekly repayment rate by 78 (see p319). If you already have one or more loans, you may also find you are offered less than you ask for. If you are unhappy about the amount awarded to you, you can ask for a review (see p324).

2   CRISIS LOANS

(i)   The basic rules

You must satisfy all the following rules in order to be eligible for a crisis loan. The rules are laid down in directions issued by the Secretary of State which are legally binding. None of the words used are defined.
- ☐ you must be 16 or over; [18] *and*
- ☐ you must not be an 'excluded person' (see 315); [19] *and*
- ☐ the loan is not for an excluded item (see p297); *and*
- ☐ the loan must not exceed an amount which you are likely to be able to repay. [20] There are maximum awards (see p318), but no minimum amount is laid down in law; [21] *and*
- ☐ you are without sufficient resources to meet the immediate short-term needs of yourself or your family [22] (see p316); *and*
- ☐ the loan is for expenses in an emergency, or as a consequence of a disaster, and is the only means by which serious damage or serious risk to the health or safety

of yourself or a member of your family may be prevented; [23] *or* the loan is for rent in advance payable to a non-local authority landlord and a CCG is being awarded to help you, or a member of your family re-establish yourselves in the community following a stay in care [24] (see p302).

(ii)   Excluded persons

The following people are excluded by the directions from getting a crisis loan, **in all circumstances.** [25]

☐   People in hospital, nursing homes or residential care homes, (private or provided by the local authority under Part III of the National Assistance Act 1948 or Part IV of the Social Work (Scotland) Act), *unless* their discharge is planned to take place within the next two weeks.

☐   Prisoners and people in custody.

☐   Members of religious orders who are fully maintained by the order.

☐   People in 'full-time relevant education' who are not entitled to IS (see p12).

The following people are excluded by the directions from getting a crisis loan except **in very limited circumstances**:

☐   Full-time students not on IS, can only claim a crisis loan for expenses arising out of a disaster. [26]

☐   People from abroad who, because of their immigration status would not be entitled to IS either at the ordinary or the urgent cases rate (see p62) can also only claim a crisis loan for expenses arising out of a disaster. [27]

Note: If you are an overstayer, subject to a deportation order, or an illegal entrant, you should not apply for a crisis loan unless you have been in touch with the Home Office to regularise your position here.

☐   People involved in a trade dispute (see p299 for details).

(iii)   The guidance

Introduction

The Secretary of State issues guidance to SFOs to help them decide who should get a crisis loan. Guidance is also issued by district office managers. This is discussed in Chapter 21. The important point about the guidance is that it is *not* legally binding. If it is helpful to your case, you can, of course, refer to it. If not, ignore it. Remember, you are eligible for a loan as long as you satisfy the basic rules above.

SFOs must consider each application on its merits, taking into account the nature, extent and urgency of the need.

The guidance reminds SFOs to use their discretion flexibly, to consider the individual circumstances of each application and to decide whether a need requires immediate relief. [28]

When applying for a crisis loan, make sure you complete the application form SF400 (see p323). Do not be put off by Benefits Agency counter staff who say you cannot get a payment. If you are *formally* refused a crisis loan and you satisfy the basic rules, you should always ask for a review (see p324).

Priorities

SFOs are told that if a crisis loan is appropriate, 'it will be rare for a payment to be refused solely because it has insufficient priority relative to other loan applications, ie, the majority of crisis loans are likely to have the higher priority.'[29]

Emergencies and disasters

Most crisis loans can only be awarded in an emergency or following a disaster (see basic rules, p314). Neither of these terms is defined. The guidance recognizes that 'individual people may be affected differently by the same situation . . . so it is not intended to give a precise definition of terms.'[30] You should always explain, therefore, why a particular situation constitutes an emergency or disaster for you or your family.

The guidance gives fire or flood resulting in significant damage or loss, as an example of a disaster.[31] A Social Security Commissioner has defined 'disaster' as something of 'a ruinous or distressing nature; a sudden or great mishap or misadventure; a calamity.'[32] Whether a payment is appropriate following a disaster depends on your resources (see below) and ability to cope.[33]

Serious damage/risk to health or safety

A crisis loan has to be the only means of preventing serious damage or risk to health or safety. You will have to show there are no other resources (see below) or ways of meeting your need. If an SFO suggests other means which are impractical or unavailable to you, ask for a review.

The potential serious risk to your health or safety might be obvious, eg, you have no money for food. If it is not, try to get supporting evidence from your doctor, social worker etc.

Resources

You must be without sufficient resources to meet the immediate short-term needs of yourself and your family. 'Resources' are not defined in the law. The guidance says all resources which ' . . . are actually available to the applicant or could be obtained in time to meet the need' should be taken into account.[34]

Resources that could count include:[35]

- ☐   cash, earnings, other income;
- ☐   capital, savings accessible with a cash card or cheque;
- ☐   credit but only if you are not on IS and if you could afford the repayments.[36]

Resources that should be disregarded:

The guidance lists the following:[37]
- [ ] other SF payments, housing benefit, disability living allowance;
- [ ] the value of your home; premises acquired for occupation within the next six months; and premises occupied by a relative, or your ex-partner;
- [ ] the value of any reversionary interest (see p278);
- [ ] your business assets;
- [ ] any sum paid to you because of damage to, or loss of, your home or personal possessions and intended for their repair or replacement;
- [ ] any sum acquired on the express condition that it is used for essential repairs or improvements to your home;
- [ ] any personal possessions, except those acquired for the purpose of qualifying for a crisis loan;
- [ ] any payments from the Independent Living Fund, and the Macfarlane Trust (see p352).

SFOs are advised to take into account help from other sources, 'if there is a realistic expectation that it would be available in time.'[38] They are told not to routinely refer applicants to employers, charities, relatives or close friends 'unless there is reason to believe their help will be forthcoming'.[39] They are reminded that social services do not normally meet financial needs.[40] Emergency payments for children should be disregarded unless they meet the need for which the crisis loan is requested.[41]

The guidance suggests it may be reasonable to disregard other resources at least for a temporary period.[42] You could argue that money set aside to meet forthcoming bills (eg, poll tax) is not available.

(iv) Guidance on crisis loan situations

The guidance gives a few examples of situations where a crisis loan may be appropriate but stresses that 'a situation not mentioned is not automatically excluded'.[43]

You could refer to the guidance if it covers your situation. Otherwise, ignore it. The guidance on disasters is discussed on p316.

Living expenses for a short period

The guidance suggests a crisis loan could be awarded to meet day-to-day living expenses in the following situations:
- [ ] You are waiting for your first benefit payment or wages (and your employer will not give you an advance).[44]
- [ ] You are suffering hardship because your employer has imposed a compulsory unpaid holiday.[45]
- [ ] You have lost money or you have lost a giro and replacement (see p108 on lost giros) is delayed.[46]
- [ ] You have been refused IS because your capital is over £8,000 but you cannot realise your assets immediately. A crisis loan can be paid to tide you over until you have raised money against your assets. SFOs are told that a crisis loan is not

appropriate where you are making no attempt to realise the asset or arrange alternative credit facilities.[47]
☐ You are homeless and need living expenses. The guidance stresses the risk to physical and mental health brought about by sleeping rough and prolonged homelessness. The threat of assault and the vulnerability of young people to the risk of drug dependency, alcohol misuse, prostitution and offending is particularly mentioned.[48] Homeless people could also get a crisis loan for items or services needed and for board and lodging charges in advance (see below).

The guidance suggests a crisis loan should only cover living expenses for more than 14 days in exceptional circumstances – eg, a continuing crisis; loss of money which would normally cover you until your next income is due; or no money because of misfortune or mismanagement.[49]

Travelling expenses

The guidance covers the following situations:
☐ You are stranded away from home, without access to your regular means of support.[50]
☐ You are a 16/17-year-old who needs the cost of a journey home after looking unsuccessfully for work or a Youth Training (YT) place elsewhere.[51] When deciding your ability to repay the loan, the SFO should take account of the fact that you should get a YT place and be paid a training allowance.
☐ The SFO will consider payment for hospital fares for you and, if necessary, an escort, where you or a member of your family need treatment and are unable to get help with fares to hospital (see p342) because, for example:
  – transport by ambulance or the hospital car scheme has been refused; *and*
  – your condition or that of a member of your family is serious; *and*
  – you cannot get the fare in advance from the hospital.[52]

Accommodation expenses

A crisis loan is payable for rent in advance to a non-local authority landlord if you are also awarded a CCG on leaving care (see p302). The rules about serious risk to health or safety do not apply.

The guidance suggests a maximum of four weeks rent is met at a weekly rate limited to the amount of HB likely to be awarded.[53] The CCG and any capital should be disregarded.[54]

If your fuel supply has been disconnected but fuel direct has been arranged (see p111), you may get a crisis loan to meet the cost of reconnection.[55] Where fuel direct arrangements have broken down but this was not your fault, the DSS may consider making an *ex gratia* payment.

(v) The amount of the loan

There is no legal minimum. There is a general legal maximum of £1,000 less any outstanding SF loan(s).[56] You also cannot be awarded more than you can afford to repay.[57] SFOs usually calculate the amount you can afford to repay by multiplying your weekly repayment rate by 78 (see below). If you already have one or more loans you may also find you are offered less than you asked for.

There are also more specific legal maximums for items, services and living expenses.

Items and services:[58] The maximum you can get is the reasonable cost of purchase (including delivery and installation) or the cost of repair, if cheaper.

Living expenses:[59] The maximum you can get is 75 per cent of the appropriate personal allowance for you and any partner (see p237), plus £14.55 for each child. If your applicable amount is reduced because of 'voluntary unemployment' (see p45) the maximum crisis loan is the total amount of IS payable, if less than the above formula.[60]

Subject to the above rules, you should be given the minimum you need to tide you over or remove the crisis.[61] For items or services, you should be paid what is reasonable. You do not normally need to supply written estimates.[62]

If you are unhappy about the amount offered, you can ask for a review (see p325).

3 REPAYMENT

All loans must be repaid to the Benefits Agency. The rate of repayment, the repayment period and the method of recovery are technically decided by the Secretary of State and not by SFOs.[63] In practice, decisions are made on his behalf at the local Benefits Agency office by SFOs wearing a different hat.

Unlike SFO decisions (eg, the amount of loan awarded), which can be challenged by review, Secretary of State decisions are not subject to review. You can request that a Secretary of State's decision is reconsidered, however, by 'making a complaint' (see p321).

There is no legislation covering how repayment rates or periods should be calculated. The information below is based on guidance alone.[64]

(i) The repayment period

The period over which a loan is expected to be repaid is determined by the size of the loan and the weekly repayment rate. The guidance says loans should normally be recovered within 78 weeks, or exceptionally, 104 weeks (eg, if a further loan is awarded)[65] The amount of a loan will usually be restricted to what you can repay within these periods).

(ii) The rate of repayment

The guidance says repayment rates should take account of what you can afford.[66] It suggests three possible weekly rates of repayment:

☐ 15 per cent of your IS applicable amount (see p236), excluding housing costs, if you have no 'existing commitments' (unspecified).[67]

☐ 10 per cent of your IS applicable amount, excluding housing costs, if you have existing commitments of up to £6.37 per week. [68]

☐ 5 per cent of your IS applicable amount, excluding housing costs, if you have existing commitments of more than £6.37 per week. [69]

A maximum repayment rate of 25 per cent of your IS applicable amount is suggested. [70]

Repayment of a crisis loan for living expenses should not begin until the end of the period covered by the loan. [71] The guidance says you should not repay more than one loan at a time. [72] Recovery of a new loan should be deferred until all other loans are repaid but all loans are expected to be repaid within a 'reasonable period' (usually 78 weeks). [73] This may mean increasing the normal weekly repayment rates for existing and new loans. [74]

Repayment terms are notified to you with the decision offering a loan. If you accept them, you should sign and return the offer form within 14 days. [75] This period can be extended. [76] If you disagree with the terms, you can make a 'complaint' (see p321).

(iii) How loans are recovered

Methods of recovery

Loans can be repaid in cash or by cheque, postal order or banker's standing order. You can make a lump-sum payment any time to partially or wholly repay a loan. [77] The DSS can tell you how much you owe at any time.

Loans are, in fact, nearly always recovered by direct deductions from benefit. The Secretary of State is legally entitled to make deductions to recover loans from the following benefits: [78]

☐ income support;
☐ family credit (but see below);
☐ unemployment benefit;
☐ sickness and invalidity benefit;
☐ severe disablement allowance;
☐ invalid care allowance (but see below);
☐ disability working allowance;
☐ disablement benefit, reduced earnings allowance and industrial death benefit;
☐ widows' benefits (excluding the lump-sum widow's payment);
☐ retirement pensions (all types);
☐ war pensions (but see below);
☐ maternity allowance.

Increases of benefit for dependants and additional benefit under SERPS are also subject to deduction.

Deductions from FC, ICA, DWA or war pensions can only commence from the start of an award of these benefits (eg, the beginning of a 26-week FC award).

Deductions are put into effect by the office responsible for payment on instruction from SF sections, who decide the rate of repayment.

Note that deductions cannot be made from child benefit, SSP or SMP, DLA, attendance allowance or HB.

From whom recoverable

A loan can be legally recovered from:
- [ ] you (the applicant);[79]
- [ ] your partner, if you are living together as a married or unmarried couple (see p229).[80]
- [ ] a 'liable relative' (see p88) or a 'sponsor' (see p66) of yours if you have claimed a crisis loan because they have stopped maintaining you.[81] If you claim IS, the crisis loan will be recovered from you. If you cannot claim IS because maintenance recommences, the crisis loan can be recovered from your liable relative or sponsor.[82]

(iv)   Challenging the rate of repayment

There is no right of review or appeal against a decision about the rate of repayment of a loan.

If you are unhappy about the repayment terms when a loan is offered, you should write to the Benefits Agency and explain why. This is technically known as 'making a complaint'.[83] You should justify asking for a lower weekly repayment by referring to your financial circumstances and commitments. You could refer to the guidance on repayment rates if it helps your case (see p319).

You should receive a written decision in response to your complaint.[84] If new terms are offered, you will be given 14 days to accept them. The Benefits Agency may want to interview you before making a decision and may offer money advice.[85] If there are doubts about your ability to repay a loan, your award could be reduced or withdrawn. You can, of course, ask for a review in these circumstances. The Benefits Agency are only likely to agree to a lower repayment rate if the loan will still be repaid within 78 (or exceptionally 104) weeks.

If you are finding it difficult to repay a loan at the agreed rate, you can write to the Benefits Agency at any time and ask for 'rescheduling', ie, lower repayments over a longer period.[86] You will need to show your current repayment rates are causing hardship.[87] The Benefits Agency can also reschedule a loan by increasing your weekly repayments if they think you can afford to pay more.[88] Rescheduling is also common when you take out a second loan.[89] The Benefits Agency often increase weekly repayments on the first loan so that both loans can be recovered within 78 weeks (exceptionally 104 weeks).

If you are having real difficulties and the Benefits Agency refuse to reduce your weekly repayments you could take the matter to your MP.

Chapter 24

Applications, payments and reviews

This chapter covers:

1 Applications (see below)
2 Decisions and payments (p324)
3 Review by a social fund officer (p324)
4 Review by a social fund inspector (p328)

1 APPLICATIONS

(i) Making an application

General matters

Applications for an SF payment must be made in writing, either on a standard application form obtainable from the Benefits Agency or in some other way which is acceptable to the Secretary of State (eg, a letter with all the necessary details).[1] If your application is incomplete, the Benefits Agency can ask you to provide additional information either in writing, or by calling in at your local office.[2]

An application can be made on your behalf by somebody else, as long as you give your written consent (this is not necessary if an appointee is acting for you – see p101.)[3]

Your application is treated as having been made on the day it is received at a Benefits Agency office.[4] If your application was incomplete and you comply with a request for additional information, your application will be treated as made on the day it was originally received.[5]

Where to apply

You should normally apply to the Benefits Agency office which covers the area in which you live.[6] If you are applying for a crisis loan, however, you can apply to the office where your need arises.[7] In an emergency, social services or other agencies, can contact the Benefits Agency 'out of hours' service on your behalf (see p4).[8]

If you are moving out of care and claiming a CCG, you should apply to the office which covers the area you are moving to unless you are only claiming removal expenses and/or fares.[9]

CCGs and budgeting loans

You should normally apply on form SF300. The form is designed to fit in with the guidance, rather than the law (see Chapter 21). Do not be put off, however, if the examples of why you need help in part 6 of the form do not apply to you. Chapter 21 covers general tactics you should be aware of when making an application.

Tips on completing the application form:
- [ ] It is usually a good idea to submit a covering letter with the form SF300, explaining your circumstances and needs in more detail. There is very little space on the form and, as noted above, its design is slanted to favour applications which fit the guidance. You should explain in your covering letter how your application satisfies one or more of the purposes for which a CCG can be awarded (see p300), and/or satisfies the purpose for which a budgeting loan can be awarded (see p313). You should also explain why your application should be given high priority, with reference to local or national guidance if it is helpful to your case.
- [ ] In part 3 of the form, you are asked whether you want a grant or loan. You should always ask for a grant if you satisfy the basic rules. You can also ask for a loan at the same time. SFOs should first consider whether to award you a CCG before deciding on the loan application.[10] Legally, your application is to the fund as a whole.[11]. The guidance says that 'Each application should be considered for a CCG, a budgeting loan and a crisis loan even if they have not been specifically requested.'[12]
- [ ] You should complete part 5 of the form with full details of what you need and the cost of each item.
- [ ] Remember to send any supporting evidence with your application – eg, from your doctor or social worker. If possible keep a copy of the form for future reference.

Crisis loans

If you are applying for a crisis loan, you will usually be interviewed at the local Benefits Agency office (or at home). Make sure that an application form SF400 is completed. Benefits Agency counter staff sometimes try to put applicants off by telling them they will not get a crisis loan which results in the form not being filled in. Make sure the form fully records your needs and circumstances before you sign it. Bear in mind the basic rules for crisis loans and the guidance if it helps (see p314). Crisis loan decisions should be based on your circumstances at the date of decision and SFOs are instructed never to deliberately delay a decision until the need has passed.[13]

(ii)   Repeat applications

If you have been awarded or refused a payment for an item or service, you cannot get a payment for the same item or service within 26 weeks of your first application unless:

either   there has been a relevant change of circumstances;
or   you are applying for a budgeting loan for which you were ineligible when you made your first application because neither you nor your partner had been on IS for 26 weeks. [14]

If your previous application was incomplete (see p322); or you withdrew it before a decision was made; or you declined a loan offer, the 26-week rule about repeat applications should not apply. [15]

A relevant change of circumstances could include any additional allocations made to the District Office budget during the year – see p326.

2   DECISIONS AND PAYMENTS

(i)   Decisions

You should receive a written decision on your application. If a payment is wholly or partly refused, the decision should explain why and state that you have the right to request a review. The reasons given are usually very general and sketchy (eg, your application is not high enough priority or is not for one of the purposes for which a payment can be made). If you are not satisfied you should always ask for a review.

There are no legal time-limits within which the Benefits Agency must make decisions. The guidance, however, says that 'All decisions should normally be made within 28 days of the date of the application.' [16] Decisions on urgent applications, eg, crisis loans, should be made within one working day. [17]

If there are unreasonable delays in getting a decision, you should complain to the SF manager in your district office. If this does not help, you should ask your MP to take up your case with the manager, the Secretary of State or the Ombudsman. The Benefits Agency has published a Customers' Charter for claimants. This gives target times for 1992/93 for processing crisis loans (the day the need arises or the application is made) and community care grants (an average of seven days). There are no targets for dealing with budgeting loans.

(ii)   Payments

You will normally be paid by giro made out to you. [18] The Benefits Agency can, however, choose to pay a supplier directly. [19] Payment can also be made in the form of travel warrants, food vouchers or cash. They can also pay you in instalments. You can ask for a review of any decision to pay a supplier rather than you, or to pay in instalments. [20]

3   REVIEW BY A SOCIAL FUND OFFICER

(i)   Introduction

There is no right of appeal to an independent body against decisions regarding the discretionary SF. There is instead a review system, which is divided into two distinct stages.

First, when you ask for a review of a decision, the Benefits Agency reconsider the decision by conducting an internal review.

Second, if you are dissatisfied with the outcome of the review, you can ask for a further review by an social fund inspector (SFI) who reconsiders the case independently of the Benefits Agency.

You should always ask for a review if you are unhappy about a decision. Although decisions are not often changed as a result of the internal review, you will often be given what you want as a result of a further review by an SFI. In 1990/91, only 18 per cent of cases which went to the SFI were confirmed as correctly decided. It is crucial, however, to pursue your review application through to the inspector stage, if necessary.

The law regarding reviews is set out in legislation and the SF directions.

(ii) Decisions subject to review

All SFO decisions are subject to review. [21] Decisions about the repayment of loans are made by the Secretary of State and not by SFOs and are, therefore, not subject to review.

The following decisions can be challenged by asking for a review:

☐ the refusal of a grant or loan;
☐ the amount awarded as a grant or loan;
☐ the award of a loan rather than a grant;
☐ the refusal to decide a repeat application (see p323);
☐ payment in instalments or to a third party (see p324).

(iii) Applying for a review

Basic rules

You must apply for a review of a decision in writing to the Benefits Agency within 28 days of the date the decision was issued to you. [22] Your application must include your grounds for requesting a review (see below, 'tactics'). [23] If somebody is making an application on your behalf, it must be accompanied by your written authority (unless the person is your appointee). [24]

The 28-day time-limit can be extended for 'special reasons'. [25] 'Special reasons' are not defined. If your application is late, you should explain why. If the Benefits Agency do not accept there are special reasons, get advice. You may have to threaten judicial review if their refusal is unreasonable (see p127).

The SFO can ask you to submit further information in connection with your application if reasonably required. [26]

You can withdraw your application in writing at any time. [27]

Tactics

☐ Your application must be in writing. Keep a copy if possible. Begin your letter by stating that you request a review and identify the decision you are unhappy about. Always quote your Benefits Agency reference number at the top of your letter. If your application is late (see above), explain in full why.

☐ Explain, as fully as possible why you disagree with the SFO's decision.

☐ CCGs are often refused on the grounds that your application was not for one of the purposes for which CCGs can be given. Such decisions are commonly based on local and national guidance rather than the law (see Chapter 21). You can challenge such decisions by stating that you are not satisfied that your needs and circumstances have been properly looked at by the SFO. You should then explain how a grant will help you move out of or stay out of care, or will ease exceptional pressures (see Chapter 22). If you have already given full details in your original application you can refer to them and add any new information.

☐ CCGs and loans are often refused on the grounds of 'insufficient priority', based on local guidance lists (see Chapter 21). You can challenge such decisions by stating you are not satisfied your particular needs and circumstances have been properly looked at. You should then explain why your application should merit high priority with reference to information already given and any further evidence or information you have.

☐ If you are unhappy about the amount you have been awarded, you should state that you are not satisfied that the SFO has assessed your needs properly. Explain why you need the amount you asked for, giving any further evidence or information which was not in your original application.

☐ If you are awarded a loan rather than a grant, you can refuse or accept the loan and also ask for a review explaining why you think you should be awarded a CCG instead.

(iv)   Review without an application

An SFO can review a decision at any time without an application.[28]
    An SFO *must* review a decision which appears:
either   to have been based on a mistake about the law or directions;
or   to have been made in ignorance of a material fact or based on a mistake about a material fact;
or   where there has been a relevant change of circumstances since the decision was given.[29]
A relevant change in circumstances could include any additional allocation to a District Office budget during the year – see p296. When this occurs, there is a strong argument that the DSS *must* review all previous decisions made during the year to refuse or restrict payments wholly or partially on budgetary grounds and issue fresh decisions. You should insist the Benefits Agency reconsider your case if this applies to you. If they refuse, get advice (see Appendix 2).

(v)   Deciding reviews

The theory

SFOs are responsible for conducting reviews.[30] The guidance says wherever practicable the SFO who made the decision being challenged should also conduct the review[31] (but not if this involves delays[32]).

When conducting a review, an SFO must have full regard to the following matters:

☐ All the circumstances of the case under review and, in particular, all the matters which have to be considered when making original decisions (see p295), including the nature, extent and urgency of the need and the size of the district budget.[33]

☐ The SF directions, the Secretary of State's national guidance and local guidance[34] (see Chapter 21).

☐ Whether the law was applied correctly when the decision under review was made. In particular, whether:

- the decision was consistent with the evidence;
- all relevant and no irrelevant considerations were taken into account;
- the law and directions were interpreted correctly.[35]

☐ Whether the SFO who made the original decision acted fairly, without bias and exercised discretion reasonably, following the required procedural steps and giving you sufficient opportunity to put your case.[36]

☐ All the circumstances which existed at the time of the original decision, any new evidence which has since been produced and any relevant changes of circumstances.[37]

The practice

Not surprisingly, SFOs rarely conduct reviews with the thoroughness demanded by the above legal requirements. They have neither the time nor the training. In practice, budget considerations and local priority lists tend to be the major determinants in reviews. Also there is a tendency for SFOs to only change their original decisions in the light of new evidence.

(vi) Review interviews

Procedure

If an SFO does not revise a decision wholly in your favour you must be given the opportunity to attend an interview.[38] You have the legal right to be accompanied by a friend or representative.[39] At the interview, you must be given an explanation of the reasons for the SFO decision and an opportunity to put your case, including any additional evidence you have.[40]

The guidance says that 'whenever possible, the interview should take place in a private interviewing room.'[41] The interview can be held in your home if, for example, you are severely disabled or ill.[42] The guidance says the interview should be with the SFO who made the original decision, unless they are unavailable.[43] The SFO must make an accurate written record of your representations, to be agreed and signed by you.[44]

Tactics

☐ Always ask to be interviewed in a private room and complain if one is not offered.

☐   Do not sign the written record unless you agree with it and everything you want to say has been recorded. You could ask to write the record yourself or provide a written statement and insist it is included in the record. If you have been told something by the SFO which you disagree with, you could refer to it in the record. It is particularly important to record any new evidence, previously unknown to the SFO.

☐   If you do not wish to attend an interview (eg, you have nothing further to add to your application), tell the Benefits Agency. The review will then automatically proceed to the next stage (see below).

(vii)   After the interview

If the SFO does not revise a decision wholly in your favour following the interview, your case must be looked at again by an SFO not below the rank of higher executive officer (HEO). [45] This is usually the SF assistant manager, who must then look at the case again taking into account all the matters set out on p327. The HEO should check that the SFO has conducted a review properly and impartially in accordance with the law, obtaining all relevant evidence. [46] S/he should then record a decision fully explaining the circumstances of the application and applicant, the evidence and how the decision was arrived at. [47]

(viii)   Getting a decision

You will be notified of the review decision in writing. There are no legal time-limits for issuing decisions. If there are unreasonable delays you should complain to the SF manager. If that doesn't help, you could ask your MP to take up your case.

4   REVIEW BY A SOCIAL FUND INSPECTOR

(i)   Introduction

If you are dissatisfied with a decision of an SFO which has been reviewed, you have a right to request a further review by a social fund inspector (SFI). [48]

SFIs are based in an office in Birmingham (see Appendix 1) and conduct their reviews independently of the Benefits Agency. SFIs tend to produce a much higher standard of decision-making than SFOs. They are generally better-trained and have more time. They tend to be less influenced by local guidance and budgets than SFOs.

You should always, therefore, ask for a further review, if necessary, as your chances of success are much higher than at the first review.

The law regarding SFI reviews is set out in legislation and SFI directions.

(ii)   Applying for a further review

Basic rules

You must apply for a further review in writing within 28 days of the date the review decision was issued to you.[49] Your application must include your grounds for requesting a further review (see below – 'tactics').[50] If somebody is applying on your behalf, you must send your written authority[51] (unless the person is your appointee). A generalised authority for somebody to act on your behalf may not be sufficient. You should specifically authorise the person to make an application for further review by an SFI on your behalf.

Late claims can be accepted for 'special reasons'[52] (see p325). You must send your application to your local Benefits Agency office and *not* directly to the SFI office in Birmingham. The local office will send your application together with all relevant papers (including copies of your original application, the review decision and details of the local budget and guidance) to Birmingham. Decisions about late or incomplete applications are made by the SFI and not the local office. The SFI will write to you direct for further information or evidence.

Tactics

☐ Submit your application in writing to your local Benefits Agency office, quoting your Benefits Agency reference number. Begin your letter by stating you request a further review by an SFI and identify the SFO review decision you are unhappy about. If your application is late, explain in full why.

☐ Explain as fully as possible why you disagree with the SFO's review decision. If the review decision you received was worded identically to the original SFO decision, you may want to simply refer to your first review application and state that you are still not satisfied that your needs and circumstances have been properly considered by the SFO. If there is any new or additional information relevant to your application, you should, of course, include it in your letter. See page 326 for examples of what you could say, if not previously included in your original review application.

☐ It is a good idea to contact the SFI office a few days after submitting your application to make sure they have received it. Local Benefits Agency offices are told to send applications on to Birmingham by courier on the day they are received if possible.[53] Complain to the SF manager and, if necessary, your MP, if there are delays.

☐ If your case is urgent, state this and explain why.

(iii) Deciding further reviews

The law

When conducting a review, an SFI is legally bound to take into account the same matters which apply to SFO reviews (see p327).[54]

An SFI review is not quite a complete rehearing of a case. It does involve, however, a thorough consideration of whether the decision under review was arrived at properly and reasonably, taking into account the law, directions, guidance and all the evidence which was before the SFO. If an SFI is satisfied a decision was reached correctly, s/he must then decide whether the decision should be changed in the light of any new evidence or changes in circumstances.

The procedure

Reviews are almost always conducted on the basis of written information. You have no right to an oral hearing although an SFI can interview you, if necessary, 'at a mutually convenient location'.[55]

You will be sent copies of all the papers which the SFI has about your case before the review takes place. You should look through the papers and send any written comments you have to the SFI on the form provided (form A). You are given two weeks to send in your comments but if you need longer, contact the SFI office and request an extension. The papers will include the full written decision of the HEO (see p328). You should read it carefully and comment on anything which is wrong, irrelevant or with which you disagree.

(iv)   SFI decisions

SFIs can:[56]
either   confirm the SFO's decision;
or   substitute their own decision;
or   refer the case back to an SFO for determination.
In 1990/91, 82 per cent of cases referred to the SFI were either substituted or referred back.

You will receive a detailed written decision. There are long delays (often several weeks) with SFI reviews and you could complain to your MP about these. Crisis loan reviews should be done urgently. If you are unhappy about an SFI decision, get advice. There is no right of appeal, but if the decision is unreasonable or wrong in law, you could ask the SFI to reconsider it,[57] or apply for judicial review in the High Court (you will need legal advice to do this).

If the SFI disagrees with the SFO decision, the case will usually be referred back to the local Benefits Agency office for redetermination. The SFI decision will give details of why the Benefits Agency decision is unacceptable. Common examples are that local guidance has been followed too rigidly or that the evidence does not support the decision given. The Benefits Agency must redetermine the case in the light of the SFI's comments.[58] You will then be issued with a fresh decision which should include full reasons, with reference to the SFI's comments, on form SF614.[59]

(v)   Second SFI reviews

If the Benefits Agency do not change a decision wholly in your favour after referral back by an SFI, you can request a second further review by an SFI. You should *always* do this if you are not satisfied that the Benefits Agency has properly taken into account the SFI's decision.

To apply for a second SFI review, you must write to your local Benefits Agency office within 28 days of being issued their last review decision. The rules and procedures are identical to first SFI reviews. Your grounds are likely to be that you are not satisfied the Benefits Agency took proper account of the SFI decision. SFIs seem generally willing to accept second applications, even if you apply late. They also commonly substitute their own decision rather than refer the case back to the Benefits Agency again. They will often find in your favour if it is clear the Benefits Agency has still failed to deal with your case properly. It is always, therefore, worth asking for a second (or even third!) SFI review, if necessary.

PART X
Other benefits

Chapter 25

Health service benefits

This chapter covers:

1   INTRODUCTION

Although the National Health Service (NHS) generally provides free health care for everybody, charges are made for prescriptions and certain treatment and appliances.

Income support (IS) and family credit (FC) claimants and their dependants are 'passported', so that they do not have to pay charges. Some people do not have to pay these charges whatever their income or savings. Other people do not have to pay the charges, or only have to pay reduced charges, if their income is low. The precise rules for each type of charge are set out in the other parts of this chapter, but the way that low income is calculated is explained here.

(i)   How low income is worked out

If you receive IS or FC, you are automatically exempt from charges. If you have over £8,000 capital, you must pay them in full unless exempted on other grounds.

Otherwise, the DSS decides if your income is low enough by comparing your 'requirements' to your 'resources'. If your 'resources' are less than, or the same as, your 'requirements' you do not have to pay anything. If they are more than your 'requirements' you may still qualify for partial help with dental costs (see p338), sight tests (see p339), glasses (see p340), wigs and fabric supports (see p341) and fares to hospital (see p342). You cannot get partial help with prescriptions. You may be better off using a pre-payment certificate.

'Requirements' and 'resources' are calculated as at the date on which you claim free or reduced dental costs, glasses, fares to hospital etc, *unless*, having already paid, you are claiming a refund, in which case it is the date you paid. [1]

(ii) Requirements[2]

Your requirements are based on the rules for calculating entitlement to IS, but more housing costs are included and some of the restrictions do not apply.

Your requirements are:
☐   your personal allowances (see p237);
☐   your premiums (see p238);
☐   rent *minus* any housing benefit you receive;
☐   80 per cent of your community charge (and your partner's) *minus* any community charge benefit you receive;
☐   your repayments (both capital and interest and including insurance payments on endowment mortgages) on mortgages and other loans secured on your home (with no reduction for the first 16 weeks and including second mortgages and regardless of the purpose for which the mortgage or loan was taken out);
☐   accommodation charges for people in residential care or nursing homes (without any restriction), *plus* an amount for meals (see p75).

The reductions which apply to IS because of voluntary unemployment or involvement in a trade dispute do not apply. Nor do the special rules for people from abroad or members of religious orders, whose requirements are calculated in the usual way.

(iii) Resources

If you have **capital** over £8,000, calculated as for IS (see Chapter 18), you will not qualify on low-income grounds. [3]

Your **income** is calculated as for IS (see Chapter 17), with the following modifications. [4]

Liable relative payments

The complicated rules for calculating liable relative payments (see p91) do not apply. Instead, **maintenance payments** are treated as follows:
☐   If you are due to receive regular payments, your normal weekly income will be:
–   the weekly amount of those payments if they are made regularly; *or*
–   the average weekly amount you have actually received in the 13 weeks immediately before you claimed, if the payments were not made regularly.
☐   Payments which are not part of a regular series (ie, lump sums), are simply treated as capital.

Earnings

☐ The rule for deciding the *period* for which income is paid (see p249) does not apply. If you receive a payment of income which does not relate to a particular period, it is likely that it will be counted as income in the week in which it is paid.

☐ The rule about *when* income is treated as paid (see p249) also does not apply, so payments will only be taken into account as your resources when they are actually paid to you.

☐ If you are affected by a trade dispute, your earnings are taken to be those you would have received had there been no dispute. [5] None of the modifications to treatment of income under IS which apply to people affected by a trade dispute apply for the purpose of calculating your resources.

Disregards

☐ There is no £15 disregard for couples who have been unemployed for two years (see p256). Instead, if you are one of a couple not entitled to a £15 disregard on other grounds, you will have £10 of your earnings disregarded. If one partner's earnings are less than £10, the remainder of the disregard can be used on any earnings of the other partner.

☐ There is no disregard of payments you receive and intend to use towards housing costs not met under the IS regulations. Of course, most of the housing costs not eligible for IS are added into the calculation on the requirements side.

☐ There is no provision for dealing with the situation in which you receive two payments of earnings or income of the same kind from the same source in the same week. Your normal income or earnings for one week should be counted in calculating your resources.

☐ The £10 disregard from student loans only applies to students eligible for a premium, deaf students, or students with a partner.

(iv) Low-income certificates

If your income is low enough to qualify for free services you get certificate AG2. If your income is not quite that low, you qualify for partial remission of charges and get certificate AG3. You get these certificates by completing form AG1, obtainable from your doctor, dentist, optician, hospital or DSS office.

These certificates last for six months. You should make a repeat claim on Form AG1 shortly before the expiry date. If your circumstances change, write to the Agency Benefits Unit – they will issue a fresh certificate if necessary. There is no right of appeal against a decision made by the Agency Benefits Unit. If you feel they have made a mistake, ask them to reconsider their decision (see Appendix 1 for address).

2 PRESCRIPTIONS

Usually, prescriptions cost £3.75, but some people do not have to pay. Those who need a lot of prescriptions can limit the cost by obtaining a pre-payment certificate (see p337).

(i) Free prescriptions

You qualify if:[6]

☐ you receive IS or FC (or you are a member of the family of someone who does – see p227); *or*

☐ your income is low enough (see p333); *or*

☐ you are under 16 or under 19 and in full-time education; *or*

☐ you are over pensionable age (65 for men, 60 for women); *or*

☐ you are pregnant; *or*

☐ you have given birth within the last 12 months (even if the child was stillborn or has since died); *or*

☐ you are a war disablement pensioner and you need the prescription for your war disability (in which case you claim from your War Pensions Office); *or*

☐ you suffer from one or more of the following conditions:
  - a continuing physical disability which prevents you leaving your home except with the help of another person;
  - epilepsy requiring continuous anti-convulsive therapy;
  - a permanent fistula, including a caecostomy, ileostomy, laryngostomy or colostomy, needing continuous surgical dressing or an appliance;
  - diabetes mellitus;
  - myxoedema;
  - hypoparathyroidism;
  - diabetes insipidus and other forms of hypopituitarism;
  - Addison's disease and other forms of hypoadrenalism;
  - myasthenia gravis.

Claims

You claim by ticking a box on the back of the prescription but, unless you are claiming on grounds of age or because you are receiving IS or FC, you must already have a certificate.

If you are a pregnant woman, you should obtain a form from your doctor, midwife or health visitor (or, in Scotland, the Primary Care Division of the Health Board) and send it to the Family Practitioner Committee (in Scotland, the Health Board). You will be sent an exemption certificate which lasts until a year after it is expected you will give birth.

If you are claiming on the ground that you have given birth within the last year (and do not already have an exemption certificate) or you are suffering from one of the conditions listed above, you should complete the form in DSS leaflet P11 which you can obtain from your doctor's surgery, a chemist or a DSS office.

If you are claiming on the ground of low income, obtain Form AG1 from your doctor, dentist, optician, hospital or a DSS office and send it off. You will be sent Certificate AG2 which you can use to get free prescriptions, free dental treatment, sight tests, glasses, wigs, fabric supports and travel to hospital, for the six months during which it is valid.

(ii) Refunds[7]

If you think you may be entitled to free prescriptions but do not have a certificate, ask the chemist for a special receipt – Form FP57 (in Scotland, EC57) – when you pay the charge. The form explains how you claim a refund. You must apply within one month of paying the charge, or three months if you have automatic exemption from paying prescription charges. These periods can be extended for as long as you can show good cause.[8]

(iii) Pre-payment certificates[9]

If you need a lot of prescriptions, but are not entitled to them free, you can still reduce the cost by buying a pre-payment certificate (sometimes called a 'season ticket'). This costs £19.40 for four months, or £53.50 for one year. It saves money if you need more than fourteen items on prescription in a year. A refund can be given if someone buys a pre-payment certificate and then, within a month, qualifies for free prescriptions, or dies. To get one, obtain Form FP95 (EC95 in Scotland) from the DSS, a post office, or chemist.

3 DENTAL TREATMENT AND DENTURES

In this section, 'dental treatment' includes dental check-ups. NHS check-ups cost £3.75. The cost of subsequent treatment varies depending on what needs to be done. However, many people are entitled to free treatment and appliances such as dentures and bridges.[10] Others need pay only reduced charges.

(i) Free dental treatment and dentures

You qualify if:[11]
- [ ] you receive IS or FC (or you are a member of the family of someone who does – see p227); *or*
- [ ] your income is low enough (see p333); *or*
- [ ] you are under:
    - 16 (for treatment, dentures or bridges),
    - 18 (for treatment),
    - 19 (for treatment, dentures, or bridges if you are still in full-time education); *or*
- [ ] you are pregnant or have given birth within the last 12 months (even if the child was stillborn or has since died); *or*
- [ ] you are a war disablement pensioner and need the treatment or appliances because of your war disability (in which case you claim from your War Pensions Office).

Claims

You claim by ticking a box on a form provided by the dentist, so tell the receptionist that you think you qualify for free treatment *before* you have it.

A woman who is pregnant or has a child under the age of one may be asked to show her Family Practitioner Committee Exemption Certificate, so it is best to get one before you go for the treatment (see p336).

If you are claiming on the ground of low income, you again need Certificate AG2. This is the same one as is used for free prescriptions. See p335 for how to get it.

(ii)   Refunds [12]

If you paid a charge when you could have had appliances or treatment free because you receive IS or FC or you have a low income, you can obtain a refund. You must apply, within one month of paying the charge, using Form AG5 (obtainable from a DSS office). This period will be extended for as long as you can show good cause for a late application.

(iii)   Reduced charges

If you do not qualify for *free* treatment on low-income grounds, but your income is nevertheless low, you may get partial help with charges for dental treatment and appliances. Your 'resources' must exceed your 'requirements' (see p333 for how these are calculated) by less than one-third of the charge, and you must have less than £8,000 capital. You will be entitled to the difference between the charge for one course of treatment, including any appliances, and three times the amount by which your income resources exceed your requirements.[13] To claim, you need Certificate AG3 which you obtain in the same way as Certificate AG2 (see p335). If you paid the full charge when you need not have done, you can obtain a refund (see above).

4   SIGHT TESTS AND GLASSES

Treatment for eye problems is free under the NHS, but sight tests are not; nor are glasses or contact lenses. However, certain people are entitled to free or reduced-cost sight tests and to vouchers which will cover all or part of the cost of glasses or contact lenses.

(i)   Free sight tests

There is no set charge for sight tests so it may be worth shopping round for them. Some opticians do not charge at all.

You qualify for a free test if: [14]

☐   you receive IS or FC (or you are a member of the family of someone who does – see p227); *or*

☐   your income is low enough (see p333); *or*

☐ you are under 16 or under 19 and in full-time education; *or*
☐ you are registered blind or partially-sighted; *or*
☐ you have been prescribed complex lenses; *or*
☐ you have been diagnosed as suffering from diabetes or glaucoma; *or*
☐ you are aged 40 or over and are the parent, brother, sister or child of someone suffering from glaucoma; *or*
☐ you are a war disablement pensioner and require the sight test because of your war disability (in which case you claim from your War Pensions Office).

To claim, tell the optician *before* you have the test. If you are claiming on the ground of low income, you need Certificate AG2 – ie, the same certificate as entitles you to free prescriptions (see p335 for how to obtain one). If you do not have Certificate AG2 before the test, you must apply for one within two weeks of the test and then apply for a refund (see below).

(ii) Reduced-cost sight tests

If your income is low but not low enough for you to qualify for *free* sight tests, you may be entitled to have the test at a *reduced* charge.[15] To claim, you need Certificate AG3 which you obtain in the same way as Certificate AG2 (see p335). You will qualify only if your 'resources' exceed your 'requirements' (see p333 for how these are calculated) by less than £11.20. You will have to pay three times the amount by which your 'resources' exceed your 'requirements'. If you do not have Certificate AG3 before the test, you must apply within two weeks of the test and then apply for a refund (see below).

(iii) 'Full-value' vouchers for glasses and contact lenses

If your sight test shows you need glasses, you are given a prescription by the optician which is valid for two years.

You will qualify for a 'full-value' voucher to meet the cost of glasses or contact lenses if:[16]

☐ you receive IS or FC (or you are a member of the family of someone who does – see p227); *or*
☐ your income is low enough (see p333); *or*
☐ you are under 16 or under 19 and in full-time education; *or*
☐ you are a Hospital Eye Service patient needing frequent changes of glasses or contact lenses; *or*
☐ you have been prescribed complex lenses.

Certain war pensioners can obtain refunds of charges for glasses or contact lenses, even though they do not qualify for vouchers (see p341).

If you qualify for a voucher, the optician will give you one if:[17]

☐ you require the glasses or contact lenses for the first time; *or*
☐ your new prescription differs from your old one; *or*
☐ your old glasses have worn out through fair wear and tear; *or*
☐ you are under 16 and have lost or damaged your old glasses or contact lenses and the cost of repair or replacement is not covered by insurance or warranty; *or*

☐   you are ill *and*, as a result of your illness, have lost or damaged your glasses or contact lenses and the cost of repair or replacement is not covered by insurance or warranty *and*
- you receive IS or FC (or you are a member of the family of someone who does – see p227); *or*
- your income is low enough (see p333); *or*
- you have been prescribed complex lenses.

The voucher is valid for six months.[18] Its value depends on the type of lenses you need, and each type of voucher is at a fixed amount.[19] It does not, therefore, automatically cover the value of your glasses. Although it should enable you to buy glasses or contact lenses (or have your existing ones repaired) without having to pay anything yourself (except in the case of complex lenses when you are expected to contribute to the cost unless you would qualify for a voucher on other grounds), you may have to shop around to find a cheap enough pair. If you cannot find a cheap enough pair, or if you choose to buy a more expensive pair, you will have to make up the difference yourself.

You must have the voucher *before* you buy the glasses or contact lenses. The circumstances in which refunds can be made are very limited (see below). This means applying for Certificate AG2 if you wish to claim on grounds of low income (see p335).

There are eight different bands of value for the vouchers ranging from £23.70 to £110.

(iv)   Reduced-value vouchers

If your income is low but not low enough to qualify for a full-value voucher, you may qualify for a voucher for a lower amount. The value of the voucher will be the value of a full-value one *less* three times the amount by which your 'resources' exceed your 'requirements' (see p333). You must apply for Certificate AG3 (in the same way as for Certificate AG2 – see p335) *before* you pay for the glasses or contact lenses.

(v)   Refunds

Sight tests

Refunds can only be made if you are entitled to free or reduced-cost sight tests on the ground of low income and apply for Certificate AG2 or AG3 within two weeks of having the test, using Form AG1 (see p325). You will get a refund if you then send Certificate AG2 or AG3 with a receipt from the optician to the Family Practitioner Committee within three months of having the test.

Glasses and contact lenses

Refunds will only be made if the glasses or contact lenses were prescribed through the Hospital Eye Service and you would have had a voucher on the ground of low income if you had had Certificate AG2 or AG3, or you are getting IS or FC. Ask the hospital or DSS for Form AG5 (and Form AG1 if you want to claim on low-income grounds and you do not hold a current AG2 or AG3 certificate). You must submit your claim within one month of the date of the receipt.

War pensioners

If you qualify for a free sight test or free glasses or contact lenses only because you are a war pensioner, you must pay the charges and then claim a refund from Treatment Group, War Pensions Branch, DSS, Norcross, Blackpool FY5 3TA.

(vi)   Home visits

If you have Certificate AG2 and you want to have your eyes tested at home, you can be visited free of charge. If you have Certificate AG3, you can put this towards the cost of the visit.

5   WIGS AND FABRIC SUPPORTS[20]

NHS wigs cost up to £119 and spinal supports cost either £16 or £21. Some people are entitled to them free or at reduced cost.

(i)   Free wigs and fabric supports

You qualify for free wigs and fabric supports if:
- [ ] you receive IS or FC (or you are a member of the family of someone who does – see p227); *or*
- [ ] your income is low enough (see p333); *or*
- [ ] you are under 16 or under 19 and in full-time education; *or*
- [ ] you are a hospital in-patient when the wig or fabric support is supplied; *or*
- [ ] you are a war disablement pensioner and need the wig or fabric support for your war injury.

You claim when you go to the hospital to have the wig or fabric support fitted. If you are claiming on the ground of low income, you need Certificate AG1 (see p335).

(ii)   Refunds

The rules are the same as for dental treatment (see p338).

(iii)   Reduced charges

The rules are the same as for dental treatment (see p338).

6 FARES TO HOSPITAL[21]

(i) Who can get help

You qualify for help if you are attending an NHS hospital or clinic for treatment or a disablement services centre and:

☐ you receive IS or FC (or you are a member of the family of someone who does – see p227); *or*

☐ your income is low enough (see p333); *or*

☐ you are a patient at a sexually-transmitted disease clinic more than fifteen miles from your home; *or*

☐ you are a war disablement pensioner and the treatment is for your war injury.

You may also get help if you live in the Highlands and Islands of Scotland or the Isles of Scilly.

You usually have to get yourself to hospital, but once you are there you are paid the cost of the return trip. However, you can ask the hospital to send you the money in advance..

If you are claiming on the ground of low income, you will need Certificate AG1 (see p336).

(ii) What costs can be paid

You can claim for:

☐ normal public transport fares;

☐ estimated petrol costs;

☐ a reasonable contribution to a local voluntary car scheme;

☐ taxi fares, but only if there is no alternative for all or part of the journey.

The travelling costs of a companion will also be paid if it is necessary for you to be accompanied.

(iii) Refunds

The rules are the same as for dental treatment (see p338).

(iv) Partial help

If your 'resources' exceed your 'requirements' and you have savings of less than £8,000, you will get the difference between your excess income and your weekly fares.

(v) Visiting patients

If you are receiving IS and are visiting a close relative or partner, you may be entitled to help from the social fund (see p310).

If you are visiting a war pensioner who is being treated for her/his war injury, you may also be entitled to help.

7   FREE MILK AND VITAMINS [22]

(i)   Free milk tokens

The following people qualify for free milk tokens:

☐ Disabled children aged 5 to 16 who cannot go to school because of their disability (claim on Form FW20).

☐ Expectant mothers who are receiving IS (or who are a member of the family of someone who is – see p227).

☐ Children under 5 whose family receives IS.

Note that expectant mothers and children under 5 also qualify for free vitamins (see p344).

The milk tokens for each person entitled can be exchanged for 7 pints/4 litres of milk a week, but if they are for a child under one they can be exchanged for 900 grammes of dried milk a week instead. You can use milk tokens at a clinic to buy dried milk or they can be exchanged for fresh milk from suppliers who are then reimbursed by the Secretary of State. Suppliers can accept milk tokens as part-payment if the milk you buy is more expensive than the basic-cost milk. [23] Otherwise you should not have to pay towards the cost of your milk, even though the DSS does not always reimburse your milk supplier for the full amount. [24] If you cannot find a supplier who will accept your tokens you can apply to the DSS to cash them. [25]

If you lose your milk tokens, the DSS may replace them, but it does not have to do so. [26] If you are turned down, you could try to negotiate, perhaps with the support of a social worker, health visitor, or your MP.

If you do not receive milk tokens to which you are entitled, they should be replaced by the DSS if 'the Secretary of State is satisfied . . . that some act or omission on his part was responsible' [27] for your failure to receive milk tokens. Again, there is no right of appeal if you are turned down, but you could try negotiating.

If you are absent from home for less than a week, with the result that you miss some of the milk covered by your token, your supplier can give you a refund for the pints you have missed. You have to ask the supplier to do this during the period within which the token is valid. [28]

(ii)   Free milk for children in day-care

Children, whether with a registered childminder, a registered day nursery or a day nursery which is not required to register, can get one-third of a pint of free milk for each day that they are in such day-care. [29] This entitlement is in addition to any entitlement you get from being in a family on IS, or having a disabled child (see above). It is the childminder or organiser of the nursery who applies to the DSS. They are then reimbursed for money spent on milk, normally every four months in arrears. Children under one are allowed one-third of a pint, or dried milk made up to one-third of a pint.

(iii)   Reduced-cost milk

Anyone attending a maternity or childcare clinic can buy dried milk at a reduced price.

Families on **family credit** with children under one can get dried milk at an even lower price from maternity and child health clinics. [30] You are allowed to buy up to 900 grammes of dried milk a week for each child under one, at a cost of £3.30. You can buy it for up to four weeks in arrears and up to four weeks in advance. You need evidence that you get family credit to buy dried milk at reduced prices from clinics, and that you get IS to get free vitamins. If you do not have this evidence through 'some act or omission' on the part of the Secretary of State, you can get a refund. [31]

(iv)   Free vitamins

The following qualify for free vitamins: [32]

☐ Expectant mothers who are receiving IS (or who are a member of the family of someone who is – see p227).

☐ Nursing mothers (ie, those breastfeeding a child/children under 30 weeks old) who are receiving IS (or who are a member of the family of someone who is – see p227).

☐ Children under 5 whose family receives IS.

Entitlement to free vitamins provides two bottles of children's vitamin drops every thirteen weeks for children, five 45-tablet containers of vitamins to nursing mothers and two 45-tablet containers of vitamins every thirteen weeks while the pregnancy lasts, to expectant mothers. [33] Vitamins are available from child health and maternity clinics.

If you are not entitled to free vitamins, you can still buy cheap ones if you are attending a maternity or childcare clinic.

Chapter 26

Local authority benefits and services

This chapter covers:

1 EDUCATION BENEFITS

(i) Free school meals

Education authorities must make such provision for meals 'as appears to be requisite' in the middle of the day,[1] but they have no responsibility to provide a suitable main meal of the day. All pupils must be charged the same price for meals, milk or other refreshments that are provided unless entitled to free meals. Education authorities have to provide such facilities as are considered 'appropriate'[2] for pupils to eat meals which they bring to the school. These do not have to be on the school premises.[3]

The only children entitled to free school meals are those who are members of the family (see p227) of a person receiving income support (IS). (This includes 16/17/18-year-olds receiving IS in their own right.) Free meals should be available for nursery children, and to young people still in education up to their 19th birthday.

(ii) Clothing grants

Education authorities may only give grants for:
☐ school uniforms;
☐ 'necessitous' clothing which is not actually school uniform. This could include sports kit.[4]
They are free to determine the level of income at which grants (if any) will be paid, and to make their own eligibility rules. Grants may be in the form of either cash or vouchers.[5] There may be rules about the number of times you can claim. It is often best to apply in the summer term for the school year commencing in September.

(iii) Educational maintenance allowances

These weekly allowances are paid to those children who stay on at school after the school-leaving age.[6] They can be paid whether or not the child has stayed on to take exams. There is considerable variation between authorities as to how much is paid, but these allowances are always paid on income grounds, and do not affect entitlement to income support (IS), family credit (FC), disability working allowance (DWA) or housing benefit (HB), unless the amount paid exceeds the amount that can be disregarded.

A child who leaves school to go to a technical college full-time might be eligible for a minor award.[7] You can find out from your education authority.

There is a scheme for giving children free places at independent, fee-paying schools if they would not otherwise be able to go there. The school fees are reimbursed by the government.[8] For more information contact the Department of Education and Science, Elizabeth House, York Road, London SE1 7PH tel: 071-934-9000.

(iv)　Free transport to school

Education authorities *must* provide free transport to school where it is not within walking distance of the child's home.[9] 'Walking distance' is defined as less than two miles for a child under 8, and less than three miles for older children. The distance between home and school is measured by the 'nearest available route',[10] which is not necessarily the shortest.[11]

Education authorities must look at the age of the pupil, the nature of the route, and alternative routes s/he could be reasonably expected to take.[12]

Education authorities *may* meet any pupil's 'reasonable travelling expenses' even where there is no duty to provide free transport.[13] However, it is rare for authorities to use this power except to reduce the walking distances required to qualify for free transport.

Students attending a college of further education may get help with the cost of fares. You can get the form from the college.

Fares to visit boarders

If your child is at boarding school in order to receive special education and you cannot afford to visit her/him, the education authority has the power to meet all or part of your fares and any other expenses involved. The Department of Education and Science has told education authorities that they can provide this help if your child's education would suffer as a result of you not being able to visit.[14] A letter from a doctor, social worker or teacher supporting your case might be helpful. If your child is being looked after by social services, and is away at school or a children's home, the Social Services Department can help you with fares.[15]

(v)　Remission of other charges

Although education authorities may charge for some educational services, the law makes it quite clear that there must be no charge for the following:

☐　an activity that occurs during school hours (with the exception of individual music tuition – but see below);[16]

☐　individual music tuition where the child is preparing for a public examination;[17]

☐　activities partly outside school hours where more than half, including travel, are in school hours;[18]

☐ activities wholly or partly outside school hours which are part of the national curriculum or part of the exam syllabus. [19]

Thus, transport, entrance fees and equipment must be free as long as they arise as part of the school curriculum.

The only exceptions are that parents may be required to pay for:

☐ board and lodging on field trips;

☐ examination fees if the child fails, without good reason, to meet any examination requirement. This will be decided by the education authority. [20]

However, *charging is optional* and no charge may be made until the governors and the education authority have decided a charging policy. Charges must not exceed the actual cost. If the pupil's parent(s) receives IS or FC at the time of a school trip, [21] any charge for board and lodging must be remitted.

Any other charge *may* be remitted if it is appropriate, whether or not the parent(s) receives IS or FC.

Under the Children Act, a local authority *must* provide supervised activities for children in need outside of school hours or during school holidays, [22] and *can* provide it for all other children. [23] Any such service provided under the Children Act must be free to any family on IS, FC and DWA. [24] In any other case, the charge cannot be more than the client can reasonably be expected to pay. [25]

Pupils who are boarding

Education authorities may charge fees if they provide board and lodging; but they cannot charge if the board and lodging is provided because education suitable to the pupil's ability, age and aptitude cannot otherwise be provided. This applies whether it is a maintained or grant-maintained school.

Fees for board and lodging may also be remitted in cases of financial hardship. [26]

(vi)   Student grants

These are beyond the scope of this *Handbook*. You can get information from your education authority or careers service, or from a welfare officer for the National Union of Students (NUS) at your college or university. The NUS provides information sheets on student grants. Write (enclosing a stamped addressed envelope) to the Student Financial Support Unit, NUS, Nelson Mandela House, 461 Holloway Road, London, N7 6LJ.

(vii)   Claiming education benefits

To find out about any of the benefits mentioned above (other than student grants), ask an education welfare officer who can be contacted via the local school or college.

2   HOUSING RENOVATION GRANTS

A local housing authority has the power to provide help with the cost of improving your home. This section describes the scheme as it applies to England and Wales. For Scotland, see the leaflet *Improve your home with a grant*, available from your local authority. The amount of financial help that you will receive depends on a means test, very similar to that for HB.

(i) Types of grant

The following grants are available:
- ☐ Renovation – for works of improvement, repair or conversion.
- ☐ Common parts – for work to common parts of a building let as flats.
- ☐ Houses in multiple occupation – for improvement or repair to a house in multiple occupation (only available to landlords).
- ☐ Disabled facilities – to make a property suitable for a disabled occupant.
- ☐ Group repair – external repairs to groups of houses which are not in reasonable repair.
- ☐ Minor works assistance.

(ii) Exclusions

You cannot apply for a grant unless the property is at least ten years old (unless you are applying for disabled facilities grant).[27] The property must not be owned by a local authority, a new town corporation, an urban development council, a housing action trust, or the Development Board for Rural Wales (except for applications for a disabled facilities grant).[28]

Restrictions are imposed which, in broad terms, require you or a family member to live in the dwelling. The exact rules vary depending on whether you are an owner-occupier, tenant or landlord applying for the grant.[29] Various other restrictions may apply related to the state of the property. The effect of these is that you are not eligible for a grant if the property is in such a poor state of repair that even when you have carried out the improvements it will still not be considered habitable.[30]

Minor works assistance grants can only be paid if you are in receipt of IS, FC, DWA, HB or CCB, and are limited to a maximum payment of £1,000 per application and £3,000 in any three-year period.[31]

(iii) Claiming

You must apply for a grant on the form supplied by the local housing authority,[32] and include two estimates for the works that are to be carried out. The local authority may agree to waive the requirement to supply two estimates. Grants are only available for work which has been approved by the local authority. If you have completed work before applying for a grant, or before a grant was approved, you get no help unless these works were necessary to comply with a statutory notice.

(iv) The means test

If you are awarded a grant, you may still have to pay something towards the total cost of the work. The local authority calculates the amount you have to pay (if any) by comparing your income with your 'needs' (called your applicable amount). These are calculated in the same way as for HB (see pp237-38 and Chapter 17), with the following main exceptions:

General

☐ The means test applies not just to you and your family, but to anyone else who has an interest in the dwelling as a joint owner or joint tenant[33] and who lives in the property, or intends to do so, and a disabled person for whom a disabled facilities grant has been awarded.

Applicable amounts

☐ This always includes a renovation grant premium of £22.[34] This may be uprated during 1992/93; check with your local authority.
☐ There is no reduction in the applicable amount if someone is in hospital.

Income

☐ Your income is normally based on the 52 weeks prior to the application, but if another period more accurately reflects your current financial situation this period should be used instead.[35]
☐ Capital over £5,000 is assumed to produce an income at the rate of £1 per £250 (or part of £250).[36]

Capital

☐ There is no upper capital limit which will bar you from making a claim but, of course, the tariff income may bar you instead.
☐ You do receive a personal allowance for a child if s/he has more than £5,000 capital.[37]

You receive the full cost of the work if *either* you are in receipt of IS *or* your income is the same or less than your applicable amount under the grants means test.

If your income is greater than your applicable amount then the grant will be reduced by multiplying the excess by £53.35 if you are an owner-occupier, or £35.37 if you are a tenant.[38] So, if the excess of your income over your applicable amount is £20, and you are an owner-occupier, the grant is reduced by £20 × £51.54 = £1,030.80. If you are a tenant the reduction is £20 × £34.62 = £692.40.

These multipliers are for 1991/92. They may be uprated during 1992/93; check with your local authority.

3   SOCIAL SERVICES

(i)   Help for children

Social services departments can give financial assistance, or assistance in kind, to safeguard and promote the welfare of children in need.[39] A wide variety of needs may be met and can include things like food, clothing, nappies, fuel bills, contributions towards the cost of a holiday and help in the home. The definition of '**children in need**' is contained within the 1989 Children Act.[40] Policy on how families can be helped varies widely between different authorities. In Scotland, the power to give financial help to children and families is provided under Section 12 of the Social Work (Scotland) Act.

(ii)   Help for sick and disabled people

A local authority has the power to provide for chronically sick and disabled people:[41]
- [ ] practical assistance in the home – eg, a home-help;
- [ ] a radio, TV, library or 'similar recreational facilities', or help in obtaining them;
- [ ] lectures, games, outings or 'other recreational facilities' outside the home;
- [ ] help in taking advantage of educational opportunities;
- [ ] help with travelling to work or recreational facilities;
- [ ] help in carrying out adaptations to the home, or in providing extra facilities designed to give 'greater safety, comfort or convenience' (eg, a ramp or building an extra room on the ground floor);
- [ ] help in taking holidays (not necessarily at holiday homes or under official holiday schemes);
- [ ] meals, at home or elsewhere;
- [ ] a telephone, and any special equipment needed in using it, and/or financial help with getting one.

A local authority sets its own criteria for deciding whether you are in need of help. But once it has admitted that the need for a service under the Act exists, it has a duty to meet it.

It may decide to charge you for that service. However, the charge must be 'reasonable' and no more than you can be reasonably expected to pay, taking your income into account.[42] This means, for example, that a local authority cannot charge everyone a flat-rate for a service unless there is also some procedure for lowering or abolishing the charge for an individual.

If you need any of the items listed above, you should apply to the local authority social services department. If they refuse, ask for a reason. If you are refused on the ground that, although it recognises the need exists it does not have the resources to help you, complain to the Minister for the Disabled at the DSS, Richmond House, 79 Whitehall, London SW1A 2NS. Give full details of your needs and circumstances and, if possible, evidence of the local authority's acknowledgement that you need the service requested. The Minister can declare the local authority in default of its duty and issue instructions as to how it should carry out that duty.

Chapter 27

Other sources of help

This chapter covers:

1 Special funds for people with disabilities (p351)
2 Help from charities (p353)

1 SPECIAL FUNDS FOR PEOPLE WITH DISABILITIES

(i)   The Family Fund

This is a government fund administered by the Joseph Rowntree Memorial Trust. It exists to provide help in the form of goods, services or a grant of money to the families of children with severe disabilities.

Who can apply

Families with a child with a very severe disability can apply to this fund. The child must live in the UK and be under 16. Examples of very severe disabilities are the loss of two or more limbs and other serious deformities, severe mental retardation, the most serious forms of visual handicap or deafness and some multiple handicaps. You can claim if your child lives permanently in a residential home or hospital and needs limited and specific provision for existing expenses which have been refused by other sources of help.

What sort of help can be provided

The Fund has wide discretion to provide help that would relieve stress arising from the day-to-day care of the child. In general, it can only help with certain needs which are not met by statutory services. You cannot get help for a foster child who is in the care of the local authority. The following are *examples* of items it has helped with:

- ☐ hire cars, taxi fares, cars and driving lessons, so that a family can go on outings;
- ☐ washing machines and dryers;
- ☐ clothing, bedding and furnishing;
- ☐ aids and adaptations (but only in very limited circumstances);
- ☐ family holidays;
- ☐ recreation equipment.

These are only some examples and parents are encouraged to ask for any items that they feel they need.

How to apply

Application forms are available from the Family Fund, PO Box 50, York YO1 1UY. When you have returned the form, you will be visited by a representative of the fund.

General family circumstances are taken into account, but there is no income test. If your application is refused you can reapply, and if it is refused again you can apply to the Management Committee of the Fund.

(ii)   Help for people with HIV infection

The **Macfarlane Trust** administers three government funds established to help people with haemophilia and HIV infection. Payments are made in the form of both grants and regular payments for living expenses (particularly for diet and heating needs). The payments do not affect tax or social security benefits, nor do you have to declare the payments to the DSS for the purpose of a claim for any means-tested benefit. You apply by writing to: The Macfarlane Trust, PO Box 627, London SW1 0QG, or by telephoning 071-233-0342.

Local AIDS charities may be able to help people with HIV infection with one-off payments. There are also national groups that give cash grants to people with HIV infection. You can obtain details by contacting your local AIDS Helpline or Gay Switchboard. Their phone number and address will be in your local phone book.

(iii)   The Independent Living Fund

The Independent Living Fund – a special trust partly financed by the government – has been established to provide extra help for people with very severe physical or mental disabilities, on low incomes, who have to pay for personal care or domestic assistance (see below) in order to live in the community.

Payments from the Fund do not affect means-tested benefits.

Who can apply

You are eligible for help if:

☐   you are aged 16 or over; *and*

☐   *either*   you live alone;

      or   you live with another person(s) who, because of old age, ill health, disability, other responsibilities or the extent of your need for care, are unable to provide the amount of 'personal care' and 'domestic assistance' needed (see below). You may still get help even if you have a person living in with you providing support on a paid or voluntary basis; *and*

☐   you receive higher rate attendance allowance or constant attendance allowance of at least the same amount; *and*

☐   you (and your partner) have savings of less than £8,000; *and*

☐   you are severely disabled.

Personal care means help with those activities that a healthy person would normally be able to do for themselves – ie, dressing, eating, washing and bathing, getting in and out of bed, getting around the home etc.

Domestic assistance is help with household activities such as cleaning and tidying, cooking and preparing meals, washing-up, essential laundering and ironing, essential shopping etc.

How to apply

Contact The Independent Living Fund, PO Box 183, Nottingham NG8 3RD, tel: (0602) 290423, for an application form – ILF100.

(iv) Help from health authorities

Health authorities can provide facilities needed to prevent illness, or to care for people who are or have been ill, if the Secretary of State considers it appropriate as part of the health service.[1] Under this provision, the health authority has the power, for example, to provide a fridge if you do not have one and your consultant says you need one in which to store drugs.

2 HELP FROM CHARITIES

If you cannot get help from the state schemes, you could apply to a charity. Your local reference library should have details of charities.

Charities are extremely varied. But *all* charities have to adhere to the terms of their trust, and so there is no point in applying if you fall outside of these terms.

It is suggested that you approach charities in the following order:

☐ Local charities.

☐ Charities connected with specific illnesses or disabilities, with specific trades or occupations, or charities for ex-servicemen and women (this may include any-one who has done National Service).

☐ National or general charities.

Some charities have to be approached via a social worker. They usually ask people to submit a statement of their problems, and sometimes this has to be on a special form.

There are two groups of charities about which little information is available to the public. These are the religious charities and charities incorporated in the National Health Service. It may be worth asking a minister of religion or a medical social worker (based in hospitals) if they know of any charity which could help you.

APPENDIX 1: Useful addresses

The president of social security appeal tribunals and regional chairpersons

The President
HH Judge Derek Holden,
Clements House,
Gresham Street,
London EC2V 7DN
Tel: 071 606 2106

The President (Northern Ireland)
Mr C.G. MacLynn,
6th Floor,
3 Donegal Square North,
Belfast BT1 5GA
Tel: 0232 249577

Regional Chairpersons

North East
Mr J.W. Tinnion,
York House,
York Place,
Leeds LS1 2ED
Tel: 0532 451246

Midlands
Mr I.G. Harrison,
Chaddesden House,
77 Talbot Street,
Nottingham NG1 5JU
Tel: 0602 472942

South East
Mr R.P. Huggins,
19-30 Alfred Place,
London WC1 7LW
Tel: 071 580 3941

North West
Mr R.S. Sim,
4th Floor,
Port of Liverpool Building,
Pier Head,
Liverpool L3 1PJ
Tel: 051 236 4334

Wales and South West
Mr C.B. Stephens,
Oxford House,
Hills Street,
Cardiff CF1 2DR
Tel: 0222 378071

Scotland
Ms L.T. Parker,
200 West Regent Street,
Glasgow G2 4SS
Tel: 041 248 2442

Offices of the Social Security Commissioners

England and Wales
Harp House,
83 Farringdon Street,
London EC4A 4DH
Tel: 071 353 5145

Scotland
23 Melville Street,
Edinburgh EH3 7PW
Tel: 031 225 2201

Northern Ireland
Lancashire House,
5 Linenhall Street,
Belfast BT2 8AA
Tel: 0232 332344

Income support – 16/17-year-olds
Severe Hardship Claims Unit,
27 Cadogan Street,
Glasgow G2 7AO
Tel: 041 204 4717

DSS Solicitor
New Court,
Carey Street,
London WC2A 2LS
Tel: 071 412 1421

Agency Benefits Unit
Longbenton,
Newcastle-upon-Tyne
NE98 1YX
Tel: 091 213 5000

Disability Working Allowance Unit
Diadem House,
2 The Pavilion
Preston PR2 2GN
Tel 0772 883300

Family Credit Unit
Government Buildings,
Warbreck Hill Road,
Blackpool FY2 0AX
Tel: 0253 500050

Office of the Social Fund Inspectors,
4th Floor, Centre City
Podium,
5 Hill Street,
Birmingham B5 4UB
Tel: 021 631 4000

Offices of the Chief Adjudication Officer
Cumberland House,
15/17 Cumberland Place,
Southampton SO9 2DD
Tel: 0703 330066

6th Floor,
Priestly House,
Park Row,
Leeds LS1 5LA
Tel: 0532 467676

Local government ombudsman

England
21 Queen Anne's Gate,
London SW1H 9BU
Tel: 071 222 5622

Scotland
Princes House,
5 Shandwick Place,
Edinburgh EH2 4RE
Tel: 031 229 4472

Wales
Derwen House,
Court Road,
Bridgend CF31 1BN
Tel: 0656 661325

Northern Ireland
Progressive House,
33 Wellington Place,
Belfast BT1 6HN
Tel: 0232 233821

APPENDIX 2: Getting information and advice

Independent advice and representation

It is often difficult for unsupported individuals to get a positive response from the DSS. You may be taken more seriously if it is clear you have taken advice about your entitlement or have an adviser assisting you.

If you want advice or help with a benefit problem the following agencies may be able to assist:
- Citizens Advice Bureaux (CABx) and other local advice centres provide information and advice about benefits and may be able to represent you.
- Law Centres who can often help in a similar way to CABx/advice centres.
- Local authority welfare rights workers provide a service in many areas and some arrange advice sessions and take up campaigns locally.
- Local organisations for particular groups of claimants may offer help. For instance, there are Unemployed Centres, pensioners groups, centres for people with disabilities etc.
- Claimants Unions give advice in some areas. For details of your nearest group contact the Federation of Claimants Unions, 296 Bethnal Green Road, London E2 OAG.
- Some social workers and probation officers (but not all) help with benefit problems especially if they are already working with you on another problem.
- Solicitors can give free legal advice under the Green Form scheme (Pink Form in Scotland). This does not cover the cost of representation at an appeal hearing but can cover the cost of preparing written submissions and obtaining evidence such as medical reports. However, few solicitors have a good working knowledge of the benefit rules and you may need to shop around until you find one who does.

If you cannot find any of these agencies in the telephone book your local library should have details.

Unfortunately, CPAG is unable to deal with enquiries directly from members of the public but if you are an adviser you can phone the advice line which is open from 2.00 to 4.00 pm on Monday to Thursday – 071 253 6569. This is a special phone line; do not ring the main CPAG number. Alternatively, you can write to us at Citizens' Rights Office, CPAG, 4th Floor, 1-5 Bath Street, London EC1V 9PY. We can also take up a limited number of complex cases including appeals to the Social Security Commissioners or Courts if referred by an adviser.

Advice from the Benefits Agency
You can obtain free telephone advice on benefits on the following numbers. These are for general advice and not specific queries on individual claims.

English 0800 666 555
Urdu 0800 289 188
Chinese 0800 252 451

Punjabi 0800 521 360
Welsh 0800 289 011

Northern Ireland 0800 616 757
Disability Benefits 0800 822 200

APPENDIX 3: Books, leaflets and periodicals

Many of the books listed here will be in your main public library. HMSO books are available from the six HMSO bookshops but also from many others. They may be ordered by post, telephone or fax from HMSO Books, PO Box 276, London SW8 5DT (tel: 071-873 9090, fax: 071-873 8463). Enquiries to PC51D, HMSO Books, 51 Nine Elms Lane, London SW8 5DR (tel: 071-873 0011).

1 Textbooks
The Law of Social Security by A.I. Ogus and E.M. Barendt (Butterworths, 3rd edn, 1988). Standard textbook on social security law.

Claim in Time by M. Partington (Legal Action Group, 2nd edn, 1989). Detailed study of the rules on the time-limits for claiming benefits. Available from Legal Action Group, 242 Pentonville Road, London N1 9UN.

2 Case law and legislation

Social Security Case Law – Digest of Commissioners' Decisions by D. Neligan (HMSO, looseleaf in two volumes). Summaries of Commissioners' decisions grouped together by subject.

The Law Relating to Social Security (HMSO, looseleaf in ten volumes). All the legislation but without any comment. Known as the 'Blue Book'. Volumes 6, 7 and 8 deal with means-tested benefits.

CPAG's Income-Related Benefits: The Legislation by J. Mesher (Sweet & Maxwell, 1992 edn available from June, £34.95 (incl. Supplement) incl p&p from CPAG Ltd, 1-5 Bath Street, London EC1V 9PY). Contains the most useful legislation with a detailed commentary. Supplement available December. If the main work and supplement are both ordered from CPAG before 29 May 1992, the total price is reduced to £31.

CPAG's Housing Benefit and Community Charge Benefit Legislation by L. Findlay and M. Ward (Sweet & Maxwell, 1992 edn available June, £33.95 (incl. Supplement) incl p&p from CPAG Ltd, 1-5 Bath Street, London EC1V 9PY). Contains the main legislation with a detailed commentary. Supplement available December. If the main work and supplement are both ordered from CPAG before 29 May 1992, the total price is reduced to £29. The reduced price of just the main volume if ordered on the same conditions is £23.

Medical and Disability Appeal Tribunals Legislation by Mark Rowland (Sweet & Maxwell), 1st edn, 1992, available from CPAG, £28 incl. p&p.

3 Official guidance

Adjudication Officers' Guide (HMSO, looseleaf in ten volumes). Volumes 3 and 4 deal with means-tested benefits.

Housing Benefit and Community Charge Benefit Guidance Manual (HMSO, looseleaf in one volume).

Income Support Manual (HMSO, looseleaf in one volume). Procedural guide issued to Benefits Agency staff.

The Social Fund Officer's Guide (HMSO, looseleaf, two volumes).

The Social Fund Administration Guide (HMSO, looseleaf, one volume).

The Social Fund Maternity and Funeral Payments Guide (HMSO, looseleaf, one volume).

The Social Fund Cold Weather Payments Handbook (HMSO, looseleaf, one volume).

4 Tribunal handbooks

Social Security Appeal Tribunals: A Guide to Procedure (HMSO).

5 Leaflets

The Benefits Agency publishes many leaflets which cover particular benefits or particular groups of claimants or contributors. They have been greatly improved in recent years and the bigger ones extend to 48-page booklets. They are free from your local Benefits Agency office or from either Benefits Agency Information Division, Leaflets Unit, Block 4, Government Buildings, Honeypot Lane, Stanmore HA7 1AY, or ISCO5, DSS, The Paddocks, Frizinghall, Bradford BD9 4HD. To put your name on the mailing list for new leaflets write to Social Security Mailing List, Room 607, Benefits Agency, Ray House, St. Andrew's Street, London EC4A 3AD. Free leaflets on HB/CCB are available from the relevant department of your local council.

6 Periodicals

The *Welfare Rights Bulletin* is published every two months by CPAG. It covers developments in social security law and updates this *Handbook* between editions. The annual subscription is £12 but it is sent automatically to CPAG Rights and Comprehensive Members.

7 Other publications – general

Rights Guide to Non-Means-Tested Benefits, £5.95 (£2.25 for claimants).

Guide to Housing Benefit and Community Charge Benefit, £7.95.

Disability Rights Handbook, £7.95

Rights Guide for Homeowners, £6.95.

Fuel Rights Handbook, £6.95.

These are available from CPAG Ltd, 4th Floor, 1-5 Bath Street, London EC1V 9PY. Prices include p&p.

APPENDIX 4: ABBREVIATIONS USED IN THE NOTES

Art(s)	Article(s)	RSC	Rules of the Supreme Court
CA	Court of Appeal	s	Section
CMLR	Common Market Law Reports	ss	Sections
ECR	European Court Reports	Sch	Schedule
para	paragraph	SF Dir	Social Fund Direction
reg	regulation	SFI Dir	Social Fund Inspectors' Direction

Acts of Parliament

CA 1989	Children's Act 1989	HSS&SSA Act 1983	Health and Social Services and Social Security Adjudication Act 1983
CBA 1975	Child Benefit Act 1975		
CC Act 1980	Child Care Act 1980		
CSDP Act 1976	Chronically Sick and Disabled Persons Act 1976	LAA 1988	Legal Aid Act 1988
		LGHA 1989	Local Government and Housing Act 1989
DWAA 1991	Disability Living Allowance and Disability Working Allowance Act 1991	NHS Act 1977	National Health Service Act 1977
EA 1944	Education Act 1944	SSA 1975	Social Security Act 1975
EA 1962	Education Act 1962	SSA 1980	Social Security Act 1980
EA 1980	Education Act 1980	SSA 1986	Social Security Act 1986
E(MP) Act 1948	Education (Miscellaneous Provisions) Act 1948	SW(S) Act 1968	Social Work (Scotland Act) 1968
ERA 1988	Education Reform Act 1988	SS(C&B)A	Social Security Contributions and Benefits Act 1992
		SS(A)A 1992	Social Security Administration Act 1992

Regulations

Each set of regulations has a statutory instrument (SI) number and a date. You ask for them by giving their date and number.

CCB Regs	The Community Charge Benefit (General) Regulations 1989 No.1321
CC(DIS) Regs	Community Charge (Deductions from Income Support) Regulations 1990 No.107
CB Regs	The Child Benefit (General) Regulations 1976 No.965
DWA Regs	The Disability Working Allowance (General) Regulations 1991 No. 2887
FC Regs	The Family Credit (General) Regulations 1987 No.1973
HB Regs	The Housing Benefit (General) Regulations 1987 No.1971
HRG(RG) Regs	The Housing Renovation Grants (Reduction of Grant) Regulations 1990 No.1189
IS Regs	The Income Support (General) Regulations 1987 No.1967
IS (Amdt 4) Regs	The Income Support (General) Regulations Amendment No 4 1991 No 1559
IS(Amdt 6) Regs	The Income Support (General) Regulations Amendment No 6 1991 No 2334
IS(LR) Regs	The Income Support (Liable Relatives) Regulations 1990 No.1777
IS(Trans) Regs	The Income Support (Transitional) Regulations 1987 No.1969
IS(Trans) Regs 1988	The Income Support (Transitional) Regulations 1988 No.1229
NHS(CDA) Regs	The National Health Service (Charges for Drugs and Appliances) Regulations 1980 No.1503
NHS(GOS) Regs	The National Health Service (General Ophthalmic Services) Regulations 1986 No.975
NHS(OC&P) Regs	The National Health Service (Optical Charges and Payments) Regulations 1989 No.396
NHS(TE&RC) Regs	The National Health Service (Travelling Expenses and Remission of Charges) Regulations 1988 No.551
SB(C&P) Regs	The Supplementary Benefit (Claims & Payments) Regulations 1981 No.1525

SF(App) Regs	The Social Fund (Applications) Regulations 1988 No.524
SF(AR) Regs	The Social Fund (Application for Review) Regulations 1988 No.34
SFCWP Regs	The Social Fund Cold Weather Payments (General) Regulations 1988 No.1724
SFM&FE Regs	The Social Fund Maternity and Funeral Expenses (General) Regulations 1987 No.481
SF (Misc) Regs	The Social Fund (Miscellaneous Provisions) Regulations 1990 No. 1788
SF(RDB) Regs	The Social Fund (Recovery by Deductions from Benefits) Regulations 1988 No.35
SOB Regs	The Scholarship and Other Benefits Regulations 1977 No.1443
SS(AA) No 2 Regs	The Social Security (Attendance Allowance) (No.2) Regulations 1975 No.598
SS(Adj) Regs	The Social Security (Adjudication) Regulations 1986 No.2218
SSCP Regs	The Social Security Commissioners Procedure Regulations 1987 No.214
SS(C&P) Regs	The Social Security (Claims and Payments) Regulations 1987 No.1968
SS(ICA) Regs	The Social Security (Invalid Care Allowance) Regulations 1976 No.409
SS(PAOR) Regs	The Social Security (Payments on Account, Overpayments and Recovery) Regulations 1988 No.664
SS(SDA) Regs	The Social Security (Severe Disablement Allowance) Regulations 1984 No.1303
SS(US&IB) Regs	The Social Security (Unemployment, Sickness and Invalidity Benefit) Regulations 1983 No.1598
SS(WB&RP) Regs	The Social Security (Widow's Benefit and Retirement Pensions) Regulations 1979 No.642
WF Regs	The Welfare Foods Regulations 1988 No.536

Other Information

AOG	The *Adjudication Officers Guide* (see Appendix 3).
Circular ES	Employment Service circulars.
Circular IS	Circulars are issued to DSS officers which update and give information additional to that contained in the *Adjudication Officers Guide*.
SF Dir	Direction on the discretionary social fund. They are printed in the *Social Fund Officer's Guide* and Mesher (see Appendix 3).
GM	The *Housing Benefit and Community Charge Benefit Guidance Manual* (see Appendix 3).
IS Manual	This is a largely procedural guide to the implementation of income support, which is issued to adjudication officers/DSS staff (see Appendix 3).
SFOG	*The Social Fund Officer's Guide* (see Appendix 3)
SFAG	*The Social Fund Administration Guide* (see Appendix 3).
SFMFG	*The Social Fund Maternity and Funeral Payments Guide* (see Appendix 3)
CWPH	*The Social Fund Cold Weather Payments Handbook*

References like CIS/142/1990 and R(SB) 3/89 are references to Commissioners' decisions (see p123).

NOTES

References are to the statutes and regulations as amended up to 1 April 1992. All regulations are (General) Regulations unless otherwise stated. There is a full list of abbreviations in Appendix 4.

References in square brackets (following references to sections of Acts) are to the equivalent sections in the consolidating Acts: the Social Security (Contributions and Benefits) Act 1992 and the Social Security (Administration) Act 1992. These come into effect on 1 July 1992.

PART II: INCOME SUPPORT
Chapter 2: The basic rules of entitlement
(pp7-19)
1 s20(3)(a) SSA 1986 [s124(1)(a) SS(C&B)A]
2 Reg 5(1) IS Regs
3 Reg 5(7) IS Regs
4 Reg 5(2) IS Regs
5 Reg 5(3) IS Regs
6 Reg 5(5) IS Regs
7 Reg 5(4) IS Regs
8 Reg 6 IS Regs
9 Regs 22-24 IS Amdt No 4 Regs
10 Reg 12 IS Regs; s2 CBA 1975 (s142 SS(C&B)A) and reg 5(2) CB Regs
11 s20(3)(d)(ii) SSA 1986 [s124(1)(d)(ii) SS(C&B)A]
12 Reg 13 IS Regs
13 R(SB) 2/87
14 Reg 12 IS Regs and reg 7 CB Regs
15 Reg 7(5) and (6) CB Regs
16 Reg 61 IS Regs
17 Reg 61 IS Regs
18 R(SB) 40/83; R(SB) 41/83
19 Reg 10(1)(h) IS Regs
20 Reg 9(1)(c),(2),(3) and (4) IS Regs
21 Reg 9(1)(c) IS Regs
22 Reg 9(1)(c) IS Regs
23 s20(3)(d) SSA 1986 [s124(1)(d) SS(C&B)A]
24 Reg 7(1)(c) IS Regs
25 Reg 8(1) and Sch 1 IS Regs
26 Regs 8(2) and (3), and 22(5) IS Regs
27 Sch 1 para 7B(1)(a) and (b), and (2) IS Regs
28 Reg 8(3) IS Regs
29 Reg 22(5) IS Regs

30 Reg 8(3) IS Regs
31 Reg 4(1) and (2)(a) and (b) IS Regs
32 Reg 4(2)(c) and (3) IS Regs
33 Sch 1 para 23 IS Regs

Chapter 3: How your benefit is calculated
(pp20-37)

2 Housing costs
(pp22-31)
1 Sch 3 para 1 IS Regs
2 R(IS) 3/91; R(IS) 4/91
3 CIS/157/1989
4 CIS/4/1988
5 R(SB) 3/87
6 Sch 3 para 5(a) IS Regs
7 Sch 3 para 9(5) IS Regs
8 Sch 3 para 9(2)(a) IS Regs
9 Sch 3 para 9(2)(b) IS Regs
10 Sch 3 para 9(2)(c) IS Regs
11 Sch 3 para 2 IS Regs; R(SB) 7/86
12 s84(1) SSA 1986 [s137(1) SS(C&B)A]; reg 2(1) IS Regs meaning of 'dwelling occupied as the home'
13 CSB/213/1987
14 Sch 3 para 3 IS Regs
15 Sch 3 para 3(1)(b) IS Regs
16 Sch 3 para 9(4) IS Regs
17 Sch 3 para 4(6)(a) IS Regs
18 Sch 3 para 4(6)(b) IS Regs
19 Sch 3 para 4(3) IS Regs
20 Sch 3 para 4(6)(c) IS Regs
21 Sch 3 para 4(5) IS Regs
22 Sch 3 para 4(7) IS Regs
23 Sch 3 para 4(7)(b) IS Regs
24 R(SB) 7/86
25 Sch 3 para 4(8) IS Regs
26 Sch 3 para 4(4) IS Regs

27 Sch 3 para 7(3) and (3A) IS Regs
28 R(SB) 46/83
29 Sch 3 para 7(4) and (4A) IS Regs
30 Sch 3 para 7(4B) IS Regs
31 Sch 3 para 7(4C) IS Regs
32 Sch 3 paras 1(a), (aa) and (b), 7(3) and (3A), and 8 IS Regs
33 Sch 3 para 7(3) IS Regs
34 Sch 3 para 3(1)(b) IS Regs
35 Sch 3 para 7(7) IS Regs
36 Sch 3 para 7(6) IS Regs; CSB/467/1983
37 Sch 3 para 7(6) and (6A) IS Regs
38 Sch 3 para 7(1)(a) IS Regs
39 Sch 3 para 7(1)(b) IS Regs
40 Sch 3 para 7(9) IS Regs
41 Sch 3 para 7(10) IS Regs
42 Reg 3A IS Regs
43 Sch 3 para 7(11) IS Regs
44 Sch 3 para 7(2) IS Regs
45 Sch 9 para 29 IS Regs
46 Sch 3 para 7(1)(b) IS Regs
47 Sch 3 para 7(6) IS Regs
48 Department of Environment Guidance: 1) Circular 78/77 Housing for One Parent Families; 2) Code of Guidance on Part III Housing Act 1985
49 Regs 42(4)(a)(ii) and 51(3)(a)(ii) IS Regs
50 Reg 54 IS Regs
51 Sch 9 para 29 IS Regs
52 Sch 3 para 8(1) IS Regs
53 Sch 3 para 8(3) IS Regs
54 para 27787 AOG
55 CSB/420/1985
56 Sch 3 para 6(1), (1A), (1B) and (1C) IS Regs
57 Reg 3 IS Regs
58 CSB/1163/1988
59 Reg 3(4) and (5) IS Regs

60   Sch 3 para 11(1) and (7) IS
     Regs
61   Sch 3 para 11(6) IS Regs
62   Sch 3 para 11(1), (2) and (8)
     IS Regs
63   Reg 5(3) IS Regs
64   Sch 3 para 11(3) and (4) IS
     Regs
65   Sch 3 para 11(5) IS Regs
66   Sch 3 para 10(3) and (4) IS
     Regs
67   Sch 3 para 10(4) IS Regs
68   R(SB)12/91
69   Sch 3 para 10(5) and (7) IS
     Regs
70   CSB/420/1981
71   CSB/617/1988
72   R(SB) 7/89
73   Sch 3 para 10(6) IS Regs
74   R(IS) 9/91
75   Sch 3 para 10(1) IS Regs
76   Sch 3 para 6(2) IS Regs
77   Sch 3 para 10(2) IS Regs
78   Sch 3 para 10(2)(a) IS Regs

3 Transitional protection
(pp31-35)
79   IS(Trans) Regs
80   Reg 17(2)-(7) IS Regs
81   Reg 17(1)(g) and Sch 3A IS
     Regs
82   Reg 17(1)(g) and Sch 3B IS
     Regs
83   IS(Trans) Regs 1988
84   Reg 69(1) SS(Adj) Regs; s52
     and Sch 7 para 4(1) SSA
     1986 (s186 and Sch 10
     SS(A)A)
85   Reg 5(2) SB(C&P) Regs
     saved by reg 12 SS(C&P)
     Amendment Regs
86   Reg 16 IS(Trans) Regs
87   Reg 10(1) IS(Trans) Regs
88   Reg 9 IS(Trans) Regs
89   Reg 10(2) IS(Trans) Regs
90   Reg 2 IS(Trans) Regs
91   Reg 14(2) IS(Trans) Regs
92   Reg 14(1) IS(Trans) Regs
93   Reg 14(1A)-(1G) IS(Trans)
     Regs
94   CSIS/30/1989
95   Reg 14(3)-(4A) IS(Trans)
     Regs
96   Reg 10(3)-(5) IS(Trans) Regs
97   Reg 15 IS(Trans) Regs
98   Reg 17(2) and (3) IS Regs
99   Reg 17(4)-(7) IS Regs
100 Reg 17(6) and (6A) IS Regs

4 Urgent cases payments
(pp35-37)
101 Reg 70(2) IS Regs
102 Reg 70(4) IS Regs
103 Reg 8(3) IS Regs
104 Reg 71(1)(a) IS Regs
105 Reg 71(1)(b) and (c) IS Regs

106 Reg 72(1) IS Regs
107 Reg 72(1)(c) IS Regs
108 Reg 72(2) IS Regs

Chapter 4: The unemployed and people on government training schemes
(pp38-51)
1   s20(3)(d) SSA 1986
     [s124(1)(d)(i) SS(C&B)A]
2   Reg 11 IS Regs
3   s17(1)(a) SSA 1975
     [s57(1)(a)]; reg 9(1) IS Regs
     and reg 7(1)(a) SS(US&IB)
     Regs
4   CSB/975/1989
5   Reg 7(1) IS Regs
6   Regs 9, 10, 11 and 12
     SS(US&IB) Regs
7   Reg 7(1)(a) SS(US&IB) Regs
     and reg 10(1)(d) IS Regs
8   Reg 10(6) IS Regs
9   Reg 10(1)(d) IS Regs
10   Reg 10(4) and (5) IS Regs
11   Reg 9(1)(b) IS Regs
12   Reg 7(c) IS Regs
13   Reg 10(1) IS Regs
14   R(U) 1/82
15   Reg 10(2) IS Regs
16   Reg 10(1)(a) IS Regs
17   Reg 12E SS(US&IB) Regs
18   R(U) 20/60; R(U) 5/71; R(U)
     2/77
19   R(U) 10/61; R(U) 15/62
20   Reg 10(1)(e) IS Regs
21   Reg 64(1) SS(Adj) Regs
22   para 25300 AOG
23   Reg 10A(3) IS Regs
24   Reg 12B SS(US&IB) Regs;
     reg 10A(3) IS Regs
25   Reg 10A(4) IS Regs; reg 12D
     SS(US&IB) Regs
26   Reg 7(2) IS Regs
27   Reg 5(1) IS Regs
28   Reg 35(1) IS Regs
29   Reg 22(6) IS Regs
30   Reg 22(4)(c)(iii) IS Regs
31   s20 SSA 1975
     [s28 SS(C&B)A]
32   Reg 12G SS(US&IB) Regs
33   Reg 12E SS(US&IB) Regs
34   s20 SSA 1975
     [s28 SS(C&B)A and reg
     22(4)(c) IS Regs]
35   s20(1) SSA 1975
     [s28(1) SS(C&B)A]
     and reg 22(4)(c) IS Regs
36   Reg 22(6) IS Regs
37   Reg 21A IS Regs
38   Reg 22(1)(a) and (b), (4)(c),
     and (6) IS Regs
39   Reg 22(2) IS Regs
40   Sch 1 para 11 IS Regs
41   Reg 2(1) and Sch 1A Part II
     IS Regs

42   s2(1)(aa) CBA 1975
     [s142(1)(b) SS(C&B)A]; reg
     7D CB Regs
43   s20(1) SSA 1975
     [s28 SS(C&B)A] and reg
     22(4)(c) IS Regs
44   Sch 2 para 12(5) IS Regs
45   Sch 9 para 13(a) and (b) IS
     Regs
46   Sch 9 para 13(b) IS Regs
47   Sch 9 para 13(c) IS Regs; Sch
     2 para 11 FC Regs; Sch 4 para
     11 HB Regs; Sch 3 para 11
     CCB Regs
48   Reg 36(2) and Sch 8 paras
     1-13 IS Regs
49   Sch 9 para 13(a) and (b) IS
     Regs; Sch 2 para 11(c) FC
     Regs; Sch 4 para 11(c) HB
     Regs; Sch 3 para 11(c) CCB
     Regs
50   Sch 10 para 30 IS Regs
51   Sch 3 para 32 FC Regs; Sch 5
     para 33 HB Regs; Sch 4 para
     33 CCB Regs

Chapter 5: Special rules for special groups
(pp52-86)

1 16/17-year-olds
(pp52-58)
1   Sch 1A IS Regs
2   Sch 1A para 1 IS Regs
3   Sch 1A para 3 IS Regs
4   Sch 1A para 2 IS Regs
5   Sch 1A para 4 IS Regs
6   Reg 7D(2)(b) CB Regs
7   Reg 2(1) and Sch 1A Part II IS
     Regs
8   Reg 13A(4)-(6) IS Regs
9   s20(4A) SSA 1986
     [s125(1) SS(C&B)A]
10   Annex B to Letters to LO
     Managers 27/11/89 RD Tech
     110/89
11   RD Tech 10/91
12   s20(4C) and (4D) SSA 1986
     [s125(3) SS(C&B)A]
13   s20(4E) SSA 1986
     [s72(1) SS(A)A]
14   Sch 2 para 1(1)(a), (b) and (c)
     and (2)(a), (b) and (c) IS Regs
15   Sch 2 para 1(1)(b) and (c), and
     (2)(b) and (c) IS Regs
16   Sch 2 para 1(3) IS Regs
17   s25(3) ERA 1988
18   sA3 Dept of Employment
     Guide 13 (M22 107/0488)
     YTS Bridging Allowances

2 People affected by a trade dispute
(pp58-62)
19   s19 SSA 1975 [s27 SS(C&B)A]

157 Sch 7 para 13(1)(a) IS Regs
158 Sch 7 para 13(1)(c) IS Regs
159 Sch 7 para (13)2 IS Regs
160 Reg 16(3)(e) IS Regs
161 Sch 7 para 13(1)(d) IS Regs
162 Regs 4 and 5 SS(AA) No 2 Regs
163 Sch 7 paras 6(2A), 7(2) and (3)(c) SS(C&P) Regs

6 People in hospital

(pp82-85)
164 Sch 3 paras 2 and 4(8)(c) IS Regs
165 Reg 16(2) IS Regs
166 Sch 2 para 13(3A) IS Regs
167 Sch 7 para 1 IS Regs
168 s37(2) SSA 1975 [s70(2) SS(C&B)A]; Sch 2 para 14ZA IS Regs
169 Sch 7 para 1(a) IS Regs
170 Sch 7 para 2(b) IS Regs
171 Sch 7 para 2(a) IS Regs
172 Sch 2 para 13(3A) IS Regs
173 Sch 7 para 1 IS Regs
174 s37(2) SSA 1975 [s70(2) SS(C&B)A]; Sch 2 para 14ZA IS Regs
175 Sch 7 para 1(b) IS Regs
176 s37(2) SSA 1975 [s70 SS(C&B)A]; Sch 2 para 14ZA IS Regs
177 Reg 4(1) and (2) SS(ICA) Regs; Sch 2 para 14ZA IS Regs
178 Sch 7 para 1(c)(i) and Sch 2 para 12(1)(c)(ii) IS Regs
179 Reg 16(2) and Sch 3 para 4(8) IS Regs
180 Sch 7 para 2 IS Regs
181 Reg 16(2) and Sch 7 para 1(b) IS Regs
182 Sch 7 para 3 IS Regs
183 Sch 2 para 14(b) IS Regs
184 Sch 7 para 18(a) IS Regs
185 Sch 7 para 18(b) and (c) IS Regs
186 Sch 7 para 18(b)(i) and (iv) 1st case IS Regs
187 Sch 7 para 18(b)(ii) 2nd case and (b)(iv) 3rd case IS Regs
188 Sch 7 para 2A IS Regs
189 Sch 7 para 7(1) SS(C&P) Regs
190 Reg 21(2) IS Regs
191 Sch 7 para 7(3)(d) SS(C&P) Regs
192 Sch 7 para 7(4A) SS(C&P) Regs; R(S) 4/84

7 Prisoners

(pp85-86)
193 Reg 21(3) IS Regs
194 Sch 7 para 8 IS Regs
195 Reg 16(3)(b) IS Regs

196 Reg 16(5)(f) IS Regs
197 Sch 7 para 8(b) IS Regs
198 See *R v Housing Benefit Review Board ex parte Robertson* 1988
199 Reg 48(7) IS Regs
200 Sch 1 para 18 IS Regs

8 People without accommodation

(p86)
201 Sch 7 para 6 IS Regs
202 para 5404 IS Manual
203 para 28503 AOG
204 para 5.407 IS Manual

Chapter 6: Maintenance payments

(pp87-99)
1 Reg 54 IS Regs
2 *Shallow v Shallow* (1979) Fam 1 (CA)
3 *Allen v Allen* (1986) 2 FLR 265 (CA)
4 *Shallow v Shallow* (1979) Fam 1 (CA)
5 *Williams v Williams* (1974) Fam 55 (DC)
6 Reg 54 IS Regs
7 Regs 54 and 55 and Sch 9 IS Regs
8 Reg 58 IS Regs
9 Reg 58(4) IS Regs
10 Reg 59(1) IS Regs
11 s27(1) SSA 1986 [s74(1) SS(A)A]; reg 7(1) SS(PAOR) Regs
12 Reg 54 IS Regs
13 *Regina v West London Supplementary Benefit Appeal Tribunal ex parte Taylor* [1975] 1 WLR 1048 (DC); *McCorquodale v Chief Adjudication Officer* (CA) reported as an appendix to R(SB) 1/88
14 Regs 54, 55, 60(1) IS Regs
15 Reg 60(2) IS Regs
16 CSB/1160/1986; R(SB) 1/89
17 R(SB) 1/89
18 Reg 57(1) IS Regs
19 Reg 57 IS Regs
20 Regs 57(4) and 59(2) IS Regs
21 s26(3) SSA 1986 [s105(3) SS(A)A]
22 s24B SSA 1986 [s108 SS(A)A]
23 s24B(5) SSA 1986 [s108(5) SS(A)A]; Reg 3 IS(LR) Regs
24 s24 SSA 1986 [s106 SS(A)A]
25 *National Assistance Board v Parkes* [1955] 2 QB 506
26 *National Assistance Board v*

Parkes [1955] 2 QB 506; *Hulley v Thompson* [1981] 1 WLR 159
27 s24(4) SSA 1986 [s106(2) SS(A)A]
28 s24A SSA 1986 [s107 SS(A)A]; reg 2 IS(LR) Regs
29 s24A(3) SSA 1986 [s107(3) SS(A)A]
30 s26(1) SSA 1986 [s105(1) SS(A)A]

Chapter 7: Claims, reviews and getting paid

(pp100-117)

1 Claims

(pp100-103)
1 Reg 4(3) SS(C&P) Regs
2 Reg 4(4) SS(C&P) Regs
3 Reg 33 SS(C&P) Regs
4 R(SB) 5/90
5 Reg 4(1) SS(C&P) Regs
6 Reg 4(5) SS(C&P) Regs
7 Reg 4(7) SS(C&P) Regs
8 Reg 4(7) SS(C&P) Regs
9 Reg 5(1) SS(C&P) Regs
10 Reg 5(2) SS(C&P) Regs
11 Reg 7(1) SS(C&P) Regs
12 R(SB) 29/83
13 Reg 7(2) SS(C&P) Regs
14 Reg 32(1) SS(C&P) Regs
15 Reg 6(1) SS(C&P) Regs
16 R(SB) 8/89
17 Reg 13(1) SS(C&P) Regs
18 Reg 19(1) and Sch 4 para 6 SS(C&P) Regs
19 Reg 19(3) SS(C&P) Regs
20 Reg 19(2) and (2A) SS(C&P) Regs
21 Reg 19(4) SS(C&P) Regs
22 s165D SSA 1975 [s68 SS(A)A]
23 R(SB) 9/84
24 CS/371/1949
25 R(P) 1/79
26 R(I) 28/54
27 R(SB) 6/83
28 CS/50/1950
29 R(U) 9/74
30 R(U) 35/56
31 R(S) 5/56
32 R(S) 14/54; R(G) 4/68; R(U) 9/74
33 R(S) 14/54
34 R(S) 11/59; R(G) 1/75
35 R(S) 10/59; R(S) 3/69; R(SB) 17/83
36 R(SB) 6/83
37 R(G) 2/74
38 R(SB) 17/83
39 R(P) 2/85
40 Reg 19(2) SS(C&P) Regs

2 Decisions and reviews

(pp103-106)
41 ss98 and 99 SSA 1975
   [s20 and 21 SS(A)A]
42 Reg 64 SS(Adj) Regs
43 Reg 63(1) SS(Adj) Regs
44 Reg 63(7) SS(Adj) Regs
45 Reg 63(5) SS(Adj) Regs
46 s99(1) SSA 1975
   [s21(1) SS(A)A]
47 *R v Secretary of State for
   Social Services ex parte
   CPAG and others*, [1989] 1
   All ER 1047 (HC) (CA)
48 s104(1) SSA 1975
   [s25(1) SS(A)A]
49 Sch 7 para 7 SS(C&P) Regs
50 Reg 69(5) and Reg 69A
   SS(Adj)
51 Reg 69(1) SS(Adj) Regs
52 Reg 64A SS(Adj) Regs
53 *Saker v Secretary of State for
   Social Services*; R(I) 2/88
54 s104(7)-(10) SSA 1975 [s69
   SS(A)A] and reg 64B
   SS(Adj) Regs

3 Payments of benefit

(pp106-112)
55 Reg 20 SS(C&P) Regs
56 para 2.902 IS Manual
57 Reg 38(1) SS(C&P) Regs
58 Reg 38(2A) SS(C&P) Regs
59 Reg 26(4) SS(C&P) Regs
60 Sch 7 para 5 SS(C&P) Regs
61 Reg 28 SS(C&P) Regs
62 Reg 26(1) and Sch 7
   SS(C&P) Regs
63 Sch 7 para 1 SS(C&P) Regs
64 Sch 7 para 6(1) SS(C&P) Regs
65 Sch 7 para 3 SS(C&P) Regs
66 Sch 7 para 3 SS(C&P) Regs
67 Reg 4 SS(PAOR) Regs
68 Reg 2 SS(PAOR) Regs
69 Reg 4 SS(PAOR) Regs
70 Regs 37, 37A and 37B
   SS(C&P) Regs
71 *Walsh v Department of Social
   Security*, Bromley County
   Court, 12 February 1990.
   Not reported – see *Bulletin 96*
72 Reg 33 SS(C&P) Regs
73 Reg 34 SS(C&P) Regs
74 Reg 35 SS(C&P) Regs
75 Sch 9 para 2 SS(C&P) Regs
76 Sch 9 para 5(1) SS(C&P)
   Regs
77 Sch 9 para 5(2) SS(C&P)
   Regs
78 Sch 9 para 5(3) SS(C&P)
   Regs
79 Sch 9 para 5(4) SS(C&P)
   Regs
80 Sch 9 para 5(1)(c) SS(C&P)
   Regs

81 Sch 9 para 5(1)(c)(ii)
   SS(C&P) Regs
82 Sch 9 para 5(1)(c)(i)
   SS(C&P) Regs
83 Sch 9 para 3 SS(C&P) Regs
84 Sch 9 para 1 SS(C&P) Regs
85 Sch 9 para 3(4) SS(C&P)
   Regs
86 Sch 9 para 4 SS(C&P) Regs
87 Sch 9 para 4(1) SS(C&P)
   Regs
88 Sch 9 para 7 SS(C&P) Regs
89 Sch 9 para 1 SS(C&P) Regs
90 Sch 9 para 7(1) SS(C&P)
   Regs
91 Sch 9 para 7(2) SS(C&P)
   Regs
92 Sch 9 para 7(7) SS(C&P)
   Regs
93 Sch 9 para 6 SS(C&P) Regs
94 Sch 9 para 6(1) SS(C&P)
   Regs
95 Sch 9 para 6(4) SS(C&P)
   Regs
96 CC(DIS) Regs
97 Sch 9 para 4A SS(C&P) Regs
98 Sch 9 para 5(6) SS(C&P)
   Regs
99 Sch 9 para 3(2) SS(C&P)
   Regs
100 Sch 9 para 6(2) SS(C&P)
   Regs
101 Reg 2 CC(DIS) Regs
102 Sch 9 para 7(3)-(6) SS(C&P)
   Regs
103 Sch 9 para 8(1) SS(C&P)
   Regs
104 Sch 9 paras 6(6), 7(8) and
   5(5) SS(C&P) Regs
105 Sch 9 para 4(2) SS(C&P)
   Regs
106 Sch 9 para 4A(3) and (4)
   SS(C&P) Regs
107 Sch 9 para 1 and 2(2)
   SS(C&P) Regs
108 Reg 2 CC(DIS) Regs
109 Sch 9 para 9 SS(C&P) Regs;
   reg 2 CC(DIS) Regs
110 Regs 15 and 16 SS(PAOR)
   Regs; reg 3 SF(RDB) Regs

4 Overpayment and fraud

(pp112-117)
111 R(SB) 2/91
112 s27 SSA 1986 [s74 SS(A)A]
113 s53 SSA 1986 [s71 SS(A)A]
114 s53(4) SSA 1986 [s71(5)
   SS(A)A]
115 CSSB/621/1988 and
   CSB/316/1989
116 CSB/688/1982
117 *Page v Chief Adjudication
   Officer (CA)*, *The Times*, 4
   July 1991
118 R(SB) 9/85

119 R(SB) 3/90
120 R(SB) 21/82; R(SB) 28/83;
   R(SB) 54/83
121 Reg 32(1) SS(C&P) Regs
122 CSB/688/1982; R(SB) 12/84;
   R(SB) 20/84; R(SB) 40/84
123 R(SB) 18/85
124 CWSB/2/1985
125 CSB/347/1983
126 R(SB) 33/85
127 R(SB) 54/83
128 CSB/393/1985
129 R(SB) 36/84; R(SB) 54/83;
   R(SB) 2/91
130 CIS/159/1990
131 R(SB) 20/84; R(SB) 24/87
132 Reg 13 SS(PAOR) Regs
133 *Commock v Chief
   Adjudication Officer* reported
   as appendix to R(SB) 6/90
134 Regs 15 and 16(3) SS(PAOR)
   Regs
135 Reg 14 SS(PAOR) Regs
136 Reg 15 SS(PAOR) Regs
137 s27(2)(b) SSA 1986
   [s74(2)(b) SS(A)A]
138 Reg 16(3) SS(PAOR) Regs
139 Reg 16(4), (5) and (6)
   SS(PAOR) Regs
140 Reg 16(6) SS(PAOR) Regs
141 Reg 17 SS(PAOR) Regs
142 *Secretary of State for Social
   Services v Solly* [1974] 3 All
   ER 922; R(SB) 21/82
143 s55 SSA 1986 [s112 SS(A)A]
144 s56 SSA 1986 [s116 SS(A)A]

Chapter 8: Appeals

(pp118-127)
1 s100 SSA 1975 [s22 SS(A)A]
   and R(IS) 7/91
2 R(SB) 29/83; R(SB) 12/89
3 Reg 63(7) SS(Adj) Regs
4 Reg 3 and Sch 2 SS(Adj)
5 Reg 3(3) SS(Adj) Regs
6 R(SB) 24/82
7 R(SB) 18/83 para 10
8 Reg 6(2) SS(Adj) Regs
9 Reg 2(1)(b) SS(Adj) Regs
10 para 38(1) *Social Security
   Appeal Tribunals: A guide to
   procedure*, HMSO
11 Reg 4(2) SS(Adj) Regs
12 Reg 4(4) SS(Adj) Regs
13 Sch 10 para 1(2) and (8) SSA
   1975 [s41 SS(A)A]
14 Regs 24(2) and 25(1) SS(Adj)
   Regs
15 Reg 25(2) SS(Adj) Regs
16 Sch 10 para 3 SSA 1975 (Sch
   2 para 7 SS(A)A)
17 Reg 24(3) SS(Adj) Regs
18 Reg 25(2) SS(Adj) Regs
19 Reg 11 SS(Adj) Regs

20 R(SB) 4/90
21 CSB/172/1990
22 Reg 10 SS(Adj) Regs
23 R(SB) 33/85; R(SB) 12/89
24 R(SB) 10/86
25 R(IS) 6/91
26 R(SB) 1/81
27 R(SB) 6/82
28 s102 SSA 1975 [s36
    SS(A)A];
    R(SB) 1/82; R(FIS) 1/82
29 Reg 5 SS(Adj) Regs
30 s20(2) SSA 1986 [s123(2)
    SS(C&B)A]
31 s97(1C) SSA 1975 [s39(2)
    SS(A)A]
32 s101 SSA 1975 [s23 SS(A)A]
33 R(I) 12/75
34 s101 SSA 1975 [s23 SS(A)A]
35 R(A) 1/72; R(SB) 11/83
36 s101(5A) SSA 1975 [s23(9)
    SS(A)A]
37 Reg 26(1) SS(Adj) Regs; reg
    3(1) SSCP Regs
38 Regs 3(3), 26 and Sch 2, para
    5 SS(Adj) Regs
39 Reg 3(1) and (3) SSCP Regs
40 Reg 3(2) and (5) SSCP Regs
41 Reg 7(1) SSCP Regs
42 Reg 5(2) SSCP Regs
43 Regs 10, 11 and 12 SSCP
    Regs
44 Reg 27(3) and (4) SSCP Regs
45 Reg 15 SSCP Regs
46 s116(1) SSA 1975 [s57
    SS(A)A]
47 Reg 17(4) SSCP Regs
48 Reg 22(2) SSCP Regs
49 s101(5)(b) SSA 1975
    [s23(7)(b) SS(A)A]
50 s101(5)(a) SSA 1975
    [s23(7)(a) SS(A)A]
51 *Innes v Chief Adjudication
    Officer* (unreported) (CA) 19
    November 1986
52 Regs 24 and 25 SSCP Regs
53 s14 SSA 1980 [s24 SS(A)A]
54 Regs 27(2) and 31(1) SSCP
    Regs
55 *White v Chief Adjudication
    Officer* [1986] 2 All ER 905
    (CA), also reported as an
    appendix to R(S) 8/85
56 s14(2)(b) SSA 1980
    [s24(2)(b) SS(A)A]
57 RSC O.59 r.21(3)
58 RSC O.3 r.5 and O.59 r.14(2)
59 RSC O.59 r.14(2), (2A), (2B)
60 RSC O.59 r.21(2)
61 RSC O.59 r.4(3)
62 *Bland v Chief Supplementary
    Benefit Officer* [1983] 1 WLR
    262 (CA), also reported as
    R(SB) 12/83
63 ss2(4)(a), 15(1) LAA 1988

**PART III: Family credit
Chapter 9: Family credit**
(pp129-138)
1 s20(5) SSA 1986 [s128(1)
   SS(C&B)A]
2 Reg 3(1) FC Regs
3 R(P) 1/78; R(M) 1/85
4 Reg 3(2) FC Regs
5 para 39043 AOG
6 s20(5)(b) SSA 1986
   [s128(1)(b) SS(C&B)A]
7 Reg 4(1) FC Regs
8 para 39326 AOG
9 Reg 4(3) FC Regs
10 Reg 4(5) FC Regs
11 Reg 4(6) FC Regs
12 R(FIS) 2/83
13 R(FIS) 6/83; R(FIS) 1/84
14 R(FIS) 6/83
15 R(FIS) 1/85; *R v Ebbw Vale &
    Merthyr Tydfil SBAT ex parte
    Lewis* [1982] 1 WLR 420
16 R(FIS) 2/81; R(FIS) 2/82
17 Reg 4(7) FC Regs
18 R(FIS) 1/83
19 R(FIS) 1/86
20 See R(FIS) 6/83; R(FIS) 1/84;
    R(FIS) 1/86
21 Reg 4(3) FC Regs
22 para 39349 AOG
23 R(FIS) 6/85; para 39338 AOG
24 Reg 4(2)(a) FC Regs
25 Reg 4(4)(b) FC Regs
26 Reg 4(4)(c)(ii)(bb) FC Regs
27 Reg 4(4)(c)(i) FC Regs
28 CIS/261/1990
29 Reg 4(4)(c)(ii)(aa) FC Regs
30 s20(5)(c) SSA 1986
    [s128(1)(c) SS(C&B)A]
31 Reg 52 FC Regs
32 s20(5)(a) SSA 1986
    [s128(1)(a) SS(C&B)A]; reg
    47(1) FC Regs
33 s21(2) SSA 1986
    [s128(2)(a) SS(C&B)A]
34 s21(3) SSA 1986 [s128(2)(b)
    SS(C&B)A]; Reg 48 FC Regs
35 Reg 46(1) FC Regs
36 Sch 4 FC Regs
37 Reg 46(4)-(6) FC Regs
38 Reg 46(2) and (3) FC Regs
39 Reg 28 SS(C&P) Regs
40 Reg 27(2) SS(C&P) Regs
41 Reg 14(1)(a) FC Regs
42 s20(6) SSA 1986 [s128(3)
    SS(C&B)A]
43 Reg 6(1) SS(C&P) Regs
44 Reg 4(7) SS(C&P) Regs
45 s165A SSA 1975; reg 19
    SS(C&P) Regs
46 Reg 5 SS(C&P) Regs
47 Reg 19 and Sch 4 para 7
    SS(C&P) Regs
48 Reg 16(1) and (3) SS(C&P)
    Regs

49 s20(6) SSA 1986 [s128(3)
    SS(C&B)A]
50 Reg 16(1B) SS(C&P) Regs
51 Reg 7(3) SS(C&P) Regs
52 para 40013 AOG
53 s99(1) SSA 1975 [s21(1)
    SS(A)A]
54 Reg 20 SS(Adj) Regs
55 Regs 20 and 27 SS(C&P) Regs
56 Reg 21 SS(C&P) Regs
57 s20(6) SSA 1986 [s128(3)
    SS(C&B)A]; reg 27(1)
    SS(C&P) Regs
58 s20(6) SSA 1986 [s128(3)
    SS(C&B)A]
59 s20(10) SSA 1986 [s128(4)
    SS(C&B)A]; reg 50 FC Regs
60 Reg 49 FC Regs
61 Reg 51 FC Regs
62 Regs 15 and 16 SS(PAOR) Regs
63 s104 SSA 1975 [s25 SS(A)A]
64 s20(6) SSA 1986 [s128(3)
    SS(C&B)A]
65 Reg 70 SS(Adj) Regs
66 s100 SSA 1975 [s22 SS(A)A]

**PART IV: Disability
working allowance
Chapter 10: Disability
working allowance**
(pp139-149)
1 Reg 7B SS(Credits) Regs
2 s20(6A) SSA 1986 [s129(1)
   SS(C&B)A]
3 Reg 5(1)(c) DWA Regs
4 s20(6A)(a) SSA 1986
   [s129(1)(a) SS(C&B)A]
5 Reg 6 DWA Regs
6 s20(6A)(b) SSA 1986
   [s129(1)(b) SS(C&B)A]
7 s27B(2) SSA 1986 [s11(2)
   SS(A)A]; reg 4 DWA Regs
8 Reg 3 and Sch 1 DWA Regs
9 Sch 1 para 24 DWA Regs
10 ss6A and 6B SSA 1986
    [s129(1) and (2) SS(C&B)A]
11 s27B(3) SSA 1986 [s11(3)
    SS(A)A]
12 s20(6A)(d) SSA 1986
    [s129(1)(d) SS(C&B)A]
13 Reg 57 DWA Regs
14 Reg 31 DWA Regs
15 s21(3A) and (3B) SSA 1986
    [s129(5) SS(C&B)A]; reg 53
    DWA Regs
16 Reg 51 and Sch 5 DWA Regs
17 Reg 4(1) SS(C&P) Regs
18 Reg 4(3A) SS(C&P) Regs
19 Reg 4(7) SS(C&P) Regs
20 Reg 5 SS(C&P) Regs
21 Sch 1 Part 1 SS(C&P) Regs
22 Reg 6(1) SS(C&P) Regs
23 Reg 6(10) SS(C&P) Regs
24 s100A(12) SSA 1975 [s30(3)
    SS(A)A]

25 Reg 6(11) SS(C&P) Regs
26 Reg 19(4) SS(C&P) Regs
27 Reg 19(2) SS(C&P) Regs
28 Reg 19(1) and Sch 4 para 11
    SS(C&P) Regs
29 Reg 19(3) SS(C&P) Regs
30 Reg 7(1) SS(C&P) Regs
31 Reg 7(3) SS(C&P) Regs
32 ss98 and 99 SSA 1975 [ss20
    and 21 SS(A)A]
33 s115C SSA 1975 [s54
    SS(A)A]
34 s100 SSA 1975 [s22 SS(A)A];
    reg 20 SS(Adj) Regs
35 Reg 16(1) and (3) SS(C&P)
    Regs
36 Reg 16(1C) SS(C&P) Regs
37 Reg 16(1B) SS(C&P) Regs
38 Reg 27(2) SS(C&P) Regs
39 s20(6F) SSA 1986 [s129(6)
    SS(C&B)A]
40 Regs 21 and 27 SS(C&P)
    Regs
41 Reg 36 SS(C&P) Regs
42 s20(6F) SSA 1986 [s129(6)
    SS(C&B)A]
43 Reg 55 DWA Regs
44 Reg 54 DWA Regs
45 Reg 56 DWA Regs
46 s100A SSA 1975 [s30
    SS(A)A]
47 Reg 26A SS(Adj) Regs
48 s104A SSA 1975 [s35
    SS(A)A]
49 ss100B and 104A(6) SSA
    1975 [ss31 and 35(8)
    SS(A)A]
50 Reg 26B SS(Adj) Regs
51 Reg 70B SS(Adj) Regs
52 s53 SSA 1986 [s71 SS(A)A]
53 s100D SSA 1975 [s33
    SS(A)A]
54 Reg 26C SS(Adj) Regs
55 Sch 10A SSA 1975 [ss42 and
    43 SS(A)A]
56 Reg 26G SS(Adj) Regs
57 s115D SSA 1975 [s55
    SS(A)A]
58 ss15(5A), 36(6C) SSA 1975
    [ss33(7) and 68(10)
    SS(C&B)A]; s16A SSPA
    1975
59 s9(5) DWAA 1991

PART V: HOUSING BENEFIT
Chapter 11: The basic rules
(pp151-167)

1 Introduction
(pp151-157)
1   s20 SSA 1986 [s130
    SS(C&B)A]
2   Reg 6(1) HB Regs

3   s20(9) SSA 1986 [s134(2)
    SS(C&B)A]; Reg 71(1) HB
    Regs
4   Reg 10(5) HB Regs
5   Reg 6(2) HB Regs; para A3.11
    GM
6   Reg 6(1)(d) HB Regs
7   s20(7)(a) SSA 1986 [s130(1)
    SS(C&B)A]; reg 5 HB Regs
8   para A3.15 GM
9   Reg 5(5)(c) HB Regs
10 Reg 5(8) HB Regs
11 Reg 5(3) and (9) HB Regs
12 Reg 5(1) HB Regs; para A3.16
    GM
13 Reg 5(5)(b) HB Regs
14 Reg 5(5)(a) HB Regs
15 Reg 5(4) HB Regs
16 Reg 5(5)(d) HB Regs
17 Reg 5(6) HB Regs
18 para A3.25 GM
19 Reg 48(A)(1) HB Regs
20 Reg 7(e) HB Regs
21 Reg 10(2)(a) and (c) HB Regs
22 Reg 2(1) HB Regs
23 Reg 7(a) HB Regs
24 Reg 2(1) HB Regs
25 para A3.29 GM
26 Reg 7(b) HB Regs
27 Reg 7(c) HB Regs
28 Reg 8(3) HB Regs
29 Reg 10(2)(e) HB Regs
30 Reg 10(2)(b) HB Regs
31 Reg 10(2)(d) HB Regs
32 Reg 7(d) HB Regs

2 'Eligible rent'
(pp157-162)
33 Reg 10(1) HB Regs
34 Reg 2(4)(a) HB Regs
35 Reg 10(3)(a) and (6) HB Regs
36 Reg 8(2)(a) HB Regs
37 Reg 10(2)(c) HB Regs
38 Reg 10(4) HB Regs
39 Reg 7(e) HB Regs
40 Reg 10(2)(e) HB Regs
41 Reg 10(2)(a) HB Regs
42 Reg 10(2)(b) HB Regs
43 Reg 10(2)(d) HB Regs
44 Reg 8(2)(b) HB Regs
45 Sch 1 Part II para 4 HB Regs
46 Sch 1 para 5(4) HB Regs
47 Sch 1 para 5(1)(a) HB Regs
48 Sch 1 para 5(4) HB Regs
49 Sch 1 para 5(1) HB Regs
50 Sch 1 para 5(2) and (2A) HB
    Regs
51 Sch 1 para 5(1)(b) HB Regs
52 Reg 10(1)(e) and (5) HB Regs
53 Sch 1 para 5(3) and Sch 6 para
    9(c) HB Regs; para A4.54 GM
54 para A4.54(ii) GM
55 Sch 1 para 4 HB Regs; para
    A4.59 GM
56 Sch 1 para 7 HB Regs
57 Sch 1 para 7 HB Regs

58 Reg 10(1)(e) HB Regs
59 Sch 1 para 1(g) HB Regs
60 Sch 1 para 1(a)(ii) HB Regs;
    para A4.42 GM
61 Sch 1 para 1(b) HB Regs; para
    A4.44 GM
62 Sch 1 para 1(a)(iv) HB Regs
63 Sch 1 para 1(b)(iv) HB Regs;
    para A4.42(iv) GM
64 Sch 1 para 1(c) HB Regs; para
    A4.45 GM
65 Sch 1 para 1(f) HB Regs; para
    A4.47 GM
66 Sch 1 para 3 HB Regs
67 Sch 1 para 1 HB Regs
68 Sch 1 para 2(1A) HB Regs;
    para A4.52 GM
69 Sch 1 para 2 HB Regs
70 Sch 1 para 1(a)(i) HB Regs
71 Sch 1 para 1A(1) HB Regs
72 Sch 1 para 1A(5) and (6) HB
    Regs
73 Reg 7(e) HB Regs
74 Reg 7(2) HB Regs
75 para A4.20 GM
76 Reg 7(3) HB Regs
77 para A4.20 GM

3 'Unreasonably high' rents
(pp162-167)
78 para A4.64 GM
79 Reg 11(2) HB Regs; para
    A4.63 GM
80 Reg 11(6)(a) HB Regs
81 para A4.63 GM
82 *Macleod v Housing Benefit
    Review Board for Banff and
    Buchan District* [1988] SCLR
    165 and *Malcolm v Housing
    Benefit Review Board for
    Tweedale* [1991]
83 Reg 11(3) HB Regs; para
    A4.64-7 GM
84 Reg 11(7) and (8) HB Regs
85 Reg 2(1) HB Regs
86 *Macleod v Housing Benefit
    Review Board for Banff and
    Buchan District* [1988] SCLR
    165
87 *Malcolm v Housing Benefit
    Review Board for Tweedale*
    [1991]
88 Reg 11(6)(b) HB Regs
89 *R v London Borough of Brent
    ex parte Connery*, QBD
    23/10/89
90 Reg 11(3A) HB Regs
91 Reg 11(4) HB Regs; para
    A4.74 GM
92 Reg 11(5) HB Regs; para
    A4.75 GM
93 para A4.73 GM
94 Reg 95(7) HB Regs
95 para A4.73 GM
96 Reg 12(b) HB Regs; para
    A4.76 GM

97 Reg 12 HB Regs; para A4.77
    GM

Chapter 12: The amount of benefit
(pp168-175)

1   Reg 61 HB Regs
2   s21(4) SSA 1986 [s130(3)(a)
    SS(C&B)A]
3   s21(5) SSA 1986 [s130(3)(b)
    SS(C&B)A] and reg 62 HB
    Regs
4   Reg 64 HB Regs
5   Reg 37 HB Regs; reg 27
    CCB Regs
6   s21(4) SSA 1986 [s130(3)(a)
    SS(C&B)A]
7   Reg 62 HB Regs
8   Reg 2 HB Regs; reg 2 CCB
    Regs
9   Reg 69 HB Regs; reg 57(1)
    CCB Regs
10 Reg 69(2)(a) HB Regs
11 Reg 69(2)(b) and (3)(b) HB
    Regs
12 Reg 70(3) and Sch 1 para
    6(2) HB Regs; para A5.46-9
    GM
13 Reg 70(3)(a) and Sch 1 para
    6(2)(a) HB Regs
14 Reg 70(3)(b) and Sch 1 para
    6(2)(b) HB Regs
15 Reg 63 HB Regs
16 Reg 3(2) HB Regs
17 Reg 3(4) and Sch 1 para 7
    HB Regs
18 Reg 63(6) HB Regs
19 Reg 63(7) HB Regs
20 Reg 63(1) HB Regs
21 Reg 63(8) HB Regs
22 Reg 63(1) and (2) HB Regs
23 Reg 4(1) HB Regs
24 Reg 4(4) HB Regs
25 Reg 4(1) and (2) HB Regs
26 Reg 4 HB Regs; para
    A5.11-14 GM
27 para A5.26-8 GM
28 para A5.13 GM
29 para A5.19 GM
30 Reg 63(3) HB Regs
31 Reg 63(5) HB Regs
32 Sch 4 para 19 HB Regs
33 Reg 20(1) HB Regs
34 Reg 20 HB Regs
35 Reg 77 and Sch 6 para 12 HB
    Regs
36 Reg 69(8) HB Regs; reg 58
    CCB Regs
37 para A5.52 GM
38 Reg 69(8) HB Regs
39 para A5.53 GM
40 ss28(6)(a) and 31B(6)(a) SSA
    1986 [ss134(8) and 139(6)
    SS(A)A]
41 ss28(7) and 31B(7) SSA 1986
    [s134(9) and 139(7) SS(A)A]

42 Reg 5(8) HB Regs
43 Reg 18(1)(a) HB Regs; reg
    9(1)(a) CCB Regs
44 Reg 18(1)(b) HB Regs; reg
    9(1)(b) CCB Regs
45 Reg 18(1)(c)(i) HB Regs; reg
    9(1)(c)(i) CCB Regs
46 Reg 18(1)(c)(ii) HB Regs; reg
    9(1)(c)(ii) CCB Regs

Chapter 13: Special rules for students
(pp176-183)

1   Reg 46 HB Regs; reg 36 CCB
    Regs
2   Reg 46 HB Regs; reg 36 CCB
    Regs
3   para C5.02 GM
4   Reg 46 HB Regs; reg 36 CCB
    Regs; para C5.03 GM
5   Reg 46 HB Regs; reg 36 CCB
    Regs
6   Reg 48A(2) HB Regs
7   Reg 6(1)(e) HB Regs
8   Reg 48A(1) HB Regs
9   Reg 48 HB Regs
10 Reg 52 HB Regs; para C5.27
    GM
11 Reg 5(8) HB Regs; para
    A3.18-20 GM
12 Reg 50(1) HB Regs; para
    C5.29 GM
13 Reg 50(2) HB Regs; para
    C5.30 GM
14 Reg 50(3) HB Regs
15 Reg 52 HB Regs; para C5.34
    GM
16 Reg 50(1) HB Regs; para
    C5.32 GM
17 Reg 49(1) HB Regs
18 Reg 49(2)(a) HB Regs; para
    C5.79 GM
19 Reg 49(2) HB Regs
20 para C5.90 GM
21 Reg 49(2) HB Regs
22 Regs 6(1)(a) and 52 HB
    Regs
23 para C5.96 GM
24 para C5.83 GM
25 para C5.81 GM
26 para C5.91 GM
27 para C5.95 GM
28 Part C5 Annex D GM
29 para C8.03(iii) GM
30 Reg 51(1) HB Regs
31 Reg 52 HB Regs
32 Reg 51(2) HB Regs; para
    C5.76 GM
33 Reg 90 HB Regs

Chapter 14: Claims, payments and reviews
pp184-211

1 Claims
(pp184-188)

1   Reg 71(1) HB Regs; para
    A2.02 GM; reg 59(1) CCB
    Regs
2   Reg 71(2) HB Regs; para
    A2.07 GM; reg 59(3) CCB
    Regs
3   Reg 71(3) and (5) HB Regs;
    para A2.03 GM; reg 59(4) and
    (6) CCB Regs
4   Reg 71(6) HB Regs; reg 59(7)
    CCB Regs
5   Reg 71(4) HB Regs; reg 59(5)
    CCB Regs
6   Reg 72(1) HB Regs; reg 60(1)
    CCB Regs
7   Reg 72(2) HB Regs; reg 60(2)
    CCB Regs
8   para A2.09 GM
9   Reg 72(7)(b) HB Regs; reg
    60(7)(b) CCB Regs
10 Reg 72(7)(a) and (8) HB Regs;
    para A2.25 GM; reg 60(7)(a)
    CCB Regs
11 Reg 74(1) HB Regs; para
    A2.19-20 GM; reg 62(1) CCB
    Regs
12 Reg 74(2) HB Regs; reg 62(2)
    CCB Regs
13 Reg 72(4)(a) and (b) HB Regs;
    reg 60(5)(a) and (b) CCB
    Regs
14 s84(1) SSA 1986 [s191
    SS(A)A]
15 Reg 72(4)(a) and (b) HB Regs;
    paras A2.10 and B2.21-4 GM;
    reg 60(5)(a) and (b) CCB Regs
16 Reg 72(4)(c) HB Regs; paras
    A2.11 and B2.23 GM; reg
    60(5)(c) CCB Regs
17 Reg 72(1) HB Regs; reg 60(1)
    CCB Regs
18 Reg 73(1) HB Regs; paras
    A2.23 and B2.26 GM; reg
    61(1) CCB Regs
19 Reg 76(2)(b) HB Regs; paras
    A6.15 and B6.2 GM; reg
    65(2)(b) CCB Regs
20 Reg 73(1) HB Regs; reg 61(1)
    CCB Regs
21 Reg 73(2) HB Regs; reg 61(2)
    CCB Regs
22 Reg 95(7) HB Regs
23 Reg 72(5)(c) HB Regs; reg
    60(6)(d) CCB Regs
24 Reg 72(5)(a) HB Regs; reg
    60(6)(a) CCB Regs
25 Reg 72(5)(b) HB Regs; reg
    60(6)(b) CCB Regs
26 Reg 72(5)(bb) HB Regs; paras
    A2.12 and B2.33 GM

27 Reg 65(1) HB Regs; reg 53(1) CCB Regs
28 Reg 72(15) HB Regs; paras A2.16 and B2.34 GM; reg 60(18) CCB Regs
29 paras A2.16 and B2.34 GM
30 Reg 72(15) HB Regs; paras A2.15 and B2.34 GM; reg 60(18) CCB Regs
31 Reg 5(6) HB Regs
32 Reg 72(11) HB Regs; paras A2.13 and B2.27 GM
33 Reg 66(1)-(3) HB Regs; paras A6.07 and B4.13 GM; reg 54(1)-(3) CCB Regs
34 Sch 6 para 9(g) and (h) HB Regs; Sch 5 para 9(c) and (d) CCB Regs
35 Reg 72(12) and (13) HB Regs; para A6.12 GM; reg 60(15) and (16) CCB Regs
36 Reg 67(a) HB Regs; reg 55(a) CCB Regs
37 Reg 72(14) HB Regs; paras A6.12 and B4.13 GM; reg 60(17) CCB Regs
38 para A6.13 GM

2 Decisions
(pp188-191)
39 Regs 76(3), 77(a) and 88(3) HB Regs; paras A6.14 and B4.16 GM; regs 64(3), 65(a) and 76(1) CCB Regs
40 Reg 76(2) HB Regs; paras A6.15 and B6.2 GM; reg 64(2) CCB Regs
41 Reg 77 HB Regs; reg 65 CCB Regs
42 paras A6.17 and B6.6 GM
43 Reg 77 and Sch 6 HB Regs; reg 65 and Sch 5 CCB Regs
44 Sch 6 para 6 HB Regs; Sch 5 para 6 CCB Regs
45 Sch 6 para 2 HB Regs; Sch 5 para 2 CCB Regs
46 Sch 6 para 3 HB Regs; Sch 5 para 3 CCB Regs
47 Sch 6 paras 9-13 HB Regs; Sch 5 paras 9-13 CCB Regs
48 Reg 77(3)-(5) HB Regs; reg 65(3)-(4) CCB Regs
49 paras A618 and B67 GM
50 para C12.10 GM

3 Payment of benefit
(pp191-195)
51 Reg 66 HB Regs; reg 54 CCB Regs
52 Reg 65(1) HB Regs; reg 53(1) CCB Regs
53 Reg 65(1) HB Regs; reg 53(1) CCB Regs
54 Reg 2(1) HB Regs; reg 2(1) CCB Regs

55 Reg 65(2) HB Regs
56 Reg 69(4)(a) HB Regs
57 Regs 5(a), 6 and 69(2)(b) HB Regs
58 Reg 66(3) HB Regs; reg 54(3) CCB Regs
59 Reg 66(2) HB Regs; paras A6.07 and B4.13 GM; reg 54(2) CCB Regs
60 Reg 66(1)(a) HB Regs; reg 54(1)(a) CCB Regs
61 Reg 66(1)(b) HB Regs; para A6.06 GM; reg 54(1)(b) CCB Regs
62 Reg 72(13) HB Regs; para A6.12 GM; reg 60(16) CCB Regs
63 Reg 66(4) HB Regs; paras A6.10 and B4.13 GM; reg 54(4) CCB Regs
64 Reg 67(b) HB Regs; paras A6.11 and B4.14 GM; reg 55(b) CCB Regs
65 Reg 67(c) HB Regs; reg 55(c) CCB Regs
66 Reg 67(a) HB Regs; reg 55(a) CCB Regs
67 Reg 72(14)(a) HB Regs; reg 60(17)(a) CCB Regs
68 Reg 67 HB Regs; para A6.11 GM; reg 55 CCB Regs
69 s28(1)(b) SSA 1986 [s134(1)(b) SS(A)A]
70 s28(1)(c) SSA 1986 [s134(1)(c) SS(A)A]; Reg 92(1) HB Regs
71 Reg 90(1) HB Regs; para A6.28 GM
72 Reg 90(2) HB Regs; para A6.31 GM
73 Reg 88(2) HB Regs; para A6.28 GM
74 Reg 90(3) HB Regs; para A6.29 GM
75 Reg 90(4) HB Regs; para A6.30 GM
76 Reg 88(1)(b) HB Regs; reg 77(1)(b) CCB Regs
77 para A6.24 GM
78 Reg 91(1) HB Regs
79 Reg 91(2) HB Regs; para A6.37 GM
80 Reg 91(3) HB Regs
81 para C9.225 GM
82 Reg 88(1) HB Regs; regs 76(1) and 77(1) CCB Regs
83 Reg 92(1) HB Regs; para A6.38 GM; reg 78(1) CCB Regs
84 Reg 92(2) HB Regs; para A.6.39 GM; reg 78(2) CCB Regs
85 Reg 92(3) HB Regs; para A6.40 GM; regs 59(4) and 78(2) CCB Regs
86 Reg 96 HB Regs; paras

A6.41-2 GM; reg 81 CCB Regs
87 Reg 93(a) HB Regs; para A6.45 GM
88 Reg 93(b) HB Regs; para A6.44 GM
89 Reg 94(a) HB Regs; para A6.43 GM
90 Reg 95(1) HB Regs; para A6.44 GM
91 Reg 95(a) and (b) HB Regs
92 Reg 95(2) HB Regs; para A6.46 GM
93 Reg 95(7) HB Regs
94 Reg 95(4) HB Regs; para A6.46 GM; reg 80(1) CCB Regs
95 Reg 95(5) HB Regs; para A6.46 GM; reg 80(2) CCB Regs
96 Reg 95(3)(a) and (b) HB Regs
97 Reg 95(6) HB Regs; para A6.47 GM; reg 80(3) CCB Regs

4 Changes in your circumstances
(pp195-197)
98 Reg 75(1) HB Regs; reg 63(1) CCB Regs
99 Sch 6 para 9(i) HB Regs; Sch 5 para 9(e) CCB Regs
100 Reg 75(1), (2)(e) and (3) HB Regs; paras A6.50 and B4.8 GM; reg 63(1), (2)(e) and (3) CCB Regs
101 Regs 73(2) and 75 HB Regs; paras A2.24 GM; regs 61(2) and 63 CCB Regs
102 Reg 75(1) HB Regs; reg 63(1) CCB Regs
103 Reg 75(2) HB Regs; paras A6.51 and B4.10 GM; reg 63(2) CCB Regs
104 Regs 2(1), 73(2) and 75(1) HB Regs; regs 2(1), 61(2) and 63(1) CCB Regs
105 Reg 68 HB Regs; reg 56 CCB Regs
106 Reg 68(1) HB Regs; reg 56(1) CCB Regs
107 Reg 68(1) HB Regs; paras A6.52 and B4.9 GM; reg 56(1) CCB Regs
108 Reg 67(a) and (b) HB Regs; reg 55(a) and (b) CCB Regs
109 Reg 68(2) HB Regs
110 Regs 26 and 68(1) HB Regs; regs 17 and 56(1) CCB Regs
111 Reg 68(3) HB Regs; 56(3) CCB Regs
112 Reg 35(4) HB Regs; reg 25(4) CCB Regs
113 Reg 68(4) HB Regs; para A6.54 GM

114 Reg 67(c) HB Regs; reg 55(c) CCB Regs

115 Reg 67(a) HB Regs; reg 55(a) CCB Regs

116 Reg 79(1)(a) and (3)(a) HB Regs; reg 67(1)(a) and (3)(a) CCB Regs

117 Reg 79(1)(a), (3)(a) and (5)(b) HB Regs; reg 67(1)(a), (3)(a) and (5)(b) CCB Regs

118 Reg 99 HB Regs; reg 84 CCB Regs

5 Overpayments
(pp197-204)

119 Reg 98 HB Regs; paras A7.2 and B5.1 GM; reg 83 CCB Regs

120 s28(1A) SSA 1986; [s134(2) SS(A)A]

121 Sch 6 para 14(b) HB Regs; paras A7.44 and B5.6 GM; Sch 5 para 13(b) CCB Regs

122 para A7.48 GM

123 ss55 and 56 SSA 1986 [ss112 and 116 SS(A)A]

124 Reg 99(2) and (3) HB Regs; para A7.22 and B5.5 GM; reg 84(2) and (3) CCB Regs

125 Reg 99(2) HB Regs; reg 84(2) CCB Regs

126 Reg 91(3) HB Regs

127 Reg 100 HB Regs; reg 85 CCB Regs

128 para 10.12-17 GM

129 Regs 79(2) and 100-102 HB Regs; regs 67(1) and 85-87 CCB Regs

130 Sch 6 para 14(d) HB Regs; Sch 5 para 13(d) CCB Regs

131 Reg 98 HB Regs; reg 83 CCB Regs

132 Reg 104(b) HB Regs; para A7.28 GM; reg 90(b) CCB Regs

133 Reg 103(1) HB Regs; reg 89(1) CCB Regs

134 Reg 103(1)(a) and (b) HB Regs; para A7.31-3 GM; reg 89(1)(a) and (b) CCB Regs

135 Reg 103(2) HB Regs; reg 89(2) CCB Regs

136 Reg 101(b) HB Regs; reg 86(1) CCB Regs

137 Reg 101(1)(a) HB Regs

138 Reg 101(2) HB Regs; para A7.35 GM; reg 86(2) CCB Regs

139 paras A7.45-7 GM

140 Reg 102 HB Regs; reg 87(1) CCB Regs

141 para A7.37(v) GM; reg 88 CCB Regs

142 paras A7.38-41 GM

143 Reg 105(2) HB Regs

144 para B5.7(iii) GM; HB/CCB(90)20 Annex A para 3

145 para A7.37(iv) GM

146 Regs 102 and 105 HB Regs; regs 87 and 91 CCB Regs

147 Reg 105(1) and (2) HB Regs; reg 91(1) and (2) CCB Regs

148 para A7.37(ii) GM

149 Reg 77(b) HB Regs; reg 65(b) CCB Regs

150 Sch 6 paras 2, 3, 6 and 14 HB Regs; para A7.44 GM; Sch 5 paras 2, 3, 6 and 13 CCB Regs

151 Reg 77(4) and (5) HB Regs; reg 65(3) CCB Regs

152 Sch 6 para 14 HB Regs; Sch 5 para 13 CCB Regs; para A7.44 GM

6 Fraud
(pp204-205)

153 s55 SSA 1986; [s112 SS(A)A]

154 ss15 and 16 Theft Act 1968

155 Reg 95(4) HB Regs; reg 80(1) CCB Regs

156 Regs 2(g) and 3(c) HB(SI) Regs

7 Reviews
(pp205-210)

157 Reg 79(1) HB Regs; reg 67(1) CCB Regs

158 Reg 79(6) HB Regs; reg 67(6) CCB Regs

159 Reg 79(3)(c) and (5) HB Regs; reg 67(3)(c) and (5) CCB Regs

160 Reg 79(2) HB Regs; reg 67(2) CCB Regs

161 Reg 79(2) HB Regs; reg 67(2) CCB Regs

162 Reg 78(3) and (4) HB Regs; reg 66(3) and (4) CCB Regs

163 Sch 6 para 3 HB Regs; Sch 5 para 3 CCB Regs

164 Reg 79(4) HB Regs; paras A6.59 and B6.9 GM; reg 67(4) CCB Regs

165 Reg 77(4) and (5) HB Regs; paras A6.18 and B6.7 GM; reg 69(5) CCB Regs

166 Reg 78(3), (4) and (5) HB Regs; paras A6.59 and B6.9 GM; reg 66(3), (4) and (5) CCB Regs

167 Sch 6 para 2 HB Regs; Sch 5 para 2 CCB Regs

168 Reg 79(2) and Sch 6 paras 4 and 5 HB Regs; reg 67(2) and Sch 5 paras 4 and 5 CCB Regs

169 Reg 79(3)(b) HB Regs; reg 67(3)(b) CCB Regs

170 Regs 79(3)(c), (5)(a) and 78(1) HB Regs; paras A6.60 and B6.10 GM; regs 67(3)(c), (5)(a) and 66(1) CCB Regs

171 Reg 81(1) and (2) HB Regs; paras A6.61-2 and B6.11 GM; reg 69(1) and (2) CCB Regs

172 Reg 78(3), (4) and (5) HB regs; reg 66(3), (4) and (5) CCB Regs

173 Reg 82(1) HB Regs; paras A6.66 and B6.12 GM; reg 70(1) CCB Regs

174 Reg 82(2) and (1A) HB Regs

175 Reg 82(3) HB Regs; reg 70(3) CCB Regs

176 Reg 82(5) HB Regs; reg 70(5) CCB Regs

177 Sch 7 HB Regs; Sch 6 CCB Regs

178 Reg 82(7) HB Regs; reg 70(7) CCB Regs

179 paras A6.64 and B6.12 GM

180 Reg 69(4) CCB Regs

181 Reg 82(2)(a) HB Regs; reg 70(2)(a) CCB Regs

182 Reg 82(2)(b) HB Regs; reg 70(2)(b) CCB Regs

183 Reg 82(2)(c) HB Regs; reg 70(2)(c) CCB Regs

184 Reg 82(9) HB Regs; paras A6.68 and B6.15 GM; reg 70(9) CCB Regs

185 Reg 82(2)(c)(ii) HB Regs; reg 70(2)(c)(ii) CCB Regs

186 Reg 82(4) HB Regs; reg 70(4) CCB Regs

187 Reg 82(5) and (6) HB Regs; paras A6.67 and B6.14 GM; reg 70(5) and (6) CCB Regs

188 Reg 83(1) HB Regs; paras A6.70 and B6.16 GM; reg 71(1) CCB Regs

189 Reg 82(8) HB Regs; reg 70(8) CCB Regs

190 Reg 83(4) HB Regs; reg 71(4) CCB Regs

191 Reg 83(2) HB Regs; reg 71(2) CCB Regs

192 Reg 83(5) HB Regs; paras A6.72 and B6.17 GM; reg 71(5) CCB Regs

193 *R v Housing Benefit Review Board of Sefton MBC ex parte Cunningham*, 22 May 1991, QBD

194 Reg 84 HB Regs; reg 72 CCB Regs

195 Reg 79(3)(c), (5) and 83(3) HB Regs; paras A6.73 and B6.16 GM; regs 67(3)(c), (5) and 71(3) CCB Regs

196 Regs 85(1) and 87(1) HB Regs; reg 73(1) CCB Regs

197 Reg 87(3) HB Regs; reg 75(3) CCB Regs
198 Reg 86(1) HB Regs; paras A6.79-82 and B6.20-2 GM; reg 74(1) CCB Regs
199 Reg 86(1) HB Regs; reg 74(1) CCB Regs
200 Reg 86(1) HB Regs; reg 74(1) CCB Regs
201 Regs 78(2) and 86(2) HB Regs; regs 66(2) and 74(2) CCB Regs
202 Reg 87(2) HB Regs; reg 75(2) CCB Regs
203 Reg 86(3) HB Regs; reg 74(3) CCB Regs
204 Reg 86(4) HB Regs; reg 74(4) CCB Regs
205 Reg 87(3) HB Regs
206 Reg 78(2) and 87(2) HB Regs

PART VI: Community charge benefit
Chapter 15: Community charge benefit
(pp213-225)
1 Reg 59(1) CCB Regs
2 Regs 46(2), 49 and 50 CCB Regs
3 Regs 46(2), 49 and 50 CCB Regs
4 Regs 46(2), 49 and 50 CCB Regs
5 Reg 47(1) CCB Regs
6 Reg 46(3) CCB Regs
7 Reg 46(4) CCB Regs
8 Reg 46(1) CCB Regs
9 ss21(5A) and 20(8E)(a) and (b) SSA 1986 [s131(10) and (6)(a)-(b) SS(C&B)A]
10 ss21(5B) and 20(8E)(c) SSA 1986 [s131(11) and (6)(c) SS(C&B)A]
11 Reg 58 CCB Regs
12 Reg 60(1) CCB Regs
13 Regs 53(2), 55(bb), 56(3A) and 60(4) CCB Regs
14 Reg 60(12) and (13) CCB Regs
15 Reg 60(14) CCB Regs
16 Reg 60(13) CCB Regs
17 Reg 60(6)(bb) CCB Regs
18 para B6.6 GM
19 Reg 65(2) CCB Regs
20 Reg 53(1) CCB Regs
21 Reg 53(3)(b) CCB Regs
22 Reg 53(2) CCB Regs
23 Reg 53(3)(a) CCB Regs
24 Reg 76(1) CCB Regs
25 Reg 76(5) CCB Regs
26 Reg 76(1) and (2) CCB Regs
27 Reg 76(1), (3) and (4) CCB Regs

28 Reg 77(1), (2) and (4) CCB Regs
29 Reg 77(3) CCB Regs
30 Reg 77(1) CCB Regs
31 Reg 78(3) CCB Regs
32 Reg 78(4) CCB Regs
33 Reg 80(1) and (2) CCB Regs
34 Reg 80(3) CCB Regs
35 Reg 80(4) CCB Regs
36 Reg 86(1) CCB Regs
37 Reg 86(2) CCB Regs
38 Reg 91(1)(a) CCB Regs
39 Regs 83 and 87(2A) CCB Regs
40 Reg 87(2)(b) CCB Regs
41 Reg 87(4) CCB Regs
42 Reg 88 CCB Regs
43 Sch 5 Part VI para 13(f) CCB Regs
44 Reg 56(2) CCB Regs
45 Reg 56(3A) CCB Regs
46 Reg 63(2) CCB Regs
47 s20(8B)(a) SSA 1986 (s131(3) SS(C&B)A)
48 Part V Chapter II CCB Regs
49 Sch 3 para 4 CCB Regs
50 Reg 36 CCB Regs
51 Reg 37 CCB Regs
52 Reg 9 CCB Regs

PART VII: Calculating needs and resources
Chapter 16: Who counts as your family
(pp227-235)
1 s20(11) SSA 1986 [s137 SS(C&B)A]
2 s20(9) SSA 1986 [s134(2) SS(C&B)A]
3 IS Reg 16(1) IS Regs
FC Reg 9 FC Regs
DWA Reg 11 DWA Regs
HB Reg 15(1) HB Regs
CCB Reg 6(1) CCB Regs
4 R(SB) 4/83
5 CSB/463/1986
6 R(SB) 13/82
7 R(SB) 8/85
8 *R v Penwith District Council ex parte Menear, The Times,* 21 October 1991.
9 s20(11) SSA 1986 [s137 SS(C&B)A] definition of 'married couple' and 'unmarried couple'
10 IS Reg 2(1) IS Regs
HB Reg 2(1) HB Regs
CCB Reg 2(1) CCB Regs
11 R(SB) 17/81
12 *Crake & Butterworth v SBC* [1980] quoted in R(SB) 35/85
13 R(SB) 35/85
14 CSB/150/1985
15 CSSB/145/1983

16 IS Reg 16(1) IS Regs
FC Reg 9 FC Regs
DWA Reg 11 DWA Regs
HB Reg 15(1) HB Regs
CCB Reg 6(1) CCB Regs
17 s20(11) SSA 1986 [s137 SS(C&B)A]; CIS/209/1989
18 Reg 15(2) HB Regs
19 Reg 6(1) CCB Regs
20 FC Reg 9 FC Regs; DWA Reg 11 DWA Regs
21 Reg 16(2) and (3) and Sch 3 para 4(8) IS Regs
22 Sch 7 paras 11 and 11A IS Regs
23 Sch 1 para 22 IS Regs
24 Sch 7 para 9 IS Regs
25 Sch 7 para 9 col (2) IS Regs
26 Sch 7 para 9 col (2) IS Regs
27 Sch 7 para 9 col (2) IS Regs
28 All s20(11) SSA 1986 [s137 SS(C&B)A]
IS Reg 17(1)(b) IS Regs
FC Reg 46(1)(b) FC Regs
DWA Reg 51(1)(c) DWA Regs
HB Reg 16(b) HB Regs
CCB Reg 7(b) CCB Regs
29 IS Reg 14 IS Regs
FC Reg 6 FC Regs
DWA Reg 8 DWA Regs
HB Reg 13 HB Regs
CCB Reg 4 CCB Regs
30 FC Reg 7(1) FC Regs
DWA Reg 9(1) DWA Regs
HB Reg 14(1) HB Regs
CCB Reg 5(1) CCB Regs
31 Reg 15(1) IS Regs
32 IS Reg 15(2) IS Regs
FC Reg 7(2) FC Regs
DWA Reg 9(2) DWA Regs
HB Reg 14(2) HB Regs
CCB Reg 5(2) CCB Regs
33 IS Reg 15(4) IS Regs
FC Reg 7(3) FC Regs
DWA Reg 9(3) DWA Regs
HB Reg 14(3) HB Regs
CCB Reg 5(3) CCB Regs
34 CIS/49/1991
35 IS Reg 16 IS Regs
FC Reg 8 FC Regs
DWA Reg 10 DWA Regs
HB Reg 15 HB Regs
CCB Reg 6 CCB Regs
36 Regs 15(3) and 16(1) IS Regs
37 HB Reg 15(5) HB Regs
CCB Reg 6(4) CCB Regs
38 FC Reg 46(6) FC Regs
DWA Reg 51(6) DWA Regs
39 All Reg 7D(1) CB Regs
IS Reg 14 IS Regs
HB Reg 13 HB Regs
CCB Reg 4 CCB Regs
40 s20(9) SSA 1986 [s134(2) SS(C&B)A]

41 **IS** Reg 14(2) IS Regs
HB Reg 13(2) HB Regs
CCB Reg 4(2) CCB Regs
42 **FC** Reg 6(2) FC Regs
DWA Reg 8(2) DWA Regs
43 **FC** Reg 6(2) FC Regs
DWA Reg 8(2) DWA Regs

Chapter 17: Applicable amounts
(pp236-245)

1 **IS** Reg 18 IS Regs
HB Reg 17 HB Regs
CCB Reg 8 CCB Regs
2 **IS** Reg 18(1)(b) IS Regs
HB Reg 17(b) HB Regs;
CCB Reg 8(b) CCB Regs
HB/CCB paras C4.05 and
C4.06 GM
3 **IS** Sch 2 para 5 IS Regs
HB Sch 2 para 5 HB Regs
CCB Sch 1 para 5 CCB
Regs
4 **IS** Sch 2 para 7 IS Regs
HB Sch 2 para 7 HB Regs
CCB Sch 1 para 7 CCB
Regs
5 **IS** Sch 2 para 3 IS Regs
HB Sch 2 para 3 HB Regs
CCB Sch 1 para 3 CCB Regs
6 Regs 15(3) and 16(6) IS Regs
7 **HB** Reg 15(5) HB Regs
CCB Reg 6(4) CCB Regs
8 **IS** Sch 2 paras 14 and 15(6) IS
Regs
HB Sch 2 paras 14 and 15(6)
HB Regs
CCB Sch 1 paras 15 and 17(7)
CCB Regs
9 **IS** Sch 2 paras 14(c),
12(1)(a)(iii) and (2) IS Regs
HB Sch 2 paras 14(c),
12(1)(a)(v) and (2) HB Regs
CCB Sch 1 paras 15(c),
13(1)(a)(v) and (2) CCB Regs
10 **IS** Sch 2 para 14(a) IS Regs
HB Sch 2 para 14(a) HB Regs
CCB Sch 1 para 15(a) CCB
Regs
11 **IS** Sch 2 para 14ZA IS regs
HB Sch 2 para 14ZA HB Regs
CCB Sch 1 para 15A CCB
Regs
12 **IS** Sch 2 para 14A IS Regs
HB Sch 2 para 14A HB Regs
CCB Sch 2 para 16 CCB Regs
13 **IS** Sch 2 para 8 IS Regs
HB Sch 2 para 8 HB Regs
CCB Sch 1 para 8 CCB Regs
14 **IS** Sch 2 paras 11 and 15(4) IS
Regs
HB Sch 2 paras 11 and 15(4)
HB Regs
CCB Sch 1 paras 12 and 17(5)
CCB Regs

15 **IS** Sch 2 para 12 IS Regs
HB Sch 2 para 12 HB Regs
CCB Sch 1 para 13 CCB Regs
16 **IS** Reg 2(1) IS Regs
HB Reg 2(1) HB Regs
CCB Reg 2(1) CCB Regs
All definition of 'attendance
allowance'
17 **IS** Sch 2 para 14A IS Regs
HB Sch 2 para 14A HB Regs
CCB Sch 1 para 16 CCB Regs
18 **IS** Sch 2 para 14B IS Regs
HB Sch 2 para 14B HB Regs
CCB Sch 1 para 16A CCB
Regs
19 **IS** Sch 2 para 12(1)(c)(ii) IS
Regs
HB Sch 2 para 12(1)(a)(iii)
HB Regs
CCB Sch 1 para 13(1)(a)(iii)
CCB Regs
20 **IS** Sch 2 para 12(1)(a)(iii) and
(2) IS Regs
HB Sch 2 para 12(1)(a)(v) and
(2) HB Regs
CCB Sch 1 para 13(1)(a)(v)
and (2) CCB Regs
21 **IS** Sch 2 para 12(1)(a)(ii) IS
Regs
HB Sch 2 para 12(1)(a)(iv) HB
Regs
CCB Sch 1 para 13(1)(a)(iv)
CCB Regs
22 **IS** Sch 2 para 12(1)(b) and Sch
1 para 5 IS Regs
HB Sch 2 para 12(1)(b) and
(6) HB Regs
CCB Sch 1 para 13(1)(b) and
(6) CCB Regs
23 **IS** Sch 2 para 12(3) IS Regs
HB Sch 2 para 12(3) HB Regs
CCB Sch 1 para 13(3) CCB
Regs
24 **R(S)** 11/51(T)
25 **IS** Sch 2 paras 11(b) and 12 IS
Regs
HB Sch 2 paras 11(b) and 12
HB Regs
CCB Sch 1 paras 12(b) and 13
CCB Regs
26 **IS** Sch 2 paras 7(1)(b) and
12(5) IS Regs
HB Sch 2 paras 7(1)(b) and
12(5) HB Regs
CCB Sch 1 paras 7(1)(b) and
13(5) CCB Regs
27 Reg 19(2) and (4) SS(C&P)
Regs and Sch 7 para 19 IS Regs
28 **IS** Sch 2 paras 9, 9A, 15(2)
and (2A) IS Regs
HB Sch 2 paras 9, 9A, 15(2)
and (2A) HB Regs
CCB Sch 1 paras 9, 10, 17(2)
and (3) CCB Regs
29 **IS** Sch 2 paras 10 and 15(3) IS
Regs

HB Sch 2 paras 10 and 15(3)
HB Regs
CCB Sch 1 paras 11 and 17(4)
CCB Regs
30 **IS** Sch 2 para 12(1)(c)(i) IS
Regs
HB Sch 2 para 12(1)(a)(ii) HB
Regs
CCB Sch 1 para 13(1)(a)(ii)
CCB Regs
31 **IS** Sch 2 para 12(4) IS Regs
HB Sch 2 para 12(4) HB Regs
CCB Sch 1 para 13(4) CCB
Regs
32 Regs 5 and 20(3) SS(SDA)
Regs
33 **IS** Sch 2 para 7(1)(a) IS Regs
HB Sch 2 para 7(1)(a) HB
Regs
CCB Sch 1 para 7(1)(a) CCB
Regs
34 *R v Secretary of State for
Social Security ex parte
Smithson*, ECJ Case C/243/90
35 **IS** Sch 2 para 10(1)(b)(ii) and
(3) IS Regs
HB Sch 2 para 10(1)(b)(ii) and
(3) HB Regs
CCB Sch 1 para 11(1)(b)(ii)
and (3) CCB Regs
36 **HB** Sch 2 para 10(3)(c) HB
Regs
CCB Sch 1 para 11(3)(c) CCB
Regs
37 **IS** Sch 2 para 10(2)(b)(ii) IS
Regs
HB Sch 2 para 10(2)(b)(ii) HB
Regs
CCB Sch 1 para 11(2)(b)(ii)
CCB Regs
38 **IS** Sch 2 paras 13 and 15(5) IS
Regs
HB Sch 2 paras 13 and 15(5)
HB Regs
CCB Sch 1 paras 14 and 17(6)
CCB Regs
39 **IS** Sch 2 para 14A IS Regs
HB Sch 2 para 14A HB Regs
CCB Sch 1 para 16 CCB Regs
40 *Foster v Chief Adjudication
Officer*, (CA) *The Times* 28
February 1991
41 **IS** Reg 3 IS Regs
HB Reg 3 HB Regs
CCB Reg 2(1) CCB Regs
definition of 'non-dependant'
42 **IS** Sch 2 para 13(3) IS Regs
HB Sch 2 para 13(3)(a) HB
Regs
CCB Sch 1 para 14(3)(a) CCB
Regs
43 **HB** Sch 2 para 13(3)(b) HB
Regs
CCB Sch 1 para 14(3)(b) CCB
Regs
44 **IS** Reg 2(1) IS Regs

HB Reg 2(1) HB Regs
CCB Reg 2(1) CCB Regs
All definition of 'close relative'
45 Sch 2 para 13(3)(c) and (4) IS Regs
46 Sch 2 para 13(3A) IS Regs
47 Reg 4(7) and (8) IS(Amdt6) Regs 1991
48 Reg 4(3)-(6) IS(Amdt6) Regs 1991
49 Reg 5 IS(Amdt6) Regs 1991
50 Reg 6 IS(Amdt6) Regs 1991
51 IS Sch 2 paras 13(2)(a)(iii) and (b), and 14ZA IS Regs
    HB Sch 2 paras 13(2)(a)(iii) and (b), and 14ZA HB Regs
    CCB Sch 1 paras 14(2)(a)(iii) and (b), and 15A CCB Regs

Chapter 18: Income
(pp246-271)

1 Introduction
(pp246-250)
1 s22(5) SSA 1986 [s136(1) SS(C&B)A]
2 Reg 23(4) IS Regs
3 s22(5) SSA 1986 [s136(1) SS(C&B)A]
4 IS Reg 44(4) IS Regs
    FC Reg 27(2) FC Regs
    DWA Reg 30(2) DWA Regs
    HB Reg 36(1) HB Regs
    CCB Reg 26(1) CCB Regs
5 IS Reg 25 IS Regs
    FC Reg 27(2) FC Regs
    DWA Reg 30(2) DWA Regs
    HB Reg 36(1) HB Regs
    CCB Reg 26(1) CCB Regs
6 IS Sch 8 para 14 IS Regs
    FC Sch 1 para 2 FC Regs
    DWA Sch 2 para 2 DWA Regs
    HB Sch 3 para 13 HB Regs
    CCB Sch 2 para 13 CCB Regs
7 IS Sch 8 para 15(b) IS Regs
    HB Sch 3 para 14(b) HB Regs
    CCB Sch 2 para 14(b) CCB Regs
8 IS Reg 44(4) and Sch 8 para 15(a) IS Regs
    HB Reg 36(1) and Sch 3 para 14(a) HB Regs
    CCB Reg 26(1) and Sch 2 para 14(a) CCB Regs
9 Reg 42(4)(a)(ii) IS Regs
10 Reg 44(2)(a) IS Regs
11 Reg 44(2)(b) IS Regs
12 Reg 44(9) IS Regs
13 Reg 44(3) IS Regs
14 para C3.89 GM
15 IS Reg 32(1) IS Regs
    FC Reg 18(1) FC Regs
    DWA Reg 20(1) DWA Regs

HB Reg 25 HB Regs
CCB Reg 16 CCB Regs
16 Reg 32(6) IS Regs
17 Reg 32(2) and (3) IS Regs
18 Reg 32(4) IS Regs
19 Reg 32(5) IS Regs
20 Reg 29(2)(a) IS Regs
21 Reg 29(2)(b) IS Regs
22 Reg 31(1)(a) IS Regs
23 Reg 31(1)(b) IS Regs
24 Reg 31(2) IS Regs
25 Reg 2(1) IS Regs
26 R(SB) 33/83
27 R(SB) 22/84; R(SB) 11/85

2 Earnings of employed earners
(pp250-256)
28 IS Reg 36(3) IS Regs
    FC Reg 20(3) FC Regs
    DWA Reg 22(3) DWA Regs
    HB Reg 29(3) HB Regs
    CCB Reg 19(3) CCB Regs
29 FC Regs 14(2) and 20(4) FC Regs
    DWA Regs 16(7) and 22(4) DWA Regs
    HB Regs 22(2) and 29(4) HB Regs
    CCB Regs 13(2) and 19(4) CCB Regs
    HB/CCB para C3.22 GM
30 HB Reg 26 HB Regs
    CCB Reg 17 CCB Regs
    HB/CCB paras C3.03 and C3.04 GM
31 R(SB) 21/86
32 IS Reg 35(1) IS Regs
    FC Reg 19(1) FC Regs
    DWA Reg 21(1) DWA Regs
    HB Reg 28(1) HB Regs
    CCB Reg 18(1) CCB Regs
33 IS Reg 35(1)(a) to (i) IS Regs
    FC Reg 19(1)(a) to (h) FC Regs
    DWA Reg 21(1)(a) to (i) DWA Regs
    HB Reg 28(1)(a) to (i) HB Regs
    CCB Reg 18(1)(a) to (i) CCB Regs
34 IS Reg 48(3) IS Regs
    FC Reg 31(2) FC Regs
    DWA Reg 34(2) DWA Regs
    HB Reg 40(3) HB Regs
    CCB Reg 30(3) CCB Regs
35 Regs 35(2)(b) and 40(4) and Sch 9 paras 1, 4 and 4A IS Regs
36 FC Reg 19(1)(g) and (h) FC Regs
    DWA Reg 21(1)(g) and (h) DWA Regs
37 FC Sch 2 paras 27 and 31 FC Regs
    DWA Sch 3 paras 27 and 31 DWA Regs
38 Reg 21(1)(i) DWA Regs
39 FC Reg 19(1) FC Regs

DWA Reg 21(1) DWA Regs
40 *See R v National Insurance Commissioner ex parte Stratton* (1979) QB 361
41 IS Reg 35(2)(a) IS Regs
    FC Reg 19(2)(a) FC Regs
    DWA Reg 21(2)(a) DWA Regs
    HB Reg 28(2)(a) HB Regs
    CCB Reg 18(2)(a) CCB Regs
42 IS Sch 9 para 21 IS Regs
    FC Sch 2 para 20 FC Regs
    DWA Sch 3 para 20 DWA Regs
    HB Sch 4 para 21 HB Regs
    CCB Sch 3 para 22 CCB Regs
43 IS Reg 48(5) IS Regs
    FC Reg 31(5) FC Regs
    DWA Reg 34(5) DWA Regs
    HB Reg 40(5) HB Regs
    CCB Reg 30(5) CCB Regs
44 Reg 48(6) IS Regs
45 IS Sch 9 para 14 IS Regs
    FC Sch 2 para 12 FC Regs
    DWA Sch 3 para 45 DWA Regs
    HB Sch 4 para 12 HB Regs
    CCB Sch 3 para 12 CCB Regs
46 IS Reg 35(2)(c) IS Regs
    FC Reg 19(2)(b) FC Regs
    DWA Reg 21(2)(b) DWA Regs
    HB Reg 28(2)(b) HB Regs
    CCB Reg 18(2)(b) CCB Regs
47 CIS/89/1989; CIS/131/1989
48 IS Sch 8 para 11 IS Regs
    FC Sch 1 para 1 FC Regs
    DWA Sch 2 para 1 DWA Regs
    HB Sch 3 para 11 HB Regs
    CCB Sch 2 para 11 CCB Regs
49 IS Sch 8 para 12 IS Regs
    FC Sch 1 para 3 FC Regs
    DWA Sch 2 para 3 DWA Regs
    HB Sch 3 para 12 HB Regs
    CCB Sch 2 para 12 CCB Regs
50 IS Reg 35(2)(d) IS Regs
    FC Reg 19(2)(c) FC Regs
    DWA Reg 21(2)(c) DWA Regs
    HB Reg 28(2)(c) HB Regs
    CCB Reg 18(2)(c) CCB Regs
51 IS Reg 40(4) and Sch 9 para 1 IS Regs
    FC Reg 24(5) and Sch 2 para 1 FC Regs
    DWA Reg 27(4) and Sch 3 para 1 DWA Regs
    HB Reg 33(4) and Sch 4 para 1 HB Regs
    CCB Reg 23(4) and Sch 3 para 1 CCB Regs
52 para 29126 AOG
53 FC Reg 19(3) FC Regs
    DWA Reg 21(3) DWA Regs
54 Reg 14(1) and (2) FC Regs

55 Reg 14(3) FC Regs
56 Reg 20(5) FC Regs
57 Reg 16(2)-(4) DWA Regs
58 Reg 19(a) DWA Regs
59 R(FIS) 1/87; R(FIS) 2/87
60 Reg 16(5) DWA Regs
61 Reg 16(3), (4)(b) and (9)(b)
    DWA Regs; s19(2)(b) SSA
    1975 [s27(3)(b) SS(C&B)A];
    R(U) 5/87
62 **FC** Regs 14(4) and 20A FC
    Regs
    DWA Reg 16(6), and 23
    DWA Regs
63 **FC** Reg 14(5) and (6) FC
    Regs
    DWA Reg 16(7) and (8)
    DWA Regs
64 **HB** Reg 22(1)(a) HB Regs
    CCB Reg 13(1)(a) CCB Regs
    HB/CCB para C3.16 GM
65 **HB** Reg 22(1)(b) HB Regs
    CCB Reg 13(1)(b) CCB Regs
    HB/CCB para C3.17 GM
66 *R v Housing Benefit Review
    Board of the London Borough
    of Ealing, ex parte Saville*,
    QBD, 2/5/86
67 **HB** Reg 22(2)(a) HB Regs
    CCB Reg 13(2)(a) CCB Regs
    HB/CCB para C3.19 GM
68 **HB** Reg 22(2)(b) HB Regs
    CCB Reg 13(2)(b) CCB Regs
    HB/CCB para C3.19 GM
69 **HB** Reg 22(3) HB Regs
    CCB Reg 13(3) CCB Regs
70 **IS** Reg 45 IS Regs
    FC Reg 28 FC Regs
    DWA Reg 31 DWA Regs
    HB Reg 37 HB Regs
    CCB Reg 27 CCB Regs
71 **IS** Reg 53 IS Regs
    FC Reg 36 FC Regs
    DWA Reg 40 DWA Regs
    HB Reg 45 HB Regs
    CCB Reg 35 CCB Regs
72 Reg 35(1)(b) IS Regs
73 Sch 8 para 1(a)(i) IS Regs
74 Sch 8 para 1(a)(ii) IS Regs
75 Reg 29(4B) IS Regs
76 Reg 48(11) IS Regs
77 Regs 29(4C) and 32(7) IS
    Regs
78 Regs 5(5) and 29(3)(a) IS
    Regs
79 Reg 29(4) IS Regs
80 Reg 29(3)(b) IS Regs
81 Sch 8 para 1(b) IS Regs
82 Sch 8 para 2 IS Regs
83 Reg 29(4) and (4C) IS
    Regs
84 CIS/104/1989
85 **HB** Sch 3 para 1(a)(i) HB
    Regs
    CCB Sch 2 para 1(a)(i) CCB
    Regs

86 **HB** Sch 3 para 1(a)(ii) HB
    Regs
    CCB Sch 2 para 1(a)(ii) CCB
    Regs
87 **HB** Sch 3 para 2 HB Regs
    CCB Sch 2 para 2 CCB Regs
88 **HB** Sch 3 para 4 HB Regs
    CCB Sch 2 para 4 CCB Regs
89 Sch 8 para 5 IS Regs
90 **IS** Sch 8 para 4(2) IS Regs
    HB Sch 3 para 3(2) HB Regs
    CCB Sch 2 para 3(2) CCB
    Regs
91 **HB** Sch 3 para 3(2) HB Regs
    CCB Sch 2 para 3(2) CCB
    Regs
92 **IS** Sch 8 para 4(4) IS Regs
    HB Sch 3 para 3(4) HB Regs
    CCB Sch 2 para 3(4) CCB
    Regs
93 **IS** Sch 8 para 4(3) and (5) IS
    Regs
    HB Sch 3 para 3(3) and (5)
    HB Regs
    CCB Sch 2 para 3(3) and (5)
    CCB Regs
94 **IS** Sch 8 para 4(6) IS Regs
    HB Sch 3 para 3(6) HB Regs
    CCB Sch 2 para 3(6) CCB
    Regs
95 **IS** Sch 8 para 7(1) IS Regs
    HB Sch 3 para 6(1) HB Regs
    CCB Sch 2 para 6(1) CCB
    Regs
96 **IS** Sch 8 para 8 IS Regs
    HB Sch 3 para 7 HB Regs
    CCB Sch 2 para 7 CCB Regs
97 **IS** Sch 8 para 7(2) IS Regs
    HB Sch 3 para 6(2)(b) HB
    Regs
    CCB Sch 2 para 6(2)(b) CCB
    Regs
98 Sch 8 para 6 IS Regs
99 Reg 3A and Sch 8 paras 4(7)
    and 6(2)-(2C) IS Regs
100 Sch 8 para 9 IS Regs
101 **HB** Sch 3 paras 5 and 8 HB
    Regs
    CCB Sch 2 paras 5 and 8
    CCB Regs

3 Earnings from self-employment
(pp256-258)
102 **IS** Reg 37(1) IS Regs
    FC Reg 21(1) FC Regs
    DWA Reg 24(1) DWA Regs
    HB Reg 30 HB Regs
    CCB Reg 20 CCB Regs
103 **IS** Reg 38(3) IS Regs
    FC Reg 22(3) FC Regs
    DWA Reg 25(3) DWA Regs
    HB Reg 31(3) HB Regs
    CCB Reg 21(3) CCB Regs
104 **IS** Reg 38(12) IS Regs
    FC Reg 22(12) FC Regs

    DWA Reg 25(14) DWA Regs
    HB Reg 31(11) HB Regs
    CCB Reg 21(11) CCB Regs
105 **FC** Reg 21(1) FC Regs
    DWA Reg 24(1) DWA Regs
106 **IS** Reg 38(3)(a), (4), (7) and
    (8)(a) IS Regs
    FC Reg 22(3)(a), (4), (7) and
    (8)(a) FC Regs
    DWA Reg 25(3)(a), (4)(a),
    (5), (6), (9) and (10)(a) DWA
    Regs
    HB Reg 31(3)(a), (4), (7) and
    (8)(a) HB Regs
    CCB Regs 21(3)(a), (4), (7)
    and (8)(a) CCB Regs
107 CFC/25/1989
108 **IS** Reg 38(6) and (8)(b) IS
    Regs
    FC Reg 22(6) and (8)(b) FC
    Regs
    DWA Reg 25(8) and (10)(b)
    DWA Regs
    HB Reg 31(6) and (8)(b) HB
    Regs
    CCB Reg 21(6) and (8)(b)
    CCB Regs
109 **IS** Reg 38(5) IS Regs
    FC Reg 22(5) FC Regs
    DWA Reg 25(7) DWA Regs
    HB Reg 31(5) HB Regs
    CCB Reg 21(5) CCB Regs
110 **IS** Reg 38(11) IS Regs
    FC Reg 22(11) FC Regs
    DWA Reg 25(13) DWA
    Regs
    HB Reg 31(10) HB Regs
    CCB Reg 21(10) CCB Regs
111 CIS/21/1989
112 Reg 30 IS Regs
113 **FC** Reg 15(1) FC Regs
    DWA Reg 17(1) DWA Regs
114 **FC** Reg 18(2) FC Regs
    DWA Reg 20(2) DWA Regs
115 **FC** Reg 17(b) FC Regs
    DWA Reg 19(b) DWA Regs
116 **FC** Reg 15(2) FC Regs
117 CFC/24/1989
118 **DWA** Reg 17(3) DWA Regs
119 **HB** Reg 23(1) HB Regs
    CCB Reg 14(1) CCB Regs
120 **IS** Reg 38(9) IS Regs
    FC Reg 22(9) FC Regs
    DWA Reg 25(11) DWA
    Regs
    HB Reg 31(9) HB Regs
    CCB Reg 21(9) CCB Regs
121 **IS** Reg 38(2) IS Regs
    FC Reg 22(2) FC Regs
    DWA Reg 25(2) DWA Regs
    HB Reg 31(2) HB Regs
    CCB Reg 21(2) CCB Regs

4 Other income
(pp258-270)
122 **HB** Reg 24 HB Regs

CCB Reg 15 CCB Regs
123 FC Reg 16(1) FC Regs
DWA Reg 18(1) DWA Regs
124 Reg 35(2) and Sch 9 para 4
IS Regs
125 IS Sch 9 para 9 IS Regs
FC Sch 2 para 7 FC Regs
DWA Sch 3 para 7 DWA
Regs
HB Sch 4 para 8 HB Regs
CCB Sch 3 para 8 CCB Regs
126 IS Sch 9 para 9A IS Regs
FC Sch 2 para 4 FC Regs
DWA Sch 3 para 4 DWA
Regs
HB Sch 4 para 5 HB Regs
CCB Sch 3 para 5 CCB Regs
127 IS Sch 9 para 33 IS Regs
FC Sch 2 para 28 FC Regs
DWA Sch 3 para 28 DWA
Regs
HB Sch 4 para 31 HB Regs
CCB Sch 3 para 32 CCB
Regs
128 IS Sch 9 para 6 IS Regs
FC Sch 2 para 4 FC Regs
DWA Sch 3 para 4 DWA
Regs
HB Sch 4 para 5 HB Regs
CCB Sch 3 para 5 CCB Regs
129 IS Sch 9 para 8 IS Regs
FC Sch 2 para 6 FC Regs
DWA Sch 3 para 6 DWA
Regs
HB Sch 4 para 7 HB Regs
CCB Sch 3 para 7 CCB Regs
130 IS Sch 9 paras 7 and 8 IS
Regs
FC Sch 2 paras 5 and 6 FC
Regs
DWA Sch 3 paras 5 and 6
DWA Regs
HB Sch 4 paras 6 and 7 HB
Regs
CCB Sch 3 paras 6 and 7
CCB Regs
131 Sch 2 para 4 FC Regs
132 Sch 3 para 46 DWA Regs
133 IS Sch 9 para 31 IS Regs
HB Sch 4 para 30 HB Regs
CCB Sch 3 para 31 CCB
Regs
134 IS Sch 9 para 38 IS Regs
FC Sch 2 para 33 FC Regs
HB Sch 4 para 37 HB Regs
CCB Sch 3 para 39 CCB
Regs
135 IS Sch 9 para 40-42 IS Regs
FC Sch 2 paras 35-37 FC
Regs
DWA Sch 2 paras 34-36
DWA Regs
HB Sch 4 paras 35-36 and 48
HB Regs
CCB Sch 3 paras 37-38 and
47 CCB Regs

136 IS Sch 9 paras 5, 44-46 IS
Regs
FC Sch 2 paras 3, 39, 41 and
42 FC Regs
DWA Sch 3 paras 3, 39 and
40 DWA Regs
HB Sch 4 paras 39, 40 and
41 HB Regs
CCB Sch 3 paras 36 and 41
CCB Regs
137 FC Sch 2 para 3 FC Regs
DWA Sch 3 para 3 DWA
Regs
HB Sch 4 para 4 HB Regs
CCB Sch 3 para 4 CCB Regs
138 IS Sch 9 para 11 IS Regs
FC Sch 2 para 9 FC Regs
DWA Sch 3 para 9 DWA
Regs
HB Sch 4 para 10 HB Regs
CCB Sch 3 para 10 CCB
Regs
139 IS Sch 9 para 47 IS Regs
FC Sch 2 para 43 FC Regs
DWA Sch 3 para 41 DWA
Regs
HB Sch 4 para 43 HB Regs
CCB Sch 3 para 42 CCB
Regs
140 IS Sch 9 para 16 IS Regs
FC Sch 2 para 14 FC Regs
DWA Sch 3 para 14 DWA
Regs
HB Sch 4 para 14 HB Regs
CCB Sch 3 para 14 CCB
Regs
141 s28(6)(a) SSA 1986 [s134(8)
SS(A)A]
142 s27(2) SSA 1986 [s74(2)
SS(A)A]
143 para C3.100 GM
144 FC Reg 16(2)(a) FC Regs
DWA Reg 18(2)(a) DWA
Regs
145 FC Reg 16(2)(b) FC Regs
DWA Reg 18(2)(b) DWA
Regs
146 FC Reg 31(6) FC Regs
DWA Reg 34(6) DWA Regs
147 s22(5) SSA 1986 [s136(1)
SS(C&B)A]
148 HB Reg 33(1) HB Regs
CCB Reg 23(1) CCB Regs
HB/CCB paras C3.88-9 GM
149 FC Sch 2 paras 13(3) and 47
FC Regs
DWA Sch 3 paras 12(3) and
13 DWA Regs
HB Sch 4 paras 13(3) and 47
HB Regs
CCB Sch 3 paras 13(3) and
46 CCB Regs
150 HB Sch 4 para 27 and Sch 3
para 9 HB Regs
CCB Sch 3 para 28 and Sch
2 para 9 CCB Regs

151 IS Reg 61 IS Regs definition
of 'grant'
FC Reg 37 FC Regs
DWA Reg 41 DWA Regs
HB Reg 46 HB Regs
CCB Reg 36 CCB Regs
152 R(SB) 20/83
153 IS Reg 61 IS Regs definition
of 'grant income'
FC Reg 37 FC Regs
DWA Reg 41 DWA Regs
HB Reg 46 HB Regs
CCB Reg 36 CCB Regs
154 Reg 61 IS Regs definition of
'grant income' (c)
155 IS Reg 62(3) IS Regs
FC Reg 38(3) FC Regs
DWA Reg 42(3) DWA Regs
HB Reg 53(3) HB Regs
CCB Reg 38(3) CCB Regs
156 IS Reg 62(4) IS Regs
FC Reg 38(4) FC Regs
DWA Reg 42(5) DWA Regs
HB Reg 53(4) HB Regs
CCB Reg 38(4) CCB Regs
157 IS Reg 62(3A) IS Regs
FC Reg 38(3A) FC Regs
DWA Reg 42(4) DWA Regs
HB Reg 53(3)(b) HB Regs
CCB Reg 38(3)(b) CCB Regs
158 IS Reg 62(2) IS Regs
FC Reg 38(2) FC Regs
DWA Reg 42(2) DWA Regs
HB Reg 53(2) HB Regs
CCB Reg 38(2) CCB Regs
159 Reg 61 IS Regs definition of
'covenant income'
160 FC Regs 37 definition of
'covenant income' and 44 FC
Regs
DWA Regs 41 definition of
'covenant income' and 49
DWA Regs
HB Regs 46 definition of
'covenant income' and 59 HB
Regs
CCB Regs 36 definition of
'covenant income' and 44
CCB Regs
161 IS Reg 63 IS Regs
FC Reg 39 FC Regs
DWA Reg 43 DWA Regs
HB Reg 54 HB Regs
CCB Reg 39 CCB Regs
162 IS Reg 64(1) IS Regs
FC Reg 40(1) FC Regs
DWA Reg 44(1) DWA Regs
HB Reg 55(1) HB Regs
CCB Reg 40(1) CCB Regs
163 IS Reg 64(2) IS Regs
FC Reg 40(2) FC Regs
DWA Reg 44(2) DWA Regs
HB Reg 55(2) HB Regs
CCB Reg 40(2) CCB Regs
164 IS Reg 65 and Sch 9 para 36
IS Regs

FC Reg 41 and Sch 2 para 29 FC Regs
DWA Reg 45 and Sch 3 para 29 DWA Regs
HB Reg 56 and Sch 4 para 33 HB Regs
CCB Reg 41 and Sch 3 para 34 CCB Regs
165 IS Reg 68 IS Regs
HB Reg 59 HB Regs
CCB Reg 44 CCB Regs
166 FC Reg 44 FC Regs
DWA Reg 49 DWA Regs
167 IS Reg 66(1) IS Regs
FC Reg 42 FC Regs
DWA Reg 46 DWA Regs
HB Reg 57 HB Regs
CCB Reg 42 CCB Regs
168 IS Reg 67 IS Regs
FC Reg 43 FC Regs
DWA Reg 48 DWA Regs
HB Reg 58(1) HB Regs
CCB Reg 43 CCB Regs
169 Reg 66(2) IS Regs
170 Reg 58(2) HB Regs
171 IS Reg 66A IS Regs
FC Reg 42A FC Regs
DWA Reg 47 DWA Regs
HB Reg 57A HB Regs
CCB Reg 42A CCB Regs
172 All definition of 'last day of the course'
IS Reg 61 IS Regs
FC Reg 37 FC Regs
DWA Reg 41 DWA Regs
HB Reg 46 HB Regs
CCB Reg 36 CCB Regs
173 IS Sch 9 para 36 IS Regs
FC Sch 2 para 29 FC Regs
DWA Sch 3 para 29 DWA Regs
HB Sch 4 para 33 HB Regs
CCB Sch 3 para 34 CCB Regs
174 IS Reg 40(3A) IS Regs
FC Reg 24(4A) FC Regs
DWA Reg 27(5) DWA Regs
HB Reg 33(3A) HB Regs
CCB Reg 23(3A) CCB Regs
175 IS Reg 66A(3) IS Regs
FC Reg 42A(3) FC Regs
DWA Reg 47(3) DWA Regs
HB Reg 57A(3) HB Regs
CCB Reg 42A(3) CCB Regs
176 Excluded from definition of 'grant' in:
IS Reg 61 IS Regs
FC Reg 37 FC Regs
DWA Reg 41 DWA Regs
HB Reg 46 HB Regs
CCB Reg 36 CCB Regs
177 IS Sch 9 para 25(2)(b) IS Regs
HB Sch 4 para 23(2)(b) HB Regs

CCB Sch 3 para 24(2)(b) CCB Regs
178 FC Sch 2 para 22(2)(b) FC Regs
DWA Sch 3 para 22(2)(b) DWA Regs
179 IS Reg 17(1)(b) IS Regs
FC Reg 46(4) FC Regs
DWA Reg 51(4) DWA Regs
HB Reg 16(b) HB Regs
CCB Reg 7(b) CCB Regs
180 IS Sch 9 para 25(2)(a) IS Regs
FC Sch 2 para 22(2)(a) FC Regs
DWA Sch 3 para 22(2)(a) DWA Regs
HB Sch 4 para 23(2)(a) HB Regs
CCB Sch 3 para 24(2)(a) CCB Regs
181 IS Sch 9 para 26 IS Regs
FC Sch 2 para 23 FC Regs
DWA Sch 3 para 23 DWA Regs
HB Sch 4 para 24 HB Regs
CCB Sch 3 para 25 CCB Regs
182 IS Sch 9 para 25(1)(b) IS Regs
FC Sch 2 para 22(1)(b) FC Regs
DWA Sch 3 para 22(1)(b) DWA Regs
HB Sch 4 para 23(1)(b) HB Regs
CCB Sch 3 para 24(1)(b) CCB Regs
183 IS Reg 48(8) IS Regs
184 IS Sch 10 para 8(b) IS Regs
FC Sch 3 para 9(b) FC Regs
DWA Sch 4 para 9(b) DWA Regs
HB Sch 5 para 9(b) HB Regs
CCB Sch 4 para 9(b) CCB Regs
185 IS Reg 48(10)(c) and Sch 9 para 39 IS Regs
FC Sch 2 para 34 FC Regs
DWA Sch 3 para 33 DWA Regs
HB Sch 4 para 34 HB Regs
CCB Sch 3 para 35 CCB Regs
186 IS Sch 9 para 39 IS Regs
FC Sch 2 para 34 FC Regs
DWA Sch 3 para 33 DWA Regs
HB Sch 4 para 34 HB Regs
CCB Sch 3 para 35 CCB Regs
187 IS Reg 48(9) IS Regs
FC Reg 31(3) FC Regs
DWA Reg 34(3) DWA Regs
HB/CCB There are no specific provisions for

HB/CCB but such payments are obviously capital
188 Reg 48(10)(a) IS Regs
189 Reg 48(10)(b) IS Regs
190 IS Sch 10 para 8 IS Regs
FC Sch 3 para 9 FC Regs
DWA Sch 4 para 9 DWA Regs
HB Sch 5 para 9 HB Regs
CCB Sch 4 para 9 CCB Regs
191 IS Sch 10 para 29 IS Regs
FC Sch 3 para 31 FC Regs
DWA Sch 4 para 31 DWA Regs
HB Sch 5 para 32 HB Regs
CCB Sch 4 para 32 CCB Regs
192 IS Sch 9 para 15 IS Regs
FC Sch 2 para 13 FC Regs
DWA Sch 3 para 12 DWA Regs
HB Sch 4 para 13 HB Regs
CCB Sch 3 para 13 CCB Regs
193 IS Sch 9 para 19 IS Regs
FC Sch 2 para 19 FC Regs
DWA Sch 3 para 19 DWA Regs
HB Sch 4 para 20 HB Regs
CCB Sch 3 para 20 CCB Regs
194 IS Sch 9 para 20 IS Regs
FC Sch 2 para 40 FC Regs
DWA Sch 3 para 38 DWA Regs
HB Sch 4 para 42 HB Regs
CCB Sch 3 para 21 CCB Regs
195 IS Sch 9 para 18 IS Regs
FC Sch 2 para 18 FC Regs
DWA Sch 3 para 18 DWA Regs
HB Sch 4 para 19 HB Regs
CCB Sch 3 para 19 CCB Regs
196 IS Sch 9 para 22(1) IS Regs
FC Sch 2 para 16(1) FC Regs
DWA Sch 3 para 16(1) DWA Regs
HB Sch 4 para 15(1) HB Regs
CCB Sch 3 para 15(1) CCB Regs
197 IS Reg 48(4) IS Regs
FC Reg 31(4) FC Regs
DWA Reg 34(4) DWA Regs
HB Reg 40(4) HB Regs
CCB Reg 30(4) CCB Regs
198 IS Sch 9 para 22(1) IS Regs
FC Sch 2 para 16(1) FC Regs
DWA Sch 3 para 16(1) DWA Regs
HB Sch 4 para 15(1) HB Regs
CCB Sch 3 para 15(1) CCB Regs

199 IS Sch 9 para 22(2) IS Regs
    FC Sch 2 para 16(2) FC Regs
    DWA Sch 3 para 16(2) DWA
    Regs
    HB Sch 4 para 15(2) HB
    Regs
    CCB Sch 3 para 15(2) CCB
    Regs
200 IS Reg 53 IS Regs
    FC Reg 36 FC Regs
    DWA Reg 40 DWA Regs
    HB Reg 45 HB Regs
    CCB Reg 35 CCB Regs
201 IS Reg 41(1) IS Regs
202 FC Reg 25(1) FC Regs
    DWA Reg 28(1) DWA Regs
203 HB Reg 34(1) HB Regs
    CCB Reg 24(1) CCB Regs
204 IS Reg 29(2)(a) IS Regs
    FC Reg 18 FC Regs
    DWA Reg 20 DWA Regs
    HB Reg 25 HB Regs
    CCB Reg 16 CCB Regs
205 IS Reg 44(1) IS Regs
    FC Reg 27(1) FC Regs
    DWA Reg 30(1) DWA Regs
206 HB Reg 39 HB Regs
    CCB Reg 29 CCB Regs
207 IS Reg 41(2) IS Regs
    FC Reg 25(2) FC Regs
    DWA Reg 28(2) DWA Regs
    HB Reg 34(2) HB Regs
    CCB Reg 24(2) CCB Regs
208 Regs 41(4) and 48(2) IS Regs
209 Reg 41(3) IS Regs
210 *R v SBC ex parte Singer
    (1973) 1 AER 931; R v
    Oxford County Council ex
    parte Jack [1984] 17 HLR
    419; R v West Dorset DC ex
    parte Poupard 28 RVR 40;
    para C3.117 GM*
211 para C2.09(xix) GM
212 *R v West Dorset DC ex parte
    Poupard 28 RVR 40*
213 IS Sch 10 para 20 IS Regs
    FC Sch 3 para 21 FC Regs
    DWA Sch 4 para 21 DWA
    Regs
    HB Sch 5 para 21 HB Regs
    CCB Sch 4 para 21 CCB
    Regs
214 IS Reg 48(2) IS Regs
    FC Reg 31(1) FC Regs
    DWA Reg 34(1) DWA Regs
    HB Reg 40(2) HB Regs
    CCB Reg 30(2) CCB Regs
215 IS Reg 48(2) IS Regs
    FC Reg 31(1) FC Regs
    DWA Reg 34(1) DWA Regs
    HB Reg 40(2) HB Regs
    CCB Reg 30(2) CCB Regs
216 Regs 41(4) and 48(2) IS Regs
217 IS Reg 40(4) IS Regs
    FC Reg 24(5) FC Regs
    DWA Reg 27(4) DWA Regs

    HB Reg 33(4) HB Regs
    CCB Reg 23(4) CCB Regs
    All Definition of
    'occupational pension' in reg
    2(1) of each of those regs
218 IS Reg 41(2) and Sch 9 para
    17 IS Regs
    FC Reg 25(2) and Sch 2 para
    17 FC Regs
    DWA Reg 28(2) and Sch 3
    para 17 DWA Regs
    HB Reg 34(2) and Sch 4 para
    16 HB Regs
    CCB Reg 24(2) and Sch 3
    para 16 CCB Regs
219 Sch 9 para 29 IS Regs
220 Sch 9 para 30(a) IS Regs
221 Sch 9 para 30(b) IS Regs
222 Sch 9 para 30(c) IS Regs
223 Sch 9 para 30(d) IS Regs
224 Sch 9 para 30(d) IS Regs
225 HB Sch 4 para 28 HB Regs
    CCB Sch 3 para 29 CCB
    Regs
226 IS Sch 9 para 11 IS Regs
    FC Sch 2 para 9 FC Regs
    DWA Sch 3 para 9 DWA
    Regs
    HB Sch 4 para 10 HB Regs
    CCB Sch 3 para 10 CCB
    Regs
227 IS Sch 9 para 2 IS Regs
    FC Sch 2 para 2 FC Regs
    DWA Sch 3 para 2 DWA
    Regs
    HB Sch 4 para 2 HB Regs
    CCB Sch 3 para 2 CCB Regs
228 IS Sch 9 para 21 IS Regs
    FC Sch 2 para 20 FC Regs
    DWA Sch 3 para 20 DWA
    Regs
    HB Sch 4 para 21 HB Regs
    CCB Sch 3 para 22 CCB Regs
229 IS Sch 9 paras 14 and 51 IS
    Regs
    FC Sch 2 paras 12 and 48 FC
    Regs
    DWA Sch 3 para 45 DWA
    Regs
    HB Sch 4 paras 12 and 49
    HB Regs
    CCB Sch 3 paras 12 and 48
    CCB Regs
230 IS Sch 9 para 43 IS Regs
    FC Sch 2 para 38 FC Regs
    DWA Sch 3 para 37 DWA
    Regs
    HB Sch 4 para 38 HB Regs
    CCB Sch 3 para 40 CCB Regs
231 IS Sch 9 para 28 IS Regs
    FC Sch 2 para 25 FC Regs
    DWA Sch 3 para 25 DWA
    Regs
    HB Sch 4 para 26 HB Regs
    CCB Sch 3 para 27 CCB Regs
232 IS Sch 9 para 27 IS Regs

    FC Sch 2 para 24 FC Regs
    DWA Sch 3 para 24 DWA
    Regs
    HB Sch 4 para 25 HB Regs
    CCB Sch 3 para 26 CCB
    Regs
233 IS Sch 9 para 10 IS Regs
    FC Sch 2 para 8 FC Regs
    DWA Sch 3 para 8 DWA
    Regs
    HB Sch 4 para 9 HB Regs
    CCB Sch 3 para 9 CCB Regs
234 IS Sch 9 para 23 IS Regs
    FC Sch 2 para 21 FC Regs
    DWA Sch 3 para 21 DWA
    Regs
    HB Sch 4 para 22 HB Regs
    CCB Sch 3 para 23 CCB
    Regs
235 IS Sch 9 para 24 IS Regs
    FC Sch 2 para 30 FC Regs
    DWA Sch 3 para 30 DWA
    Regs
    HB Sch 4 para 32 HB Regs
    CCB Sch 3 para 33 CCB
    Regs
236 IS Sch 9 para 48 IS Regs
    FC Sch 2 para 44 FC Regs
    DWA Sch 3 para 42 DWA
    Regs
    HB Sch 4 para 44 HB Regs
    CCB Sch 3 para 43 CCB
    Regs
237 IS Sch 9 para 49 IS Regs
    FC Sch 2 para 45 FC Regs
    DWA Sch 3 para 43 DWA
    Regs
    HB Sch 4 para 45 HB Regs
    CCB Sch 3 para 44 CCB
    Regs
238 IS Sch 9 para 50 IS Regs
    FC Sch 2 para 46 FC Regs
    DWA Sch 3 para 44 DWA
    Regs
    HB Sch 4 para 46 HB Regs
    CCB Sch 3 para 45 CCB
    Regs

5 Notional income
(pp270-271)
239 IS Reg 42(1) IS Regs
    FC Reg 26(1) FC Regs
    DWA Reg 29(1) DWA Regs
    HB Reg 35(1) HB Regs
    CCB Reg 25(1) CCB Regs
240 IS Reg 42(2) IS Regs
    FC Reg 26(2) FC Regs
    DWA Reg 29(2) DWA Regs
    HB Reg 35(2) HB Regs
    CCB Reg 25(2) CCB Regs
241 paras C3.98-102 GM
242 IS Sch 10 para 7(b) IS Regs
    FC Sch 3 para 8(b) FC Regs
    DWA Sch 4 para 8(b) DWA
    Regs
    HB Sch 5 para 8(b) HB Regs

CCB Sch 4 para 8(b) CCB Regs
243 Reg 42(3) IS Regs
244 Reg 70(2)(b) IS Regs
245 Reg 42(5) IS Regs
246 Reg 2 SS(PAOR) Regs
247 IS Reg 42(4)(a)(ii) and (9) IS Regs
FC Reg 26(3)(a) FC Regs
DWA Reg 29(3)(a) DWA Regs
HB Reg 35(3)(a) and (8) HB Regs
CCB Reg 25(3)(a) and (8) CCB Regs
248 Reg 42(4) IS Regs
249 IS Reg 42(4)(b) IS Regs
FC Reg 26(3)(b) FC Regs
DWA Reg 29(3)(b) DWA Regs
HB Reg 35(3)(b) HB Regs
CCB Reg 25(3)(b) CCB Regs
250 IS Reg 42(6) IS Regs
FC Reg 26(4) FC Regs
DWA Reg 29(4) DWA Regs
HB Reg 35(5) HB Regs
CCB Reg 25(5) CCB Regs
251 R(SB) 13/86
252 R(SB) 13/86
253 IS Reg 42(6) IS Regs
FC Reg 26(4) FC Regs
DWA Reg 29(4) DWA Regs
HB Reg 35(5) HB Regs
CCB Reg 25(5) CCB Regs
254 *Sharrock v Chief Adjudication Officer* (CA) 26 March 1991
255 CIS/93/1991

Chapter 19: Capital
(pp272-284)

1 Introduction
(p272)
1 HB Sch 5 para 5 HB
CCB Sch 4 para 5 CCB Regs
2 IS Reg 45 IS Regs
FC Reg 28 FC Regs
3 DWA Reg 31 DWA Regs
HB Reg 37 HB Regs
CCB Reg 27 CCB Regs
4 IS Reg 53(1) IS Regs
FC Reg 36(1) FC Regs
DWA Reg 40(1) DWA Regs
HB Reg 45(1) HB Regs
CCB Reg 35(1) CCB Regs
5 IS Reg 53 IS Regs
FC Reg 36 FC Regs
DWA Reg 40 DWA Regs
HB Reg 45 HB Regs
CCB Reg 35 CCB Regs
6 s22(5) SSA 1986 [s136(1) SS(C&B)A]
7 IS Reg 47 IS Regs
FC Reg 30 FC Regs
DWA Reg 33 DWA Regs
HB Reg 39 HB Regs

CCB Reg 29 CCB Regs
8 IS Reg 17(1)(b) IS Regs
FC Reg 46(4) FC Regs
DWA Reg 51(4) DWA Regs
HB Reg 16(b) HB Regs
CCB Reg 7(b) CCB Regs
9 IS Reg 44(5) IS Regs
FC Reg 27(3) FC Regs
DWA Reg 30(3) DWA Regs
HB Reg 36(2) HB Regs
CCB Reg 26(2) CCB Regs
10 IS Reg 17(1)(b) IS Regs
FC Reg 46(4) FC Regs
DWA Reg 51(4) DWA Regs
HB Reg 16(b) HB Regs
CCB Reg 7(b) CCB Regs

2 What counts as capital
(pp272-275)
11 para C2.09 GM
12 IS paras 30010 and 42010 AOG
HB/CCB para C2.08 GM
13 R(SB) 35/83
14 IS/FC Reg 2 SS(PAOR) Regs
HB Reg 91(1) HB Regs
15 R(SB) 12/86
16 R(SB) 53/83; R(SB) 1/85
17 R(SB) 49/83
18 para 30027 AOG
19 R(IS) 1/90
20 R(SB) 23/85
21 IS Reg 48 IS Regs
FC Reg 31 FC Regs
DWA Reg 34 DWA Regs
HB Reg 40 HB Regs
CCB Reg 30 CCB Regs
22 paras 40144, 40152-3 AOG
23 FC Reg 31(6) FC Regs
DWA Reg 34(6) DWA Regs
24 IS Sch 9 para 32 IS Regs
FC Sch 2 para 26 FC Regs
DWA Sch 3 para 26 DWA Regs
HB Sch 4 para 29 HB Regs
CCB Sch 3 para 30 CCB Regs

3 Disregarded capital
(pp275-279)
25 IS Sch 10 para 1 IS Regs
FC Sch 3 para 1 FC Regs
DWA Sch 4 para 1 DWA Regs
HB Sch 5 para 1 HB Regs
CCB Sch 4 para 1 CCB Regs
26 IS Reg 2(1) IS Regs meaning of 'dwelling occupied as the home'; R(SB) 13/84
FC Sch 3 para 1 FC Regs
DWA Sch 4 para 1 DWA Regs
HB Sch 5 para 1 HB Regs
CCB Sch 4 para 1 CCB Regs
27 IS Sch 10 para 1 IS Regs
FC Sch 3 para 1 FC Regs
DWA Sch 4 para 1 DWA Regs

HB Sch 5 para 1 HB Regs
CCB Sch 4 para 1 CCB Regs
28 R(SB) 1/85
29 IS Sch 10 para 25 IS Regs
FC Sch 3 para 26 FC Regs
DWA Sch 4 para 26 DWA Regs
HB Sch 5 para 24 HB Regs
CCB Sch 4 para 24 CCB Regs
30 IS Sch 10 para 27 IS Regs
FC Sch 3 para 28 FC Regs
DWA Sch 4 para 28 DWA Regs
HB Sch 5 para 26 HB Regs
CCB Sch 4 para 26 CCB Regs
31 IS Sch 10 para 26 IS Regs
FC Sch 3 para 27 FC Regs
DWA Sch 4 para 27 DWA Regs
HB Sch 5 para 25 HB Regs
CCB Sch 4 para 25 CCB Regs
32 para 30211 AOG
33 R(SB) 32/83
34 IS Sch 10 para 28 IS Regs
FC Sch 3 para 29 FC Regs
DWA Sch 4 para 29 DWA Regs
HB Sch 5 para 27 HB Regs
CCB Sch 4 para 27 CCB Regs
35 IS Sch 10 para 3 IS Regs
FC Sch 3 para 3 FC Regs
DWA Sch 4 para 3 DWA Regs
HB Sch 5 para 3 HB Regs
CCB Sch 4 para 3 CCB Regs
36 R(SB) 14/85
37 IS Sch 10 para 2 IS Regs
FC Sch 3 para 2 FC Regs
DWA Sch 4 para 2 DWA Regs
HB Sch 5 para 2 HB Regs
CCB Sch 4 para 2 CCB Regs
38 IS Sch 10 para 8(a) IS Regs
FC Sch 3 para 9(a) FC Regs
DWA Sch 4 para 9(a) DWA Regs
HB Sch 5 para 9(a) HB Regs
CCB Sch 4 para 9(a) CCB Regs
39 IS Sch 10 para 8(b) IS Regs
FC Sch 3 para 9(b) FC Regs
DWA Sch 4 para 9(b) DWA Regs
HB Sch 5 para 9(b) HB Regs
CCB Sch 4 para 9(b) CCB Regs
40 IS Sch 10 para 9(a) IS Regs
FC Sch 3 para 10(a) FC Regs
DWA Sch 4 para 10(a) DWA Regs
HB Sch 5 para 10(a) HB Regs
CCB Sch 4 para 10(a) CCB Regs
41 IS Sch 10 para 9(b) IS Regs
FC Sch 3 para 10(b) FC Regs

DWA Sch 4 para 10(b) DWA Regs
HB Sch 5 para 10(b) HB Regs
CCB Sch 4 para 10(b) CCB Regs

42 IS Sch 10 para 37 IS Regs
FC Sch 3 para 39 FC Regs
DWA Sch 4 para 38 DWA Regs
HB Sch 5 para 37 HB Regs
CCB Sch 4 para 36 CCB Regs

43 para 30208 AOG

44 IS Sch 10 para 4 IS Regs
FC Sch 3 paras 4 and 30 FC Regs
DWA Sch 4 paras 4 and 30 DWA Regs
HB Sch 5 para 4 HB Regs
CCB Sch 4 para 4 CCB Regs

45 HB Sch 5 para 24 HB Regs
CCB Sch 4 para 24 CCB Regs

46 IS para 30237 AOG
HB/CCB para C2.12a and b GM

47 FC Sch 3 para 4 FC Regs
DWA Sch 4 para 4 DWA Regs

48 IS Reg 2(1) IS Regs definition of 'relative'
FC Reg 2(1) definition of 'close relative' and Sch 3 para 4 FC Regs
DWA Reg 2(1) definition of 'close relative' and Sch 4 para 4 DWA Regs
HB Reg 2(1) HB Regs definition of 'relative'

49 CSB/209/1986; CSB/1149/1986; R(SB) 22/87

50 IS Sch 10 para 10 IS Regs
FC Sch 3 para 11 FC Regs
DWA Sch 4 para 11 DWA Regs
HB Sch 5 para 11 HB Regs
CCB Sch 4 para 11 CCB Regs

51 IS Sch 10 para 8(a) IS Regs
FC Sch 3 para 9(a) FC Regs
DWA Sch 4 para 9(a) DWA Regs
HB Sch 5 para 9(a) HB Regs
CCB Sch 4 para 9(a) CCB Regs

52 IS para 30271 AOG
FC para 42271 AOG

53 IS Sch 10 para 6 IS Regs
FC Sch 3 para 6 FC Regs
DWA Sch 4 para 6 DWA Regs
HB Sch 5 para 7 HB Regs
CCB Sch 4 para 7 CCB Regs

54 FC Sch 3 para 7 FC Regs
DWA Sch 4 para 7 DWA Regs

55 IS Sch 10 para 19 IS Regs
FC Sch 3 para 20 FC Regs
DWA Sch 4 para 20 DWA Regs

HB Sch 5 para 20 HB Regs
CCB Sch 4 para 20 CCB Regs

56 IS Sch 10 para 7 IS Regs
FC Sch 3 para 8 FC Regs
DWA Sch 4 para 8 DWA Regs
HB Sch 5 para 8 HB Regs
CCB Sch 4 para 8 CCB Regs

57 IS Sch 10 para 41 IS Regs
FC Sch 3 para 43 FC Regs
DWA Sch 4 para 42 DWA Regs
HB Sch 5 para 38 HB Regs
CCB Sch 4 para 37 CCB Regs

58 IS Sch 10 para 36 IS Regs
FC Sch 3 para 38 FC Regs
DWA Sch 4 para 37 DWA Regs
HB Sch 5 para 36 HB Regs
CCB Sch 4 para 35 CCB Regs

59 IS Sch 10 paras 31, 32 and 33 IS Regs
FC Sch 3 paras 33, 34 and 35 FC Regs
DWA Sch 4 paras 33, 34 and 35 DWA Regs
HB Sch 5 paras 28, 29 and 42 HB Regs
CCB Sch 4 paras 28, 29 and 41 CCB Regs

60 IS Sch 10 para 15 IS Regs
FC Sch 3 para 16 FC Regs
DWA Sch 4 para 16 DWA Regs
HB Sch 5 para 16 HB Regs
CCB Sch 4 para 16 CCB Regs

61 IS Sch 10 para 11 IS Regs
FC Sch 3 para 12 FC Regs
DWA Sch 4 para 12 DWA Regs
HB Sch 5 para 12 HB Regs
CCB Sch 4 para 12 CCB Regs

62 IS Reg 41(2) IS Regs
FC Reg 25(2) FC Regs
DWA Reg 28(2) DWA Regs
HB Reg 34(2) HB Regs
CCB Reg 24(2) CCB Regs

63 IS Sch 10 para 5 IS Regs
FC Sch 3 para 5 FC Regs
DWA Sch 4 para 5 DWA Regs
HB Sch 5 para 6 HB Regs
CCB Sch 4 para 6 CCB Regs

64 IS Sch 10 para 12 IS Regs
FC Sch 3 para 13 FC Regs
DWA Sch 4 para 13 DWA Regs
HB Sch 5 para 13 HB Regs
CCB Sch 4 para 13 CCB Regs

65 R(SB) 2/89

66 IS Sch 10 paras 40 and 46 IS Regs
FC Regs 24 and 29 FC Regs
DWA Regs 27 and 32 DWA Regs
HB Regs 33 and 38 HB Regs

CCB Regs 23 and 28 CCB Regs

67 *Thomas v Chief Adjudication Officer* (appendix to R(SB) 17/87)

68 IS Sch 10 para 13 IS Regs
FC Sch 3 para 14 FC Regs
DWA Sch 4 para 14 DWA Regs
HB Sch 5 para 14 HB Regs
CCB Sch 4 para 14 CCB Regs

69 IS Sch 10 para 14 IS Regs
FC Sch 3 para 15 FC Regs
DWA Sch 4 para 15 DWA Regs
HB Sch 5 para 15 HB Regs
CCB Sch 4 para 15 CCB Regs

70 IS Sch 10 para 16 IS Regs
FC Sch 3 para 17 FC Regs
DWA Sch 4 para 17 DWA Regs
HB Sch 5 para 17 HB Regs
CCB Sch 4 para 17 CCB Regs

71 IS Sch 10 para 23 IS Regs
FC Sch 3 para 24 FC Regs
DWA Sch 4 para 24 DWA Regs
HB Sch 5 para 30 HB Regs
CCB Sch 4 para 30 CCB Regs

72 IS Sch 10 para 23 IS Regs
FC Sch 3 para 24 FC Regs
DWA Sch 4 para 24 DWA Regs
HB Sch 5 para 30 HB Regs
CCB Sch 4 para 30 CCB Regs

73 IS Sch 10 para 24 IS Regs
FC Sch 3 para 25 FC Regs
DWA Sch 4 para 25 DWA Regs
HB Sch 5 para 31 HB Regs
CCB Sch 4 para 31 CCB Regs

74 IS Sch 10 para 11 IS Regs
FC Sch 3 para 12 FC Regs
DWA Sch 4 para 12 DWA Regs
HB Sch 5 para 12 HB Regs
CCB Sch 4 para 12 CCB Regs

75 IS Sch 10 para 12 IS Regs
FC Sch 3 para 13 FC Regs
DWA Sch 4 para 13 DWA Regs
HB Sch 5 para 13 HB Regs
CCB Sch 4 para 13 CCB Regs

76 IS Sch 10 para 17 IS Regs
FC Sch 3 para 18 FC Regs
DWA Sch 4 para 18 DWA Regs
HB Sch 5 para 18 HB Regs
CCB Sch 4 para 18 CCB Regs

77 IS Sch 10 para 38 IS Regs
FC Sch 3 para 40 FC Regs
DWA Sch 4 para 39 DWA Regs
HB Sch 5 para 39 HB Regs
CCB Sch 4 para 38 CCB Regs

78 IS Sch 10 para 39 IS Regs

FC Sch 3 para 41 FC Regs
DWA Sch 4 para 40 DWA Regs
HB Sch 5 para 40 HB Regs
CCB Sch 4 para 39 CCB Regs
79 IS Sch 10 para 40 IS Regs
FC Sch 3 para 42 FC Regs
DWA Sch 4 para 41 DWA Regs
HB Sch 5 para 41 HB Regs
CCB Sch 4 para 40 CCB Regs
80 IS Sch 10 para 18 IS Regs
FC Sch 3 para 19 FC Regs
DWA Sch 4 para 19 DWA Regs
HB Sch 5 para 19 HB Regs
CCB Sch 4 para 19 CCB Regs
81 IS Sch 10 paras 42 and 43 IS Regs
FC Sch 3 paras 44 and 45 FC Regs
DWA Sch 4 paras 43 and 44 DWA Regs
HB Sch 5 paras 43 and 44 HB Regs
CCB Sch 4 paras 42 and 43 CCB Regs
82 IS Sch 10 para 29 IS Regs
FC Sch 3 para 31 FC Regs
DWA Sch 4 para 31 DWA Regs
HB Sch 5 para 32 HB Regs
CCB Sch 4 para 32 CCB Regs
83 IS Sch 10 para 22 IS Regs
FC Sch 3 para 23 FC Regs
DWA Sch 4 para 23 DWA Regs
HB Sch 5 para 23 HB Regs
CCB Sch 4 para 23 CCB Regs
84 IS para 30476 AOG
HB Reg 73(1) HB Regs
CCB Reg 61(1) CCB Regs
85 IS Sch 10 para 34 IS Regs
FC Sch 3 para 36 FC Regs
DWA Sch 4 para 36 DWA Regs
HB Sch 5 para 38 HB regs
CCB Sch 3 para 40 CCB Regs
86 IS Sch 10 para 30 IS Regs
FC Sch 3 para 32 FC Regs
DWA Sch 4 para 32 DWA Regs
HB Sch 5 para 33 HB Regs
CCB Sch 4 para 33 CCB Regs
87 IS Sch 10 para 21 IS Regs
FC Sch 3 para 22 FC Regs
DWA Sch 4 para 22 DWA Regs
HB Sch 5 para 22 HB Regs

CCB Sch 4 para 22 CCB Regs
88 IS Sch 10 para 20 IS Regs
FC Sch 3 para 21 FC Regs
DWA Sch 4 para 21 DWA Regs
HB Sch 5 para 21 HB Regs
CCB Sch 4 para 21 CCB Regs

4 Notional capital
(pp280-283)
89 IS Reg 51(6) IS Regs
FC Reg 34(6) FC Regs
DWA Reg 37(6) DWA Regs
HB Reg 43(6) HB Regs
CCB Reg 33(6) CCB Regs
90 IS Reg 51(1) IS Regs
FC Reg 34(1) FC Regs
DWA Reg 37(1) DWA Regs
HB Reg 43(1) HB Regs
CCB Reg 33(1) CCB Regs
91 CIS/124/1990;
CSB/1198/1989
92 CSB/626/1989
93 CIS/124/1990
94 CIS/40/1989
95 CIS/264/1989
96 R(SB) 38/85
97 IS para 30323 AOG
FC para 42323 AOG
HB/CCB para C2.67 GM
98 IS Reg 51(1) IS Regs
FC Reg 34(1) FC Regs
DWA Reg 37(1) DWA Regs
99 IS Reg 51(7) IS Regs
FC Reg 34(7) FC Regs
DWA Reg 37(7) DWA Regs
100 IS Reg 51(6) IS Regs
FC Reg 34(6) FC Regs
DWA Reg 37(6) DWA Regs
HB Reg 43(6) HB Regs
CCB Reg 33(6) CCB Regs
101 IS Reg 51A IS Regs
FC Reg 34A FC Regs
DWA Reg 38 DWA Regs
HB Reg 43A HB Regs
CCB Reg 33A CCB Regs
102 R(IS) 1/91
103 Lord Henley, *Hansard*, 25 June 1990
104 para C2.69 GM
105 IS Reg 51(2) IS Regs
FC Reg 34(2) FC Regs
DWA Reg 37(2) DWA Regs
HB Reg 43(2) HB Regs
CCB Reg 33(2) CCB Regs
106 IS Reg 51(3)(a)(ii) and (8) IS Regs
FC Reg 34(3)(a) FC Regs
DWA Reg 37(3)(a) DWA Regs
HB Reg 43(3)(a) and (7) HB Regs
CCB Reg 33(3)(a) and (7) CCB Regs
107 IS Reg 51(3)(b) IS Regs
FC Reg 34(3)(b) FC Regs

DWA Reg 37(3)(b) DWA Regs
HB Reg 43(3)(b) HB Regs
CCB Reg 33(3)(b) CCB Regs
108 IS Reg 51(4) IS Regs
FC Reg 34(4) FC Regs
DWA Reg 37(4) DWA Regs
HB Reg 43(4) HB Regs
CCB Reg 33(4) CCB Regs
109 IS Reg 51(5) IS Regs
FC Reg 34(5) FC Regs
DWA Reg 37(5) DWA Regs
HB Reg 43(5) HB Regs
CCB Reg 33(5) CCB Regs
110 IS para 30371 AOG
FC para 42371 AOG

5 How capital is valued
(pp283-284)
111 IS Reg 49(a) IS Regs
FC Reg 32(a) FC Regs
DWA Reg 35(a) DWA Regs
HB Reg 41(a) HB Regs
CCB Reg 31(a) CCB Regs
112 R(SB) 18/83
113 R(SB) 6/84
114 CIS/24/1990
115 IS Reg 49(a)(ii) IS Regs
FC Reg 32(a)(ii) FC Regs
DWA Reg 35(a)(ii) DWA Regs
HB Reg 41(a)(ii) HB Regs
CCB Reg 31(a)(ii) CCB Regs
116 R(SB) 27/84
117 R(SB) 2/83; R(SB) 31/83
118 CSB/1198/1989
119 IS Reg 49(a)(i) IS Regs
FC Reg 32(a)(i) FC Regs
DWA Reg 35(a)(i) DWA Regs
HB Reg 41(a)(i) HB Regs
CCB Reg 31(a)(i) CCB Regs
120 IS Reg 49(b) IS Regs
FC Reg 32(b) FC Regs
DWA Reg 35(b) DWA Regs
HB Reg 41(b) HB Regs
CCB Reg 31(b) CCB Regs
121 IS Part 30 Appendix 2 AOG
HB/CCB C2: Annex B GM
122 IS Reg 52 IS Regs
FC Reg 35 FC Regs
DWA Reg 39 DWA Regs
HB Reg 44 HB Regs
CCB Reg 34 CCB Regs
123 IS Reg 49(a) IS Regs
FC Reg 32(a) FC Regs
DWA Reg 35(a) DWA Regs
HB Reg 41(a) HB Regs
CCB Reg 31(a) CCB Regs
124 R(SB) 18/83; R(IS) 2/90
125 IS para 30131 AOG
FC para 42132 AOG
HB/CCB para C2.34 GM
126 *Peters v Chief Adjudication Officer* (appendix to R(SB) 3/89)

127 IS Reg 50(a) IS Regs
     FC Reg 33(a) FC Regs
     DWA Reg 36(a) DWA Regs
     HB Reg 42(a) HB Regs
     CCB Reg 32(a) CCB Regs
128 IS Reg 50(b) IS Regs
     FC Reg 33(b) FC Regs
     DWA Reg 36(b) DWA Regs
     HB Reg 42(b) HB Regs
     CCB Reg 32(b) CCB Regs
129 IS Sch 10 para 21 IS Regs
     FC Sch 3 para 22 FC Regs
     DWA Sch 4 para 22 DWA
     Regs
     HB Sch 5 para 22 HB Regs
     CCB Sch 4 para 22 CCB Regs

**PART VIII: THE
REGULATED SOCIAL
FUND**
**Chapter 20: The regulated
social fund**
(pp285-289)
 1 Reg 5(1) SFM&FE Regs
 2 Reg 6 SFM&FE Regs
 3 Reg 5(2) SFM&FE Regs
 4 Reg 9(1) SFM&FE Regs
 5 Reg 9(2) SFM&FE Regs
 6 Reg 9(3)(b) SFM&FE Regs
 7 Reg 3(1) SFM&FE Regs
    meaning of 'confinement'
 8 Reg 5(1)(b)(ii) SFM&FE
    Regs
 9 Reg 4(2) SFM&FE Regs
10 Reg 6(1) SS(C&P) Regs
11 Reg 19 and Sch 4 SS(C&P)
    Regs
12 Reg 7(1) SFM&FE Regs
13 para 2060 SFMFG
14 Reg 7(2) SFM&FE Regs
15 Reg 8 SFM&FE Regs
16 Reg 9(1) SFM&FE
17 Reg 9(2) SFM&FE Regs
18 Reg 9(3)(b) SFM&FE Regs
19 Reg 9(3)(a) SFM&FE Regs
20 Reg 9(3)(c) SFM&FE Regs
21 Reg 6(1) SS(C&P) Regs
22 Reg 19 and Sch 4 SS(C&P)
    Regs
23 Reg 35(2) SS(C&P) Regs
24 CIS/616/1990
25 s32(4) SSA 1986 [s78(4)
    SS(A)A]
26 Reg 2(1)(a) SFCWP Regs
27 Reg 1A SFCWP Regs
28 Reg 1(2) SFCWP Regs
29 Sch 1 SFCWP Regs
30 Reg 3 SFCWP Regs
31 SFCWP Regs as amended;
    para 25 CWPH
32 para 82 CWPH
33 paras 135-6 CWPH

**PART IX: THE
DISCRETIONARY
SOCIAL FUND**
**Chapter 21: General
principles**
(pp291-299)
 1 s32 SSA 1986 [s167 SS(A)A]
 2 s33(9) SSA 1986 [s140(1)
    SS(C&B)A] Bill
 3 ss32(2)(b) and 33(10) SSA
    1986 [s140(2)-(4) SS(C&B)A]
 4 SF(App) Regs; SF(AR) Regs;
    SF(RDB) Regs; SF(Misc)
    Regs
 5 s33(10) SSA 1986 [s140(2)
    SS(C&B)A]
 6 paras 1046, 1047, 3007, 3042
    and 5045 SFOG
 7 s32(11) SSA 1986 [s140(5)
    SS(C&B)A]
 8 s32(11) SSA 1986 [s140(5)
    SS(C&B)A]
 9 s32(8A) and 8C SSA 1986
    [s168(1) SS(A)A]
10 para 5 App 3 SFAG
11 SF Dir 41
12 para 2144 SFOG
13 para 2063 SFOG
14 para 2063 SFOG
15 SF Dir 42
16 s32(8C)(c) and (d) SSA 1986
    [s168(3)(c) and (d) SS(A)A]
17 paras 7 and 8 App 3 SFAG
18 s33(9)(e) SSA 1986
    [s140(1)(e) SS(C&B)A]
19 SF Dir 40
20 para 2141 SFOG
21 SF Dir 41
22 paras 2124-2126 SFOG
23 para 1027 SFOG
24 paras 1080-1103 SFOG
25 SF Dirs 12, 23 and 29
26 para 3203 SFOG
27 para 3204 SFOG
28 para 3223 SFOG
29 para 3224 SFOG
30 para 3240 SFOG
31 para 3241 SFOG
32 SF Dirs 12(o) and 23(f)
33 para 3061 SFOG
34 paras 5286-5302 and
    5465-5468 SFOG
35 para 5544 SFOG
36 SF Dir 29
37 SF Dir 12(n)
38 SF Dir 23
39 s32(2)(b) SSA 1986
    [s138(1)(b) SS(C&B)A]
40 Reg 3 SFM&FE Regs meaning
    of 'funeral'
41 SF Dir 4(b)(ii)
42 SF Dir 26
43 para 6043 SFOG
44 para 6045 SFOG
45 paras 6041, 6042 SFOG

46 SF Dir 8
47 SF Dir 17

**Chapter 22: Community
care grants**
(pp300-311)

1 Introduction
(pp300-302)
 1 SF Dir 6
 2 SF Dir 25(a)
 3 SF Dir 25(b)
 4 SF Dir 27
 5 SF Dir 27(2)
 6 para 5102 SFOG
 7 SF Dir 28
 8 SF Dir 4
 9 paras 5005 and 5045 SFOG
10 para 5045 SFOG
11 para 5023 SFOG
12 para 5024 SFOG
13 SF Dir 28
14 para 5120 SFOG

**2 Moving out of institutional or
residential care**
(pp302-305)
15 SF Dir 4(a)(i)
16 paras 5005 and 5045 SFOG
17 para 5162 SFOG
18 *R v Secretary of State for
    Social Security ex parte
    Healey, The Times*, 22/4/91
19 *R v The Social Fund Inspector
    Ex parte Sherwin, The Times*,
    23/2/90
20 paras 5141-5142 SFOG
21 paras 5169-5170 SFOG
22 para 5120 SFOG
23 paras 5171-5172 SFOG
24 para 5120 SFOG
25 paras 5180-5184 SFOG
26 paras 2024-2025 SFAG
27 paras 5185-5186 SFOG
28 paras 5200-5202 SFOG
29 paras 5240-5243 and
    5263-5265 SFOG
30 paras 5260-5262 SFOG
31 paras 5220-5221 SFOG
32 SF Dir 4(a)(iv)
33 paras 5500-5502 SFOG

**3 Staying out of institutional or
residential care**
(pp305-307)
34 SF Dir 4(a)(ii)
35 paras 5045 and 5364 SFOG
36 para 5281 SFOG
37 para 5283 SFOG
38 para 5280 SFOG
39 paras 5285, 5324, 5341, 5345
    and 5361 SFOG
40 paras 5284-5308 SFOG
41 paras 5286-5287 SFOG
42 para 5120 SFOG
43 paras 5300-5302 SFOG

44 para 5301 SFOG
45 para 5302 SFOG
46 para 5303 SFOG
47 paras 5304-5306 SFOG
48 paras 5307-5308 SFOG
49 paras 5321-5329 SFOG
50 paras 5343-5346 SFOG
51 paras 5340-5342 SFOG
52 5360-5362 SFOG

**4 Easing exceptional pressures
on families**
(pp307-309)
53 SF Dir 4(a)(iii)
54 paras 5005, 5045 and 5392
    SFOG
55 para 5380 SFOG
56 para 5381 SFOG
57 *R v Secretary of State for
    Social Security ex parte
    Healey, The Times*, 22/4/91
58 CIS/104/1991
59 paras 5400-5420 SFOG
60 paras 5421-5423 SFOG
61 paras 5424-5429 SFOG
62 paras 5440-5443 SFOG
63 paras 5469-5470 SFOG
64 paras 5465-5468 SFOG
65 paras 5460-5464 SFOG
66 paras 5483-5484 SFOG
67 paras 5480-5482 SFOG

5 Travelling expenses
(pp309-311)
68 SF Dir 4(b)
69 SF Dir 4(b)(i)
70 paras 5520-5524 SFOG
71 para 5544 SFOG
72 paras 5526-5528 SFOG
73 para 5529 SFOG
74 para 5544 SFOG
75 paras 5542-5548 SFOG

Chapter 23: Loans
(pp312-331)

1 Budgeting loans
(pp312-314)
1 SF Dir 5
2 SF Dir 8(1)(a)
3 SF Dir 8(1)(c)
4 SF Dir 8(2)
5 para 3124 SFOG
6 SF Dir 2
7 SF Dir 10
8 SF Dir 11
9 para 3060 SFOG
10 para 3042 SFOG
11 para 3080 SFOG
12 para 3061 SFOG
13 para 3062 SFOG
14 para 3063 SFOG
15 SF Dir 10
16 para 3163 SFOG
17 para 3163 SFOG

2 Crisis loans
(pp314-319)
18 SF Dir 14(a)
19 SF Dirs 15, 16 and 17
20 SF Dir 22
21 SF Dir 21; para 4183 SFOG
22 SF Dir 14(b)
23 SF Dir 3(a)
24 SF Dir 3(b)
25 SF Dir 15
26 SF Dir 16
27 SF Dir 16
28 paras 4040 and 4063 SFOG
29 para 4042 SFOG
30 para 4007 SFOG
31 para 4402 SFOG
32 R(SB) 1/83
33 para 4402 SFOG
34 para 4101 SFOG
35 para 4101 SFOG
36 para 4102 SFOG
37 paras 4103-4122 SFOG
38 para 4126 SFOG
39 para 4127 SFOG
40 para 4128 SFOG
41 para 4103 SFOG
42 para 4124 SFOG
43 para 4400 SFOG
44 paras 4440-4442 SFOG
45 para 4443 SFOG
46 paras 4422-4423 SFOG
47 paras 4444-4445 SFOG
48 paras 4463-4467 SFOG
49 paras 4424-4426 SFOG
50 para 4420 SFOG
51 para 4421 SFOG
52 paras 4460-4461 SFOG
53 paras 4480-4481 SFOG
54 para 4481 SFOG
55 para 4462 SFOG
56 SF Dirs 18, 20 and 21
57 SF Dir 22
58 SF Dir 21
59 SF Dir 18
60 SF Dir 20
61 para 4181 SFOG
62 para 4225 SFOG

3 Repayments
(pp319-321)
63 s33(5) and (6) SSA 1986
    (s78(1) and (2) SS(A)A)
64 Part 3 SFAG
65 paras 3002-3003 SFAG
66 para 3004 SFAG
67 para 3007 SFAG
68 para 3008 SFAG
69 para 3009 SFAG
70 para 3010 SFAG
71 para 3011 SFAG
72 para 3012 SFAG
73 para 3013 SFAG
74 para 3014 SFAG
75 Reg 2 SF(Misc) Regs
76 Reg 2(2) SF(Misc) Regs
77 paras 3120-3121 SFAG

78 Reg 3 RDB Regs
79 s33(7)(a) SSA 1986 [s78(3)(a)
    SS(A)A]
80 s33(7)(b) SSA 1986 [s78(3)(b)
    SS(A)A]
81 s33(7)(c) SSA 1986; para 3051
    SFAG [s78(3)(c) SS(A)A]
82 para 3051 SFAG
83 para 3501 SFAG
84 App 2 SFAG
85 para 3502 SFAG
86 para 3503 SFAG
87 para 3040(1) SFAG
88 para 3040(2) SFAG
89 para 3040(3) SFAG

**Chapter 24: Applications,
payments and reviews**
(pp322-331)
1 Reg 2(1) and (2) SF(App) Regs
2 Reg 2(5) SF(App) Regs
3 Reg 2(4) SF(App) Regs
4 Reg 3(a) SF(App) Regs
5 Reg 3(b) SF(App) Regs
6 para 2100 SFOG
7 para 2101 SFOG
8 paras 2080-2086 SFAG
9 paras 2103-2105 SFOG
10 para 2002 SFAG
11 para 1043 SFOG
12 para 1043 SFOG
13 paras 4081-4082 SFOG
14 SF Dir 7
15 paras 3100, 4080 and 5060
    SFOG
16 para 2062 SFOG
17 para 2061 SFOG
18 para 2068 SFAG
19 s33(1A) SSA 1986 [s138(3)
    SS(C&B)A]
20 para 7022 SFOG
21 s34(1) SSA 1986 [s66(1)(a)
    SS(A)A]
22 Reg 2(1) and (2)(a) SF(AR)
    Regs
23 Reg 2(4) SF(AR) Regs
24 Reg 2(6) SF(AR) Regs
25 Reg 2(3) SF(AR) Regs
26 Reg 2(5) SF(AR) Regs
27 SF Dir 37
28 s34(1)(b) SSA 1986 [s66(1)(b)
    SS(A)A]
29 SF Dir 31
30 s34 SSA 1986 [s66 SS(A)A]
31 para 7050 SFOG
32 para 4005 SFAG
33 s34(6) SSA 1986 [s66(6)
    SS(A)A]
34 s34(7) SSA 1986 [s66(7)
    SS(A)A]
35 SF Dir 39(a)
36 SF Dir 39(b) and (c)
37 SF Dir 32
38 SF Dir 33
39 SF Dir 33

40 SF Dir 34
41 para 7140 SFOG
42 para 7140 SFOG
43 para 7141 SFOG
44 SF Dir 35
45 SF Dir 36
46 para 7242 SFOG
47 para 7129 SFOG
48 s34(3) SSA 1986 [s66(3)
    SS(A)A]
49 Reg 2(1) and (2)(b) SF(AR)
    Regs
50 Reg 2(4) SF(AR) Regs
51 Reg 2(6) SF(AR) Regs
52 Reg 2(3) SF(AR) Regs
53 para 4046 SFAG
54 s34(6) and (7) SSA 1986; SF
    Dirs 1 and 2 [s66(6) and (7)
    SS(A)A]
55 para 8011 SFOG
56 s34(4) SSA 1986 [s66(4)
    SS(A)A]
57 s34(5) SSA 1986 [s66(5)
    SS(A)A]
58 SF Dir 38
59 para 7224 SFOG

PART IX: Other benefits
Chapter 25: Health benefits
(pp333-344)
1   Reg 6(2) NHS(TE&RC) Regs
2   Sch 1 para 3 and Table B
    NHS(TE&RC) Regs
3   Reg 4(e) NHS(TE&RC) Regs
4   Sch 1 para 1 and Table A
    NHS(TE&RC) Regs
5   Reg 6(5) NHS(TE&RC) Regs
6   Regs 3, 4, 5 and 6 NHS(CDA)
    Regs
7   Reg 9 NHS(CDA) Regs
8   Reg 8(2) NHS(TE&RC) Regs
9   Reg 8(5) NHS(CDA) Regs
10 Regs 3 and 4 NHS(TE&RC)
    Regs

11 Sch 12 paras 2(4) and 3(4)
    NHS Act 1977
12 Reg 8 NHS(TE&RC) Regs
13 Reg 5(3) NHS(TE&RC) Regs
14 Reg 13 NHS(GOS) Regs
15 Reg 3 NHS(OC&P) Regs
16 Reg 8(2) NHS(OC&P) Regs
17 Regs 9(4) and 17 NHS(OC&P)
    Regs
18 Reg 12(1) NHS(OC&P) Regs
19 Sch 1 NHS(OC&P) Regs
20 Reg 5 NHS(TE&RC) Regs
21 Reg 3 NHS(TE&RC) Regs
22 Reg 3 WF Regs
23 Reg 12 WF Regs
24 Reg 12(2A) WF Regs
25 Reg 9A WF Regs
26 Reg 16(2) WF Regs
27 Reg 9 WF Regs
28 Reg 12 WF Regs
29 Reg 4 WF Regs
30 Reg 5 WF Regs
31 Regs 10 and 11 WF Regs
32 Reg 3 WF Regs
33 Reg 3 and Sch 2 WF Regs

Chapter 26: Local authority benefits and services
(pp345-350)
1   s77(2) SSA 1986
2   ss22(1)(b) and 23(1)(b) EA
    1980
3   s77(1) SSA 1986
4   Reg 4(a) SOB Regs as
    amended
5   s5(2) and (3) E(MP) Act 1948
    as amended by s29(1) EA
    1980
6   Regs 4(e)(i) and 6 SOB Regs
7   s2 EA 1962
8   s17 EA 1980
9   ss55 and 39 EA 1944
10 s39 EA 1944

11 *Rogers v Essex* CC 1986 3
    WLR 689, HL
12 s53 Education (No.2) Act
    1986
13 s55(2) EA 1944
14 Administrative Memorandum
    6/66
15 Sch 2 para 16 CA 1989
16 s106 ERA 1988
17 s106 ERA 1988
18 s107 ERA 1988
19 s107 ERA 1988
20 s108 ERA 1988
21 s110 ERA 1988
22 s18(5) CA 1989
23 s18(6) CA 1989
24 s29(3) CA 1989
25 s29(2) CA 1989
26 s111 ERA 1988
27 s103 LGHA 1989
28 s104 LGHA 1989
29 ss104, 105 and 136 LGHA
    1989
30 s107 LGHA 1989
31 s131 LGHA 1989
32 s103 LGHA 1989
33 Reg 3 HRG(RG) Regs
34 Reg 8 HRG(RG) Regs
35 Regs 17, 18 and 19 HRG(RG)
    Regs
36 Reg 37 HRG(RG) Regs
37 Reg 12(b) HRG(RG) Regs
38 Reg 10 HRG(RG) Regs
39 s17(6) CA 1989
40 s17(10) CA 1989
41 s2 CSDP Act 1976
42 s17 HSS&SSA Act 1983

Chapter 27: Other sources of help
(pp351-353)
1   s3 NHS Act 1977

Index